Framing Celebr

Celebrity culture has a pervasive presence in our everyday lives – perhaps more so than ever before. It shapes not simply the production and consumption of media content but also the social values through which we experience the world. This collection analyses this phenomenon, bringing together essays which explore celebrity across a range of media, cultural and political contexts.

The authors investigate topics such as the intimacy of fame, political celebrity, stardom in American 'quality' television (Sarah Jessica Parker), celebrity 'reality' TV (*I'm a Celebrity … Get Me Out of Here!*), the circulation of the porn star, the gallery film (*David*/David Beckham), the concept of cartoon celebrity (*The Simpsons*), fandom and celebrity (k.d. lang, *NSYNC), celebrity in the tabloid press, celebrity magazines (*heat*, *Celebrity Skins*), the fame of the serial killer and narratives of mental illness in celebrity culture.

The collection is organized into four themed sections. **Fame Now** broadly examines the contemporary contours of fame as they course through new media sites (such as 'reality' TV and the internet) and different social, cultural and political spaces. **Fame Body** attempts to situate the star or celebrity body at the centre of the production, circulation and consumption of contemporary fame. **Fame Simulation** considers the increasingly strained relationship between celebrity and artifice and 'authenticity'. **Fame Damage** looks at the way the representation of fame is bound up with auto-destructive tendencies or dissolution.

Dr Su Holmes is Lecturer in Film and Television at the University of Kent. She is the author of *British TV and Film Culture in the 1950s: Coming to a TV Near You!* (2005) and co-editor of *Understanding Reality Television* (Routledge, 2004).

Dr Sean Redmond is Senior Lecturer in Film Studies at the University of Victoria, Wellington, New Zealand. He is the co-editor of *The Cinema of Kathryn Bigelow: Hollywood Transgressor* (2003) and the editor of *Liquid Metal: The Reader in Science Fiction Film* (2004).

Framing Celebrity

New directions in celebrity culture

Edited by Su Holmes and Sean Redmond

Taylor & Francis Group

LONDON AND NEW YORK

First published 2006
by Routledge
2 Park Square, Milton Park, Abingdon, Oxon OX14 4RN

Simultaneously published in the USA and Canada
by Routledge
270 Madison Ave, New York, NY 10016

Routledge is an imprint of the Taylor & Francis Group, an informa business

Typeset in Perpetua and Bell Gothic by Bookcraft Ltd, Stroud, Gloucestershire
Printed and bound in Great Britain by
TJ International Ltd, Padstow, Cornwall

British Library Cataloguing in Publication Data
A catalogue record for this book is available from the British Library

Library of Congress Cataloging in Publication Data
Framing celebrity : new directions in celebrity culture/edited by Su Holmes and Sean Redmond
p.cm.
Includes bibliographical references and index.
ISBN 0-415-37709-9 (hardback : alk. paper) – ISBN 0-415-37710-2 (pbk. : alk. paper)
1. Popular culture—United States. 2. Celebrities in mass media. 3. Mass media—
Social aspects—United States. I. Holmes, Su. II. Redmond, Sean, 1967–
E169.Z83F68 2006
306'.0973090511—dc22   2005033385

ISBN10: 0-415-37709-9 (hbk)
ISBN10: 0-415-37710-2 (pbk)
ISBN13: 978-0-415-37709-6 (hbk)
ISBN13: 978-0-415-37710-2 (pbk)

Contents

Illustrations

Part openings

Chapters

Notes on Contributors

Kristina Busse teaches at the University of South Alabama. She has written a variety of essays on fan fiction and has co-edited the the essay collection *Fan Fiction and Fan Communities in the Age of the Internet* (McFarland, 2006).

Ramona Coleman-Bell is a doctoral candidate in American Culture Studies at Bowling Green State University, Bowling Green, Ohio. Her research interests range across representations of race and gender in American media and culture, and African American literature. She is the author of 'Narrating Nation: Exploring the Space of Americanness and the Place of African American Women through the Works of June Jordan', in Valerie Kinloch and Margret Grebowicz (eds), *Still Seeking an Attitude: Critical Reflections on the Work of June Jordan* (Boulder, CO: Lexington Books, 2004).

Philip Drake is a Lecturer in Film and Media Studies at the University of Stirling. He has published numerous articles on celebrity and stardom, screen performance, memory and film music, and intellectual property rights. He is currently writing a book on the political economy of stardom in Hollywood cinema and is co-editing a forthcoming edition of the journal *Cultural Politics* on the politics of celebrity.

Rebecca Feasey is a Lecturer in Film and Media Communications at Bath Spa University. She has published in the areas of cult film and the contemporary star system, and is currently writing about reader-responses to celebrity gossip magazines. She has contributed articles on the politics of taste to Mark Jancovich (ed.), *The Cult Film Experience* (Routledge, 2003), and Julian Stringer (ed.), *Movie Blockbusters* (Routledge, 2003).

Catherine Fowler is a Senior Lecturer in Film at Otago University, New Zealand. Her research interests include women filmmakers, European cinema and the film/art axis of influence. She is the editor of *The European Cinema Reader* (Routledge, 2002).

Judith Franco is a Senior Lecturer in the department of Arts, Media and Technology at the Utrecht School of the Arts (the Netherlands), where she teaches courses on cultural studies, film and television genres, and feminist theory. She has published in *Tijdschrift voor Genderstudies*, *European Journal of Cultural Studies*, *Quarterly Review of Film Studies* and other collected works.

Stephen Harper is Senior Lecturer in Media Studies at the University of Portsmouth. His research focuses on health issues in the media and on gender representation. He has also published articles and edited books in the area of cult film, including '"They're Us": Representations of Women in George Romero's "Living Dead" Series', *Intensities: The Journal of Cult Media*, 3, Winter (2003).

Michael Higgins is a Senior Lecturer in Media and Cultural Studies at the University of Sunderland. He has published numerous journal articles on media and politics in publications such as *Discourse & Society* and *Journalism: Theory, Practice and Criticism*. He is currently writing a book, *The Media and its Public*, for Open University Press, and is co-editing the forthcoming *Cambridge Companion to Modern British Culture*.

Matt Hills is a Senior Lecturer in the Cardiff School of Journalism, Media and Cultural Studies at Cardiff University. He is the author of *Fan Cultures* (Routledge, 2002), *The Pleasures Of Horror* (Continuum, 2005) and *How To Do Things With Cultural Theory* (Hodder Arnold, 2005). He has written on media fandom for a wide range of journals and edited collections.

Su Holmes is a Lecturer in Film and Television at the University of Kent. She is the author of *British TV and Film Culture in the 1950s: Coming to a TV Near You!* (Intellect, 2005) and co-editor of *Understanding Reality Television* (Routledge, 2004). Her key research interests are in British TV history, reality TV, and the subject of celebrity, and she has published widely on these topics in journals such as *Screen*, *Continuum*, *International Journal of Cultural Studies* and *Television and New Media*.

Deborah Jermyn is a Senior Lecturer in Film and TV at Roehampton University, UK. She has published widely on the representation of women in popular culture, and her edited collections include *The Cinema of Kathryn Bigelow: Hollywood Transgressor* (Wallflower Press, 2003) and *Understanding Reality Television* (Routledge, 2004). She is currently writing a book on *Sex and the City*.

Sofia Johansson is a doctoral candidate at the University of Westminster. Her research interests cover the press, popular culture and media reception, and her thesis examines the relationship between audiences and tabloid journalism (working title 'Reading Tabloids'). She is the author of '"They Just Make

Sense": Tabloid Newspapers as an Alternative Public Sphere', in Richard Butch (ed.), *Media and Public Spheres* (forthcoming) and is a founding member of the journal *Westminster Papers in Communication and Culture.*

Adam Knee is Assistant Professor and MA Programme Coordinator in the Ohio University School of Film, and he has previously taught in Thailand, Taiwan and Australia. His research interests include Asian film, race and celebrity in American film, and issues of genre. His writing has appeared in such journals as *Quarterly Review of Film and Video* and *Asian Cinema*, and in such anthologies as Steven Jay Schneider and Tony Williams (eds), *Horror International* (Wayne State, 2005), and Pamela Robertson Wojcik and Arthur Knight (eds), *Soundtrack Available* (Duke, 2001).

Adrienne Lai is a visual artist, writer, independent curator, and educator. She graduated with a BFA from Emily Carr Institute in 1998 and received her MFA from the University of California, Irvine in 2001. She has exhibited across Canada and the United States and her writing has been published in *Fuse, Parachute* and a number of exhibition catalogues. Adrienne's research interests are located at the intersections of contemporary art, technology, popular culture, social identity and memory.

David Magill is Assistant Professor of English at the University of Pittsburgh at Johnstown, where he teaches courses in American and African American literature and culture. He is currently completing his manuscript *Modern Masculinities: Modernist Nostalgia and Jazz Age White Manhood* which examines the production of white masculinities in the 1920s United States. His latest work focuses on contemporary examinations of the civil rights movement.

John Mercer is Field Chair in Film Studies at Buckinghamshire Chilterns University College. His research interests include issues surrounding sexuality, representation and identity and film melodrama. He has published articles on the generic conventions of gay pornography in *Paragraph: The Journal of Homosexuality*, and he has contributed an essay to the collection by Todd G. Morrison (ed.), *Pornocopia: Eclectic Views of Gay Pornography* (Haworth Press, 2005). He is co-author (with Martin Shingler) of *Melodrama: Genre, Style, Sensibility* (Wallflower Press, 2004).

Sean Redmond is Senior Lecturer in Film Studies at the University of Victoria, Wellington, New Zealand. He is the co-editor of *The Cinema of Kathryn Bigelow: Hollywood Transgressor* (Wallflower Press, 2003) and the editor of *Liquid Metal: The Reader in Science Fiction Film* (Wallflower Press, 2004). He has research interests in film authorship, film genre, black and Asian cinema, and stars and celebrities.

Suzanne Rintoul is a PhD candidate in the department of English and Cultural Studies at McMaster University. Her primary research interests include Victorian fiction, celebrity culture, and Canadian Literature. Suzanne is currently writing her thesis entitled *Displaced Domestic Violence in Victorian Literature*, and has published work in *M/C Journal* and *Eighteenth-Century Fiction*.

David Schmid is an Associate Professor in the Department of English at the State University of New York, Buffalo, where he teaches and researches in the areas of twentieth-century literature, popular culture, and cultural studies. He is the author of *Natural Born Celebrities: Serial Killers in American Culture* (Chicago, 2005).

Sheila Whiteley is Professor of Popular Music at the University of Salford, Greater Manchester. Her publications include *The Space Between the Notes: Rock and the Counter Culture* (Routledge, 1992), *Women and Popular Music: Sexuality, Identity and Subjectivity* (Routledge, 2000) and *Too Much Too Young: Popular Music, Age and Gender* (Routledge, 2005). She is editor of *Sexing the Groove: Popular Music and Gender* (Routledge, 1998) and is co-editor (with Jennifer Rycenga) of *Queering the Popular Pitch* (Routledge, forthcoming).

Acknowledgements

Where do books come from? The idea for them seems to magic out of thin air – the alchemy of good conversation, pleasurable negotiation, academic provocation, and hard-fought debate. They start off with an explosive energy and an outpouring of thoughts, arguments, concepts and theories. Books to be written are like fireworks or comets blazing a trail. They emerge from intensive intellectual labour: the hard graft of extensive research, the constant drafting and re-drafting of sentences, paragraphs and chapters, and the following of false trails, as well as the search for new horizons. Books are the product of journeying.

On this particular journey a great many friends, colleagues, and students have helped steer us in the right direction. We would like to thank our contributors for their energetic support for this collection. Their essays are the fireworks and comets that light up a project like this. We would like to thank Rebecca Barden for initially commissioning the book at Routledge. We would like to thank our long-standing (and long-suffering) friends and colleagues – Deborah Jermyn, Cathy Fowler, David Lusted and Karen Randell – for endless rounds of juicy star-gossip and emotional support. Finally, we would like to thank our students in the UK and New Zealand for allowing us to play out the game of fame in lectures and seminars.

SH: with particular thanks to Nick Rumens and Aylish Wood for hearing many stories about that 'Celebrity Book', and to *heat* magazine for keeping me up to date with what 'Everyone's Talking About ...'.

SR: enormous thanks to Louise Brooks, Charlie Chaplin, Rita Hayworth, Marlon Brando, Elvis Presley, David Bowie, Cassius Clay, George Best, Mickey Rourke, and Leif Memphis – you know why! And to Carla, Joshi, Caitlin and little Erin, for putting up with me.

Chapter 1

Introduction

Understanding celebrity culture

The I and the Me of fame

I want to be a star. I want to be adored. I want to see and hear the screams of *my* fans and the roar of an ecstatic applause. I want my name in neon lights and my handprints on the Hollywood Boulevard. I want money. I want *lots* of money. I want a heavenly mansion in Beverley Hills and a string of servants to pay my bills. I want wealth. I want to land a helicopter on my luscious lawn. I want sex. I want drug and alcohol excess. I want boys and girls and I want boys and girls to want me. I want a size 8 supermodel in my heart-shaped swimming pool. *Give me luxury leather.*

I want to be a celebrity. I want to be loved. I want the glitz, the glamour, the sparkle and the existential glow. I want the red carpet treatment. I want VIP champagne parties. I want TV chat show hosts to fawn (fall) over me. I want to be harassed and harangued by the tabloid press. I want to be on the cover of *Hello* magazine. I want fame. I want celebrification. I want to be holy, extra special, a precious metal, worshipped and loved. I want a statue of me on Wellington's Lambton Quay. I want the key to my home city.

I want to be the star of a blockbuster film. I want to be Colin Farrell. I want to be a hard-bodied action hero, a smooth-talking Irish romancer, and an icon of male perfection. I want to be Kelly McGillis, in *Top Gun*, kissing Tom Cruise. I don't want to be a nobody. I want to be the centre of attention. I want to be someone called ... Leif Memphis ...

As one of the co-editors of this book, this is how Sean introduces fame to his undergraduate students. As he begins to take on the persona of 'Leif Memphis', PowerPoint slides of the objects/events/possessions being referenced appear on the giant screen behind him. The students laugh, thankfully, but they also begin to get an intimate sense of the footprints of contemporary stardom and celebrification that the lecture goes on to explore. In fact, the introduction to the lecture sets up many of the dominant themes of star and celebrity analysis that are taken up in this edited collection. 'The Leif Memphis Story' is very much the story of this book, as we now go on to outline briefly.

Adulation, identification and emulation are key motifs in the study of celebrity culture. The *desire* for fame, stardom, or celebrification stems from a *need* to be wanted in a society where being famous appears to offer enormous material, economic, social and psychic rewards (Gamson, 1994; Rojek, 2001; Turner, 2004). Nick Couldry (2000, 2003) argues that, in the modern world, being famous gives one access to a social space that sits at the centre of meaning generation and belonging. If you are *not* famous then you exist at the periphery of the power networks that circulate in and through the popular media. If you are *not* famous you help make up the legions of fans that celebrate the famous. If you are *not* famous you become part of the deifying crowd who help co-produce (along with the popular media) the overriding impression that stars and celebrities are indeed at the centre of things. Contemporary fame circulates in a spider-web-like tautology: it is at the beginning and end of a great many important social relations.

This particular discursive strand of 'me, me, me' fame also relates to what one might refer to as the egotistical, fractured, or incomplete nature of (post)modern identity. On the one hand, it is argued that the modern self is overly vain, narcis-sistic and increasingly founded on possessive qualities – qualities that the star or celebrity best embodies. The 'possessive individual' (Abercombie *et al.*, 1986; Pateman, 1988) understands the self to be 'a kind of cultural resource, asset or possession' (Lury, 1996: 8) that has to be styled or accessorized in the same way that famous people are. The possessive individual measures their self-worth in terms of the way they look, which is part dependent on the clothes, jewellery and beauty products they own – consumption choices strongly influenced by the stars and celebrities who are 'in fashion' at any one particular moment. On the other hand, the modern self is said to be marked by a great deal of anxiety, doubt and confusion over who- and how-to-be in a world where identity is felt to be more malleable, more questionable, and much more decidedly manufactured. According to Kobena Mercer, 'in political terms, identities are in crisis because traditional structures of membership and belonging inscribed in relations of class, party and nation-state have been called into question' (1994: 4). The alienated individual of the modern age, then, may feel homeless, and in a perpetual state of dislocation.

The I/Leif Memphis personae come into being along this representational axis. Leif Memphis exists as the epitome of the successful, narcissistic star, made to be in love with his own idolized image. He is an idealized male who loves to be loved. He is 'onstage' (Braudy, 1986: 549), in public view, and such visibility guarantees his selfhood. By contrast, the possessive 'I' of the narrative wants to be famous (to become Leif Memphis), so that he can live in the social centre, where material wealth and psychic good health supposedly lie. But the 'I' is also a split figure, dissatisfied and unhappy with his lot in the world, desperately reaching out for that which he thinks will bring him plenitude or ontological and existential wholeness. His desire to be famous reveals emptiness at the core of his being. Yet one could also argue that Leif Memphis has a similar, if perhaps inverted, incomplete subjectivity. The surface level and commodity-driven nature of his imagined life can be said to be devoid of meaningful intimacy. The drink and the booze can be said to be a coping, but a nonetheless destructive, device to deal with the constant glare of fame. The (perhaps ironic) desire to be hounded by the press reveals a fear or loathing of its intrusive and unkind gaze – a gaze that leaves Leif without a 'private' world into which to escape. Across these vacillating subject positions, then, a story of fame emerges that is shot through with uncertainty, ambiguity and unfulfilled desire: one is or one wants to be somebody else, somewhere else, continually. In the modern world one is psychologically damaged, whether it is as an anomic fan or a lonely famous person. This version of existential drift is compounded by the way stardom or celebrification are made synonymous with one another. The 'I' can see little difference between them, and only simultaneity in the utopian promises and dystopian consequences they both offer. To be famous is *to be famous* and that is all that matters.

The wider context of the para-social relationship that emerges between the fan and the star or celebrity is important in the analysis of fame. Stars and celebrities have often been perceived as performing a surrogate function, standing in for absent or non-existent friends and family (Schickel, 1985). Anomic, atomized individuals reach out for idealized stars and celebrities in what might be called a self-directed healing process. In the modern world where real face-to-face intimacy, with people you know, has arguably decreased, fandom involves an 'illusion of intimacy' that aims to compensate for such loneliness (ibid.: 4). But the para-social relationship may also involve a much more productive or life-affirming connectivity. The fan/star/celebrity relationship may actually be one of the most intimate and far-reaching forms of sociability in the modern world (Elliott, 1999). Fandom is often a creative enterprise, involving the production of artwork, fiction and dedicated websites. Fandom opens up new networks of communication and interaction between and across fan communities. Gossip about stars and celebrities can be understood 'as an important social process through which relationships, identity, and social and cultural norms are debated, evaluated, modified and shared' (Turner, 2004: 24). In this context, the star or celebrity is not just a desired object but also an intimate doorway for connecting people. If Leif Memphis were real (authentic), then his stardom would also be a productive and affective cultural force.

Fandom, and the construction of stars and celebrities, has always involved the 'search' for the 'authentic' person that lies behind the manufactured mask of fame (Dyer, 1998). However, this 'game' of star and celebrity hide-and-seek seems to be an increasingly important one given the amount of 'extra' artifice and simulation in the modern world. New and old media technologies have enabled stars and celebrities to be endlessly circulated, replayed, downloaded and copied. Their images, qualities and cultural values are found almost everywhere, invading or affecting many areas of social life. At the same time, the digital and the virtual media technologies have also opened up the number of spaces where the star or celebrity can be found out, re-written, and seen *in the flesh* as they really are. The desire, by both the popular media and fans/consumers, to get behind or to see through the manufactured nature of the star or celebrity image is one of the over-riding discourses for the way contemporary fame is circulated and interpreted (Gamson, 1994). The body of the star or celebrity is key to this search for the 'truth' about the star or celebrity. If one can see the famous person stripped of all their finery, then one is supposedly getting unrestricted and unfiltered access to gaze at, and be intimate with, their primal state. If one gets to see the star or celeb-rity body as flawed (fat, spotty, wrinkled), then one is supposedly getting a more natural or unmediated picture of them. The bare flesh either confirms them as desirable beings or as beings whose flesh disappoints, perhaps just like our own skin and bone. The bare flesh confirms them as idealized beings or as beings who are as materially fallible as we are. It also confirms or helps to disrupt the gendered and sexual nature of hegemonic desire. The body of the star or celebrity either func-tions to reproduce dominant culture's patriarchal, racial and heterosexual gaze, or it allows transgressive, oppositional, and queer feelings and fantasies to emerge. Of course, the naked body of the star or celebrity is not an indicator of authenticity, nor can it ever be 'pure' or 'natural'. Images are touched-up, shot in soft focus, or digitally manipulated, and the persona of the star or celebrity (which may in any case be built on nudity) always haunts the representation. And with cosmetic surgery and the emergence of digital stars (such as Lara Croft) there is no longer a 'real' body referent to anchor this anyway.

Bodies surround the imagined star persona of Leif Memphis. He is a figure of idealized sexual attraction and corporeal desirability, and he craves the bodies of groupies who will confirm his own physical perfection. The 'I' of the passage is an embodied fan, too, wanting to be the body (of Leif Memphis) and to have the bodies of fans that such stardom would bring. The body is imagined to be the vessel that will grant intimacy, authenticity, and guarantee present/future film parts, photo-shoots, and front-page newspaper and magazine coverage. The body is both felt to be authentic and a saleable commodity. But the body is also sexu-ally fluid and promiscuous: desire oscillates between straight, queer and trans-gender identification. The fantasy 'I' imagines itself as both a famous female and a male body, and desires bodies that are young and which will keep its body feeling young. As such, the 'I' of the passage is also a cipher for subversive, marginal fans who seek identificatory pleasures through the re-inscription and appropriation of the famous body. Leif Memphis's desired body is not his own, it belongs to the cultural industries; and it belongs to the fans who can make of it what they will.

To return to the performance in the lecture hall, it is also an embodied one. The lecturer pretends to be the possessive 'I' and the desired/desirable Leif Memphis. He tries to literally bring the discourses of fame into the lecture space – embodying a figure that dresses, talks and walks for the part. The lecture ends with a 'publicity' photograph of Leif, in close-up, that is signed with the inscription, 'with love, Leif Memphis xxx'. In this sense fame has entered academia in two ways: it provides the performative material out of which lectures can be delivered (Sean has also 'starred' as Charlie Chaplin and David Bowie), and it provides the issues and debates that drive many film, television, cultural and media studies courses. Of course, academic fame exists in other forms. There is the star academic whose work is publicly well known and who regularly turns up on television to provide authoritative commentary. There is the star academic fêted within the academic community, whose name guarantees a publishing contract (in the same way as a Hollywood star can guarantee funding for a movie), and who is invited to star at conventions and symposia. At the 2005 Society for Cinema and Media Studies (SCMS) conference, Richard Dyer's plenary speech was delivered from what can only be described as a stage. His entrance was greeted with ecstatic applause and he delivered a paper that was full of witticisms, jokes and self-reflexive innuendo, all signifiers of the Richard Dyer star persona. We loved it, lapped it up and crowded around him afterwards – fans of an academic star who had just delivered a star performance. Richard, of course, is the author of *Stars* (1979), arguably the most important (*famous*) study of this phenomenon, and the book that launched his academic career. Richard, then, is an academic star in part because of the study of stars.

In a sense, then, the story of the possessive 'I' and of the desired/desirable Leif Memphis is the story of this edited collection. The themes of belonging, identification, empowerment, psychic loss, authenticity, intimacy, affect, corporeality and dislocation/damage reoccur across the essays and the sections the book is composed of. These are decidedly contemporary concerns: the collection speaks to the here-and-now of fame culture – although of equal concern is how the present is situated in complex articulations with historical trajectories of stardom and celebrification. The collection aims to address how the production, circulation and consumption of fame have been transformed by new media technologies, formats and (post)modern sensibilities. More specifically, the collection attempts to situate the study of stars and celebrities in relation to new or under-researched sites of analysis. Fame is made sense of in terms of its ubiquitous presence in all areas of modern life. Fame is analysed in terms of its increasingly simulated nature but also through the sense that it is now often represented as less authorized and therefore more authentic. Fame is understood to be centred on the body and there is an emphasis on how corporeality drives the production and consumption of stars and celebrities. Lastly, fame is explored in terms of the destructive damage it does to the famous and the fans of the famous. Modern or postmodern fame is often apocalyptic in nature, with hate and despair – as much as love and desire – at its burning centre.

We suggest that this collection has something new (even profound) to say about the processes and practices of stardom and celebrification as they are played out in the modern world today. However, at the same time, we fully acknowledge that the idea of what is 'new' is both highly complex and open to interpretation, and that history is always written into the present of any phenomenon that comes into social existence. As Jessica Evans has observed of contemporary celebrity culture: '[C]hange often happens in a small-scale, piecemeal fashion, so that elements of the "old" are reformulated and combined with new developments' (2005: 16). One of the challenges here, then, is to keep this balance in play.

Talk About Fame

Did you see such-and-such on TV last night? Didn't she look beautiful! Don't think much of him though ... they'll never last, mind you ...

Braudy argues that we 'live in a society bound together by the talk of fame' (1986: 1). If we take 'talk' to encompass both social interaction and media discourse, then it is this dialogue which constitutes the very concept of celebrity. The famous are constructed, circulated and consumed through the busy channels of media production, as well as the social networks with which they intersect, and in debating how we might explore this phenomenon, the student or academic has to find a way to enter (and even 'pause') this flow, which has perhaps never seemed so prominent and pervasive. Celebrity clearly courses through these cultural circuits in many different ways, shaped by a myriad of different contexts, technologies and interactions. Within this environment, Graeme Turner observes the range of ways in which the question of 'what is a celebrity?' might be understood:

First, commentary in the popular media ... tends to regard the modern celebrity as a symptom of a worrying cultural shift: towards a culture that privileges the momentary, the visual and the sensational over the enduring, the written, and the rational. Second, those who consume and invest in celebrity tend to describe it as an innate or 'natural' quality ... [here] the defining qualities of the celebrity are both natural and magical ... Third, and in striking contrast to this, the academic literature ... has tended to focus on celebrity as the product of a number of cultural and economic processes (2004: 4).

This is certainly useful in indicating the different discursive investments in celebrity. Rather than echoing the discourse of 'broadsheet think-pieces railing against the C-list celebs infecting our culture' (Hilton, 2004: 21), academic comment indeed aims to analyse celebrity – examining its historical development, cultural, political and economic functions, or its social and cultural use value for the audience. Rather than dismissing it as the ultimate symbol of cultural decline, it aims to explore, then, why and how it *matters*. At the same time, such boundaries are not as clear-cut as they might first appear, particularly when it comes to situating the role of academic analysis. Issues of 'taste' and cultural value have long since shaped conceptions of celebrity, and the contemporary lament over the empty status of modern fame is deafening. Indeed, the claim that there is something 'new' or different about celebrity in contemporary culture is often a political act – it is rarely neutral (see Evans, 2005). Reality TV, for example, has become a particularly visible site for debate here. While academic analysis has undoubtedly provided far more reflective and complex accounts of such fame when compared to the 'sound-bite' assertions in the press, it still inhabits the same cultural framework. Reality TV contestants can be described in academic contexts – as indeed they are in the press – as 'the epitome of the fabricated celebrity' (Turner, 2004: 60), or as 'a bottom level of regularly replenished celebrity' (Corner and Pels, 2003: 5). Furthermore, in terms of this arena in particular, the discursive environment has fostered roles which are somewhat interchangeable: academic comment is used to contextualize comment on fame in the press, public intellectuals can even *become* contestants/participants,[1] contestants can become media 'commentators' on fame, and the perspectives of producers now appear in academic collections (e.g. Carter, 2004). As 'The Story of Leif Memphis' has already (and perhaps provocatively) suggested, despite traditional conceptions of academic 'objectivity', academics get close to the stars and celebrities they write about: their case studies or approaches can often be shaped by an affective connection with the famous figure in question. One only has to read Richard Dyer's oft quoted end to *Stars*, to see (*feel*) the emotional investment in the stars and celebrities that he chooses to study:

When I see Marilyn Monroe I catch my breath; when I see Montgomery Clift I sigh over how beautiful he is ... While I accept utterly that

> beauty and pleasure are culturally and historically specific, and in no
> way escape ideology, none the less they are beauty and pleasure and I
> want to hang on to them in some form or another (1998: 162).

On a number of different levels, then, it is worth returning to Leo Braudy's
comment that we should be wary of the easy 'pose of objectivity that steals into
language' when we talk and write about fame (1986: 11). The point made above
is less intended to 'rehabilitate' the cultural value of celebrity in reality TV, than
to emphasize the difficulty of positioning academic comment on celebrity as an
entirely autonomous sphere, separate from – and only commenting on – the
wider circuits which constitute celebrity culture. While it certainly has its own
particular aims and agendas which differ from popular media commentary,
academic comment is always part of the cacophony of voices discussing fame in
any one moment, shaped by its contexts in a range of different ways. For
example, 'academic' texts such as those by Daniel Boorstin (1961) and Leo
Lowenthal (1961) are now read as elucidating something of the history of fame –
the discourses in operation during the time in which they were writing. From
this perspective, we might ask about the status and role of our own comment
here, and what it reveals about celebrity in the *here and now*.

So, in relation to discourses of cultural value, we make two points here. First, it
is impossible to discuss contemporary celebrity without *also* addressing such judgements – they form such an integral part of how celebrity circulates in the public
sphere. Essays dealing with the porn star, the celebrity 'skin' or gossip magazine,
celebrity reality TV, or boyband fans on the internet, necessarily confront these
judgements in a number of different ways. Second, issues of cultural value simultaneously (and necessarily) structure the varying perspectives our contributors offer
on celebrity – some keen to defend and rehabilitate their topic of concern, others
more openly ambiguous and critical. What emerges in this talk of fame is a
searching and kinetic exploration of its textures, forms and processes.

Furthermore, and as perhaps another example of the ubiquitous nature of
fame, it is worth noting that compiling an academic collection on celebrity has
connections with the processes of fame which structure a celebrity magazine –
even though we might conceive of them as radically different media forms.
Framing Celebrity is a text which is capitalizing on the popular, as well as the
academic, interest in contemporary celebrity. At the level of content, there is
also the need to consider whether the stars/celebrities discussed garner a sense of
national and international appeal, whether they have enough 'cultish' capital, or
whether their fame carries a certain market value. In fact, the economic 'worth'
of the star or celebrity often influences their potential visibility in the pages of
academic analyses. In addition to this, and as noted above, academia has been
conceived as operating its own form of 'star system', with the fame of authors

functioning to market the appeal of academic works.[2] Tim Spurgin has fascina-tingly distinguished between 'star academics', 'superstars' and 'megastars' (2001: 2), bringing out how the 'academic star system' both compares to, yet differs from, the circulation of fame in wider cultural contexts. The Su Holmes and Sean Redmond of this edited collection, then, are perhaps hoping for their own bit of academic stardom.

Celebrity matters

Although it did not mark the beginning of intellectual comment on stardom (Barker, 2003: 5), Richard Dyer's work had a seminal influence on the field, and his books *Stars* (1998, originally 1979) and *Heavenly Bodies* (1986) continue to be canonical texts. Dyer famously argued for the analyses of stars in the realm of representation and ideology. Stars could be understood as 'signs' – read as 'texts' and 'images' – and investigated using the tools of semiotics (Barker, 2003: 6). Paul McDonald, for example, summarizes Dyer's approach as the investigation of how 'cinema circulates the images of individual film performers and how those images may influence the ways in which we think of the identity of ourselves and others' (1998: 176). For Dyer, stars articulate what it means to 'be human' in capitalist society, dramatizing 'ideas of personhood, in large measure shoring up the notion of the individual but also at times registering the doubts and anxieties attendant on it' (Dyer, 1986: 6). Dyer's broader argument here is that stars func-tion to work through useful questions about personhood (as the example of Leif Memphis at the beginning of this section also suggests). It is precisely the medi-ated status of stars and celebrities, and the highly performative context in which they appear, that activates this contradictory dynamic, fostering questions such as: Is there a distinction between our 'private' and 'public' selves? Do we have any unique, essential, 'inner' self, or are we simply a site of self-performance and public presentation? Dyer's *Heavenly Bodies* also went on to offer a more detailed framework for conceptualizing and researching the star image (Dyer, 1986), situ-ating it within the myriad of historical, social and cultural contexts from which it emerged. Film studies arguably remains the most developed field in this respect, and it has increasingly widened its focus on stardom in recent years, addressing in more detail questions of political economy, histories of stardom, and the role of the audience (see McDonald, 1998; Barker, 2003).

Exploring the relationship between identity and the cultural functions of celeb-rity has permeated much of the work in the field, and this focus is further pursued by the essays collected here. But in media and cultural studies (as well as sociology or sports studies and beyond), it is fair to suggest that this subject has also been approached as a set of broader cultural and political processes which are not necessarily anchored to, or explored through, a particular star/celebrity image (Turner, 2004) (e.g. see Braudy, 1986; Marshall, 1997; Rojek, 2001).[3] From this perspective, wider questions are asked about the cultural functions of celebrity. Chris Rojek (2001) for example, examines the phenomenon in relation to the historical contours of community and religion, while John Corner and Dick Pels (2003) have been among those to explore the relationship between celebrity and discourses of modern citizenship, particularly in terms of its implications for the political arena. As briefly referred to above, Nick Couldry (2000, 2003, 2004) has pushed at the traditional parameters of the field in a fascinating set of analyses, raising new questions about the role of celebrity in producing and legitimating the media's (wider) symbolic power. Rather than asking questions about the cultural functions of celebrities once they take up their place on the media stage, Couldry has questioned why it seems 'natural' to create this arena *in the first place*. Couldry argues that the media constructs and maintains a symbolic hierarchy between media/ordinary worlds, in which the media is presented as the privileged '"frame" through which we access the reality that matters to us as social beings' (2004: 58). This is what he terms the 'myth of the media centre', in which mediated space is constructed as 'special' and significant, and to enter it, or even briefly pass through it, is to receive a form of symbolic capital. Reality TV has epitomized this assumption, and is seen as catering to a new era of public narcissism ('pick me!') in which the self is validated by performing for the gaze of others. This perspective suggests a wider view, one in which we need to address how public visibility *in itself* functions to validate social identity and belonging – a means by which we can ensure we 'really' do (or did) exist (Braudy, 1986; Littler, 2004).

This brief outline of disciplinary contexts is important here, as this collection draws upon the heritage of these different spheres. It explores the construction of particular star/celebrity images, while it also gives attention to a much broader set of questions about how celebrity functions. But it is crucial to pause here given that mapping this terrain also raises the issue of terminology – the categories used to explore and conceptualize fame. The terms fame, stardom and celebrity have a degree of liquidity, as our discussion so far has no doubt suggested. In fact, the malleable and porous nature of these concepts is taken up and contested in this collection (see David Schmid's essay). For example, in film studies, where the term 'star' is most commonly used, stardom was understood to mean the product of an interaction between on- and offscreen construction, a dialogue between the performing presence, and the 'private' life of the star (deCordova, 1990; Ellis, 1992), while it also carries auratic, glamorous and desirable connotations. (There are of course also other terms which could be placed above or alongside this, such as icon or idol.) In comparison, the term 'celebrity' has historically had a more contradictory and often less prestigious lineage, in terms of both its popular and its academic use. As P. David Marshall demonstrates, the use of the 'term *celebrity* in its contemporary (ambiguous) form developed in the nineteenth century' (1997: 4; italics in original); Marshall provides more detail of its historical trajectory than is possible here, and illustrates clearly how the term's shifting significance is bound up with its changing relations with cultural value. This in turn is a trajectory which is inextricably linked to the rise of capitalism (and celebrity is conceived as its product). While originally indicating an 'affinity with piety and religion' (ibid.), by the nineteenth century celebrity had become 'a term that announce[d] a vulgar sense of notoriety', and 'some modern sense of false value' (Marshall, 1997: 5, 4). From this perspective, then, celebrity is historically conceptualized as a particular form of fame – one which is the product of capitalism, and which implies a particular connection to the historical evolution of public visibility, and its relations with the mass media and changing notions of achievement.

This shift is seen to be intimately intertwined with the democratization of fame: as fame becomes more ubiquitous, so its currency is seen to be devalued, at least at the level of public discourse. Indeed, the term celebrity has increasingly come to be used in a highly playful and usually derogatory sense – from the irreverent and cheeky peep into 'celebville' provided by publications such as *heat* magazine (Holmes, 2005), to the joke that celebrity can now be referred to as the alternative 'C-word'. Even here, however, we might note that with the designation of categories from the A- to the Z-list of celebrities now a part of popular cultural discourse, there is a bid to establish an ordered taxonomy of fame. This is perhaps a good example of how it remains a deeply hierarchical phenomenon, even while it seems to proliferate and expand (Turner, 2004).

The term celebrity has various uses in academia. It can function to indicate how the media contexts of fame are now less specific, with individual celebrities rarely restricted to a single media form (Bonner, 2005: 65). It is also used to indicate the broad category of being famous, as now defined by public, mass-mediated, visibility. Rojek describes how 'celebrity = impact on public consciousness' (2001: 10), while Marshall conceives of celebrities as 'overtly public individuals' who are permitted to 'move on the stage while the rest of us watch' (1997: ix). The term can also be used to indicate the broader redefinition of the public/private boundary where the construction of the famous is concerned: where the primary emphasis is increasingly on a person's 'private' life or lifestyle rather than their professional role – if indeed they have one at all (Geraghty, 2000). It is not difficult to see how celebrity then becomes a general term in this respect, given that the emphasis above now characterizes the dominant way in which people are made legible in the public sphere. As Turner comments:

> We can map the precise moment a public figure becomes a celebrity. It occurs at the point at which media interest in their activities is

transferred from reporting on their public role ... to investigating the
detail of their private lives (2004: 8).

So the term celebrity is ambiguous in its meanings, and we have noted how it can
also imply (or confer) judgements about the topic or figure under discussion. (As
Christine Geraghty has observed, for example, women 'are particularly likely to
be seen as celebrities whose working life is of less interest than their personal
life'; 2000: 187.) Nevertheless, we have used it in the title of this book to signify
its contemporary currency in describing mass-mediated fame, and to encompass
the scope of its cross-media focus. At the same time, the authors of the essays
have used different terms, as shaped by their particular media focus or perspective. They have also used the same terms in different ways.

   All of the approaches in this book work from the premise that celebrity is less a
property of specific individuals. Rather, it is constituted discursively, by the way
in which the individual is represented' (Turner et al., 2000: 11). As indicated
above, it may well be true that the significance of celebrity as a discursive category has taken on a particular significance in the contemporary cultural climate.
This emerges from the suggestion that it may increasingly be a 'generic' mode of
representation, a set of discursive structures through which the famous are
constructed, shuttled and consumed. This is an idea that is usually articulated
with a sense of alarm and distaste, and Turner notes David Giles' suggestion that
'the brutal reality of the modern age is that all famous people are treated like
celebrities by the mass media, whether they be a great political figure, a worthy
campaigner, an artist "touched by genius", a serial killer or [a reality TV star]'
(Giles, 2000: 5, cited in Turner, 2004: 7). This effectively prioritizes the
'authorship' of the apparatus over the celebrities it produces, reflecting the argument that the publicity machine has become a highly visible player in the cultural
fabrication of celebrity, 'as much an object of fascination as the individuals it
promotes' (Mole, 2004). These debates are particularly important in relation to
this collection, given that it explicitly aims to offer a cross-media, cross-disci-
plinary focus.

   The study of stardom and celebrity was for some time reliant on a small range
of canonical texts, and while it has represented an expanding field of publishing
in recent years, edited collections have not been especially prominent. More
importantly, and despite the arguments about the blurring of categories above,
they have been organized around a particular media/cultural focus – such as
cinema or sport (e.g. Gledhill, 1991, Babington, 2001, Andrews and Jackson,
2001). What we want to suggest here is that, in the contemporary media environment, a range of studies from different contexts can productively speak to
one another in a dynamic and broader dialogue about fame. The form of the
edited collection is unique in enabling a number of arguments, approaches and

perspectives to unfold, and we suggest that this is highly suited to the far-reaching and often contradictory rhythms of celebrity culture.

This also requires qualification. The collection indeed ranges across some of the figures mentioned by Giles above – 'the genius', the serial killer, the reality TV star – but that is not to imply that their 'celebrity' is interchangeable. To assert this would surely be a woeful neglect of their discursive construction, or the affective relations they may foster with the audience. Equally, while the media contexts of fame have become more blurred, many faces *do* remain associated with a particular media context or role. John Mercer's essay here is interested in the textual and cultural specificity of the male porn star, while Sheila Whiteley examines how the generic norms of popular music have shaped the political contours of celebrity at the level of gender, subjectivity and transgression. This is evidence of the need to balance the 'discursive regime' of celebrity with the more localized attention to detail, case study and context. At the same time, other contributors are interested in movement *across* such boundaries: how rock/film stars move into politics (see Drake and Higgins' essay), how a tennis player travels across promotional intertexts (Ramona Coleman-Bell's essay), or how a famous footballer is quite literally reframed as the subject of a video portrait in a gallery (see the essay by Catherine Fowler). But while it is true that earlier work perpetuated restrictive media categories that are now (in part) outdated (Deborah Jermyn's essay in this collection revisits the earlier dichotomy of the film star versus the 'TV personality') (see Ellis, 1992), debates about the overriding significance of the celebrity *apparatus* also give rise to other ways of conceptualizing media specificity. If earlier work anchored this to a particular media role, many of the essays collected here are interested in how particular genres or media formats – through which a range of celebrities may move – give rise to their own ways of understanding fame, and its aesthetic, technological or ideological implications. Contributors explore how the internet, the magazine, the tabloid newspaper, the gallery film, celebrity photography, or celebrity reality TV, demand a consideration of how celebrity culture travels *across* and through the contemporary media landscape, bringing out what can be seen as differences, as well as commonalities.

This internal flexibility is respected by the sections, which organize the essays according to overriding themes. It will also become clear that a range of other concerns interweave between these categories. For example, something which deserves a particular mention here is the contemporary interest in rendering celebrities, and the idea of being a celebrity, more 'ordinary' – an idea which pivots on the related discourse of 'democratization'. These (symbiotic) claims have certainly been part of the mythic construction of fame for some time, and there is ample evidence to suggest that the concept of democratization brought the modern phenomenon of celebrity into being (see Marshall,

1997). But these discourses do seem to be articulated with more fervour and frequency, albeit with different points of reference. We might refer to how the famous are constructed for public consumption (the boisterously democratic attempt to capture them looking the worse for wear, the desire to 'starve' them in reality shows, and the move to invade every waking minute of their lives), to who gets to *become* famous, and the routes through which this can be attained ('ordinary' people in reality TV, the DIY celebrity culture of the internet). Whether the observer adopts the perspective of cultural decline, in which modern celebrity is viewed as a fall from an earlier period when fame had more scarcity and prestige, or celebrates the freedom of an apparently populist democracy, both arguments agree that fame has opened its doors to more 'ordinary' people in recent years (Evans, 2005: 14). As Nick Stevenson describes, audience members

> are now increasingly likely to perceive themselves as potential stars and celebrities, rather than being content to admire others from afar. However, we need to be clear that most of the audience are still *unlikely to become* either stars or celebrities [our emphasis] (2005: 159).

As this suggests, critics have been sceptical as to whether this 'shift' undermines the traditional economic, ideological or political structures of celebrity in significant ways. Even if the celebrity, and the idea of *becoming* a celebrity, is increasingly promoted as 'ordinary', this far from indicates an equality of opportunity. Furthermore, it is perhaps easy to forget that any claims to 'democratization' always sit on the fault-line of an unassailable contradiction. As McDonald usefully reminds us: 'Fame, like power, could never be evenly distributed, for even if it were possible that we could all be famous, if everyone were famous then no one would be famous' (1995: 65). The contributors in this collection further reflect on the political dimensions of these claims, bringing into focus new perspectives, sites of analysis and case studies.

Inside this book: Exclusive! Uncut! And only in *Framing Celebrity* ...

Framing Celebrity is organized into four themed sections. Each section addresses what the editors and contributors consider to be a particular dominant feature of stardom and celebrity as it is configured in the modern world. Nonetheless, while each section makes a case for its own purchase on the play of fame, conversations, interconnections and arguments emerge in and across the book.

Part I, 'Fame Now', broadly examines the contemporary contours of fame as they course through new media sites (such as reality TV and the internet), and different social, cultural and political spaces. The section considers the pervasive nature of fame and its impact on everyday life, while also examining how contemporary fame circulates within – and is profoundly shaped by – its different cultural, political and technological contexts. Key issues and terms that emerge in this section include authenticity, ordinariness, intimacy, televisual stardom, the celebritization of politics and the phenomenon of subcultural celebrity.

Part II, 'Fame Body', attempts to situate the body of the star or celebrity at the centre of the production, circulation and consumption of contemporary fame. The hard, soft, black, white, partially-dressed or pornographic celebrity body is positioned as central to processes of audience identification, emulation and desire, and to the transmission of powerful ideological messages about race, class, gender and sexuality. Stars and celebrities communicate through their flesh: the popular media produces a gaze that focuses on the shape, size, *look* of the body, and fans idolize and decry the famous on the basis of the perfect (and increasingly) imperfect bodies they display. Key issues and terms which emerge in this section include corporeal anxieties, muscularity, queer desire, physical agency, flesh-as-authenticity, and the relationship between the celebrity body and feminine/feminist self-affirmation.

Part III, 'Fame Simulation', considers the increasingly strained relationship between stardom and celebrity and artifice and authenticity. One of the central paradoxes of the construction and consumption of stars and celebrities rests on the supposed 'unmediated' nature of people's relationship with them, and the highly manufactured way they are brought into vision. A range of new media technologies and formats has made this dialogue between actuality and fakery much more charged. Famous people are now often captured in the raw, 'up close and personal', and yet they are also fabricated by the ever-expanding reach of PR networks and digital technologies which manipulate and distort the 'real'. Key issues and terms that emerge in this section include postmodern subjectivity, hyperreality, self-reflexivity, performativity, democratization and mediation.

Part IV, 'Fame Damage', looks at the way the representation of fame is bound up with auto-destructive tendencies or dissolution. One of the dominant scripts of stardom and celebrity now centres on the real and symbolic pain fame brings to those who exist in the glare of the media spotlight, and who live a life of material and sexual excess. At the same time, the popular media are increasingly involved in 'damaging' the image of the star or celebrity through salacious, critical and unflattering reportage. The famous find themselves subject to existential loss and despair – the object of media representation that brings negation to their doors. Key issues and terms in this section include the decline of individuality, catharsis, narratives of mental illness, trauma, transgression, celebrity-'bashing' and celebrity gossip.

Summaries of each essay can be found in the Introduction to each section. We hope that the direction taken by this collection makes for an enriching, provocative and perhaps even intimate journey for the reader in its bid to contribute to an exciting and expanding area of scholarship.

Notes

1 We refer here to the example of Germaine Greer who entered the *Celebrity Big Brother* house in the UK in 2005. After leaving voluntarily, Greer returned to her role as intellectual critic of the format, foregrounding its exploitative nature.

2 There may of course be objections to the notion that we can describe academia in these terms, as perhaps countered by the suggestion that academic stardom is based on a deserving meritocratic ethos, and that it is name and intellect, rather than persona and personal life, which characterize 'fame' here. These are doubtless fair points, but this is still a system which recognizes achievement through individuation and recognition.

3 This is not necessarily to point to a 'deficiency' in the approach adopted by film studies, but merely to emphasize the different disciplinary influences in operation here.

Part I

Fame Now

Introduction

In 2005, UK terrestrial television screened the documentary *Abi Titmuss: A Modern Day Morality Tale* (Channel 4, 19 May 2005). Although undoubtedly a figure of national, rather than international, fame, Abi achieved celebrity status during 2003, when her celebrity boyfriend, John Leslie, was accused of raping another woman. Abi stood by her partner throughout the trial and Leslie, a former children's TV presenter turned daytime TV host, was subsequently acquitted of the crime. But the intense media focus on the event also meant that Abi, a middle-class former nurse, had edged into the media spotlight. With his image irrevocably tarnished by the media coverage, Leslie has since receded from public view, while Abi has enjoyed immense visibility, whether through glamour modelling for 'lads' mags', the circulation of pornographic footage on the internet, appearances in celebrity reality shows, or relationships with male celebrities. The documentary followed the intimate details of Abi's daily life, particularly her celebrity engagements, and placed a particular emphasis on capturing Abi's attitudes toward her new-found fame. How did she feel about being voted 'the world's most pointless celebrity' by a magazine poll? ('I think it's quite funny actually.') How much money has she made and how much is she worth? ('Well, I'm not quite a millionaire yet but …') The documentary also showed how part of Abi's daily existence involved paying a personal paparazzi photographer to trail her. The photographer relentlessly snapped 'paparazzi' pictures of Abi to sell to tabloid newspapers and magazines, thereby ensuring constant media exposure. Recognizing that this may be an exposé too far, Abi rather weakly insists, 'Stop, don't film that …'. Caught in the act of producing her own fame, she blushes, and turns away from the documentary camera.

The documentary seemed to play out a number of discourses which permeate contemporary celebrity culture. It circled around a fascination with the processes and practices of fame-making, perhaps more so than the celebrity herself (see Mole, 2004); it flagrantly displayed the production and manufacture of celebrity, while aiming to negotiate a discourse of intimacy and authenticity around its subject. It expressed an implicit disapproval about the flourishing of such fame, while simultaneously celebrating it as the ultimate triumph, and it offered an intriguing dramatization of the power dynamics which structure relations between the production of celebrity and the economic and cultural entity this creates. In this respect it is worth acknowledging that Abi's celebrity is very gendered in nature (she was initially famous for her association with a famous male partner and then later for her body), but she also represents a woman who has confidently exploited the apparatus of fame, even while – as the documentary makes clear – she struggles to maintain control of the image it has produced.

There was much about this documentary that appeared to play out something of the *here and now* of celebrity. It proffered a sense of 'newness' (Abi was implicitly held up as the epitome of cultural shifts in celebrity), while its perspective now also seemed increasingly familiar and routine. The burgeoning academic interest in celebrity both reflects and contributes to an energy around the subject, producing books 'with the regularity that echoes the celebrity system's own production process' (Marshall, 2004). This urgency has suggested a desire to address not only the history but also the particular, contemporary moment of fame, circling around its changing character, innovation and indeed difference from the past. At the same time, however, what this actually constitutes is hard to pin down and articulate. Viewing the documentary above may confirm the sense that something 'feels' different about contemporary celebrity (compared to even five or ten years ago), but how can that sense be anchored, articulated and explored? Part I has what is perhaps the broadest scope, aiming, in various ways, to capture something of fame in the contemporary moment. We acknowledge that this may be no simple task, but aim to offer case studies which stimulate this debate in wide-ranging and provocative ways.

In concluding his extensive history of fame, Leo Braudy writes:

> Fame is an elusive idea that I have tried to set to words, one of its older mediums … But because the nature of fame is defined by context, both historical and immediate … no pattern traced here has the force of determining causality. Fame is metamorphic … There can be no single perspective, no secret key by which we can unlock what it really is (Braudy, 1986: 591).

Braudy captures here how fame is 'both fickle and incredibly enduring' (Marshall, 2004); it has a history – both in terms of its development and the public individuals it produces – while it also revels in the ephemeral flash of the moment. It leaves behind traces of representation – 'in which people tell stories about themselves and stories are told about them' (Braudy, 1986: 591) – and these shape our understandings of the past. But Braudy's statement also invites a plural perspective, indicating not only the *constantly* changing nature of fame but also its many sites of origin and transformation.

This sense of plurality is useful, as it also captures the differing interpretations of these histories, and by implication, the relationship between the past and the present. Braudy's *The Frenzy of the Renown* (1986) has arguably offered the most mammoth history in this respect, investigating the 'will to fame' from Roman times until (at the time when he was writing) the present day. According to Braudy, since 'fifth-century Athens, fame has been a way of expressing … the legitimacy of the individual within society' (1986: 585), and he invokes a long historical sweep that sometimes conflicts with more contemporary assessments. As Graeme Turner asserts, Braudy 'is one of the … few to have addressed contemporary celebrity … by insisting on its continuity with earlier versions of fame' (2004: 9), given that others position modern celebrity as fundamentally a phenomenon of the mass media (Turner, 2004; Rojek, 2001). It thus follows that there are different interpretations as to the relationship between contemporary celebrity and its longer historical trajectory. Some emphasize that it is the '*perva-siveness* of celebrity [our italics]' that should prompt us to regard it as a new development (Turner, 2004: 4), a term which might encapsulate its spread across media forms and outlets, its infusion into 'every facet of everyday exis-tence' (Andrews and Jackson, 2001: 2), or the literally more ubiquitous currency of celebrityhood. (Abi might variously be described as famous-for-being-famous, famous for having been *made* famous, to famous-for-knowing-the-famous: Liddiment, 2005.)

But then we are faced with the question of what constitutes the 'past', and the identification of key points of change. In concluding his *Picture Personalities: The Emergence of the Star System in America* (1990), Richard deCordova suggested that 'in conducting this study, I have been struck by … how little the star system has changed, at how stable the discourses of stardom have been over the last sixty-five years' (1990: 142), while Braudy concludes that the last great shift 'in the history of fame was in the wake of World War Two, and I cannot see that anything very new has happened since, only an increase of volume, and an added detachment about the process' (1986: 596). Whether with respect to film stardom (Austin and Barker, 2003) or wider media celebrity (Biressi and Nunn, 2005), others would disagree, and of course we can only speculate as to what these earlier authors would make of contemporary celebrity. Such 'disagree-ments' actually appear to be quite productive, and a greater self-reflexivity about them may prove to be useful in furthering debate in the field. But to return to the example used at the beginning of this section, what 'Abi' would mean, and how she might be placed in the history of celebrity, would slip and slide across these different accounts. Pinning down exactly how she speaks to contemporary celeb-rity is very much an interpretive act.

While many of the essays in this book clearly aim to contribute to this exploring of the here and now of contemporary celebrity, Part I expands and focuses this discussion across a range of media, cultural and geographical sites, whether the internet, celebrity reality TV, American quality television, the fan culture, or the political arena. It goes without saying that this cannot offer an exhaustive or indeed coherent picture, and nor does it aim to do this. Rather, it seeks to present a range of nodal points that we hope will prompt debate and shape future avenues of enquiry. But we argue here that if we are considering whether/how the nature of fame is changing, this crucially also means *revisiting* key aspects of star and celebrity theory (see also Austin and Barker, 2003). This is a process to which this section in particular aims to contribute, even while it remains central to the collection as a whole. Hills, for example, revisits the traditional polarity constructed between the position of fan/celebrity, while Jermyn revisits conceptions of the 'television personality'. The theoretical and methodological approaches we use to analyse celebrity should also be the subject of continual rewriting, scrutiny and revision – much like the history of fame itself.

Summaries

Sean Redmond's essay 'Intimate fame everywhere' opens the section, exploring – and bringing together – a number of themes which structure the collection as a whole. Redmond is interested in mapping how fame flows in and out of everyday life, as a 'dominant discursive formation' which shapes social relations, identity and in fact our very sense of the world in meaningful and complex ways. As it exists across reality TV, celebrity magazines, weblogs, the Oscar ceremonies, advertising billboards or pop concerts, fame may articulate ideas about individual success, operate as 'the "glue" that holds the cultural centre together', offer 'a site of para-social relations', or stand tall as a gleaming 'symbol of western democratisation'. But while celebrities may indeed embody the benefits of capitalism, playing out 'the utopian promise of material and symbolic rewards', they are also increasingly a site upon which ideas of 'failure' as well as success take hold. As Redmond points out, 'the suffering and damage of fame' is now also a prevalent discursive force in the construction and circulation of celebrity culture (see also Part IV). For Redmond, then, fame has both transgressive and dominant ideological implications as it circulates in – and through – the spaces and relations which constitute the fabric of social existence. But crucially, and as the title of the essay implies, Redmond is interested in how 'contemporary fame speaks and is spoken about through the language of intimacy'. Rather than seeing the relations between celebrities and consumers as negatively 'para-social' (the terms in which such interactions were traditionally cast), Redmond rejects a real/unreal binary in arguing that such 'para-social connectivity is as "real" as anything can be in a cultural universe made out of simulacra, and that the relationships which emerge between star/celebrity and fan/consumer fill the world with productive, surplus emotionality that cannot be easily channelled or "sucked up" by capitalism, and which offers people transgressive models of identity'.

The idea that celebrity culture beckons us with the promise of 'intimate' access to the famous pervades many of the essays in this collection. Celebrity reality TV has emerged as a key site in playing this out. As noted in Chapter 1, reality TV has emerged as a particularly visible site for debates over the status of modern fame, but the focus here is *celebrity* reality formats, where a degree of celebrity status is a prerequisite for entering the show. While fame in reality TV has often invoked discourses of 'democratization', so this perspective has had a currency where celebrity formats are concerned. In programmes such as *I'm a Celebrity ... Get Me Out of Here!* or *Celebrity Fear Factor*, there is a claim to render the celebrity 'ordinary', and to offer a space in which such 'celebrity baiting ... may ... be the last simmering refuge of populist hatred for the spoiled rich' (Sconce, 2004: 255). Su Holmes' essay 'It's a jungle out there!: the game of fame in celebrity reality TV' interrogates these arguments by exploring the British version of *I'm a Celebrity*, considering how the programme shapes our access to, and the circulation of, the celebrities it displays. Celebrity reality TV offers us an extended space to become intimate with its participants, and the essay explores how the format negotiates the 'authenticity' of the celebrity self, and invites the audience to *play* with this concept as integral to the process of the game. But is there anything intrinsically new about how such formats circulate celebrities for our consumption? As Holmes points out, it is not new to encounter claims to 'democracy' and 'ordinariness' in the cultural construction of fame, and she remains sceptical of the format's political implications. The essay concludes that '*I'm a Celebrity* offers a fascinating and heightened commentary on the discursive construction of celebrity, but one which ultimately draws upon highly traditional structures'.

If Holmes is interested in interrogating claims to change here, this is also true of Deborah Jermyn's essay, '"Bringing out the ★ in you": SJP, Carrie Bradshaw and the evolution of television stardom'. Building on the earlier attempts to theorize the technological, ideological and cultural specificities of television fame (particularly as compared to the film star; Langer, 1981, Ellis, 1992), Jermyn revisits these debates from a contemporary perspective. She does so via the example of 'SJP', the actress famous for her role as Carrie Bradshaw in the hugely successful American quality television (AQT) series, *Sex and the City*. In describing SJP's status as a 'trend-setting icon', Jermyn emphasizes how 'what makes her stardom all the more intriguing ... is the means through which it has come about; that SJP is a figure who is ... most prominently known and feted for her work on *television*'. This is 'intriguing' in the context of earlier work which insisted that 'stardom' was the province of the cinema, while television offered a 'personality' system – with the absence of glamour, aura and adulation that this implies. Yet Jermyn asks: 'What might the fortunes of SJP suggest ... about the changing nature of the relationship between TV and stardom in the contemporary media landscape?' Analysing the construction of SJP in a range of media intertexts, Jermyn suggests that she provides a timely and productive insight into the increasingly complex circulation of television fame.

In 'I'm a celebrity, get me into politics: the political celebrity and the celebrity politician', Philip Drake and Michael Higgins intervene in debates about the increasingly inextricable relationship between celebrity culture and the sphere of politics. Debate on this matter usually adopts a negative rhetoric (in which a 'mist of fame and glamour' is seen as intruding into the political arena). Drake and Higgins by no means suspend these concerns, but they also explore an alternative perspective which suggests that the interrelationship between celebrity and politics 'needs to take into account the quality of the political arguments offered, the integrity of the mediated persona involved, and the success or otherwise of their performance'. Drawing upon Irving Goffman's (1974) concept of 'keying' in the performative frame, they focus on two particular case studies. The first is the example of the Irish rock star Bono and his speech on tackling poverty in Africa at the annual Labour Party conference (UK, 2004), and the second is Hollywood film star turned state governor Arnold Schwarzenegger, and his speech to the 2004 US Republican Party Convention. While remaining ambivalent about the political implications of such relations, Drake and Higgins conclude that it may be unhelpful to entrench generalized arguments about the relationship between celebrity and politics when we have recourse to the more illuminating specificity of the case study. From this perspective the analysis of 'celebrity performance in the political sphere may offer a useful means through which we can conceptualize the contemporary circuit between politicians, celebrities, and the public presentation of political issues'.

Lastly, Matt Hills' essay, 'Not just another "powerless elite"?: when media fans become subcultural celebrities' aims to explore how the pervasive nature of contemporary fame has penetrated the fan culture. His analysis begins from the premise of what he describes as an 'unusual collision' between fan theory and star theory: while fans have been described as a 'powerless elite' (Tulloch and Jenkins, 1995), possessing the power to interpret a text but not to shape its production, so Francesco Alberoni (1972) famously described stars as a 'powerless elite', an apparently privileged group which have little access to real political power. Hill suggests that if both fans and stars are seen as occupying somewhat ambiguous relations with power, 'then it may be rather unhelpful to view cultural power as being entirely housed or possessed by celebrities and concomitantly lacked by fans'. This argument is explored within the context of 'subcultural celebrity': when fans achieve a certain level of celebrity status within their own fan community. Historically, we have conceptualized these spheres as distinct, with the (mass) audience confirming and venerating the status of the (individual) celebrity. But Hills explores how fans can become widely known within their fan culture, whether through print or internet cultures, running fan clubs, or even working on the TV show which is the focus of their fan interest. Hills distinguishes this from mass-mediated celebrity, since 'fan-celebrities are not directly known by other fans, but instead typically acquire fan-cultural reputations and recognition via the subcultural, niche mediation of their names and their work'. Intersecting with a long history of work which investigates the power relations inherent in fan production/consumption, Hills explores the extent to which celebrity operates within the context of the fan network, internally stratifying the fan culture at the level of cultural capital and prestige. This is not to suggest the symbolic inequalities inherent in the fan/celebrity relationship are redundant, but to foreground how power relationships also operate *within* these spheres, calling into question their conventional separation. As Hills concludes, 'to consider media fandom as a "powerless elite" misses its own subcultural stratifications, and its own hierarchies of subcultural celebrity, in which not all fans are similarly "elite" or equally "powerless"'.

Chapter 2

Intimate fame everywhere

Sean Redmond

Introduction

In this essay I want to explore the frameworks of fame in two specific but related ways. First, I want to set out to establish that fame is a ubiquitous and dominant cultural phenomenon, a meta-discourse that shapes, in profound and meaningful ways, social and everyday life for the great many touched by its mediagenic fingers. Fame, I will contend, is everywhere, and the cultural centrality of fame needs unpacking and greater critical understanding. In this respect I will be following the work of writers such as Joshua Gamson (1994), Chris Rojek (2001), and Graeme Turner (2004), who contend, albeit in different ways, that the modern world is distinctly marked by the practices and processes of fame. Second, I will argue that the everywhere of fame has the potential to offer new and liberating interactions and engagements for all those who are 'made-up' in fame, or for all those who regularly consume its stars, celebrities and personalities. My argument will be that *fame culture* offers 'ordinary' and 'extraordinary' people the chance of a heightened level of intimacy, an intimacy that potentially, perhaps inevitably, destabilizes the borders and boundaries of identity, and which energizes or electrifies one's experience of the world.

Fame everywhere

In the modern world the instances and footprints of fame can be found everywhere. So-called 'ordinary' people, for example, find themselves, sometimes 'accidentally', on television, online, in front of the roving film/documentary/ stills camera, in the newspaper, and in the promotional and publicity material for *real* stars and celebrities. Ordinary people become 'accidental celebrities' (Turner *et al.*, 2000) because they know or work with someone famous, or because a newsworthy event or action on their part (such as a kidnapping and a daring escape) thrusts them into the limelight. Ordinary people often exist in the visual arena or slipstream of the famous, with shots of the adoring crowds – at a pop concert, film premiere, or book signing – providing one of the intertextual symbols for the glory and power of stardom and the worship it entails. The video footage of the girls who sobbed and screamed at Robbie Williams's performance at Live 8 is a recent example of bringing into vision, into representation, such star-studded infatuation. Ordinary people provide the vox pop for radio and television news, they star in docu-soaps, game and talent shows, and they populate the universe of reality TV. In fact, as Frances Bonner (2002) argues in her research on what she calls 'ordinary television' in the UK and Australia, one is now more likely to be someone, or to know someone, who has been on television.

Being ordinary, authentic or 'real' is a dominant rhetorical device of fame that has increasingly found its logical point of reference in the onscreen and online antics of extraordinary and ordinary people supposedly *just* being themselves (Holmes, 2004; Biressi and Nunn, 2004). Hot and cold celebrities turn up on reality TV using the format to suggest they are free of the chains of performativity and artifice. The 'play' that viewers get to see them in is marked by their sincerity, honesty and openness; and by their willingness to be just like us, even if this warts-and-all authenticity is a strategy to propel them to greater celebrification, far, far away from such ordinariness. Supposedly free of publicists and public relations, rehearsal and training/coaching, everyday people on reality TV appear as if they are *really* at home, at work, and/or with friends and family. And this representation of life 'caught unawares', this process of catching the individual both in the moment before fame and in the present of fame unfolding, validates them for 'just being who you are, every day' (Turner, 2004: 63).

Certain blog websites extend the reach of the celebrification of the ordinary by making famous those who write honestly and intimately about their everyday lives. Heather Armstrong, for example, became a celebrity blogger for diarizing her dislike of her colleagues and the general day-to-day crassness of her working life. On Monday, 4 February 2002, under the heading 'Reasons the Asian Database Administrator is so Fucking Annoying', Armstrong writes:

> Because he always assumes that when you say 'The Asian Database Administrator' you're talking about him. Because he stares at your ear when you try to ask him why he didn't run those scripts. Because he didn't run those scripts after you'd reminded him four different times, 'You have to run those scripts.' Because you found him stuffing Oreos from the kitchen into his pockets instead of running those scripts. Because when you ask, for the last time, 'Why haven't you run those scripts?' he can't really explain because his mouth is full of cookies. Because he wears Looney Tunes socks (www.dooce.com/archives/daily/02_04_2002.html).

Armstrong has acquired cult status among blog users for her personal/political reflections: she was fired soon after the above entry was recorded and her website, Dooce, now attracts to its pages over 55,000 people a day. Armstrong has become an extraordinary figure through an engagement with the most ordinary aspects of her everyday life.

Ordinary people, then, are also increasingly given the opportunity to demonstrate that they are really, truly, extraordinary – waiting in the wings as writers, dancers or singers – with lashings of 'natural' talent and 'essential' charisma which floods out of them once they are given the chance to 'shine'. The global format of *Pop Idol* auditions would-be hopefuls on the overriding premise that they are looking for 'raw talent', the 'perfect package', that 'certain charisma' which is 'out there' waiting to be 'discovered' (quotes taken from *NZ Idol*, 2005). With the proliferation of shows and series that offer the rewards of fame to the ordinary/extraordinary many, this chance to shine is seen to be repeatedly given in what has been provocatively called the demotic or democratic turn of fame where one and all are potentially welcomed through its glittering doors (Braudy, 1986; Gamson, 2001; Turner, 2004).

Ordinary/extraordinary people do this willingly because to be offscreen, offline, or out of print is, as Nick Couldry (2003) argues, no longer satisfactory, or empowering, in a world where the acquisition of fame is the affirmation of the self. Fame, stardom, celebrification, or 'minor' moments of media personalization promise 'acceptability, even if one commits the most heinous crime, because thereby people will finally know who you are, and you will be saved from the living death of being unknown' (Braudy, 1986: 562).

Magazine and television adverts and billboards are shrines to the commodity value of the star or celebrity. On any given week, the iconic faces and perfect bodies of the celebrated will be attached to a brand that fuses their values together, and marketed in fantasy-based adverts that, in a push for sales, are 'splashed' across the relevant publications, and/or aired on prime-time television slots. For example, Britney Spears' recently launched (2004) perfume, Curious, was promoted, in (pre-)teen magazines such as *Bliss*, through a range of 'coy' adverts that attempted to connect her sexual ambivalence – is Britney a good/bad girl? – to the intended enigmatic meaning of the scent. The value transference on offer for the potential female purchaser becomes loaded with heterosexual and famed desire: buy, be *curious*, put on the scent and become, for the man/boy of your dreams, a tantalizing enigma, a scented 'star' that stands out from the she-crowd.

Girls' and women's magazines extend the reach of fame in another way. They promote and produce, as Susan Hopkins (2002) has argued persuasively in relation to girls' magazines, a cult/culture of celebrity way beyond the fame fantasy networks found in adverts. According to Hopkins, girls' magazines increasingly suggest to girls that individual success is measured through the fame that they acquire. Magazines support this fantasy rhetoric of self-plenitude through 'becoming famous' advice that instructs the readers on how to look and behave like the stars they (are often told they should) so admire. In the July 2005 edition of *New Ideas* (a New Zealand publication aimed at women aged 20+) a regular 'beauty' feature runs with the headline, 'Star Appeal: give yourself a celebrity makeover by following our step-by-step guide to make-up magic' (40–1). The two-page feature gives readers the opportunity to glamour-up like 'Classic Hollywood Siren' Kate Beckinsale, and/or 'Fresh and Natural' Sienna Miller. In so doing, the feature suggests, they will be able to get Kate's 'sultry eyes' or Sienna's 'luscious' lips; and they will have access to the essential ingredients of what it means to be a sex-siren star (Kate) or a natural, pure, heavenly star (Sienna). The feature offers them the brand names of the beauty products that will secure the success of this transformation, and consequently cements the 'necessary' relationship between the individual, the star, and the commodity. In this respect, Chris Rojek argues that there is a close correlation between fame, selling and desire:

> Capitalism requires consumers to develop abstract desire for commodities ... Celebrity culture is therefore partly the expression of a cultural axis organized around abstract desire. It is an essential tool of commodification since it embodies desire. In particular, it provides consumers with compelling standards of emulation (2001: 187).

All manner of goods and services are used, worn, held, driven and put on by the famous elite. The literal and symbolic value of having someone famous 'live' in your clothes, wear your sunglasses, or drive your sports car, is immense. Icons of pop and sport propel the sales of goods that have their image/brand/logo on, they 'guarantee' the sale of tickets to their concerts and games, and they can determine the share price of the corporations they work for. British footballer David Beckham was reckoned to have cost his PR company tens of million of dollars in lost sponsorship deals because of his alleged infidelity with Rebecca Loos. The David Beckham 'brand', partly constructed on his role as a loving husband and model father, was said to be badly damaged by the accusation of adultery (see also Catherine Fowler's essay in this collection).

It can be argued that the consumption of commodities by stars and celebrities serves another, perhaps more important, cultural function: they fuel a general desire among people for such commodities and they promise the 'good life' for all if such commodities are indeed purchased. Such 'idols of consumption' (Lowenthal, 1957) come to embody the benefits of capitalism; and they *play* out, in fantasized form, the material and symbolic rewards of working for a living (King, in Dyer, 1998: 43).

One can analyse the Academy Awards ceremony in terms of how it operates in a vortex of 'commodities for sale' and manufactures the success myth, or the belief 'that American society is sufficiently open for anyone to get to the top, regardless of rank' (Dyer, 1998: 42). Oscar night is one gigantic promotional arena for car manufacturers, hair and make-up stylists, fashion/clothes designers, caterers and chefs, jewellers and watchmakers, and, of course, for the whole synergetic Hollywood machine. Oscar night sells the worldwide audience its beautiful stars, its spectacular films, its commodity-inflected dreams, and its transnational media companies that peddle these stars and films across the globe in a range of ancillary texts and products. In particular, the glamorous stars who arrive in limousines and designer outfits, who walk down the red carpet that help separate the 'crowd' from the 'special' few, and who give out or receive awards, resonate as cultural figures who 'speak' to the needs, drives and processes of capitalism and its corollary, individualism. Halle Berry's highly emotional, 'best actress' winning speech, in 2002, illustrates wonderfully the way that stars function as commodity enterprises, as ideal social types, and as vehicles for/of social equality. Dressed in a see-through Elie Saab dress, and choking back the tears, Berry dedicated her Oscar accordingly:

> This moment is for Dorothy Dandridge, Lena Horne, Diahann Carroll. It's for the women that stand beside me – Jada Pinkett, Angela Bassett and it's for every nameless, faceless woman of colour that now has a chance because this door tonight has been opened. Thank you. I'm so honoured. I am so honoured and thank the Academy for choosing me to be the vessel from which this blessing might flow. Thank you.

Halle Berry's performance is seemingly contradictory. Her reference to the colour bar that has operated in Hollywood, and in American society more generally, draws direct attention to the social inequality, racism and exploitation faced by African American artists, and to the great 'mass' of black women who cannot even be named so anonymous, so culturally prevalent, are they. And yet Berry also references herself as the 'vessel' that will put a stop to such racism; and as someone (black and female) who has been rewarded for her talents, hard work and determination. Berry, then, ultimately confirms the success myth – by thanking the Academy for recognizing her talent she is also confirming that America is (now) a meritocracy, and that black women in the future, if they are talented and work hard enough, will also be able to make it to the top. Of the elements that make the success myth work, according to Richard Dyer, at least three are in play here: 'that ordinariness is the hallmark of the star; that the system rewards talent and "specialness"; and that hard work and professionalism are necessary for stardom' (1998: 42). In a related argument, Anita Biressi and

Heather Nunn (2004) contend that the success myth has found its logical point of reference in reality TV formats, but here the process of hard work and talent is elided. Working-class people are witnessed climbing up the social strata to the dizzy heights of fame but this is attributed to leisured success and free time.

But Berry, of course, is also functioning here as an 'extraordinary' figure, a beautiful creature, and as a commodity intertext with huge earning potential. The lavish (media) setting, the glamorous designer dress, the 'next' film role, and present/future endorsements and promotions are all wrapped up in the emotion-centred performance that she gives. Berry has already walked through the glittering doors of fame and she stands there as a symbol of its reach, potential and availability for all.

Film stars are central to the way the Hollywood machine works. At the 'pitching' and pre-production stage, a star's name can ensure that a project is given the 'green light'. In so-called vanity or star-vehicle projects, stories are conceived and written with the attributes or 'values' of the star in mind (Dyer, 1998: 2). The marketing machinery then utilizes the star's image to sell the film to the audience. At the time of writing this essay, Tom Cruise has been feverishly promoting *War of the Worlds* (Spielberg, 2005), one of the summer's key 'event' movies. He has appeared on American and European chat shows, has taken part in countless interviews, attended numerous red-carpet premieres, and his star name is used to anchor posters and trailers for the film. Cruise offers the audience a particular set of action and performance traits and in terms of this film, he resonates as an archetypal white American hero. It has to be also noted, however, that his 'media-managed' relationship with Katie Holmes at this time has produced a counter-discourse, one which threatens the stability of his image. At present, the more Cruise tries to demonstrate how 'real' his love is for Katie the more he seems lost in the artifice of his own star image.

Newspapers, magazines, and a whole range of official and unofficial web-based media sites fill their pages with stories and pictures that lionize, idolize, ironize and (increasingly) defame and decry those who they put in the public eye. In fact, the 'downmarket' reporting of the famous is often about bringing the heavenly star or glitzy celebrity back down to earth with an almighty 'bang', as a sort of just desserts or social levelling for their showy affluence and/or 'lack of talent' in the first place.

For example, the supermodel Naomi Campbell has been regularly attacked by the British press for being an arrogant and manipulating prima donna. In particular, the *Daily Mirror*, a tabloid newspaper, has run countless stories on her alleged poor or violent treatment of employees, mental instability, drug addiction and failed sexual relationships. This hounding reached its peak with the publication in February 2001 of a report about her drug addiction, including a photograph of her leaving a Narcotics Anonymous meeting in King's Road,

Chelsea. Campell took the *Daily Mirror* to court for breach of confidentiality, a case that she eventually won. However, Piers Morgan, the *Daily Mirror* editor, continued his own 'bringing down' of the star through vitriolic copy:

> This is a very good day for lying drug-abusing prima donnas who want to have their cake with the media, and the right to then shamelessly guzzle it with their Cristal champagne.

A range of media sites and agencies exist to show us the famous at their worst, most 'ugly' and most corrupt. As Graeme Turner argues, 'among the appeals of celebrity journalism is its revelation of the scurrilous, the pathetic and the phoney' (2004: 49). The activities of the paparazzi, gossip columns, celebrity skin magazines and 'tabloid' TV function to show us the star, celebrity or personality as blotchy, spotty, over/underweight, drunk and disorderly, dishevelled, drugged, angry, violent, deceiving, hiding, lying, stealing, naked, knickerless, bra-less, lewd, promiscuous, or metaphysically 'lost'. In the week up to 18 July 2005, the 'bad boy' actor Colin Farrell takes legal action to try to stop a 14-minute videotape of him having sex with a Playboy model from going public; the 'troubled' rock singer Courtney Love is snapped being taken to a Los Angeles hospital after 'feeling faint' and is later praised by an LA judge for progressing well on a court-ordered drug rehabilitation programme; the 'strange' and 'deviant' Michael Jackson reportedly fails to show up to a hearing in a case brought by Joseph Bartucci, who claims he was abused by the singer; the film director Roman Polanski wins his libel case against *Vanity Fair* over an article (published in July 2002) saying he tried to seduce a Scandinavian 'beauty' soon after his wife was murdered while eight-and-a-half months pregnant; and the Indian film star Salman Khan is headline news as he stands trial for allegedly having links with Mumbai's underworld crime syndicates.

Joshua Gamson (1994) has suggested that in the latter half of the twentieth century fame has been increasingly produced and consumed in terms of critical self-reflexivity: the media often represent stardom and celebrity as forms of 'construction' and fans are asked to take part in this mockery of the manufactured. Joke Hermes (1999) and Jo Littler (2004) have both examined the pleasure that women get from the media 'bringing down' the famous. Hermes' research on readers of women's celebrity gossip magazines in Holland revealed that women got through the difficulties in their own lives by comparing it to the 'misery of others'. Hermes argues that this 'repertoire of melodrama' is constituted not only by reference to 'misery, drama and by its sentimentalism and sensationalism, but also by its moral undertone. Life in the repertoire of melodrama becomes grotesquely magnified' (1999: 80). In a similar fashion, Jo Littler has analysed the UK magazine *heat*, concluding that 'Reading *Heat* provides one

outlet in which by reading it you can register your criticism, your cynical awareness and your knowledge of how the celebrity system works' (2004: 23).

Increasingly one can argue that the suffering and damage of fame is a prevalent
trend in the production and consumption of stars, celebrities, and personalities.
In fact, psychosis, madness, depression, drug and sex addiction, and suicidal
tendencies mark out the representational trajectory of a great many famous
people. Similarly, stalking and obsessive behaviour by fans make headline news
on a regular basis. Both of these aspects of what I would like to term fame
damage can be argued to be predicated on the intensity of being a star/celebrity,
or on so desperately wanting/desiring a star/celebrity, in a world where 'post-
God celebrity is now one of the mainstays of organising recognition and
belonging in a secular society' (Rojek, 2001:58).

While it has always been true that the famous have been identified as having a
close relationship to madness and genius (Stephen Harper explores this in his
essay in this collection), modern fame seems particularly centred on the politics
of dissolution. Not only are much of the mass and narrowcast media geared up to
attacking the famous, but the famous seem increasingly unable to deal with the
amount of (hostile) exposure they get. The intensity of the glare and the totalized
nature of the surveillance that they are put and put themselves under creates a
vision regime that leaves little if any space for them to be offscreen, out of print,
switched off. The famous are caught in the collapse of the public/private and are
often forced to be continually in role, in performance, as media beings. So much
so, perhaps, that they exist literally only in and through media representation: as
made-up beings, with no 'consciousness' beyond that. Tom Cruise, then, can
only 'love' Katie Holmes in and through the garments of stardom: Tom, Katie,
Tom and Katie together, are simply no more real than their images allow. Celebrities appear on reality TV pretending to be 'themselves' because without the
referentiality of fame they no longer exist at all.

The adoring, obsessive fans play their part in this dissolution of the famous:
they live their lives in and through the stars and celebrities they come to worship.
They put them under a panopticon of fame which itself can extend into the
realms of the psychotic. Obsessive fans blur and confuse the real and the fictional
so that the star or celebrity is imagined to respond to, or get in the way of, their
wishes and desires. As Chris Rojek suggests:

> In extreme cases the veridical self of the fan voluntarily submits to be
> substantially engulfed by the public face of the celebrity. This can lead to
> hopeless and painful feelings of resignation when the imaginary relation-
> ship with the celebrity is unconsummated, or to aggressive feelings of
> resentment against the celebrity (2001: 196).

Dawnette Knight was recently sentenced to three years in prison for stalking and threatening the Hollywood star, Catherine Zeta Jones. Knight had become infatuated with Michael Douglas, Jones's film star husband, constructing a narrative in which the two were lovers. Knight wrote more than two dozen letters to Douglas and stated in one, with reference to Jones, that 'We are going to slice her up like meat on a bone and feed her to the dogs'. The reality collapse is significant here: the 'made-up' star, who is no more or less than a famous being, is imagined to be real and a part of a real person's fantasy life which is itself written as if it is a 'stalking' Hollywood script.

There is, however, another inflection to the 'second-order intimacy' (Rojek, 2001: 52) created between stars/celebrities and fans/consumers. This is what might be termed a productive intimacy where stars and celebrities feel they are an important and valued part of everyday life, and fans/consumers employ stars/celebrities to extend and enrich their everyday world and the face-to-face interactions that take place there. Joke Hermes suggests that celebrity gossip enables 'readers to live in a larger world than in real life', mobilizing the stories of the famous to increase the number of people in their social network and to talk about the problems and crises that emerge in such exchanges (Hermes, 1999: 80).

The intimacy between the star/celebrity and the fan/consumer seems particularly heightened and extended because everything knowable, every verifiable fact, every salacious allegation, every bare centimetre of star/celebrity flesh, is reported upon and dwelt over by the mass and narrowcast media, and utilized by fans/consumers to help them make sense of their lives. The famous are increasingly brought into view through what is presented or reported and perceived to be an 'unmediated' close-up of their actually lived existences (Holmes, 2004). It is as if one has unfettered access to their lifestyles, behaviours, hang-ups, material bodies and interior selves. So, in direct counterpoint to the argument that modern fame is about distancing techniques and critical self-reflexivity, one can contend that the apparent closeness and realness of the star/celebrity image to the reader/viewer creates a 'relationship' that is experienced as first-hand, a priori, and as essentially meaningful to both parties.

In summary, one can argue that the reach, scope and intensity of fame has and continues to have fundamental cultural consequences for the way people live and understand the way they live. Fame can be argued to be a 'new' dominant discursive formation that shapes subjectivity, identity and belonging, and which 'speaks' in articulating frameworks about relations of power and the merits of individual success (Marshall, 1997; Dyer, 1998; Littler, 2004). Fame can be understood to be the 'glue' that holds the cultural centre together and which offers the alienated and anomic forms of para-social relations that make them feel complete and a part of a material culture that they can invest in and which 'invests' in them (Rojek, 2001; Hermes, 1999). Fame can be named as the vehicle for, or the symbol of, Western democratization, or, conversely, as the very thing that effaces democracy because of its 'trivialisation of public affairs' (Gitlin, 1997: 35). Fame can be identified as a central part of the core fabric of postmodern life where the surface and the mirror continually reflect off one another, free of referent, cut loose from 'depth' (Baudrillard, 1994). Fame can be argued to be the key resource for the playing out of spectacular, mediated events that are meant to fill the world with awe, desire and wonder (Kellner, 2002). Fame, in fact, can be understood to be so central to everyday life that it warrants placing in a field of reference that expresses that centrality in terms of a fame *culture*. As Graeme Turner suggests,

> it is the pervasiveness of celebrity across the modern mass media that encourages us to think of it as a new development, rather than simply the extension of a long-standing condition. The exorbitance of celebrity's contemporary cultural visibility is certainly unprecedented, and the role that the celebrity plays across many aspects of the cultural field has certainly expanded and multiplied in recent years (2004: 4).

There is a 24-hour, global clock of fame with someone – potentially anyone – constantly being brought onto the mediated world stage for hailing, adoring or despising. In the modern world, scientists, politicians, generals, terrorists, literary authors, poets, artists, musicians, film directors, stalkers, serial killers, and *especially* the man and woman next door can be – are all – caught in the panoptic glare of a culture that sets its sights on bringing into vision a revolving and relatively ephemeral celebrated elite (who, ironically, now encompass the many). I would now like to argue that this is an intimate vision that electrifies one's experience of human relations and the material world.

Intimate fame everywhere

If one were to retrace the footsteps of this essay so far one would find a weight of evidence to suggest that the production and consumption of fame is orientated around desire, authenticity, emotional investment, attachment, para-social inter-action and emulation. Contemporary fame speaks and is spoken about through the language of intimacy: it is a word, concept, practice, sellable commodity that smoulders at its very core. New media and information technologies; print, film and television formats; the discourses of authenticity, self-reflexivity and cultural closeness; the economic and political organization of late capitalism; these draw stars/celebrities and fans/consumers into ever decreasing circles of affective connectivity. One such instance of this is the celebrity confessional where through 'the combination of reflexivity about the business of being a celebrity, emotional interiority and self criticism on offer' one is 'invited to feel with their feelings' (Littler, 2004: 13, 18). Through the confessional text the celebrity attempts to speak openly and honestly about where they have come from – their humble beginnings; the troubles, hardships and corruption they may have faced along their journey to fame; who they really are underneath the fame gown; and how alike they are to the everyday people who watch their films, buy their records, go to their concerts and watch their soccer or tennis matches.

In this respect, one can usefully return to Halle Berry's 'best actress' winning speech and read it as an intimate confessional moment laced with political anger about her plight and the plight of black women in racist America. The worldwide audience are asked to identify and empathize with Berry: to see her as she really was and is now, and to ignore the glamour, the stage, the artifice around her, which is, at an existential level, somehow less than the sum of her parts; and, ultimately, to *feel* those tears as they fall down her cheeks and to cry a few tears of their own. As Jo Littler observes, 'anchoring the celebrity's image in relation to a "real moment before fame" invites us to feel closer to celebrities and to suggest our proximity to their emotions' (ibid.: 18).

Berry's 'best actress' winning speech touches many of the core human issues that trouble and motivate people: discrimination, inequality, honesty, fairness, openness, and the idea of the shared community. Her speech, then, has the potential to 'crack open', or at least draw attention to, the capitalist ideology that is seeking to contain and commodify her. The oppositional power of the speech is communicated through not just sentiment but also the heartfelt intensity of its delivery. Berry's speech is an electrified, fully embodied, charge against the Hollywood machine and it has the potential to reverberate in the cultural universe – in people's consciousness – long after the ceremony has closed.

Walter Benjamin argues that the 'celebrity achieves an aura through mass reproduction' and that the reproduction of a celebrity image makes seeing them 'in the flesh' even more captivating (1999: 236). For Benjamin, then, the power of the blown-up star or celebrity image, which is often of the face in radiant close-up, actually resides in the relational desire/opportunity that one might get to really see the heavenly body/face in the material world. So, the 'special' opportunity through which fans were able to meet and talk in person to Tom Cruise at the premiere of *War of the Worlds* works actually to heighten his auratic quality and to increase the desire for his onscreen image.

However, I would like to suggest that the star or celebrity's image is, in many instances, already *seeing in the flesh*. Their mediagenic aura is built upon the impression of uniqueness, on an intense one-to-one correspondence with the viewer/reader. When shot in close-up, for example, it is as if the star is looking at *you*, into *your* eyes, and when he smiles he is smiling at and for *you*. And what you *see* is the 'complete' figure and a high degree of interiority. In the intimacy of the close-up 'we can see to the bottom of a soul by means of such tiny movements of facial muscles which even the most observant partner would never perceive' (Balazs, 1985: 260). One takes the eyes and the smile as a doorway into something deeper and very personal. The screen dissolves or melts away in the unfolding moment and one comes into direct contact with the star or celebrity. What comes into being is an intimate flesh-to-flesh encounter, a free-forming collision, existentially grafted across time and space, and this all in spite of the technological apparatus that fires the star/celebrity/ fan relationship. In these highly charged moments, Halle Berry is talking to *me* about my awful life. Tom Cruise is smiling at *me* and I can see (feel) the love he has for me. Berry's speech and Cruise's smile have corporeal consequences: they have the potential to affect me in my body and effect the way I see myself in relation to the social world.

Nonetheless, one could still argue that this is an example of what has so far been referred to as a para-social or second-hand intimacy: a simulated intimacy that has been filtered through the tube, magazine column, film role, rock video or associated advertisement. There has been no face-to-face interaction; no conventional sense of getting to know the star or celebrity in the flesh, and no literal meeting of people present in simultaneous space. For a number of scholars, including Chris Rojek (2001), this is actually a type of false intimacy that helps commodify desire, and which enables alienated and isolated people to get by. The intimacy works in the service of a social and economic system that needs abstract desire, and not against it. As Rojek concludes:

> Celebrity culture is one of the most important mechanisms for mobi-
> lizing abstract desire. It embodies desire in an animate object, which
> allows for deeper levels of attachment and identification than with inani-
> mate commodities. Celebrities can be reinvented to renew desire, and
> because of this they are extremely efficient resources in the mobilization
> of global desire. In a word, they *humanize* desire (2001: 189).

However, what I would like to suggest is that this type of para-social connectivity is as 'real' as anything can be in a cultural universe made out of simulacra, and that the relationships that emerge between star/celebrity and fan/consumer fill the world with productive, surplus emotionality that cannot be easily channelled or 'sucked up' by capitalism, and which offers people transgressive models of identity.

The relationship between the star or celebrity and the commodity is a useful reference point to return to. It is suggested that through advertisements, endorsements, and 'lifestyle' choices, stars and celebrities work in the interests of capitalism (Marshall, 1997). The commodified celebrity peddles the myth of the autonomous individual and the value of consumption for a full and happy life. But the famous also work to replenish and motivate desire for constantly changing and updated goods and services since 'capitalism can never permit desire to be fulfilled, since to do so will neutralise desire and thus, forfeit economic growth. Market organization is actually founded on the perpetual replenishment and development of desire through commodity and brand innovation' (Rojek, 2001: 189). In this understanding of the star/celebrity–commodity nexus there is argued to be a perpetual cycle of famous people being attached to 'new' goods and services, creating and re-creating demand and desire for these things that 'have a provisional quality' (ibid.: 189). In this argument, desire becomes a deeply unsatisfying experience or quality because 'consumers under capitalism do not experience unifying fulfilment when desire is matched with possession. For the abstract quality of desire means that wants are never satisfied by possessing a particular commodity' (ibid.: 187). It is these observations that I would like to take issue with.

First, at the precise moment of the consumption of a celebrity 'thing', for example, when an expensive perfume is first sprayed over a neck, a designer dress first worn, or a piece of jewellery first put on, the intensity of that thing, imbued as it is with the pregnant aura of the star or celebrity, is immense. The thing itself radiates like the star or celebrity and the level of 'self-identification', when 'involvement has reached the point at which the audience-member places himself in the same situation and persona of the star' (Tudor, quoted in Dyer, 1998: 18), is in perfect material and psychological unison. On the one hand, the celebrity-inflected thing becomes a fantasy time and space device 'transporting' the consumer to the privileged exterior/interior world of the famous. On the other, the celebrity-inflected thing transforms the material present, or the here-and-now, filling it and the person with a heightened, perhaps even an out-of-body, sense of the real, of the self, of who one is as a *living thing*. There is, then, a period of time when the use of the shiny commodity-celebrity thing increases one's self-worth and self-esteem, when one feels empowered by the thing, and more alive than one did before it was possessed. The commodity thing itself seems to have feelings, emotions that one can access through the signification chain that accompanies it. You, the thing, and the star or celebrity (now) within you, are expanses of light. The transient nature of the relationship is itself pleasurable since there is a constant promise of renewal and of transformation with each new famous-commodity encounter.

But in these epiphany moments there is also the chance that in seeing oneself differently one also sees oneself *accurately*. There is the possibility that one also sees oneself both before the possession of the commodity thing, and after the initial euphoria of having experienced it. There is the possibility, then, that one sees oneself as exploited, alienated and duped by the 'thing' that promised so much in its primal state. There is always the possibility that one sees capitalism *accurately*. This has the potential to be a double reward: while the first rush of the commodity thing gives one an uplifting, transcendental experience, the second gives one a critical insight into the mechanics of late capitalism and one's place within it.

Second, the celebrity-commodity thing is often represented in terms of transgressive values or attributes that potentially work against the dominant ideology of late capitalism. The themes of sexual adventure, 'excessive' forms of embodiment, rebellion and resistance to 'normative' behaviour, reoccur in the fantasy settings of a great many adverts and billboards, pop and rock videos, films and television programmes. Celebrity-commodity intertexts leak, they are ideologically porous, and countervalues emerge in their sign systems. One can re-read the representation of Britney Spears' perfume Curious in this way. The barely concealed connotation of the perfume's name and supporting imagery – with Britney dressed provocatively and pouting at the imagined purchaser – is for girls to experiment, to try out sexual scenarios and encounters, both with boys and other girls. The subtext here is about sexual freedom, and choice, on the girl's terms. There is much more, then, than simple heterosexual desire at play in the fantasy Britney household. As such, the advert/perfume/Britney offers the purchaser, at least in representational terms, a form of self-identity and self-awareness that does not easily sit with patriarchy and stereotypical gender norms. In this sense, one can buy star- or celebrity-inflected goods without buying into dominant ideology as well. In summary, transcendence, transformation, empowerment and a critical consciousness can all rise up out of the scorching ashes of celebrity-capitalism.

There is one final kinetic attribute to the star or celebrity/fan relationship that I would like to briefly explore. This is a connectivity that explicitly exists at a heightened level of intimacy and of transgressive, transformative power. In this respect, *fame damage* seems be a particularly potent form of identification and an increasingly common way for stars and celebrities to be produced and consumed. This damage of fame not only draws people closer to the injured star or celebrity, but it offers up the potential for resistant behaviour and for a critique of the machinery of fame (and capitalism) to emerge. The damaged famous, and the fans of the damaged famous – who often see themselves as similarly damaged – form resistant, symbiotic 'relationships' that work against the grain of dominant ideology and the 'artifice' of fame.

Richard Dyer has argued in relation to Hollywood stardom that 'both consumption and success are from time to time shown to be wanting. Consumption can be characterized as wastefulness and decadence, while success may be short-lived or a psychological burden' (1998: 44). The damaged star or celebrity can suffer any one of a number of mythic tragedies; fame is felt to be short-lived or not 'bright' enough; success and wealth is said to ruin the star or celebrity because it takes them too far away from their common 'origins'; fame is said to isolate and alienate them and they turn to drink, drugs and suicide to escape the loneliness of their lives; and fame is said to offer the star or celebrity too much of everything that is vacuous and surface level, and very little of the intimate, the psychologically deep, or the long-lasting, and this destroys their ability to be happy and contented. While the damaged star or celebrity is as much a construction as the replenished figure of fame their identity crisis resonates in ways that signify beyond the discourse that they are made up in.

The isolated, alienated famous figure exists in a realm of alienation and 'exclusion' that is familiar to ordinary individuals in crisis who exist outside the social communities or family networks that would otherwise help them feel like they belonged. While one is trapped in the 'artifice' of fame the other is trapped in the 'reality' of social exclusion. Through these mirrors of likeness, the lonely star and the anomic fan 'speak' to each other about the harsh realities of modern living and about their own sense of worthlessness. The fading celebrity and the failing (in life) fan 'talk' to one another about the deceiving and exploitative nature of late capitalism: the ruined star shows that fame doesn't work (when it is prophesied to be the very definition of commodity success) and the ordinary fan shows that life is awful (and this is the fault or responsibility of an alienating system). These are often the most intimate – if seemingly destructive – of cultural exchanges, scripted in suicide diaries/notes (Kurt Cobain, Lesley Cheung), written on the flesh (Richey Edwards), sung out in heartfelt exposition (Judy Garland, Elvis Presley), or in verified mental breakdowns (Ian Holmes). But these exchanges can also be productive because the message of damage is also about enabling the fan to see through and beyond the pain and suffering that they are experiencing and which they are sharing with the wounded star or celebrity. This is particularly true when marginal identities are drawn into the affective equation. The repressed and resistant figure of fame communicates or resonates with the 'outsider' about the liquid, troubling nature of (their) identity and the ways that one can get through the maelstrom of everyday life. In this respect, Richard Dyer reads Judy Garland as an emotive figure of crisis who had 'a special relationship to suffering' (1986: 143), a 'gay sensibility' (ibid.: 154) that gay men particularly identified with. When Judy Garland sings there is an 'intensity and irony' (ibid.: 154) to the performance that extends out from beyond the screen to profoundly connect with the experiences of gay men. In a similar way, one can argue that Halle Berry's performativity screams out to the 'racial Other' about her/their exploitation; that Tom Cruise's ambivalent masculinity whispers to the closet gay about the fascism of normative sexuality; and that Britney Spears' representational curiosity stimulates real sexual curiosity in the legion of young female fans who adore her.

When fame doesn't work, when it destroys and negates and critically self-reflects on its trajectories and outcomes (through biography, confessional, irony and mockery), it shows up stardom and celebrification to be faulty enterprises. The burnt-out star, wasted on pills, fat on glamour and sick on wealth is one of the most haunting, or charged images in the hall of fame. In the blown-up face and the bloodshot eyes one is required to stare directly into the unmediated 'truth' of the star or celebrity, laid bare, at the existential level, before us.

I would like to end this essay with my own confessional moment. I am aged 10 and I am about to watch on TV a re-run of Elvis Presley's 1967 *Comeback Special*, a few months after his death. I am a huge fan of the pre-Vegas Elvis, so much so that I pretend to be Elvis whenever and wherever I can (including the Irish clubs we would go to as a family, at the weekend). The day he dies I cry uncontrollably. The images of the bloated, rambling Elvis that surface after his death upset me greatly: in fact I honestly believe that they are not of him. I have been told the *Comeback Special* is a must-see: it is Elvis at his best. In anticipation I have turned off the lights and closed the curtains.

Elvis arrives on screen, in figure-hugging black leather, with quivering lips and hips. It is as if the TV is shaking. His raw, anthemic voice and the vocal inflection rhythmically echo the hypersexual, masculine identity that is dancing on screen before me. But there is no screen there. Elvis is in my living room and I am on stage with him, and he is singing and swaying to and for me. And I am Elvis, hypersexual and masculine. In those moments, in the half-light, I couldn't be happier: Elvis and I have shared real flesh-to-flesh intimacy. And those death pictures haunt me no more.

Bibliography

Balazs, Bela (1985) 'The Close-Up', in Gerald Mast and Marshall Cohen (eds), *Film Theory and Criticism*, Oxford: Oxford University Press, pp. 255–64.

Baudrillard, Jean (1994) *Simulacra and Simulation*, trans. Sheila F. Glaser, Ann Arbor: University of Michigan Press.

Benjamin, Walter (1999) *Illuminations*, London: Pimlico.

Biressi, Anita and Nunn, Heather (2004) *Reality TV: Realism and Revelation*, London: Wallflower Press.

Bonner, Frances (2002) *Ordinary Television*, London: Sage.

Braudy, Leo (1986) *The Frenzy of Renown: Fame and its History*, Oxford: Oxford University Press.

Couldry, Nick (2003) *Media Rituals: A Critical Approach*, London: Routledge.

Dyer, Richard (1998) *Stars*, 2nd edn, London: Routledge.

—— (1986) *Heavenly Bodies: Film Stars and Society*, New York: St Martin's Press.

Gamson, Joshua (1994) *Claims to Fame: Celebrity in Contemporary America*, Berkeley: University of California Press.

Gitlin, Todd (1997) 'The Anti-Political Populism of Cultural Studies', in Marjorie Ferguson and Peter Golding (eds), *Cultural Studies in Question*, London: Sage, pp. 25–38.

Hermes, Joke (1999) 'Media Figures in Identity Construction', in Pertti Alasuutari (ed.), *Rethinking the Media Audience: The New Agenda*, London: Sage, pp. 69–85.

—— (1995) *Reading Women's Magazines: An Analysis of Everyday Media Use*, Cambridge: Polity.

Holmes, Su (2004) 'All You've Got to Worry About is the Task, Having a Cup of Tea, and Doing a Bit of Sunbathing', in Su Holmes and Deborah Jermyn (eds), *Understanding Reality TV*, London: Routledge.

Hopkins, Susan (2002) *Girl Heroes: The New Force in Popular Culture*, Sydney: Pluto Press.

Kellner, Douglas (2002) *Media Spectacle*, London: Routledge.

Littler, Jo (2004) 'Making Fame Ordinary. Intimacy, Reflexivity and "Keeping it Real"', *Mediaactive* 2: 8–25.

Lowenthal, Leo (1961) 'The Triumph of Mass Idols', in *Literature, Popular Culture and Society*, Palo Alto, CA: Pacific Books, pp. 109–40.

Marshall, P. David (1997) *Celebrity and Power: Fame in Contemporary Culture*, London: University of Minnesota Press.

Rojek, Chris (2001) *Celebrity*, London: Reaktion.

Turner, Graeme (2004) *Understanding Celebrity*, London: Sage.

Turner, Graeme, Bonner, Frances, and Marshall, P. David (2000) *Fame Games: The Production of Celebrity in Australia*, London: Cambridge University Press.

Chapter 3

It's a jungle out there!

Playing the game of fame in celebrity reality TV

Su Holmes

Celebrity reality TV describes formats where a degree of celebrity status is a prerequisite for entering the show. Initially, perhaps, it appeared to be a less successful, interesting or spectacular version of reality TV based around 'ordinary' people. This was at least true of the UK, and, as Nick Couldry observed after the first series of *Celebrity Big Brother* in 2001,

> With celebrities, not 'ordinary people' as inmates of the house, it was much less clear what was being 'revealed' during the climax of the game: we know, of course, that celebrities are *in fact* 'ordinary', and there was no excitement in seeing a celebrity confirm his or her existing status by winning the game (2002: 288–9).

Since this time, the concept of celebrities entering reality TV, whether in designated formats of their own (*The Osbournes, The Anna Nicole Show, I'm a Celebrity ... Get Me Out of Here!, The Games, Celebrity Boxing, Back to Reality, Celebrity Love Island*), or in celebrity versions of existing series (*Celebrity Big Brother, Celebrity Fame Academy*), has accelerated in both prevalence and popularity.[1] It is now difficult to accept Couldry's suggestion that celebrity reality TV may be less fascinating to the public, after the third series of *I'm a Celebrity* emerged as the most successful UK reality series to date (Born, 2004: 3). With the final in 2004 attracting a 62 per cent viewer share (6 in 10 of the total TV audience), the show offered ITV1 its largest peak-time audience in more than two years (ibid.). In this respect, it seems that the textual structures and appeal of celebrity reality TV are worth some thought, particularly in terms of their comparative relationship with wider reality TV. The spectacle of 'ordinary' people grabbing the media spotlight, 'without overtly drawing on education, entrepreneurial skills or even ... obvious talent' (Biressi and Nunn, 2005: 145), has emerged as a particularly visible site for debates over the status of contemporary fame. Here, the emphasis has been on discourses of democratization, whether this is read as a worrying cultural shift or as a populist challenge to more elite societal structures. But, as Couldry's comment suggests, there has also been a push toward conceptualizing celebrity formats within their own discourses of democratization. As Phil Edgar-Jones, executive producer of the UK *Celebrity Big Brother* confirms: 'With normal *Big Brother* we're making ordinary people extraordinary. With this, we're making famous people very, very ordinary' (cited in Biressi and Nunn, 2005: 147). Edgar-Jones emphasizes the format as almost a deconstruction of the celebrity façade. In comparison, and in discussing the US shows *Celebrity Boxing* and *Celebrity Fear-Factor*, Jeffrey Sconce foregrounds an impetus toward democratization from a different perspective, and more forcefully invokes the power relationship between celebrity and audience. In applauding the fact that the 'humiliation of debased, frustrated, and faded celebrity has now found a mass audience', Sconce notes that 'in a culture that chooses to repress the politics of class division, celebrity baiting ... may well be the last simmering refuge of populist hatred for the spoiled rich' (2004: 255). While the debate surrounding reality TV has ventured that anyone can be a celebrity, the currency of democracy in relation to celebrity formats pivots on the context in which participants are placed, their 'journey' within the reality space, and the investment that is offered to the audience. But discourses of democracy have long since been woven into the tapestry of modern fame (Gamson, 1994), and it is easy to forget that this essentially individualistic and hierarchical phenomenon is a *deeply* paradoxical place for this to occur (Turner, 2004; Littler, 2004). Indeed, while they might appear to originate from a similar perspective, it is difficult to reconcile the claim that celebrity reality TV makes its subjects 'ordinary' with the notion that it provides an outlet for our collective frustration with the (hierarchical) difference between 'them' and 'us'. The heritage of star and celebrity studies has *long* emphasized how the claim to the 'ordinary' functions as part of the mythic construction of fame, more often aiming to assuage class resentment than stoke its fires. (Sconce's comment about the repression of class difference above may well point to elements of national specificity, but I refer here to discourses which are primarily associated with American stardom – the ordinary/extraordinary paradox, or the success myth: see Dyer, 1998.) In relation to the UK version of *I'm a Celebrity*, I want to expand this perspective, situating it within a wider context which considers how the authenticity of the celebrity is negotiated by the text, and how (and why) its framework engages the audience in the cultural production of fame. *I'm a Celebrity* offers a fascinating and heightened commentary on the discursive construction of contemporary celebrity, but it is one which ultimately draws upon highly traditional structures. Indeed, when the current watchword in media commentary appears to be *change* – the prevalent sense that modern celebrity represents a qualitative break with the past – it is sometimes difficult, and almost unfashionable, to pause and interrogate these claims to the new. It is precisely for this reason that such a task remains important.

Catch a falling star ...

While initially dubbed 'Celebrity Survivor' (the originators of *Survivor* attempted to sue Granada for format theft: Brenton and Cohen, 2003: 77), *I'm a Celebrity* originated in the UK. It has been sold as an international format, although with varying degrees of success. With participants conceived as 'the usual hotch-potch of has-been[s]',[2] principally appearing on the show to 'beef-up their flagging careers' (ibid.), celebrity reality TV is often peopled by faces who have experienced a decline in auratic status, names jostling for the chance to relaunch or reinvent their personae. If, as current wisdom would suggest, fame has become increasingly detached from notions of 'talent' and 'hard work' (which are in themselves problematic constructs: Littler, 2004), this also has the effect of suggesting that it is more of a 'risky lottery of opportunity' than a 'birthright for the righteously dedicated' (ibid.: 8). The notion of luck has long since permeated mythic constructions of fame (Dyer, 1998; Gamson, 2001), but the ever more ephemeral nature of contemporary celebrity, and the increasing number of faces crowding to get in, may well offer this discourse new impetus. It is surely in part the notion of celebrity as a 'risky lottery' that fosters interest in the time-line of fame: we only need think of the magazine/television appetite for featuring articles and programmes on celebrities before or after 'they were famous'. While these suggest different perspectives on and investments in celebrity, interest partly emerges here from tracking a trajectory through the *process* of fame, and its temporal impact on the physical, cultural and economic fortunes of the self. This offers a further perspective on the argument that there is a contemporary fascination with the mechanisms of the celebrity *apparatus* itself (Gamson, 1994), perhaps considerably more so than the people it produces (Mole, 2004).

It seems only natural that people should want to climb back up what Leo Braudy describes as the 'ladder of the renown' (1986: 5), yet this is natural only in a society where celebrity suggests economic and symbolic empowerment and anonymity suggests economic and symbolic *dis*empowerment (Littler, 2004). In this respect, Nick Couldry has usefully drawn attention to how celebrity functions to entrench a broader symbolic boundary which is constructed between 'media' and 'ordinary' worlds, a hierarchy which functions to naturalize media power. To step into television is culturally conceived as entering a form of privileged reality, a 'special place' (Couldry, 2004: 47), and what occurs within this space is coded as more significant than what occurs outside it. The emergence of a category of programming called 'reality TV' has arguably only propagated this claim in a more explicit form (Couldry, 2004). In a culture which tells us we 'should [be famous] if we possibly can, because it is the best, perhaps the only, way *to be*' (Braudy, 1986: 6), the media value of celebrity suggests that the 'ordinary' world must be escaped from although it is paradoxically by making a claim to the 'ordinary' that this very process occurs. This is because in order to claim a privileged access to reality, the media must also be invoked as a shared space, thus *also* representing the world of 'the everyday' (Couldry, 2000: 47). Conversely, it is from this perspective that the term 'ordinary' can be used interchangeably with the notion of 'real' people – without undermining the symbolic hierarchy above.

In celebrity reality TV, the notion of having slipped somewhat from this privileged space does establish a power relationship between participants and audience. Reality TV has in general foregrounded the (interactive) power of the audience, constructing the viewer as the ultimate conferrer of public visibility ('pick me': Holmes, 2004a, 2004b). But in celebrity reality TV, the fact that these people were once *more* famous (they 'had it' and 'lost it') doubly invokes this discourse. At the same time, it is crucial to note that this varies according to the individuals who are cast to appear. Some participants were indeed at the height of their fame over twenty years previously (the Sex Pistols' Johnny Rotten, ballet dancer Wayne Sleep, 1980s pop star Toyah Wilcox, or DJ Tony Blackburn), some two to three years before (former girl group singers such as Natalie Appleton or Kerry McFadden), or somewhere in-between (athletes John Fashanu or Diane Modahl, Australian pop singer Peter Andre). (See Figure 3.1 for the cast of series 3, 2004.) Other participants were at the height of their careers at the time of entering the show, already enjoying varying degrees of public visibility (models Jordan or Sophie Anderton, make-over TV presenter Linda Barker, TV chef Anthony Worral-Thompson, socialite Tara Palmer-Tomkinson). In contrast, others were virtually unknown to many viewers (Lord Brocket, or Fran Cosgrave – then the ex-boyfriend of Atomic Kitten singer Natasha Hamilton). When compared to more youth-orientated shows such as *Big Brother,* this temporal range is also important to the family appeal of the series and in the UK, particularly to the more generalist address of ITV1. But despite this diversity, what apparently unites the participants, as the Executive Producer claims, is that they are not 'really really famous' people. This, he explains, wouldn't work because:

> While casting is crucial, part of the reason [we select the celebrities for the programme] is that ... there's always a ... question mark about why they're famous. It gives that slight edge to it – just the way they all compete with each other for the camera.[3]

Here, the claim is that *I'm a Celebrity* revels in the decline of a merited claim to fame, which is apparently integral to the entire dynamic of the show. However, a closer consideration reveals a more careful negotiation of celebrity status, and I draw here on Joshua Gamson's work (1994, 2001) which has usefully traced the ways in which historical explanations of fame have shifted over time.

Figure 3.1 From left to right (back): Diane Modahl, Peter Andre, Mike Read, Neil 'Razor' Ruddock, 'Johnny Rotten' (John Lydon), Lord 'Charlie' Brocket. From left to right (front): Jennie Bond, Kerry McFadden (now Katona), 'Jordan' (Katie Price), Alex Best.

In examining the historical development of celebrity, Gamson argues that different explanations of fame have battled for cultural legitimacy at different times. In its early stages fame was largely limited to figures such as political and religious elites, with discourses constructing it as the province of 'the top layer of a natural hierarchy' (Gamson, 2001: 260). Yet with the growth of arts and technologies, by the middle of the nineteenth century celebrity was becoming established as a mass – and more democratic – phenomenon. With the Hollywood studio system representing celebrity's later period of industrialization, and with a controlled production system producing celebrities for a mass audience, the earlier theme of 'greatness' became muted into questions of 'star quality' and 'talent' (Gamson, 2001: 264), mediating between the concepts of an elitist meritocracy and an 'egalitarian democracy' (ibid.: 261). However, the increasing visibility of the publicity machine gradually began to pose a threat to this myth. The explosion of media outlets in the second half of the twentieth century witnessed the increasing prevalence of the manufacture discourse (that celebrities are produced and made and not 'born'), where it henceforth becomes a 'serious contender' in explaining celebrity (Gamson, 1994: 44). It is not that the older narratives of fame are rendered redundant, but rather that the two explanations jostle for cultural legitimacy in the same space. Gamson suggests that by the late twentieth century, it was possible to discern strategies intended to *cope* with the increasing disjuncture between the claims-to-fame stories. He points toward the devices of 'exposing' the process (inviting us behind-the-scenes of celebrity production), the construction of an ironic and mocking perspective on celebrity culture, and an increased emphasis on the power of the audience.

'You really can't act all the time': capturing authenticity

We only need to look at contemporary celebrity texts to see the relevance of Gamson's paradigm here. While celebrity magazines such as *heat* and *Now* have trailblazed a less reverential approach to the famous (see Feasey in this collection, and Holmes, 2005), there are many ways in which reality TV's coverage of celebrity complements this boisterously democratic approach to the famous. *I'm a Celebrity* drops its participants in an inhospitable environment, and encourages the audience to relish the power of determining their fate in the obligatory bush-tucker trials – which the celebrities must endure in exchange for basic necessities such as food. It equally adopts a somewhat irreverent attitude to its participants. The comedic Geordie presenting duo Ant and Dec are key to the success of the UK version. Although ultimately framing the programme with a good-natured and certainly affectionate attitude toward the celebrities (through which Ant and Dec foreground their 'ordinariness' and efface their own celebrity status), the presenters adopt a slightly ironic distance from the proceedings. They always refuse to defer to the celebrity status of the participants – rolling their eyes at blatant celebrity plugs, taking the mickey out of the celebrities' intelligence (e.g. when Peter Andre tried to write 'OZ' on his face with charcoal, but without the help of a mirror it came out as 'ZO'), or barely stifling giggles and sneaking asides to the camera as the celebrities screech and scream their way through grue-some trials. These are also important framing devices in how the programme cues us to respond to the concept of celebrity status in the show.

But this takes place alongside a fervent negotiation of authenticity. In many ways harking back to pre-modern models of the self, the jungle terrain is offered as stripping away the trappings of modern life – consumer culture, technology and mass communication – and, by implication, revealing more of the 'real' person beneath. This claim is more highly charged in light of the aim to display *celebrities* within this context, not least of all because this rhetoric always struc-tures celebrity coverage. Particularly when contemporary celebrity is primarily defined as a consumer lifestyle, this charge firstly emerges from conceptions of a privileged existence. Before returning to a live link from Ant and Dec in the studio, the end of each edited segment is signified by a dissolve to a range of possible images which stage the meeting, and supposed mismatch, between celebrity culture and the jungle climate. These include an image of a mobile phone slipping slowly into a swamp, crickets crawling up a glass of sparkling champagne, a frog sitting on the end of a gentleman's cane, a snake slithering through a diamond-encrusted sandal and a kangaroo chewing on the end of a pink feather boa. With the exception of the mobile phone, these objects are all signifiers of a once upper-class, or even aristocratic status, curiously harking back to older, elite definitions of social status and economic privilege which the growth of celebrity culture has itself helped to undermine. The persistent drawing of this boundary seems to have a number of significant functions.

First, despite their radically different levels of public fame (as discussed, some are essentially unknown to the audience) this establishes all the participants as celebrities upon entrance into the show. In simple terms, this cues the notion that we should be interested in them and how they cope in this environment. It also homogenizes them as a group in other ways. While the producer dismissed a merited claim to fame as shaping the selection criteria for the show (the question mark over why they were/are famous), the participants collectively emerge from a *range* of cultural domains which in fact have different explanations of fame attached to them. Sport, for example, continues to be associated with discourses of talent and meritocracy (Giles, 2000, cited in Turner, 2004: 18). In a programme apparently unconcerned with passing judgement on explanations of fame (Why *are* they here? *Should* they be?), explaining celebrity as an economic status is more clear-cut, and not necessarily problematic. The programme, like reality TV in general, delights in putting a range of class, as well as ethnic and sexual, identities in camp, but the strategy above uncouples notions of economic and class status: celebrity is *apparently* open to all, while it is simultaneously defined by elite privileges once you get in. (As discussed later in the article, the programme also very much *retains* the idea that class is significant, particularly when it comes to judging and validating the selves which are put on display.) What of course really unites the participants as a group is their past and more crucially present *media*tion: i.e. literally being *in* the programme itself. While the programme ostensibly seems to be unconcerned with traditional, merited explanations of fame, this fact would surely reveal too nakedly the arbitrary nature of celebrity,[4] while it would also of course be intangible to image. But perhaps more importantly, this would reflect back on how, far from a democratizing arena, this represents a highly privileged space. Indeed, as they guzzle the glass of champagne that is handed to them upon their exit, it is amusing to watch the celebrities feigning relief upon being voted out ('I couldn't have stood *another* minute'), as the presenters construct their exit as a well-earned and privileged release: 'You're a celebrity, get yourself *out* of here!' In having their spell of unprecedented public visibility cut short, we all know that, if offered the chance, many would often leap right back in.

The categorizing of the celebrities as different on an economic level enables the show to construct a visible, tangible dichotomy between a celebrity world of wealth and privilege and the seemingly democratizing space of reality TV. However playfully, this indeed invites a reading of the text in which, returning to Sconce's argument, it beckons a cathartic release of a 'populist hatred for the spoiled rich' (even if many of the participants are not actually that wealthy) (2004: 255). It is presumably within this framework that it is inappropriate for the celebrities to win prize money on the programme, particularly as it is provided from our pockets via the telephone/digital voting on the show. This contradictory framework points to how the programme carefully constructs a *symbolic boundary* between the celebrities and their audience so that the game can begin. Within this framework, the celebrities are to appear as different from us, but not *too* different. Indeed, if celebrityhood and social mobility are defined here as dependent on consumption, this is relatively superficial and surface, as the entire notion of the primitive jungle terrain aims to make only too clear. In short, a boundary is drawn between 'them' and 'us' but only in such a way that it can be lessened or blurred throughout the trajectory of the show.

Like all celebrity coverage, as well as much of reality TV, we are invited to become acquainted with the 'real' selves on display, although this is negotiated within the specificity of the format. For example, to return to the comparison with the magazine and its negotiation of authenticity, one of *heat*'s regular columns is 'Spotted: They Can't Get Away from Us', while with reality TV there is no chance of escape and thus no need to chase. This convenience means making sacrifices where the rhetoric of authenticity is concerned. The magazine image trades on the belief in 'the higher truth of the stolen image' (Sekula, 1984: 29, cited in Becker, 1992: 142) – 'Scandal!', '100% Unapproved' – but reality TV's claim to present the real, to strip away the celebrity persona, comes into conflict with its status as an openly performative space which is deeply self-conscious about its mediated status. In *I'm a Celebrity*, we witness singers bursting into song, ex-athletes doing press-ups, models modelling (dressing-up tasks are often devised), dancers dancing, make-over experts designing (decorating the camp) and TV chefs cooking. In being thus reminded of their pre-existing media personae, we know that far from being a forbidden peep into celebrity culture this text is clearly very *aware* of being watched. This is arguably even more charged with the celebrity formats, as giving a performance is literally recognized as part of the skill of the celebrity persona. At the same time, like many reality TV formats (*Big Brother* in particular), this contradiction must be continually negotiated in order to validate the authenticity of events which occur. The claim which most encapsulates this tension, and tries to reconcile its contradictions, is that you are 'aware that there are cameras about, but some of the time you forget … You really, really can't act *all* the time' (Jordan, series 3, 7 February 2004).

It is partly because of this ongoing dialectic that the bush-tucker trials are structurally important. Jostling for space alongside the more self-reflexive discourses of performance, the daily trials, which range from plunging one's head into a eel-filled helmet to eating the local delight of a kangaroo's testicle, are intended as visceral shocks, both physical and mental. They seem to insist that surely *this* is *real* (terror, fear or revulsion)?

This ever-present oscillation seems entirely appropriate for a form of programming in which, as Annette Hill's audience research has highlighted, viewers have not so much abandoned the '*idea* of authenticity' as they aim to search out the moment when people seem to be 'really' themselves in an unreal environment (Hill, 2002: 337). This structure is in many ways resonant of our relations with the textual construction of celebrity: we understand the mediated nature of the celebrity image, but we are perpetually encouraged to search the persona for elements of the real and authentic, beckoned by the promise of intimate access to their 'real' selves (Dyer, 1998).

But more recent comment on celebrity might question whether there is a neat fit here, or whether this conception of reality TV fully captures the degree of playfulness in audiences' relations with celebrity. Dyer famously argued that stars articulate ideas about personhood and, in particular, discourses of individualism. For Dyer, the continual insistence on 'authenticity' in the star image, or the perpetual claim to 'really', pivoted upon a particular model of selfhood which endorsed the notion of a 'separable, coherent quality, located "inside" consciousness and variously termed "the self", "the soul", "the subject"' (Dyer, 1986: 9). But within the context of postmodern and poststructuralist strands of thought, such a depth model of the self has become somewhat unfashionable. Barry King's argument, for example, is a challenge to Dyer's when he draws attention to the changed 'existential parameters of stardom ... Today's stars ... epitomise the postmodern self, a decentred subject, deeply reflexive and disdainful of claims to identity' (King, 2003: 45). He invokes here Gamson's (1994) research into audiences' relations with celebrity. Particularly as correlated with their awareness of the production process, this revealed a continuum of categories ranging from 'traditionalists' or 'believers', who read the celebrity text as realistic, to 'game players', who read the text as semi-fictional and are unconcerned with questions of truth and authenticity. Rather, the celebrity system becomes a source of play, a 'pleasurable dance of appearances' in which the reader can 'continually *ride* the belief/disbelief and fiction/reality axes with no particular destination' (Gamson, 1994: 178). But this provides no straightforward challenge to Dyer's argument. First, Gamson's emphasis is on how the celebrity system mobilizes a *wide* range of reading strategies, and how this works to *sustain* rather than threaten its status. Such constructions are actively intended to solicit game-playing, and of course, celebrity producers were always aiming to keep us interested – not shore up a

particular model of individualism and selfhood. But, in returning to Dyer, it
seems rash to dismiss the negotiation of authenticity simply because the arena
appears to be playful (a complexity arguably incorporated into Dyer's thesis
anyway: Dyer, 1986: 15). However self-reflexive and playful the contexts may
have become, it is evident that the illusion of access and intimacy remains the
dominant structuring force in celebrity texts. This constitutes a beckoning which,
on some level at least, continues to arouse audience interest.

When we talk about the search for the 'real' or the authentic where celebrity
is concerned, the meanings of these terms are not easily pinned down (Dyer,
1998). They differ across performance contexts and historically, have often been
shaped by discourses of class (and ethnicity) (see Littler, 2004). Furthermore, we
need to consider them in the context of reality programming. Drawing on Martin
Montgomery's useful taxonomy of 'authentic talk' in broadcasting, Hill emphasizes how authenticity in this respect has a range of different meanings:

> First there is talk that is deemed authentic because it does not sound
> contrived, simulated or performed but rather sounds natural, 'fresh',
> spontaneous. Second, there is talk that is deemed authentic because it
> seems to truly capture or present the experience of the speaker. Third,
> there is authentic talk that seems to truly project the core self of the
> speaker – talk that is true to the self of the speaker in an existential
> fashion (Montgomery, 2001, cited in Hill, 2005: 75).

Particularly when it comes to rendering the celebrity accessible and 'ordinary',
each of these seems important to the discourses of selfhood in *I'm a Celebrity*. A
premium value is certainly placed on moments of emotional intimacy with the
participants, whether it be Kerry McFadden crying to the diary camera, 'It's *so*
hard, I miss my kids … You have no idea how *much* I want to make my family
proud … I can't *take* it here', or Peter Andre tenderly confessing his emerging
feelings for fellow contestant Jordan –'I could just watch her *all* day … [shy
pause as he drops his head]. Does that sound stupid?'. In this respect, the
programme undoubtedly provides an extended – and apparently more intimate
and 'real' – space for an emphasis on the therapeutic discourse of selfhood which
pervades reality TV. Reality TV has established a new televisual realism in the
digital age, founded on the concept of self-revelation and (often) personal development as a privileged signifier of authenticity (Biressi and Nunn, 2005: 104).
But the idea of a confessional and therapeutic discourse also very much infuses
identity construction in celebrity culture (see also Stephen Harper's essay in this
collection), from 'raw' 'tell-all' biographies, to the self-revelations of magazine
and chat show interviews. Celebrity reality TV, then, perhaps represents the ultimate synergy of these conceptions. With its reality aesthetic, version of a diary

room, and serial form, *I'm a Celebrity* less invents this discourse than it fosters a greater illusion of intimacy, and a more extended narrative space for self-exploration to occur. Indeed, while I argue throughout that the programme negotiates a fervent insistence that the 'real' (celebrity) self is both locatable and valuable, it by no means imagines this entity as static, finished and whole. The often highly vague approximation of a therapeutic discourse means that participants are invited to explore different facets of their identity, with the hutcam in particular providing what Biressi and Nunn elsewhere describe as 'updates on personal progress and identity' (2005: 105).

Notions of intimacy and authenticity are often equated with 'ordinariness' here, and celebrity has long since been constructed through an apparent paradox of the ordinary/extraordinary (Dyer, 1998; Ellis, 1992). Functioning as something of a transhistorical myth, this paradox is necessarily vague, and it has been interpreted in different ways. For example, in respect to the classic Hollywood period it is often understood to suggest a combination of some 'special talent or position' with an emphasis on 'ordinary' hobbies or feelings (Ellis, 1992: 95), or a contrast between a glamorous lifestyle and the 'surprisingly ordinary domestic life of the star' (Geraghty, 2000: 184). This is invoked in various ways in the reality format. For regular viewers in particular, the show carefully and repetitiously fosters the *shared* pleasures of becoming familiar with the intimate routines (and jokes) of the camp life. We know how many cups of tea Jennie Bond drinks each day, and that comedian Joe Pasquale likes to take the baby emus for a daily walk, as well as the minutiae of who is constipated by jungle food (or the lack of it), and the rhythms of the fitness routines that sustain the celebrity bodies we see on display. The notion of equating a (performance of) the 'ordinary' with the everyday and the routine of course also emerges from reality TV in general (e.g. *Big Brother*). But this concept of 'ordinariness' – again as seen in wider reality TV – is most clearly anchored to conceptions of the 'real' self. It is difficult for the programme to suggest that the experience makes the celebrity 'ordinary', unless it works hard to engage the possibility that we have access to them in the first place. How this process is dramatized is explored below.

'It's a little bit like Clark Kent and Superman': searching for the self

In celebrity reality TV, participants enter the text with certain meanings already attached to them, whether these stem primarily from an onscreen public image (e.g. former BBC Royal Correspondent Jennie Bond, Linda Barker from makeover TV), from 'private'/offscreen narratives and associations (Alex Best as George Best's long-suffering wife, glamour model Jordan for her night-clubbing exploits), or from an interaction between the two (former *EastEnders* star

Danniella Westbrook, famous for playing soap character Sam Mitchell and for her struggle with cocaine addiction). Part of the interest and attraction here emerges from seeing how their image in the reality space compares to the existing expectations we may hold.

One of the most fascinating and explicit examples of this play centred on Jordan, in the third series. Often seen to exemplify the utter triviality of contemporary celebrity, the 26-year-old glamour model has found fame in Britain largely due to the size of her surgically-enhanced breasts (she is thus doubly defined through discourses of the false and synthetic). It is not difficult to see that Jordan's celebrity, initially for her body, sexual exploits and partying lifestyle, is very gendered in nature. Given the gendering of the personal as female and the fact that women's work is valued less than men's, the concerns of physical appearance and private life are more likely to colonize conceptions of female celebrity (Geraghty, 2000). Jordan undoubtedly received the most coverage in the programme and its surrounding media commentary, not least because of the machinations of her onscreen romance with Australian pop star, Peter Andre (initially famous in Britain in the 1990s). The romance on the programme in fact led to their marriage in 2005, and the couple now staunchly occupy a regular place in the weekly output of the tabloid press and celebrity magazines. But in the programme itself and its surrounding media coverage, there emerged an *extraordinarily* self-conscious debate about the relationship between 'Jordan', the media image, and the person known in reality as 'Katie Price',who was perceived by the show as being her 'real' self. Katie, it seemed, didn't wear make-up in camp, ate rice from a can, selflessly endured tough bush-tucker trials, and may have genuinely romantic feelings for Peter. At the same time, she was seen to be lazy around camp, posed in skimpy bikinis and flashed her breasts at the camera, and teased and taunted Peter with open sexual display. Where did Jordan end and Katie begin?

From day one, there was an apparent slippage between these concepts with participants calling her by different names. As Kerry McFadden asked the model upon entering the camp: 'So are you going to be "Jordan" in here or "Katie"?' (26 January 2004). She was the first to use Katie as the preferred name for the model, implying that there was somebody behind the image. Presenter Dec explained halfway through the series that 'the rest of the camp have started to spot the difference between Katie Price and Jordan. It's a little bit like Clark Kent and Superman ... Which is the real her?' (7 February 2004). On one occasion the celebrities were given costumes for a task. With Jordan sporting a white tutu, and Kerry wearing a white lace dress with puffed sleeves ('I feel like an 80s bride!'), the women sang Madonna's 'Like a Virgin'. As the routine progressed and Jordan writhed sexily in her outfit, Kerry shouted: 'Katie! I mean *Jordan*! Get back in your box!' (7 February 2004). Positioned on all fours with the camera filming in close-up, Jordan later sang the famous words from the musical *Grease*, 'Look at me I'm Sandra Dee, lousy with virginity …', before turning to the camera and mouthing 'That [tutu] cuts me up in *just* the right place'. Kerry chastized the model again, with the implication that she was letting her public, exhibitionist persona intrude into the camp which, as discussed, pivots on the ideology of claiming to show the celebrities' 'real' selves.

The press and magazine coverage equally worked through the complexities of the relationship between Jordan and Katie, narratives which took a further turn when the celebrities, Peter Andre in particular, re-emerged from the camp. *Now* reported that

> Peter … was wary of her teasing in the jungle and wondered whether he had got to know Jordan, the brazen sexpot and night-clubbing model, or Katie Price … [He] admits it's sometimes hard to differentiate between [them] … 'I loved the person that I met' he said. 'When she doesn't turn into that other person, she's her sweet self. And I love her. I genuinely like her' (Ewbank and Julien, 2004: 18).

As part of the magazine's long-running coverage of the unfolding relationship, *heat*'s 'Jordan and Peter: They've Fallen for Each Other!' similarly quoted Peter as saying 'I don't like Jordan, but I like Katie … She's completely wonderful' (21–27 February 2004: 4). The magazine later ran the headline 'Katie Kills Off Jordan For Love' (28 February–5 March: 5), and Jordan was even quoted as saying, 'Jordan is a slag, slut and bitch, and Katie likes to stay at home'. It is difficult not to observe here that these comparisons validate particular ideologies of femininity based around monogamy, domesticity and the containment of female sexuality. The quote also reveals how discourses of class function to regulate ideals of femininity (Biressi and Nunn, 2005: 150). Jordan was evidently too 'trashy' and offended 'good taste'. Much of reality TV pivots on the idea of judging the selves that are put on display, particularly with the invocation of audience interactivity. As Biressi and Nunn note, the relevant criteria here are often articulated in vague terms – identification, appreciation, dislike or disdain – but this is in fact often a system of judgement and classification which pivots on discourses of class (2005: 151). While I later discuss how *I'm a Celebrity* often values working-classness as 'authenticity', this is of course also a marker which can be used to ridicule and exclude identities, particularly when they enjoy the 'undeserved' trappings of social wealth. Indeed, despite the fact that (corporeal, sartorial and consumer) 'excess' is deliberately cultivated by Jordan's persona, the media construction of the couple after the show has regularly focused on their lack of cultural capital (Bourdieu, 1986): foregrounding their trashy and 'tasteless' displays of celebrity wealth, and particularly the much publicized event of their 'chavtastic'[5] wedding which was 'snubbed' by other famous names. But whether invoked in a negative or positive sense, both perspectives adopt the ideologically reassuring idea that class is an 'essential' part of one's identity.

This complements, in broader terms, the ideologies of selfhood on display in *I'm a Celebrity*: the notion that there is a 'core' to be found, even if this is partly 'in process' in the camp. What is important in the magazine quotation above is the general suggestion that the public (celebrity) self and the private ('real') self may well be blurred, but they can ultimately be separated. In other words, the contemporary celebrity persona can indeed be taken on and off at will, but there is still a 'real' lurking *beneath*. In this particular piece there was a clear pull toward foregrounding the truth or 'reality' of the relationship, and the romantic and sexual activities of celebrities have long since been a privileged site (in Foucauldian terms) for seeking out the essence of the star's private self (deCordova, 1990). But in *I'm a Celebrity*, this quest has to continually negotiate a number of obstacles or contradictions. This is where its highly self-reflexive rhetoric about celebrity construction – and the potential threats to this enterprise – becomes crucial. The first of these is the commercial discourse of celebrity construction, something which can be linked to Gamson's (1994) emphasis on manufacture as the primary explanation for modern fame. For example, the programme, as well as its surrounding media coverage, self-consciously interrogated the pairing of Peter and Jordan in relation to the economic rules of the celebrity game: the idea that a celebrity couple are understood as having a higher news (and thus economic) value than celebrity individuals. Jordan in particular seemed to actively encourage such discussion while on the show. Lying on her bed next to Peter and showing an acute awareness of how the programme (and the popular press) were choreographing her media image, she enquired, 'It *must* look like me and Peter are an item like this – does it?' Fellow participant Lord Brocket replied, 'It looks good for the cameras Katie', while Kerry confirmed, 'It's what the cameras and the audience want to hear [sic]' (7 February 2004).

This returns us to the emphasis on the agency of the audience which structures the show on a number of different levels. In Gamson's analysis, an increasing emphasis on the power of the audience has worked to mediate between potential tensions in shifting explanations of fame. But as Gamson explains,

> Celebrities at the service of the audience, however, brought about a new problem: the suspicion that the images presented were constructed to gain an audience ... The more active the audience, the more celebrity is suspect as an artificial image created and managed to pander to that audience (2001: 265, 269).

Yet the notion that images are 'constructed to gain an audience' ('it's what the audience want to hear') is openly and playfully articulated in *I'm a Celebrity* in ways which apparently conflict with the promise that the celebrities may forget that the cameras are whirring ('You really, really can't act *all* the time'). This self-reflexivity is conflated with the notion of *inter*activity when presenter Ant explains, near the end of the third series,

> Now it's time to see our celebrities chasing your votes again, and now they can see the finish line, they are getting really desperate. Honestly, these people will do *anything* to keep you guys happy. Next they'll be singing and dancing, wandering around in next-to-nothing [and referring to Peter and Jordan] pretending to get off with each other – all in the name of getting votes (7 February 2004).

Furthermore, the economic exchange value of celebrity also surfaces explicitly in the text, and is hardly smuggled under its ideological door. Like other singers who have appeared in the show (American singer Sheila Ferguson from The Three Degrees in particular), Peter Andre was often breaking into song in camp. Such scenes were placed in the context of the presenters' good-natured jibes at his performances, and images showing the other celebrities smirking at his unashamed bid for media exposure. More explicitly, and referring to the song Peter claimed to have penned spontaneously while in the jungle, he was asked by Lord Brocket, 'Are you going to try for a [record] contract when you get out of here? ... Are you going to do one called "Insania"?' (6 February 2004). Peter replies, 'I'd love to', while Brocket immediately quips, 'It doesn't sound right – we give it the thumbs down'. The link back to studio shows Ant performing mock incredulity and mouthing 'Not *sure* about it?', as Dec hums in the background 'This is insania, *doo doo doo*'. This exchange typifies the way in which Andre was constructed as a slightly deluded fame-seeker on the show – 'naff' and laughable but also ultimately lovable. (In fact, Peter re-released his earlier hit 'Mysterious Girl' which immediately charted at number one. 'Insania' was released, although to less success, not least of all because it had become something of a joke.) But what is clear here is that the commercial structures of celebrity, and the fact that these people are explicitly commodities, are turned into an object of humour in the interplay between celebrities, presenters and audience.

The notion of the celebrities acquiring media deals after exiting the show has become increasingly acknowledged in the programme as further series have been produced, whether in terms of relaunching previous media careers, moving into new roles, or entering into product endorsement and sponsorship deals. The apparently explicit play surrounding this may well work to negotiate claims to artifice and self-interest by 'exposing' it ('nothing else to see here'), while also flattering the audiences' superior perspective on these aspirant media ambitions, which would normally be associated with 'ordinary' people. This is particularly so when the highly visible and lucrative nature of such media deals has attracted some disapproval.[6] Yet again, this still appears to be simply a more self-conscious dramatization of the cultural rules which always structure our relations with celebrity, particularly in terms of television appearances. On chat shows, for example, it is understood that celebrities will often be plugging their latest or future product in exchange for which they will offer some intimate and 'private' access to their lives (Bonner, 2003: 84). This is what Frances Bonner elsewhere describes as 'privacy for free advertising time … It is not that there is necessarily a naivety about the process, rather a feeling that it is a good trade' (ibid.). During their time in camp, the celebrities are primarily 'advertising' themselves as saleable commodities rather than promoting a particular product per se (although this may certainly come after). Yet *I'm a Celebrity* can surely be conceived as a similar kind of trade. What I am suggesting, then, is that the emphasis on audience agency (the action may be manipulated to please us), as well as the open play with commercial discourse on celebrity production, function as further frameworks to be negotiated in approaching authenticity in the text: the solicitation to search for the 'real' self. Of course, these perspectives are not necessarily antithetical: we have long since been asked to *buy* into the 'real' self.

'Honest, and completely natural'

Within the welter of performance and self-promotion, the 'real' self may be difficult to find, but it is constantly and quite sincerely invoked as a discursive ideal. Significantly, as is the case with the construction of winning contestants from reality TV more widely (Holmes, 2005), the winning celebrity is often perceived as having 'been themselves' throughout the show. In the UK, it has been those who appear more unassuming – celebrities who are central to the series, but are not seen to be aggressively grabbing the spotlight or making the most naked bids for media exposure. When Kerry McFadden emerged as the first female winner of *I'm a Celebrity* in series three ('If the public want me to be the queen of the jungle, I'll piss my pants'), often quoted were such comments as 'what the viewers have seen on screen is Kerry as she is – no games, no pretence, just the great girl she is … She's honest, open, caring and completely natural' (Sleep, 2004: 7). In this respect, celebrity reality TV is highly traditional in its construction of the celebrity self, particularly when we note Dyer's argument that 'sincerity and authenticity are two qualities greatly prized in stars' (1986: 11). As Dyer makes clear, we have historically valued stars who appear to 'bear witness to the continuousness of their own selves' (ibid.). We value them because they are (seem) who they *appear* to be. In making a seemingly backstage perspective so central to the construction of the celebrity's image, reality TV in fact pushes for a more traditional coincidence between public and private personae – striving for the ideological coherence that deCordova (1990) associates with the emergence of the Hollywood star system. But this emphasis on the 'continuousness of the self' also demands qualification where the extended and serialized space of celebrity reality TV is concerned. 'Being yourself' is valued, but there is paradoxically also the suggestion that this self was in part 'found' or released by the reality experience, and its vaguely therapeutic and transforming qualities. Indeed, headlines proclaimed Kerry as moving from 'whinger to winner!' (she nearly left the programme at the start), and she was applauded for having 'learnt a lot about herself in there', and for experiencing one 'hell of a journey over the last two weeks' (Sleep, 2004: 7). At the same time, this is imagined as having brought forth the real self which was there ('inside') all along. Now that we have got to know the real self, the implication is that we can see why 'we' were right to make it famous (Gamson, 2001: 270).

But discourses of class are important here. In the UK version (and at the time of writing),[7] celebrities conceived as 'working-class made good' have been more likely to emerge as winners. Kerry's singing career had ended some years before entering the show, to be followed only by minor TV presenting roles, yet she was already understood to be wealthy given her marriage to the then successful Westlife singer, Bryan McFadden.[8] But her win was attended by explicit stories about her impoverished class upbringing, telling horrors of how 'Three weeks before I joined [pop group] Atomic Kitten, I had to sell my parrot for 20 quid to buy Tampax – that's how bad it was'.[9] Here then, the programme's insistence on the possibility of a core self is deeply intertwined with discourses of class. That is not to imply (on the limited evidence presented here) that the UK programme constructs some kind of a metanarrative around the relationship between celebrity and class. Rather, it is to note how its conservative ideologies of selfhood are necessarily intertwined with wider conceptions of cultural identity. Even though working-classness is here invoked to signify authenticity, there is still the suggestion that – unlike the attributes of celebrity status – class is not a 'vestment or trapping' that can be taken on and off at will: it is part of one's essential identity (Biressi and Nunn, 2005: 152). This is evidently far from a radical gesture, and in wider terms, it naturalizes social hierarchies and the imbalance of power on which they are based.

Biressi and Nunn have emphasized how, as celebrity has become increasingly detached from traditional structures of influence such as talent, education and inheritance, and instead defined more and more by conspicuous consumption, there has been an increasing emphasis on the negotiation of some 'hidden essence of "true" working-class identity concealed beneath the "glitz"' (2005: 146). While they are emphasizing a shift here (the apparent elision of a merited claim to fame is a crucial part of the appeal), they rightly note that such discourses are prefigured by a longer historical trajectory where the relationship between stardom and the mythologization of working-class mobility are concerned (see also Dyer, 1998). Indeed, this seems to be paradigmatic of aspects of the ordinary/extraordinary paradox into which class is often woven: the notion that the famous are 'ordinary people who live more expensively than the rest of us but are not essentially transformed by this' (Dyer, 1998: 43). As established, the jungle environment in many ways sets out to *prove* this highly conservative discourse, before returning the inhabitants back to their celebrity lives anew.

This journey through *I'm a Celebrity* suggests that it is premature to assert that 'in this new post-Warholian future, ten minutes of fame will cost you five more of public mockery and loathing' (Sconce, 2004: 256). The programme *does* speak to an increasingly less reverential attitude toward the famous – where a tank of rats may replace the pedestal – and a desire to boisterously strip away wealth and privilege from a celebrity class who do not appear to 'deserve' it. The increasing decline of more meritocratic ideologies of fame also beckons this on with new energy and fervour. But this is surely to take a somewhat surface reading of the text: it is this very perspective, albeit in a playful and good-humoured manner, which the format initially works so hard to set up.

But beyond this, any populist desire to take a punitive or cynical attitude toward celebrity is precisely evoked so that, as Littler observes in relation to *heat* magazine, it can then be 'channelled straight back into feeding it' (2004: 22). In fact, in so far as it resonates with Gamson's discursive paradigm, if *I'm a Celebrity* exemplifies constructions of contemporary celebrity, it is because it carefully negotiates the *threats* to its status – whether through seemingly exposing the commercial discourses of fame, invoking the power of the audience, or dramatizing the process of ordinarization to apparently new heights. It is important to remind ourselves that both intimacy and 'ordinariness' are prevalent tropes in contemporary celebrity culture which potentially function to 'paper the gap' between media and ordinary worlds, compensating for their inevitable *imbalance* of power (Littler, 2004: 23).

The programme undoubtedly addresses an audience highly conversant in the concept of celebrity image production and construction, inviting us not simply to seek out the 'real' self behind the image but also to (apparently) view the processes of fabrication and performance which constitute this entity. But it seems important that it actively precipitates this play as integral to its viewing pleasure. Nor does this seem to be a radical gesture, aiming to foster the notion that 'If there is a problem in peeling away the veneer, viewers need simply be given better viewing tools' (Gamson, 2001: 274). Enter the extended and intimate space of celebrity consumption promised by *I'm a Celebrity*, where the dance of images which constitutes the performance of celebrity can apparently entertain us for hours. An objection here may indeed be that I have presented a textual reading of the show, an imaginary subject position, while Sconce's reading may tap into the more various political perspectives adopted by the audience. Of course, celebrity producers have always aimed to negotiate the authenticity of the celebrity self, the capitalistic belief in the 'really' here sells the celebrity and the products they promote (Littler, 2004: 12). But it also seems problematic to downplay the careful negotiations performed by these textual frameworks, or to imply that, in our contemporary age, such shows are being viewed simply 'ironically'. As one journalist in fact noted of the third series of *I'm a Celebrity*, 'of course we know it's all about performance, this is a very media aware age. But still, it was difficult not to feel moved by ... [Kerry's] win. Fantastic stuff ...'[10]

Reflecting the discussion of fame surrounding reality TV in general, as well as the desire to reassert more meritocratic ideologies of fame, critics may gleefully point out that for many jungle participants fame from the show is fleeting, and does not always lead to the sustained rejuvenation of a career. For others, the rewards are quite literally rich (on the back of series three, Jordan and Kerry in particular have enjoyed extensive media exposure, and Jordan is now said to enjoy an annual income of £5 million).[11] But far from being evidence of the excessively manufactured celebrity on these shows (and the audiences' unwillingness to invest in its mystifying project), this framework in fact perpetuates more traditional myths of fame. It naturalizes the deeply capitalistic belief, as Paul McDonald notes in a different context, 'that life has its winners and losers and that is only natural' (1995: 65). With contemporary celebrity imagined as more of a 'risky lottery' than perhaps ever before, this returns us to where we began – with a willing line of celebrities waiting to be rejuvenated by the apparatus of the show.

Notes

1 At the same time, the popularity of these formats is clearly unpredictable: ITV1's *Celebrity Wrestling* and *Celebrity Love Island* in 2005 were not ratings successes.

2 'Everyone's Talking About.... I'm a Celeb', *heat*, 14–20 February 2004: 3.

3 *Tonight with Trevor McDonald* (ITV1, 13 February 2004).

4 In this respect, it is worth noting the relative failure of Channel Five's *Back to Reality* (2004) in the UK. This programme grouped together people who had only recently been made famous by reality TV.

5 Reflecting an upsurge of popular class distaste in Britain, the word 'chav' has recently risen to prominence, delineating a subculture of white working-class identity/behaviour (male and female). Although the use of the term 'chav' does vary, it circles around ideas of uneducated, 'uncultured' and often anti-social forms of identity, while also taking in motifs of dress and appearance. Flashy jewellery and designer brands (complete with prominent logos) are invoked as key signifiers in this respect, indicating the bid to extend one's consumption practices outside the 'appropriate' boundaries of class identity.

6 Ironically, given that it emerges from the same channel as *I'm a Celebrity*, ITV1's *Tonight with Trevor McDonald* devoted an entire programme to this issue following the end of series three (13

February 2004). It was highly critical of the 'easy' economic profit to be gained from 'instant television fame' – discussing the celebrities within the same moralistic framework that usually structures the critique of wider reality TV.

7 This was originally October 2004. Since this time Carol Thatcher (the daughter of ex-Prime Minister Margaret Thatcher) has won *I'm a Celebrity ... Get Me Out of Here!*, in December 2005. Although Thatcher's persona was constructed in terms of a decidedly *upper-class* eccentricity, she was still valued for being 'ordinary' – highly willing to put up with the living conditions of camp life (and thus putting her mother's famous stoicism to 'good' use). The class roots of the Thatcher family are also less privileged than Carol's demeanour on the programme implied.

8 Shortly after the programme the couple split up, an event that has attracted an enormous amount of coverage in celebrity magazines. Kerry then changed her name back to Kerry Katona.

9 FemaleFirst:' Kerry McFadden had to sell parrot to buy tampons', found out [accessed 21 April 2004].

10 As cited on *Richard and Judy* (C4, 18 February 2004).

11 'Celebrity Gossip', *Now*, 27 April 2005: 26.

Bibliography

Becker, Karin E. (1992) 'Photojournalism and the Tabloid Press', in Peter Dahlgren and Colin Sparks (eds), *Journalism and Popular Culture*, London: Sage, pp. 130–52.

Biressi, Anita and Nunn, Heather (2004) 'The Especially Remarkable: Celebrity and Social Mobility in Reality TV', *Mediactive* 2: 44–58.

—— (2005) *Reality TV: Realism and Revelation*, London: Wallflower.

Bonner, Frances (2003) *Ordinary Television*, London: Sage.

Born, Matt (2004) 'I'm a Celebrity draws record 16 million viewers', *Daily Telegraph*, 11 February: 3.

Bourdieu, Pierre (1986) *Distinction: A Social Critique of the Judgement of Taste*, London: Routledge.

Braudy, Leo (1986) *The Frenzy of Renown: Fame and its History*, Oxford: Oxford University Press.

Brenton, Sam and Cohen, Reuben (2003) *Shooting People: Adventures in Reality TV*, London: Sage.

Couldry, Nick (2000) *The Place of Media Power: Pilgrims and Witnesses of the Media Age*, London: Routledge.

—— (2002) 'Playing for Celebrity: *Big Brother* as Ritual Event', *Television and New Media* 3/3: 283–93.

—— (2004) 'Teaching us to Fake It: The Ritualized Norms of Television's "Reality" Games', in Susan Murray and Laurie Ouellette (eds), *Reality TV: Re-making Television Culture*, New York: New York University Press, pp. 57–74.

deCordova, Richard (1990) *Picture Personalities: The Emergence of the Star System in America*, Urbana and Chicago: University of Illinois Press.

Dyer, Richard (1998) *Stars*, 2nd edn, London: BFI.

—— (1986) *Heavenly Bodies: Film Stars and Society*, London: Macmillan.

Ellis, John (1992) *Visible Fictions: Cinema, Television, Video*, London: Routledge.

Ewbank, Tim and Julien, Selina (2004) 'It's On Again', *Now*, 18 February: 18.

Gamson, Joshua (1994) *Claims to Fame: Celebrity in Contemporary America*, Berkeley: University of California Press.

—— (2001) 'The Assembly Line of Greatness: Celebrity in Twentieth-Century America', in C. Lee Harrington and Denise D. Bielby (eds), *Popular Culture: Production and Consumption*, Oxford: Blackwell, pp. 259–82.

Geraghty, Christine (2000) 'Re-examining Stardom: Questions of Texts, Bodies and Perfor-mance', in Christine Gledhill and Linda Williams (eds), *Reinventing Film Studies*, London: Arnold, pp. 183–201.

Giles, David (2000) *Illusions of Immortality: A Psychology of Fame and Celebrity*, London: Macmillan.

Hill, Annette (2002) '*Big Brother*: The Real Audience', *Television and New Media* 3/3: 323–41.

—— (2005) *Reality TV: Audiences and Popular Factual Television*, London: Routledge.

Holmes, Su (2004a) '"Reality Goes Pop!": Reality TV, Popular Music and Narratives of Stardom in *Pop Idol*', *Television and New Media* 5/2: 147–72.

—— (2004b) 'But This Time *You* Choose!: Approaching the Interactive Audience of Reality TV', *International Journal of Cultural Studies* 7/2: 213–31.

—— (2005) '"Off Guard, Unkempt, Unready?": Deconstructing Contemporary Celebrity in *heat* Magazine', *Continuum: Journal of Media and Cultural Studies* 19/1: 21–38.

King, Barry (2003) 'Embodying an Elastic Self: The Parametrics of Contemporary Stardom', in Thomas Austin and Martin Barker (eds), *Contemporary Hollywood Stardom*, London: Arnold, pp. 29–44.

Littler, Jo (2004) 'Making Fame Ordinary: Intimacy, Reflexivity, and "Keeping it Real"', *Mediactive* 2: 8–25.

McDonald, Paul (1995) 'I'm Winning on a Star: The Extraordinary Ordinary World of *Stars in their Eyes* ', *Critical Survey* 7/1: 59–66.

Mole, Tom (2004) 'Hypertropic Celebrity', *Media/Culture* 7/5, found at: http://journal.media-culture.org.au/0411/01 (accessed 2 December 2004).

Montgomery, Martin (2001) 'Defining "Authentic Talk"', *Discourse Studies* 3/4: 397–405.

Sconce, Jeffrey (2004) 'See You in Hell, Johnny Bravo!', in Susan Murray and Laurie Ouellette (eds), *Reality TV: Re-making Television Culture*, New York: New York University Press, pp. 251–67.

Sekula, Alan (1984) *Photography Against the Grain*, Halifax: The Press of Nova Scotia College of Art and Design.

Sleep, Wayne (2004) 'Kerry's a cutie who deserved to win', *Now*, 18 February, 2004: 7.

Turner, Graeme (2004) *Understanding Celebrity*, London: Sage.

Chapter 4

'Bringing out the ★ in you'

SJP, Carrie Bradshaw and the evolution of television stardom

Deborah Jermyn

A cab crosses a bridge towards the skyline of a glittering night-time metropolis. Across town, as her date approaches, a woman takes a shower, soaping herself in luxuriant foam. They meet and the couple is seen sitting in the back of the cab, the woman now clothed in a shimmering dress. The cab turns a corner and happens upon a crowd of photographers and public, lining a red carpet that leads to security staff guarding the entrance to some kind of exclusive party or premiere. The woman ponders a moment and the cab pulls up alongside a parked limousine. Leaving the cab, she sneaks in one passenger door of the limo and emerges from the other onto the red carpet. Walking towards the club entrance, the photographers' flash bulbs erupt as she smiles, sashays, swivels down the red carpet. As she moves her body fragments, splits, freezes, morphs through a 'flash trail effect',[1] mimicking the frozen images captured on a score of cameras, and she transforms. The anonymous woman becomes Sarah Jessica Parker, for this stolen moment, she becomes a star. Confirming the metamorphosis we have seen, next to the final image of a bottle of Lux shower gel, the advertising tagline is displayed: 'Brings out the ★ in you.'

With its chic mise-en-scène, glamorous settings, striking photographic effects and funky music,[2] the 2004/5 Lux TV and poster campaign (see Figure 4.1) was an enjoyable piece of advertising promotion which pulled off its stylish venture with flair. But beneath the sophisticated veneer, the obvious expense of its high production values was matched by the essential simplicity of the message at its core. The Lux promise is plain in this ad: this product, with its 'pearls of rich fruit oils', will envelop your senses in such a way that you will feel as if you've transformed into a star. In buying Lux, even you, the woman on the street, can buy into some of the glamour, self-indulgence and decadence of the charmed life of a star. In short, recognizing and fulfilling the frustrated desires and dreams in all of us, Lux will 'bring out the star in you'. To underline all this, of course, a star was needed to front the campaign. A woman whom the target audience of young-to-middle-youth women with moderate disposable income might seek to emulate; a woman whom they admired, who embodied some of their desires and fantasies. Who could best crystallize the transformative qualities of Lux? Enter Sarah Jessica Parker, aka SJP.

In this essay I want to examine the repercussions of the premise at the core of the Lux campaign and its decision to adopt SJP as its star. The very simplicity of its slogan and concomitant use of SJP encapsulates the extent to which SJP's self-evident 'star quality' has become so instantly recogniszable, so widely and tacitly understood, and so desired, in contemporary popular culture. If one of the markers of having attained Hollywood A-list status is to be recognized and denoted through a single (above-the-title) name (cf. Pacino, Schwarzenegger, *et al.*), it is perhaps testimony to Sarah Jessica Parker's remarkable media presence that she needs only initials. Since playing the romantically challenged fashion maverick Carrie Bradshaw in the internationally syndicated *Sex and the City* (SATC) (HBO 1998–2004), a series credited with having 'brought exclusive designer labels and couturiers into the mainstream' (McCabe and Akass, 2004: 10), 'SJP' has come to denote a kind of 'brand' on the modern media landscape. She has come to embody a particular type of quirky but directional style along-side a capacity for classical glamour, which is showcased with quite remarkable ubiquity in the pages of celebrity, women's and fashion magazines. In the April 2004 UK edition of *In Style*, for example, her picture accompanied no fewer than four feature articles; the first, on her fondness for the Marni label; ditto, the second on designer Tom Ford; in the third she was seen in attendance at a Golden Globes party; while the final one, a feature on A-list 'body-shaping strat-egies', dedicated special attention to her Pilates training. Beyond an actress, then, she is a trend-setting icon and personal-grooming guru, a prime aspirational figure for contemporary 'middle-youth' (and arguably white, middle-class) women, where a nexus of desires surrounding femininity, feminism and fashion meet.[3] All this in itself marks her as one of the most noteworthy and absorbing female stars of the twenty-first century. What makes her stardom all the more intriguing, however, is the means through which it has come about; that SJP is a figure who is, or was primarily at the time of the Lux campaign at least, most prominently known and fêted for her work on *television*.

What does it mean that a brand trying to sell its product in a campaign which absolutely hinges on the fantasy of stardom would choose an actress best known from television to front it? Critical consensus in film and television studies has long held that 'stardom' is the exclusive preserve of *cinema*. What might the fortunes of SJP suggest, then, about the changing nature of the relationship between TV and stardom in the contemporary media landscape? Indeed, Lux is a brand which can lay claim to having sought and won endorsement from some of the most adored women stars of cinematic history. When SJP was appointed to the campaign, 'she followed in the footsteps of undisputed beauty icons Marilyn Monroe, Elizabeth

Figure 4.1 'Bringing out the ★ in you' – SJP fronts the Lux 2004/5 campaign

Taylor and Sophia Loren as the new face of cult beauty brand Lux'.[4] This pedigree, which can be traced back further still to Susan Hayward and Claudette Colbert, clearly acknowledges and trades on the enormous investment, both emotional and financial, that female audiences have long placed in their favourite women stars (Stacey, 1994). Through examining the intertextual promotion and circulation of her image, and its relationship with Carrie Bradshaw, in a range of media and advertising texts, this paper argues that SJP's career trajectory offers a timely and persuasive insight into the increasingly complex relationship between television and stardom, pointing to the inadequacies of our existing conceptualizations in this respect. While I reflect here on some of the conditions that have enabled the recent evolution of TV stardom embodied by SJP, it is not my intention to try and offer conclusions about this changed and changing landscape. On the contrary, the profusion of debates, questions and paradoxes that emerge from interrogating SJP's star status seems in many ways to be what is most valuable here when revisiting debates about media specificity and fame. It is these tensions that promise to prove productive in prompting further work on this theme; work which must address the real need for Television and Film Studies to build new models and theoretical paradigms with which to examine the dynamic relationship between contemporary stardom and television.

How does she wear it?

Such was SJP's star power in this period, in fact, that she also fronted another major advertising campaign in 2004/5, for Gap. The first of these featured the star in a variety of Gap outfits alongside the tagline 'How do you wear it?'.[5] Of course, there is a long and acknowledged history of how the fashion and other retail industries have called on celebrity endorsement and media 'tie-ins' as a means of promoting consumerism and maximizing sales (Eckert, 1990; Herzog and Gaines, 1991) and both Lux and Gap were quick to realize the mileage that could be had from SJP's star persona following her role as Carrie Bradshaw. In the UK, as in the US, Gap ran a limited offer at the start of the campaign where customers buying a particular line of jeans could have them specially customized, in effect making their pair unique. For these keen Gap customers the answer to the question 'How do you wear it?' was evidently 'I make it my own' and, in effect, this too was SJP's unspoken answer to the question at the core of the campaign.

SJP – style guru, personal grooming idol, fashion aficionado – would never take an ordinary pair of Gap jeans ('the new low rise jean') off the rail and 'just' wear them. As the images in the campaign underlined, through an unexpected brooch pinned here, or a surprising choice of jacket teamed there, SJP would make these jeans more than, something other than, a mass-produced commodity available to everyone from this 'midpriced international chain store' (Epstein, 2000: 197). This quality – a capacity, according to a generation of fashion writers, for quirky, individuated and typically (though not unfailingly) skilfully judged fashion statements – undoubtedly made SJP a dream face to front the new

Gap campaign, bringing her reputation for fashion innovation to bear on a store most enduringly associated with simple fashion perennials.

But of course, there was a hazy crisis of identity blurring the exact nature of the figure at the core of the campaign. One particular aspect of the campaign seemed to capture this 'blurring' especially well, where – beyond wide coverage in Gap stores, TV, magazines and poster sites – the SJP campaign was also carried on the exterior of some London buses. For anyone holding even a passing familiarity with SATC, a fragment of the programme would have echoed when seeing the images in this way. In a moment approaching something like *déjà vu*, the bus campaign mirrored the show's memorable opening credits where, next to the tagline 'Carrie Bradshaw knows good sex', the image of a prostrate Carrie adorns the side of a New York bus advertising her newspaper column. Embodying the contemporary, consuming *flâneuse*, both the bus campaign and opening credits figure the woman at their core traversing public space, a woman who is marked as both being 'a face in the crowd' *and* as standing out from that crowd. For the knowledgeable spectator standing in the street and catching the images in this way, 'real life', fictional narrative and television iconography would have coalesced in this instant as the wisdom of those astute Gap marketing executives crystallized. The prestige held by SATC as a trend-setting fashion arbiter (and its attendant exoneration of pleasure in consumption) was quite effortlessly harnessed to a store still arguably best known for its reliable sartorial basics, despite its efforts to diversify. And the more pertinent question at the core of the campaign revealed itself to be not 'How do you wear it?' but rather 'Who is wearing it?' – namely, SJP or Carrie Bradshaw?

Desperately seeking (the real) SJP

These advertising campaigns are just two instances of the media's wider reflexive play with, and an often intriguing apparent collapse of, distinctions between the actress and the character she plays. While playing Carrie Bradshaw in SATC catapulted SJP to A-list status, her transformation and visibility as such have been largely maintained by a continuing series of red-carpet moments, beloved of women's, fashion and celebrity magazines, which seem to confirm her own 'real' aptitude for trend-setting. It is this SJP whom we see echoed in the Lux campaign where, in line with the TV advert described above, one of the posters simply comprised the image of her disembarking from a limousine onto a red carpet. For example, in the 'Star style' pages of *heat* in December 2004, a feature asking 'How to wear your hair this season?' answered 'The only way is up, baby', and showed how 'stylish star' SJP (along with Jessica Simpson and Jada Pinkett Smith) was leading the way with a 'twisted bun' (4–10 December 2004: 52). Indeed (just as a number of Carrie's fashion initiatives such as name-plate

Figure 4.2   From haute couture to high street – *heat* magazine instructs readers how to steal SJP's style.

necklaces, flat caps and flower corsages filtered down from SATC into the high street), a week later, in the 'Star style' pages again, *heat* showed how readers could 'steal her style' with details of affordable versions of her prom-style dress and accessories (11–17 December 2004: 90; see Figure 4.2). Elsewhere, in the 'trend-spotter' pages of *Hot Stars* (free with *OK!* magazine) it was revealed that, 'thanks to the stars', lace 'has been given a fab new lease of life'; a pronouncement given weight by a picture of SJP in said fabric alongside copy noting, 'The style icon can't go wrong' (23 November 2004: 34).

The spectacular growth and changed nature of celebrity magazines such as these in recent years offers yet another motive to revisit theoretical approaches to stardom (see, for example, Holmes, 2005). The hierarchy once headed by cinematic stars has apparently shifted as glamorous names from film, TV and other arenas feature alongside one another as equal objects of desire and public interest. They are all as likely as one another to appear as designer muses and devotees, a shift which has been central in discourses bemoaning the 'decline' of contemporary celebrity. More specifically for my purposes here, the implicit collapse of distinctions in the above coverage, or what Dyer has similarly identified as the 'elision of star as person and star as image' (1979: 23), incurs a process where one of the 'defining' qualities of SJP/Carrie – fashion trailblazing – is apparently, and crucially, shared by them both. As one magazine article put it, 'It's in their insatiable appetite for fashion that the worlds of Sarah Jessica Parker and Carrie Bradshaw really collide' (Holgate, 2003: 405).

Linked to all this, there has been considerable academic interest in the extent to which stardom pivots on the '*duality of image* ... a duality which emphasises a balance between the site of the fictional performance and life outside' and which in classical cinema typically pivoted on 'a contrast between the glamorous film world and the surprisingly ordinary domestic life of the star' (italics mine) (Geraghty, 2000: 184–5). Equally, however, suggesting a greater sense of confluence, Dyer's seminal work on stardom notes that 'the roles and/or the performance of a star in a film were taken as revealing the personality of the star' (1979: 22), though, as is still undoubtedly the case, this 'real' 'personality' in itself was inevitably (at least something of) a construction. Certainly, star studies has attested to how the move from early Hollywood cinema's 'picture personalities' (deCordova, 1990) to the undisputed 'stars' proffered by Classic Hollywood was marked by a major shift regarding the perception of this 'duality': namely, that 'the disarticulation of the 'true' identity of the star from the aggregated personalities they played on screen' became the 'key symptom' in the emergence of stardom (Turner, 2004: 13).

In 1982, John Ellis's seminal *Visible Fictions* (revised in 1992) helped push debates around stardom in another direction with regards to the pertinence of the concept for analysis of television. He argued that stardom proper could not be bestowed by the more 'intimate' medium of television, since its performers were constructed to appear as a 'known and familiar person rather than a paradoxical figure, both ordinary and extraordinary' (1992: 106). His position held much in common with John Langer who, in an essay published just prior to *Visible Fictions,* had similarly suggested that the consumption of TV in the home, the medium's fondness for direct address and its routinized scheduling all functioned to reduce a sense of 'distance' between the medium and the viewer. In Langer's formulation, cinematic stars form a stark contrast to the 'personalities' produced by television:

> Whereas stars emanate as idealizations or archetypal expressions, to be contemplated, revered, desired and even blatantly imitated, stubbornly standing outside the realms of the familiar and routinized, personalities are distinguished for their representativeness, their typicality, their 'will to ordinariness', to be accepted, normalized, experienced as *familiar* (Langer, 1981: 355).

Notably, for both Ellis and Langer, a significant result of the differences between cinema and television, and one initially apparently borne out by the slippage between SJP/Carrie, is that television posits 'a drastic reduction in the distance between the circulated image and the performance. The two become very much entangled, so that the performer's image is equated with that of the fictional role (rather than vice-versa)' (Ellis, 1992: 106).

Langer's work was one of the earliest and most expansive efforts to try and conceptualize the particular attributes of television, and its performers, in comparison to cinema (a project which has always been bound up with discourses of cultural value). But his argument that television had constructed a 'personality system' as opposed to a cinema-style 'star-system' was somewhat flawed by a troubling lack of attention to the *distinctiveness* of how fiction/non-fiction television each constructed their 'personalities'. This is not to disavow many of the convincing differences between film and TV that Langer describes, for example, in terms of predominant forms and modes of address. Much of what he delineates in his account of the TV 'personality' still seems valid for understanding today's TV news reporters or talk-show presenters, for example, and perhaps this is why his kind of approach was in many ways later endorsed by P. David Marshall, who similarly concluded that the medium of television reduced the 'aura' of its celebrities (1997: 121). More recently, Graeme Turner has also observed that 'Langer's remains a well caught distinction, particularly when we reflect on its parallel with De Cordova's history of the picture personality in early Hollywood' (2004: 15). But the growth of 'quality' television, the promotion of both those who star in television fictions and the programmes themselves, and the wider celebrity culture of which they are a part, have contributed to so many shifts in television culture in recent years that the conceptualization of television's 'personality system' must also now be due revision.

Reflecting on this existing body of work, then, and how it might pertain to the spectacular rise of SJP, discrepancies and paradoxes emerge which underline how this paradigm has long been problematic. In fact, the apparent 'elision' of Carrie/SJP is not consistent at all and exists largely in relation to the promotion of both as *fashionistas*, a quality which constitutes only one dimension of each of these multifaceted figures. For example, while it would be most misleading to suggest that SATC is not in some sense(s) 'political', all its characters, including Carrie, have been recurrently denounced for their 'superficiality' in critiques where their conspicuous consumption is constructed as having precluded them from more 'serious' interests. The 'real' SJP, however, is a member of Hollywood's Women's Political Committee who grew up attending Democratic Party rallies with her struggling working-class family (Anon, 2000) and who has been vocal in criticizing the Bush administration (Millea, 2002: 112). Having been born in Ohio to a large family, and having lived on welfare before her child-star earnings took off, SJP's roots carry a resonance of 'poor white trash' which clearly informs her commitment to liberal politics and which underlines her star image as one marked by work rather than privilege. Most predominantly, however, beyond her regular place in red-carpet fashion photo-montages, popular coverage of SJP simultaneously routinely delights in detailing her 'other' role as a home-maker, her 'ordinary domestic life', as Geraghty put it above in relation to discourses common to classical Hollywood stars. These reports continually espouse the fact of her happy, monogamous relationship (she married her long-term partner actor Matthew Broderick in 1997) and, more recently, her joy at becoming a mother for the first time (son James was born in 2002). Interestingly, in many ways they parallel stories common in the discourses which constituted the transition from 'picture personalities' to cinematic stars around 1913–14, as documented by deCordova, during which time intense interest began to develop around stars' domesticity and attention 'focused specifically on the family lives of the players. This was the most important aspect of "the private" as it was invoked to constitute the star' (1990: 105). The stories in both eras could be said to work similarly at an ideological level in seeking to promote and consolidate the desirability of the institutions of marriage and family; particularly, in the first instance, for a fledgling film industry eager to disassociate itself from the 'moral laxity' and scandals common to coverage of theatre stars (ibid.: 102) and in the latter case, to distinguish SJP from 'sleep-around single gal' Carrie Bradshaw (Anon, 2000).

Such coverage strives to situate SJP and her husband as an ordinary young couple juggling work and parenthood, regularly sighted or 'papped' on the streets of New York in 'civilian' attire, downplaying the trappings of their glamorous profession (indeed these 'grunge' images of stars caught 'off-guard' are another cornerstone of the celebrity magazine market which negotiate the ordinary/extraordinary paradigm). The images accompanying a *Vogue* 2003 feature on SJP, 'Girl's World' (Holgate, 2003), humorously and self-consciously play with this contradiction, where SJP-as-housewife meets SJP-as-high-fashion-high-maintenance-screen-goddess. In the first of these parodic and reflexive images, a sultry-looking SJP wears a lacy turquoise bra and knickers beneath an open Hermés shirt, accessorized with 6-inch Manolo Blahniks and a £12,000 Fred Leighton diamond necklace while, caught in a moment of domestic duty, she irons a man's shirt. Sitting on the sofa over the page, she wears a sequinned Celine mini-dress while cosily knitting a pair of baby booties, the ball of blue wool unravelling from her exclusive gold Louis Vuitton handbag. More sombrely, in the interview she underlines her desire to be an ordinary mum when she bemoans paparazzi attention only for the way in which it intrudes on her relationship with her son 'and separates me from the other mothers in the playground'. Of her life with her husband she describes how, unlike the shining star of the Lux adverts, '"We're not public in any way, really ... we don't have limousines; we don't have bodyguards; we live on the streets of New York."' The writer agrees, comparing them favourably to tabloid regulars Jennifer Lopez and Ben Affleck whose on-off relationship and assorted antics were rarely out of the papers at this time: 'It's true ... There is something refreshingly ordinary about them. The Jen 'n' Ben show this ain't' (Holgate, 2003: 348).

Elsewhere, in a 2003 *Elle* feature/cover story about the star, both dimensions of SJP's persona – the glittering *fashionista* versus married mum – are similarly engaged by interviewer Rebecca Lowthorpe. She moves seamlessly from the starry-eyed (if SJP could wear only three designers for the rest of her life, who would they be?) to the mundane (has motherhood changed her marriage?), while SJP recalls that she married in a black dress and confides that

> I begged Matthew recently, 'Please, let's renew our vows so I can wear a pretty white gown' ... By all accounts they live in blissful harmony ... '[I] would definitely like to have more children', she says, fishing around in her bag ... in search of a picture of her son. When she realises she's left it at home she looks somewhat dejected (Lowthorpe, 2003: 80).

The stable, conventional picture of culturally sanctioned domesticity, femininity and motherhood implicit in these narratives lies in stark contrast to the party-hopping, bachelorette lifestyle of Carrie Bradshaw, who in one episode (4: 15) was so averse to the prospect of her imminent marriage that she suffered a violent allergic reaction after trying on a wedding gown. While the endless stream of pictures of SJP on the red carpet premiering her latest fashion initiative seems to correspond perfectly with Carrie's glamorous and frenetic lifestyle, then, stories of the 'private' SJP often contrast with and remove her from this arena. Indeed, in one *Red* magazine article, psychiatrist Dr Az Hakeem 'deciphers the meaning behind the look' of SJP at an event to mark the end of SATC. His analysis of her picture seems to strive to make sense of the 'public' persona in the light of our knowledge of the 'private' one and to reconcile the SJP/Carrie dyad. Of the image of a typically glamorous looking SJP, wearing impossibly high heels and surrounded by flash bulbs, he notes,

> With hair blow-dried straight and sleek, it's obvious that Sarah Jessica Parker has long been growing out of singleton Carrie's chaotic curls, and this mature look is arguably more in keeping with the married mother that she is in real life. It was SJP who allegedly called an end to the series, perhaps conscious of the danger that, despite the differences in their personal lives, she was almost synonymous in the public's mind with Carrie – a comparison encouraged by their near-identical dress sense. Here, we see a hint of both character and actress (Hakeem, 2004: 126).

On the one hand such discourses work to diffuse some of the progressive potential offered by Carrie – in Hakeem's analysis, identification with this rare model of a thirty-something woman who has not embraced the dominant paths of marriage and/or motherhood is something that a 'mature' woman will 'grow out of'. Furthermore, particularly since in 'real life' she *has* chosen these paths, it is implied that SJP would be right to want to distance herself from Carrie. But equally, these are discourses which very much consider SJP in relation to the 'ordinary/extraordinary' paradigm once said to be the exclusive preserve of *cinematic* stardom.

'I enjoy being a girl!'

This paradigm also seems especially relevant to the construction of SJP's star persona with regard to her physical appearance. While she has the supremely youthful, petite and athletic frame of a dancer, and a lush mane of hair which has been admiringly scrutinized by many a fashion feature, she is also characterized by a somewhat pronounced jaw and nose and the distinctive mole on her chin which she has steadfastly refused to have removed. Though clearly such matters are somewhat subjective, many would agree she does not possess the kind of innate 'natural' beauty which, however cosmetically enhanced, is *de rigeur* among so many other women stars.[6] Indeed, her early TV role in *Square Pegs* (US, 1982–3) cast her as bespectacled, awkward, teenage nerd Patty Greene, while commentators continue to make regular jibes about her looks; for example, A. A. Gill's delicately made observation in the *Sunday Times* that she 'has a face like a shaved Staffordshire bull terrier' (2001). Despite/because of this, there is something of the enduringly appealing, classical 'ugly-duckling-turned-swan' star narrative about SJP. Much of her contemporary status as a 'style-icon' who is to be desired and imitated – quite unlike Langer's formulation of the TV 'personality' cited above (1981), and despite the fact that she 'isn't a stereotypical Hollywood beauty' (Lowthorpe, 2003: 80) – has apparently been brought about through work, grooming and learned skills rather than 'God-given' beauty. This has arguably made her something of a beacon of hope for the 'ordinary' woman, even though access to these 'skills' is arguably largely determined by wealth. Of course, this also alerts us to the constructedness of on- and offscreen personae again; just as stylist Patricia Field is credited as having been the major creative force behind the styling of SATC, and despite Parker's evident passion for fashion as described in many feature articles about her, SJP's 'taste' is in all probability at least partly assisted by a team of professional advisers. Throughout all this, the pertinence of the 'ordinary/extraordinary' paradigm to SJP evidences the degree and nature of public fascination she has given rise to. It is just one of the ways in which her star image (and its relationship with Carrie) can be seen to be polysemic and fractured, rather than consistent or stable, and in which some of the existing theoretical models about the status and nature of television fame, and its theoretical parameters and possibilities, start to seem increasingly fragile.

Furthermore, the fact that SJP lacks what one might call conventional beauty arguably contributes to the sense that she is very much a *woman's* star; a woman championed, admired and desired most predominantly by other women. Gap again capitalized on this feature of her star persona in their spring 2005 'Pretty Khaki' campaign (Figure 4.3). This featured a particularly feminine SJP dressed up as a vision in pink, in her dressing room and dancing down the street in a classic Hollywood-style Technicolor musical pastiche-cum-homage, singing happily, 'I enjoy being a girl!' More specifically, what is arguably promoted as 'enjoyable' here are the opportunities for consumerism which the securing and maintenance of 'being a girl' demands/offers. This campaign again very much echoed the world of SATC and the *flâneuse*, where Carrie was similarly seen countless times vibrantly skipping down her stoop and into the streets of New York. Indeed, more broadly, the acquisition of 'television stardom' generally is perhaps particularly pertinent to understanding women stars and women audiences. In Hollywood cinema, women's star-power has never fully recovered from the decline that set in following the demise of the classic era, so that the biggest salaries and 'Top 10 Box Office' names since that time have come to be consistently dominated by men. By contrast, in television, throughout TV history and very much into the present day, significant numbers of women have attained A-list status. Two factors seem pertinent here. First, as raised above, the rise of celebrity magazines, and the coverage of celebrity

Figure 4.3 SJP or Carrie Bradshaw? – The face of Gap's Spring 2005 'Pretty Khaki' campaign

fashion in a still broader range of popular magazines predominantly bought by women, gives many women TV stars a vivid extra-textual existence that consistently underlines and contributes to their status. Second (and still linked to this first point), with its close links to the domestic, television has long been perceived as something of a feminized/feminizing medium, and it may be that this enduring notion continues to particularly facilitate the rise of women TV stars.

SJP's status as a 'woman's star' was effectively summarized by British *Vogue* in October 2003 when she featured as their cover model, with the heading next to her picture reading, 'Sarah Jessica Parker: The girl's girl'. This is not to say that her women fans wouldn't opt for 'stereotypical Hollywood beauty' for themselves given the choice. Rather, it is as if she wins admiration (and perhaps inspires a certain optimism) from others for the manner in which she demonstrates what imagination and good grooming *can* achieve, given that she did not start out with the benefit of supermodel features. Furthermore, for all the endless column inches and photo-montages dedicated to her in women's and fashion magazines, there is a conspicuous lack of interest in her emanating from the 'lads' mags' market. While she certainly can be found posed in sexy attire in high-end women's fashion mags like *Vogue* and *Elle*, SJP is not a star who one generally expects to find appearing as a cover girl in the men's 'lifestyle' section. Indeed, in contrast again to the kind of sexually liberal politics characteristic of SATC, SJP insists on working with a no-nudity clause, a position she gamely parodied in her role as a precious actress in *State and Main* (Mamet, 2000) and another way in which she has strived to differentiate her lifestyle choices from Carrie's. As an *Elle* article put it as early as 2002, even before the birth of her son, '[F]ashion passions aside, it's a well known fact that Sarah *is completely unlike her character*, sex columnist Carrie Bradshaw. "Any talk of sex and I clam up," she says. "I even smoke fake cigarettes during filming"' (Millea, 2002: 111, italics mine; see also Radner, 2004). What all this draws attention to, then, is a multitude of apparent continuities and contradictions around the meanings of SJP and Carrie: the way a star image can encapsulate both a sense of closeness to and of difference from a signature role; and how a television performance/performer now has the capacity to inspire and maintain the breadth of speculation and fascination that only a *star*, and not a mere 'personality', can occupy.

Constructing a televisual firmament

Some two decades after they first formulated their arguments, then, it seems an appropriate juncture to revisit and reconsider Langer and Ellis's contention that television produces 'personalities' rather than stars. Ellis bases his argument partly on the fact that television lacks cinema's 'photo-effect', a term he borrows from Barthes to describe the quality of 'present absence' in cinema: 'the irreducible separation that cinema maintains (and attempts to abolish), the fact that objects and people are conjured up yet known not to be present' (1992: 58–9). Karen Lury has taken issue with Ellis's premise here, arguing that 'the pro-filmic moment is as much a part of television as it is of film, so that what is represented in two-dimension on screen is also a demonstration that there was something (three dimensional, solid) there *once*' (1995: 117–18). Looking beyond the somewhat problematic appropriation of Barthes at the centre of Ellis's argument for a moment, and reflecting further on SJP's spectacular rise to iconic status in recent years, it seems indisputable that this status has been conferred by television and that it speaks of a changing landscape in the relationship between stardom and television.

Interestingly, since making her acting debut as a child star on stage, SJP's career trajectory has actually traversed *both* media, from TV (*Square Pegs*) to Hollywood – including *LA Story* (Jackson, 1991) and *Honeymoon in Vegas* (Bergman, 1992) – and back again. While both *LA Story* and *Honeymoon in Vegas* were mainstream successes featuring accomplished performances by SJP, they failed to match the visibility brought to her by SATC; in the words of one commentator, she is 'an actress whose movie career promised much, but never quite delivered' (Holgate, 2003: 348). All this points to a fluidity increasingly common in contemporary stardom where movement between the two media appears to be burgeoning and where *television*, rather than film, may operate as the primary medium in bestowing A-list status; the careers of Gillian Anderson, Jennifer Aniston or George Clooney, for example, would also make instructive case studies in this respect.[7] Of course, it is not mere coincidence that all these stars are American; not only does US TV have greater international syndication, offering its actors the promise of a greater media presence, but for non-US audiences the programmes' geographical distance feeds in to a sense of their stars being less immediately ordinary and familiar, and perhaps more particularly 'desirable'. In this respect it is interesting, too, that writing in a British context about television's capacity to produce only 'personalities', Ellis's examples are predominantly British (1992). Within this discussion, the most recent renaissance of 'American quality television' (AQT), in which the makers of SATC, HBO, have played a prominent role, has further underlined the sense in which contemporary television can confer professional credibility, as well as a regular mass audience, on an actor. SJP enjoys not merely public devotion but critical acclaim, having won four Best Actress Golden Globes (www.thegoldenglobes.com) and the 2004 'Outstanding Lead Actress in a Comedy Series' Emmy for her role as Carrie.[8] Indeed, it is overwhelmingly evident that the individuals we might term 'television stars', who obtain the degree of international reach and kudos this term suggests, emanate from a particular *kind* of television, drawn from a particular national context, and underline the import of AQT as a kind of breeding ground for TV stardom.

Furthermore, the refinement of TV and 'home-cinema' technologies, the advent of DVD and the expansion of multi-channel television with its continuous reruns of top series, have changed the way audiences can engage with both film *and* television, empowering and encouraging many more viewers to become television connoisseurs as deeply passionate, reflective and knowledgeable about TV as film buffs are about cinema. In fact, linked to the above, it is very often AQT that produces these kinds of intense audience/TV text relationships, marked by recurrent viewing or the purchase of box-sets and so forth. A week, a year, or more, after the demise of SATC, for example, seeing its unforgettable quartet of women friends walk along the streets of NYC together in the final episode for the last time, knowing the series/the narrative/these characters are now forever lost to them yet forever theirs, the dedicated SATC fan is surely every bit as able to feel Ellis's 'intolerable nostalgia' (1992: 59) as the fan of old movies. In bringing her a level of visibility and public fascination which cinema did not while transforming her into a 'style icon', with all the connotations of 'distance' that such status inescapably brings (paradoxically alongside the simultaneous 'intimacy' of imitation), SJP's appearance in SATC on the small screen for six years both *has* and *has not* made her 'familiar'.

Lux, like Gap, turned to SJP to head their campaign for the way she, both in 'herself' and through Carrie, has come to be a prime aspirational figure for contemporary women belonging, or seeking entry into, a certain demographic group arguably marked by whiteness, middle-youth, professional status and disposable income. Inherent in this too is the appeal which SJP holds as a star so intrinsically associated with 'the city'; and not just any city, but Manhattan, with all its romantic, potent (and, interestingly, largely cinematic) connotations of modernity, glamour and reinvention. Consequently, more detailed analysis of the ways in which her star image engages with the particular social contexts of the early twenty-first century, how audiences identify with (or resist) this star image, SJP's 'own' knowing, sometimes parodic invoking of it – and what all these processes signify about the status of contemporary stardom – has the potential to enrich and expand star studies beyond what the modest space afforded to me here allows.

What is required is a new conceptualization of the relationship between TV and stardom which recognizes how some of the differences that were once held to exist between TV 'personalities' and cinematic stars have been eroded and yet nevertheless retains a sense of the distinctiveness of each medium. For example, the longevity of a TV role, as acknowledged here, undoubtedly means a TV star is likely to have a longer and more particular association with a specific role than is the case of a cinematic star; but is it not perhaps time to revisit the notion that stardom 'proper' (i.e. as it has come to be constructed in a cinematic context) must emerge from a succession of separate roles? Furthermore, the excitement and anticipation that still greets a cinematic star doing a TV cameo appearance speaks of an ongoing fascination with how big-screen stars will appear (and whether they will be 'different') on the small screen, suggesting audiences do maintain a sense of such distinctions. We must also reflect on how the shifts noted here have repercussions for stars emerging from other arenas and media, for example, the music or sports industries. This is significant particularly since it is the changing nature not only of television but also of those intertexts that help construct stardom – for instance, the celebrity and women's magazines discussed here – that has undoubtedly played a major role in the fracturing of the traditional hierarchies of stardom which once privileged cinema. For now, we can but watch and await the fortunes of SJP with interest, especially since it could be argued that the sheer number of high-profile ad campaigns she is fronting at the time of writing threaten, ironically, to over-expose and thus devalue her star-status. With her own perfume, Lovely, just launched in summer 2005 and with a number of big-screen roles in the offing, it will be fascinating to see whether SJP's star finally eclipses Carrie.

Acknowledgements

An abridged version of part of this research was published in the first online edition of *Critical Studies in Television* (Jermyn, 2005). Many thanks to Janet McCabe there and to friends and colleagues for their feedback on earlier versions of this essay presented at University of Warwick Film and TV Studies Graduate Seminar Series, November 2004; Roehampton University CRFAC Seminar Series, February 2005; the SCMS Annual Conference, London, April 2005; to editors Su Holmes and Sean Redmond; and to my 'research associates', Fabrice Bana, Mo Bharwani, Nova Matthias and Shân Pope, for all being a ★.

Notes

1 As explained on www.virtualcamera.com/ttsw_lux.html (accessed 2 February 2006). The effect is not unlike Edward Muybridge's early 'serial photography' experiments.

2 'Dumb' by The 411.

3 That said, critical analysis of any star must note with caution that their 'meaning' can not be thought of as entirely fixed nor universally shared, whether approached synchronically or diachronically. Cultural specificity is of course a factor in this. For instance, it is interesting to note that the Lux campaign proved controversial in Israel where offended rabbis called for the posters of SJP to be banned, leading Unilever to adapt the campaign so that she appeared in a rather more demure dress (see for example Anon, 2004).

4 www.xtremeinformation.com/page/home

5 She was also one of a number of stars who advertised Garnier Nutrisse hair colorant in 2004.

6 However, there has been speculation that SJP has had plastic surgery; a montage of photos ranging from the 1980s to the present on one internet site, for example, traces what appears to be a series of subtle changes in the shape of her nose (www.awfulplasticsurgery.com/archives/000463.html, accessed Feb 2 2006). SJP has denied having any cosmetic surgery (Lowthorpe, 2003: 78).

7 In terms of more historical precedents, it would be intriguing to make some comparative analysis between the star profiles and career trajectories of SJP and women such as Lucille Ball or Mary Tyler Moore; indeed before 'SJP', 'MTM' could also lay claim to requiring only initials where others need a name.

8 Her reputation as a gifted actress is also undeniably enhanced by the critical praise she has won for her theatre work on and off-Broadway

Bibliography

Anon (2000) 'Naughty But Nice: Squeaky Clean, Happily Married and Ready for Kids, Sex and the City's Sarah Jessica Parker Makes her Mark as a Sharp-tongued Sleep-around Single Gal', *People Weekly* 54/14, 2 October: 116ff.

Anon (2004) 'Ad Nauseam', *Private Eye* 1121, 10–23 Dec: 9.

deCordova, Richard (1990) *Picture Personalities: The Emergence of the Star System in America*, Urbana and Chicago: University of Illinois Press.

Dyer, Richard (1979) *Stars*, London: BFI.

Eckert, Charles (1990) 'The Carole Lombard in Macy's Window', in Jane Gaines and Charlotte Herzog (eds), *Fabrications: Costume and the Female Body*, London: Routledge, pp. 100–21.

Ellis, John (1992) *Visible Fictions: Cinema, Television, Video*, 2nd edn, London: Routledge.

Epstein, Rebecca (2000) 'Sharon Stone in a Gap Turtleneck', in David Desser and Garth Jowett (eds), *Hollywood Goes Shopping*, Minneapolis and London: University of Minnesota Press, pp. 179–204.

Geraghty, Christine (2000) 'Re-examining Stardom: Questions of Texts, Bodies and Performance', in Christine Gledhill and Linda Williams (eds), *Reinventing Film Studies*, London: Arnold, pp. 183–201.

Gill, A. A. (2001) 'Time for the Awful Truth: Television', *Sunday Times* ('Culture' section), 11 March: 12.

Hakeem, Az (2004) 'What Was She Thinking? Sarah Jessica Parker', *Red* , June: 126.

Herzog, Charlotte Cornelia and Gaines, Jane Marie (1991) '"Puffed Sleeves Before Tea-time": Joan Crawford, Adrian and Women Audiences' in Christine Gledhill (ed.), *Stardom: Industry of Desire*, London: Routledge, pp. 74–91.

Holgate, Mark (2003) 'Girl's World', *Vogue* (UK edn), October: 344–9, 405.

Holmes, Su (2005) '"Off-guard, Unkempt, Unready?": Deconstructing Contemporary Celebrity in *heat* Magazine', *Continuum* 19/1: 21–38.

Jermyn, Deborah (2005) '"How Does she Wear it?": Shopping with SJP and Carrie Bradshaw in the Age of Television Stardom', *Critical Studies in Television* 1/1, available online at www.criticalstudiesintelevision.com/tvshorts/jermynd.

Langer, John (1981) 'TV's Personality System', *Media, Culture and Society* 4: 351–65.

Lowthorpe, Rebecca (2003) 'Downtown Girl', *Elle* (UK edn), December: 74–80.

Lury, Karen (1995) 'Television Performance: Being, Acting and "Corpsing"', *New Formations* 26: 114–27.

McCabe, Janet with Akass, Kim (2004) 'Introduction: Welcome to the Age of Un-innocence', in Akass, Kim and McCabe, Janet (eds) *Reading Sex and the City*, London: IB Tauris, pp. 1–14.

Marshall, P. David (1997) *Celebrity and Power: Fame in Contemporary Culture*, Minnesota: University of Minnesota Press.

Millea, Holly (2002) 'Groovy Baby!', *Elle* (UK edn), September: 109–14.

Radner, Hilary (2004) 'Between Feminism and Femininity: Style and the City: Reading Sarah Jessica Parker as a Fashion Icon', *The Space Between – textiles, art, design, fashion*, conference held at Curtin University of Technology, Perth, Western Australia, conference proceedings available on cd-rom, ed. Moira Dropoulos, Anne Farren and Suzette Worden, ISBN 0-9752106-2-9, vol 2.

Stacey, Jackie (1994) *Star Gazing: Hollywood Cinema and Female Spectatorship*, London and New York: Routledge.

Turner, Graeme (2004) *Understanding Celebrity*, London: Sage.

Chapter 5

'I'm a celebrity, get me into politics'

The political celebrity and the celebrity politician

Philip Drake and Michael Higgins

The aim of this chapter is to examine the endorsement of politicians by celebrities and the increasingly interwoven nature of celebrity and politics. Although our focus will be on contemporary matters, the introduction of celebrity into the political sphere is by no means a recent phenomenon. Indeed, anxiety over the perceived influence of celebrity upon the political process – and upon the public at large – has been a concern for much of the twentieth century. The sociologist Leo Lowenthal (1944), for instance, examined the evolution of the popular biography and noted that there had been a shift in media coverage from 'idols of production', such as industry leaders and politicians, to 'idols of consumption', such as film and sports stars. Just over a decade later C. Wright Mills (1956) argued that the increasing power of celebrities had enabled them to become a new 'power elite' to be ranked alongside the political elite.

Developing these critiques, P. David Marshall (1997) takes a neo-Marxist approach in arguing that modern celebrity is a direct product of late-capitalist society. For him there is a 'convergence in the source of power between the political leader and other forms of celebrity' (1997: 19). Marshall argues that celebrities and politicians are commodities sold to audiences, and the relationship developed in capitalist societies between the 'leader' and the 'crowd' is central to the creation of both, suggesting that 'in the rationalization of the social, the celebrity ... celebrates the potential of the individual and the mass's support of the individual in mass society' (1997: 43). According to this argument, both celebrities and politicians promote similar myths of individualism, and construct a public form of subjectivity that expresses freedom and aspiration in a capitalist democratic society. However, Marshall also acknowledges the operation of different kinds of celebrity (with varying demands placed upon them by the public), noting that 'in politics, a leader must somehow embody the sentiments of the party, the people, and the state [whereas] in the realm of entertainment, a celebrity must somehow embody the sentiments of an audience' (1997: 203). We shall suggest that the distinction between the two, the subject of this chapter, is not always straightforward and that the division between these spheres of activity has become increasingly blurred. In an age dominated by mediated politics, politicians also need to address their electorate as audiences. Granted, by relating celebrity to the processes of capitalism, Marshall usefully debunks the idea that celebrity is simply a status rewarded to talented individuals. However, his analysis of the celebrity politician is limited by a focus on the system in which celebrity is produced, thus neglecting to fully distinguish between different kinds of politicians and celebrities, and the ways in which they present themselves to the wider public. Through political campaigning and image management, the politician – like the celebrity – aims to appeal to a mass audience, but, we shall argue, this is not accomplished in quite the same terms. A key aim of this chapter is to address this distinction through an analysis of celebrity and political performance.

With the rise in influence and power of celebrities identified by Lowenthal and Mills, the political sphere has become intertwined with celebrity and the value that celebrity endorsement can bring to political causes. Just as in advertising, gaining the support of prominent celebrities functions as a means of promoting product (in this case a political agenda) and leveraging media coverage. Examples of this include John F. Kennedy's links to Hollywood stars such as Frank Sinatra and Marilyn Monroe, and, more recently, the courting of rock stars (Oasis, Bono, Paul Weller and others) by New Labour in Britain. At the same time, celebrities have increasingly entered the domain of formal politics. The rise of Hollywood film star Ronald Reagan to the Presidential Office and the recent successful election of Arnold Schwarzenegger as governor of California are the most obvious examples, although the UK also has cases of its own, such as the elections of actress Glenda Jackson and journalist Martin Bell as Members of Parliament.

Another indicator of the traffic between the political and celebrity spheres is that politicians are increasingly seen in popular formats such as the television talk show. Thus the appearance of Bill Clinton performing saxophone on the *Arsenio Hall Show* (Paramount, 1989–94) or the seven appearances of former UK Liberal Party leader Charles Kennedy on the topical BBC comedy show *Have I Got News For You?* (1990–) – leading to his nickname of 'chat-show Charlie' – are now almost to be expected. Contemporary politicians are aware that an appearance on a popular television show enables them to reach a wider public and circulate their image more effectively than any conventional political speech in parliament. Perhaps concerned that a disaffected public has lost interest in formalized politics, politicians also often attempt to use celebrities to garner media coverage at moments of political need. Hence in 2004 Bruce Springsteen, REM, Dave Matthews and Pearl Jam performed 'Vote for Change' concerts across the USA in support of John Kerry, the Democrat presidential candidate. In the same year the rock star Bono, of the band U2, garnered widespread media coverage by telling the UK Labour Party conference that Tony Blair and Gordon Brown were the 'Lennon and McCartney' of politics, and the governor of California, Arnold Schwarzenegger, endorsed George W. Bush by defending his policies through reference to his own celebrity past – a performance that was widely reported across national and international news networks.

Contemporary political culture and the rise of performative politics

As we have outlined, there is a widespread critical belief that the development of celebrity has contributed to a change in contemporary political, democratic culture. In their introduction to a recent collection on the 'restyling' of politics, John Corner and Dick Pels (2003) argue that this can be broadly divided into two positions. The first is pessimistic, based on the view that contemporary party politics has come to rely too much on image and spin and not nearly enough on rational argumentation. Nick Jones (1999) describes the emergence of an industry of 'spin doctors', dedicated to refashioning political culture and debate to suit the aesthetic needs of the media and the marketplace. Citing the guidance of these image managers, and the collaboration both of politicians themselves and of mainstream media, Bob Franklin (2004) argues that politics has begun to be 'packaged' for sale like any other consumer product. The result of this is an emphasis on the immediate palatability of the image rather than on the intricacies and social consequences of policy content. For Franklin, the election of Arnold Schwarzenegger to major political office served to verify the extent of this 'supremacy of style over substance', and the descent of democracy into a pool of artifice and trivia (2004: 12).

The second position is more optimistic. Corner and Pels suggest that a 'performative restyling' of politics does not have to be viewed in a negative manner but might be fashioned to the service of a more inclusive political culture (2003: 16). Invoking performance theory drawn from theatre and anthropology, they suggest that this perspective allows a greater understanding of how a largely mediated political culture can attract and engage with its audience. Corner (2003) argues that the 'mediated persona' – the public image of an individual – functions as a central, and perhaps necessary, aspect of contemporary mediated democracy. He suggests that politicians are required to perform a personalized 'self' to the public, and need to attempt to convince us that this self operates congruently with the political demands placed upon it. Sometimes this performance appears to reveal aspects of a private self and at other times is called upon to maintain an unflappable public authority. As well as offering a potential means of insight into the character and intentions of political actors, Corner suggests that a historically and technologically informed view of the 'mediated persona' enables a more productive and transparent relationship between the political process and the cultural dimension in which it operates.

John Street also addresses the politician as performer and argues that 'the style is part of a process, just as is marketing and branding. Styles are manufactured too, but in analysing this process we need to appreciate the appropriate analogy – not commerce but celebrity, not business but show-business' (2003: 97). He too stresses the need to view politics as a form of performance and discusses the need for politicians to adapt different styles to different settings. This is accomplished by varying their mode of performance across media appearances and deploying a recognizable 'idiolect' – the particular repertoire of voice, expressions, gestures and styles associated with their persona. Just as with actors, skilled politicians vary their performance according to the demands placed upon them by different media genres, and so assessment of their performances will also vary according to the context in which they appear. Appearing on the topical television satire *Have I Got News For You?*, for instance, demands a more self-reflexive, informal and comedic political performance than that appropriate to a more formal political context such as a policy speech.

We will now consider some examples of the intersection between politics and celebrity, looking in more detail at Bono and Arnold Schwarzenegger. Both examples are speeches given to political party gatherings in 2004 and both were given widespread media coverage. We turn first to an address to the 2004 UK Labour Party annual conference by the Irish rock star Bono, on tackling poverty in Africa, and then consider the speech given by Hollywood movie star turned state governor Arnold Schwarzenegger to the 2004 US Republican Party Convention, in which he advocates President George W. Bush's election for a second term.

Bono as a political celebrity

Bono is an interesting case because he is not a politician by occupation but a highly recognizable international celebrity. The source of his fame and personal wealth is his position as lead singer of the successful rock group U2. Yet, as Street (2004) warns, this does not mean that the form of celebrity exemplified by Bono should be read as apolitical. Throughout their careers, the members of U2 have produced overtly political songs, such as 'Sunday, Bloody Sunday' and 'Mothers of the Disappeared', and have dedicated their albums to various political causes. They also appeared at both the 1985 Live Aid and 2005 Live 8 concerts in support of ending Third World poverty. Bono has continued to use his individual renown to sit on the Commission for Africa and intervene in debates concerning the relief of poverty, to the extent that Bill Clinton names him as 'the person most responsible' for the passage of a bill on Third World debt relief through the US Congress (Varga, 2003). Bono has sought to exert his influence on British political policy as well, and John Street describes a photograph from summer 1999 showing Bono and Bob Geldof discussing debt relief, with Prime Minister Tony Blair wedged between them 'listening intently' (2002: 434).

The point we should take from this as we look at Bono's performance is that it would be misleading to examine his words in isolation from his celebrity persona. Bono is known as a kind of entertainer who, in John Street's words, 'pronounces on politics and claims the right to represent people and causes ... without seeking or acquiring elected office' (2004: 438). Bono's address therefore operates in parallel with the subtext of his image as someone who holds political views and has a history of putting them into action, all from the position of detached integrity that comes from occupying a space outside of the main political apparatus. We will try to show, however, that although his renown undoubtedly gives Bono substantial political influence, he must also deal in his address with the lack of democratic mandate implied by his celebrity status. In other words, as well as reflecting on the access and apparent influence politically active celebrities such as Bono may enjoy, our reading of the celebrity advocate must take account of the widely held view (especially by journalists) that the engagement of celebrities within politics brings substantial dangers of obscuring political debate in a mist of fame and glamour. As both of our examples are political speeches, the focus in this chapter will be primarily on verbal performance and the rhetorical construction of Bono's political claims. While we acknowledge that Bono's speech is clearly a bodily performance, the reason for our focus is that it addresses a tendency within writing on celebrity to privilege visual signifiers over other aspects of performance.

Bono's speech is quite complex, as it needs to address and reconcile several aspects of his public persona. To consider how he does this, it is useful to draw upon Erving Goffman's (1974) book *Frame Analysis* and his concept of 'keying'. Goffman defines the key as 'the set of conventions by which a given activity, one already meaningful in terms of some primary framework, is transformed [temporarily into] ... something quite else' (1974: 44–5). This is useful here because if one of the goals of a lengthy political monologue is that the audience remain attentive for its duration, it is usually necessary to break from the main political frame with recollections and humorous asides. Keying simply refers to the means by which the speaker manages these asides; how they switch from their primary role as political advocate to such secondary roles as perhaps 'practically-minded businessperson', or 'stand-up comedian', or even 'bashful rock musician'. To engage in keying is therefore to temporarily shift the terms of an interaction and the way in which it should be read, in a manner that suits the needs of the matter in hand. The cues that signal such shifts can be semantic, but in contexts such as political speeches – and, in this case, in Bono's delivery – cues can also take the form of a switch in posture and tone of voice.

Bono's speech is a complex of keying instances, but two main patterns seem to develop. The first is that he manages his credentials in the speech by brief periods of 'keying down'. These are moments in which he seems to temporarily concede to doubts concerning his right to speak, which are then followed by transitions in which he reconciles his celebrity position with his holding the political stage. What follows are two examples from Bono, both of which call attention to his position as a rock musician:

> [You're probably better off asking] anyone but a rock star. I mean, get yourself a source you can trust – one who, say, when he hears the word 'drugs', probably thinks 'life-saving' rather than 'mind-altering'.

> Can you take this from a rock star? 'All you need is love' when all you need are groceries?

What these extracts have in common is that they are certainly intended to be funny. Both examples draw upon and toy with the popular image of the rock star as drug-addled on the one hand, or naïve and other-worldly on the other. At the same time, both are also based on a conceit of self-depreciation that assumes the presence of a sympathetic and friendly audience. These lines could be counted upon to raise a laugh – which of course they did – because all those present would be more than familiar with Bono's sober and practical approach to the eradication of Third World poverty, in spite of his being a rock star. Yet for all that, the humour depends upon the very currency of these negative images of celebrity. Indeed, when we factor in the infinitely more diverse television audience, an interpretation emerges in which, for all its immediate comedy, Bono's approach has the dual function of addressing and diffusing the negative impact his rock star status may have on his credibility to offer political advice.

The second pattern relates to the overall development of the speech. At the beginning of the address, a distinction is maintained between the political elements of the discourse and Bono's celebrity credentials. This section of the speech steps along on such political assertions as 'this is not about charity, it's about justice' and 'the war against terror is bound up in the war against poverty' (a line that he subsequently attributes to Colin Powell, and has re-used in speeches across the world), while also invoking broad, mutually reassuring notions of a British and Irish disposition towards charity. However, by the time we get to the second main section of political discussion in the speech, and after he keys down and offers a transition passage, Bono has started to embellish the political frame with narratives of the personal, and speaks on the basis of his own upbringing and social background on the streets of Ireland. He then returns to a conventional political frame, before keying down again (conceding 'he is just a rock star'). However, after a brief transition, his return to the main political frame has a significant new element – this time the address proceeds on the basis of his celebrity rock star experiences. This section of Bono's performance begins with the following passage, teasing the Prime Minister and Chancellor of the Exchequer:

> Now you know why Tony Blair and Gordon Brown are really excited
> that U2's got a new album coming out – why?
>   Because I'll be away on tour next year.
>   But even from a tour bus I can be a pain in the arse. That's my job.
>   And I've got some very interesting friends, there's as many of them
> in mothers' unions as trade unions.
>   It's not just purple Mohawks we've got going, it's blue rinses.

Again, humour plays a significant part in reading Bono's address. Contrasting pairs are offered, placing the expected alongside the unexpected, and a form of lexical choice normally ill-suited to the frame is utilized. That is, political speakers, used to selling themselves to their public, rarely define their occupation as being 'a pain in the arse', but rock stars can. Having then asserted his celebrity status as one from which to speak with force, he then engages in a final keying down, although this time it could be better described as a mock keying down in which he apes the cynic's ironic interpretation of his being there:

> I am Tony Blair's apologist. The rock star pulled out the hat at the
> Labour Party conference.

Of course, Bono's humour is necessarily controlled and instances of keying must remain answerable to the dominant frame. Accordingly, he immediately reins back from this aberrant explanation by reassuring the assembled delegates:

> I've more faith in the room than that. I've more faith in your leaders
> than that.

Bono here emphasizes the benefit of his experience as a celebrity, and dismisses potential objections that he acts as a stooge. He then moves to conclude his speech with a passage in which he implicitly claims equal credentials with the audience and recasts the political element of the speech within an inclusive mode of address, saying 'We're serious, this is gigantic' and culminating in a final plea beginning 'Do we have the will to make poverty history?'

The most interesting aspect of Bono's performance is the amount of rhetorical effort he must expend to account for the possibility that his celebrity credentials might impede his right to speak, while he also stresses the political experience and reputation for action he has gained as a result of his celebrity activities. Bono's need throughout to shift position – or engage in keying – shows his ability to assert the validity of his position as a celebrity speaker offering political endorsement, while for our purposes it also typifies a broader necessity to deal simultaneously with negative and productive associations of celebrity.

However, as we have indicated earlier, this analysis is still insufficient: a further dimension needs to be taken into account. Bono and U2 frequently lampoon celebrity culture in their songs, videos and rock concerts (most famously in their 'Zoo TV' tour which satirized global media culture). Bono's star image is therefore one that is self-reflexive and self-mocking, often ironic, yet at the same time invested with sincerity, performing Irishness in its stereotypical sense. (He is thus also seen as an amiable, funny, religious, working-class 'rascal'.) Alongside his trademark visual signs – the ever-present wrap-around sunglasses, his grungy rock star attire – Bono is a determinedly embodied performer. In his live performances he throws himself around the stage, shifts between different personae, and he frequently intersperses U2's songs with speeches about social and political issues. Analysis of his political pronouncements needs to be contextualized through his public image, the songs that he writes, and the politically charged speeches that he gives on stage. The affective and connective power of Bono's presence in politics should be understood in terms of his overall celebrity, and this is brought to bear in his political performance.

Arnold Schwarzenegger as celebrity politician

Unlike Bono, Schwarzenegger speaks in his capacity as an elected politician. In John Street's (2004: 437) schema, Schwarzenegger is an example of someone who trades on his celebrity background with the purpose of getting or maintaining political office. Indeed, as his role on this occasion is to endorse George W. Bush for re-election as president, Schwarzenegger also speaks as a representative of the Republican Party at large. But of course the reason that Schwarzenegger is known internationally, and by those who do not maintain a keen interest in state politics, is his hugely successful movie career. Having grown up in Austria, Schwarzenegger rose to prominence for his hypermasculine physique in the films *Pumping Iron* (1977) and *Conan the Barbarian* (1982), before taking an iconic role in James Cameron's 1984 film *The Terminator*. Since then, Schwarzenegger's career has continued through such star vehicles as *Total Recall* (1990), the self-reflexive *Last Action Hero* (1993), as well as reprising his

Terminator role in two highly successful sequels. Alongside his action hero persona he also appeared in successful comedies that effectively played upon and sent up his star image, including *Twins* (1988), *Kindergarten Cop* (1990) and *Junior* (1994). Schwarzenegger became a US citizen in 1983, and has been involved in political activities on behalf of the Republicans since the 1990s, to the extent that he was appointed as chairman of the President's Council of Physical Fitness and Sports by President Bush senior (BBC, 2004). Importantly, in terms of his image, he is married to Maria Shriver, a member of the Democrat Kennedy family, jointly presenting an unusual crossing of political divides.

Schwarzenegger's political career has drawn heavily upon the opportunities presented by the extent of his movie stardom. He decided to run for election as governor of California in late 2003, the same year as the international release of *Terminator 3: Rise of the Machines*. As Rachel Smolkin (2003) points out, the degree of attention given to his campaign was far greater than could be expected of any aspiring politician who did not also happen to be a movie star. Schwarzenegger was accorded the platform of *The Tonight Show with Jay Leno* to announce his candidature, and attracted a press entourage that saw reporters from *Access Hollywood* jostling for position with correspondents from the *Washington Post* (Smolkin, 2003: 42). Schwarzenegger was able to use his celebrity profile to engineer the tone of his media appearances and limit scrutiny of his policies. He opted to restrict interviews to either relatively informal chat formats (with such other celebrities as Oprah Winfrey and Howard Stern) or to remain with the more politically sympathetic media outlets (such as the pro-Republican Fox News channel). Throughout, the experience and renown of Schwarzenegger's stellar movie career has been a key feature of the management of his political career, and he has frequently cross-referenced this in his political appearances.

There is a crafted articulation between celebrity and the political establishment that is also apparent in the widely reported political speech by Schwarzenegger that we have chosen to examine. In comparison to Bono's performance, Schwarzenegger's speech has much more of the structure of a traditional piece of political oratory, with a few reasonably subtle but extremely significant differences from the commonplace politician. Traditional oratory techniques employed by Schwarzenegger include hailing an upright and virtuous 'us' in opposition to an inferior and sinister 'them' (Atkinson, 1984: 37), and 'projecting' his announcement of the name of the US President to maximize the enthusiasm of the audience reaction (Atkinson, 1984: 49). In common with Bono, however, Schwarzenegger takes to the stage and immediately refers to his celebrity status:

> Thank you. What a greeting. This is like winning an Oscar. As if I would know.

Like Bono, Schwarzenegger uses humour to address and foreground the reason for his fame. Moreover, his status as a movie star is drawn upon in a manner that assumes fairly substantial prior knowledge on the part of the audience. That is, Schwarzenegger takes for granted not only that the audience know he is a movie star but that they are able to share in a critical judgement on the supposed standard of his acting abilities, or are at least familiar with the widely circulated view that Schwarzenegger is a star known for his action and comedic rather than actorly performances, and that these modes of performance are often accorded a low cultural status (Drake, 2004: 80). Whereas Bono marshals the jokes towards addressing doubts of his right to be there, Schwarzenegger's speech begins on the assumption that the audience are in a position to participate in the pretend mocking of the calibre of his acting. This, however, has the similar effect of demonstrating to the audience his own sense of humour, an ability to make a joke at his own expense, and his general ease in front of an audience. In Goffman's terms, by commenting upon the terms of his framing through his movie star persona, Schwarzenegger is able to construct a mode of engagement less susceptible to awkward political interrogation.

In his address, Schwarzenegger embarks on a fairly lengthy personal reflection. His movie star status is placed temporarily to one side, and this section of the performance is devoted to the construction of a personal narrative of delicate humility and a background of former political oppression, typified by politically convenient statements such as 'My family lived in fear of the Soviet boot' and 'I finally arrived here in 1968. I had empty pockets, but I was full of dreams'. Apart from one intertextual reference to his future celebrity, drawing upon his self-referencing movie role in *Last Action Hero* – 'I was a little boy, I wasn't an action hero back then' – references to his personal success at this stage of the address are oblique enough to be included in a broad discourse of opportunity for all and 'you can achieve anything'. The concept of democratic inclusion and 'equal' opportunity is central to constructions of both political participation and mythic ideologies of stardom.

Schwarzenegger's speech is most conventional, however, in its extensive use of what Maxwell Atkinson (1984) calls the 'claptrap'. While the term has gathered negative connotations to refer to outwardly pleasing but empty talk, Atkinson uses the idea of the claptrap to explore rhetorical devices or techniques that motivate and choreograph audience applause. For example, in the following list of points given by Schwarzenegger later in the speech, the repeated resolution 'then you are a Republican' has the dual function of using what Atkinson calls an 'us term', while at the same time signalling the audience to respond. That we have reached the last item on the list is flagged by introducing it 'And, ladies and gentlemen', thereby ensuring that the pause that follows is filled by sustained and rapturous applause:

If you believe your family knows how to spend your money better than the government does – then you are a Republican!

If you believe our educational system should be held accountable for the progress of our children – then you are a Republican!

If you believe this country, not the United Nations, is the best hope of democracy in the world – then you are a Republican!

And, ladies and gentlemen, if you believe we must be fierce and relentless and terminate terrorism – then you are a Republican!

Yet in spite of these traditional political elements, celebrity remains central to understanding the power of this speech because the impact of these devices is made considerably greater by intertextual references to Schwarzenegger's movie star career. We have already looked at his opening quip about the likelihood of his winning an Oscar, and his citation of *Last Action Hero*, and to these we can add a reference from the *Saturday Night Live* television show to those advocating an alternative economic policy as 'girlie men'. And, of course, a movie reference to *The Terminator* ('terminate terrorism') has been engineered into the last and climactic item of his list reflecting upon what it is to be a Republican.

Perhaps inevitably, however, the speech itself climaxes in Schwarzenegger's *pièce de résistance* 'I'll be back', again from *The Terminator* series of movies, and an expression subsequently pivotal to his celebrity image. This is developed into the 'list of three', a technique that Atkinson (1984: 57) describes as the ideal claptrap formulation, this time asserting national resurgence. Conceivably because the reference itself has become such a clichéd one, so central is it to his star image, Schwarzenegger actually delivers this particular line by placing it in a quotation from someone else:

[On an injured soldier] And do you know what he said to me then? He said he was going to get a new leg and get some therapy – and then he was going back to Iraq to serve alongside his buddies. He grinned at me and said, 'Arnold – I'll be back.'

Ladies and gentlemen, America is back – back from the attack on our homeland, back from the attack on our economy, back from the attack on our way of life.

This example deliberately recalls those scenes from the Terminator movies where Schwarzenegger's hard-bodied action hero is repaired and made fit for active service again. At the same time, it demonstrates a knowing and comic self-reflexive awareness of his own image. However, it is again significant for the speech that Schwarzenegger is able to assert his credentials to speak, not only through his action-hero persona but through his formal political position 'as governor of the great state of California'. To recap, in spite of the traditional elements present, we want to suggest that the celebrity of Schwarzenegger is central to understanding his performance, such that it is assumed throughout that the audience are familiar not only with him, but with his movie roles and his ongoing status as a Hollywood star. In other words, the speech endorsing the President was delivered on the basis of a shared understanding in and acceptance of the terms of Schwarzenegger's celebrity.

While Bono and Schwarzenegger might be said to present quite different cases – where one is elected and the other is not – it does seem that the case of Schwarzenegger shows a greater fusing of the celebrity and political status in claiming the right to speak and to offer endorsement on political issues. Certainly, we should take into account that Schwarzenegger is the elected governor of California, but it remains that his speech involves none of the activities of concession-making that we see in Bono's approach. In part, this may be due to differences between the American and British political spheres, and indicate a greater ease in the former of such an intersection of celebrity and politics than might be deemed acceptable in the latter. Indeed, Schwarzenegger's use of his celebrity credentials throughout his campaign is consistent with a high degree of contentment at being both celebrity and politician simultaneously.

Although Schwarzenegger is more content than Bono to explicitly link his political and star personae, what both celebrities have in common is that they seek to harness their fame to position themselves outside of the political mainstream, albeit in slightly different terms. In Marshall's account (1997: 226), both are staking a claim to represent political issues to the public in a way that is uniquely theirs, by juxtaposing their exceptionalness with a claim to be somehow 'ordinary', and therefore better able to represent the views of the popular audience and voting public. Added to his departure from conventional political rhetoric, even Bono's instances of 'keying down' and his deliberate distancing of himself from formal politics (still claiming he can be a 'pain in the arse') may be read as reaffirming his status as an ordinary man, able to voice popular opinion amongst politicians distanced from their public. Schwarzenegger, for his part, deploys his immigrant status and avoids complex political arguments in order to show that he is a 'regular guy' just keen to 'get things moving', in opposition to a supposedly self-interested, traditional political elite.

Both in the structure and content of the speeches and in their bodily performances, the rhetorical emphasis on the personal backgrounds and activities of Bono and Schwarzenegger feed into what Corner has termed the 'kinetic' element of an energetic political persona (2003: 69). That is, both speeches project the image of an individual in constant and productive movement, even while speaking from behind a podium. Bono's performance is of a restless rock star, with a lilting, emotional voice railing impatiently against the slow pace of politics and willing it to make progress, whilst Schwarzenegger performs with a distinctive physicality embodied by his intimidating presence (his body is sculpted, muscled and barely contained by his suit) and his staccato Germanic vocal delivery that insistently recalls his career-making *Terminator* performances. Thus, in the matter of iconic display the 'demeanour, posture and associative contexts of the political self' are invariably presented through the prism of celebrity (Corner, 2003: 69), albeit that Schwarzenegger wears the suit and tie that his state office demands, while Bono's self-consciously alternative rock star garb is offered as indexical of a different, new, exciting, perhaps more trustworthy form of political representation.

Conclusion

This chapter has focused upon two case studies: the celebrity endorsement of New Labour by rock star Bono, and the self-referencing movie-star performance of Arnold Schwarzenegger as politician. These examples, one of a political celebrity and the other a celebrity politician, raise a number of wider questions about the intersection between celebrity and politics. First, to what extent do celebrities, and politicians endorsed by celebrities, engage a public disengaged from formal politics: that is, do they enable political issues to be aired to a wider audience? Such an argument suggests that celebrities perform a public service in bringing politics to an audience that traditionally feels excluded from political discourse. Second – the contrary view – to what extent does endorsement of particular political causes by celebrities actually make it more difficult for the mediated political process to operate effectively? That is, do celebrities who come to dominate media coverage of political issues without any electoral mandate actually worsen rather than address a democratic deficit?

Our chapter has tried to consider the celebritization of politics through the examination of two celebrities: Bono and Arnold Schwarzenegger. Both examples demonstrate the re-framing of political debate through celebrity discourse, and both performers make knowing reference to their respective celebrity images. However, we have suggested that this is done on different terms. The performance frame adopted by Bono is one that clearly indicates his independence from but influence over the political sphere (hence his criticism of Tony Blair's involvement in the Iraq war) and through this his reliability and integrity are emphasized, simultaneously both supporting and critiquing New Labour. Schwarzenegger, by constantly referring to his movie star past, keys his performance such that his actions and policies are justified by the conviction, force and high visibility of his action-hero screen persona. What this reveals is that an analysis of the relationship between celebrity and politics needs to take into account the *particular* celebrity, the mode of performance they adopt, their earlier image, and the political claims that they make. Overall, celebrity performance in the political sphere should be seen in the context of the increased profile of career politicians as celebrities in their own right. We have therefore argued for the continued prominence of the constructed persona as an important means of delivering politics via the mass media. To dismiss celebrity as a mere symptom of the trivialization of politics would be to fail to recognize its significance as a means of contemporary political engagement.

Bibliography

Atkinson, J. Maxwell (1984) *Our Masters' Voices: The Language and Body Language of Politics*, London: Routledge.

BBC (2004) 'Profile: Arnold Schwarzenegger' in www.bbc.co.uk, accessed 25 March 2005.

Corner, John (2003) 'Mediated Persona and Political Culture', in John Corner and Dick Pels (eds), *Media and the Restyling of Politics: Consumerism, Celebrity and Cynicism*, London: Sage, pp. 67–84.

Corner, John and Pels, Dick (2003) 'Introduction: The Restyling of Politics', in John Corner and Dick Pels (eds), *Media and the Restyling of Politics: Consumerism, Celebrity and Cynicism*, London: Sage, pp. 1–18.

Drake, Philip (2004) 'Jim Carrey: the Cultural Politics of Dumbing Down', in Andrew Willis (ed.), *Film Stars: Hollywood and Beyond*, Manchester: Manchester University Press, pp. 71–88.

Franklin, Bob (2004) *Packaging Politics: Political Communications in Britain's Media Democracy*, London: Arnold.

Goffman, Erving (1974) *Frame Analysis: An Essay on the Organisation of Experience*, Boston: Northeastern University Press.

Jones, Nicholas (1999) *Sultans of Spin: The Media and the New Labour Government*, London: Victor Gollancz.

Lowenthal, Leo (1961) [1944] 'The Triumph of Mass Idols', *Literature, Popular Culture and Society*, Palo Alto, CA: Pacific Books, pp. 109–40.

Marshall, P. David (1997) *Celebrity and Power: Fame in Contemporary Culture*, Minneapolis: Minnesota University Press.

Mills, C. Wright (1956) *The Power Elite*, New York: Oxford University Press.

Smolkin, Rachel (2003) 'Star Power', *American Journalism Review*, December 2003/January 2004: 42–6.

Street, John (2002) 'Bob, Bono and Tony B: The Popular Artist as Politician', *Media, Culture & Society* 24: 433–41.

—— (2003) 'The Celebrity Politician: Political Style and Popular Culture', in John Corner and Dick Pels (eds), *Media and the Restyling of Politics: Consumerism, Celebrity and Cynicism*, London: Sage, pp. 85–98.

—— (2004) 'Celebrity Politicians: Popular Culture and Political Representation', *British Journal of Politics and International Relations* 6: 435–52.

Varga, George (2003) 'Part-time Rocker, Full-time Humanitarian: Bill Clinton, Others Sing Bono's Praises', *Union-Tribune*, 2 March.

Chapter 6

Not just another powerless elite?

When media fans become subcultural celebrities

Matt Hills

As Su Holmes has noted, 'in academic analyses [of celebrity] there often remains a perpetuation of rather restrictive categories' (2004: 115; see also Hills, 2003b). In this chapter I want to consider one such restriction on what has been counted and theorized as celebrity, namely the fact that celebrities have been addressed as culturally ubiquitous and mass-mediated figures. Viewed in this limited light, the celebrity (construed as mass-mediated text) has carried a related binary — that of the fan (construed as dedicated audience member). Fans have frequently been analysed as passionate consumers of celebrity-related texts and intertexts (as in, for example, Barbas, 2001; Stacey, 1994; Staiger, 2005; Thompson, 1995). These categories have typically been treated and reified as separate text versus audience phenomena, resulting in the discussion of 'extreme symbolic differentials between celebrities and so-called "ordinary" individuals' (Holmes, 2005: 211). 'Mass recognition' is said to be concentrated on a symbolic elite of celebrities, who 'belong to a very restricted visibility class' (Holmes, 2005: 213), meaning that the media world is effectively divided into two groups: those who are visible in the media, and so possess high status, and those who are invisible — the far lower-status audience of fan-consumers. As David Holmes puts it, this 'boundary division ... traps the star as much as the fan' (2005: 214) in alienated social interactions defined by the presence/absence of symbolic power.

What Holmes takes as a self-evident 'boundary division' has been largely replicated in academic work on celebrity and media fandom, especially given that this work has tended to progress on two parallel but distinct tracks (on celebrity see Giles, 2000; Marshall, 1997; Rojek, 2001; and for major work on media fandom see Jenkins, 1992; Hills, 2002; Sandvoss, 2005). A foundational assumption here has, indeed, remained that fandom and celebrity correspond to two different orders of being within mediated society, representing divisions of labour between media production and consumption. It is this restriction that I want to centrally challenge in what follows, as I will suggest that celebrity and fandom may not, after all, constitute entirely reified and separable concepts/experiences. In fact, Leo Braudy's history of fame, *The Frenzy of Renown* (1986), doesn't entirely render celebrity and fandom distinct, noting that the 'advent of the fan' means that it is possible to be 'a fan before [becoming] a star' and observing of twentieth-century mass-mediated fame that 'there have now grown up several generations of fans who in their turn have become looked at themselves' (1986: 407, 572).

Of course, it can also be argued that a series of cultural and new media developments have led to fandom and celebrity blurring together more generally in unprecedented ways. For example, the rise of reality television as a genre of TV programming has spurred on the construction of a type of TV celebrity premised on their prior (and semiotically retained) connotation as an 'ordinary' member of the TV audience (see Holmes, 2004; Littler, 2004). And beyond this specific genre, the internet has offered a potentially liminal cultural space where the usual mechanisms of media-industry celebrity cultivation can be supplemented or even side-stepped, as in the generation of 'net celebrities' where cultural consumers turn producers by setting up their own commercial websites (see Marshall 2004: 10–11, on this 'cultural production thesis'). Media fandom and celebrity may now be less clearly bounded concepts or entities than ever before (see also Kristina Busse in this collection). Rather than holding on to a singular conceptual version of 'celebrity', contemporary audiences – not to mention scholars – may thus need to ever more reflexively distinguish between different levels, types and taxonomies of celebrity, ranging from the media industry's various mass-mediated products through to audience-constructed and perhaps more subcultural celebrity personae. Following and sharing such concerns, in this chapter I will refrain from approaching celebrity and fandom as two opposed terms – where celebrity is assumed to be primary and the fan secondary (see Hills, 2005) – and will instead analyse how these cultural identities can meaningfully intersect, and how their hybridization can result in specific types of celebrity.

John Tulloch and Henry Jenkins have described media fans as a 'powerless elite' (1995: 144) who are generally unable to directly influence the content of their favoured TV shows, but who nevertheless possess great expertise in terms of their knowledge of a series' history. This description usefully points to the potential contradictoriness of fan identities: fans may have the power to produce an aesthetic history of their beloved texts (1995: 145), yet they are not economically/industrially significant to media producers where they constitute only a very small percentage of the overall audience (see also Hills 2002: 37). However, Tulloch and Jenkins's rendering of fans as a 'powerless elite' tends to place all fans in a similar position of cultural (dis)empowerment relative to media producers and professionals, suggesting that fans can be thought of in clear opposition to media-professional celebrities. By way of starting to unravel this blanket characterization, I want to note that (purely coincidentally) Francesco Alberoni

(1972: 75) actually uses the exact same term, 'powerless elite', to depict media celebrities, suggesting that their 'institutional power is very limited or non-existent' while their actions nevertheless 'arouse a considerable ... degree of interest' (1972: 75). Given that both celebrities and fans may, therefore, possess uneasy and ambiguous relationships to forms of cultural power, it may be rather unhelpful to view cultural power as being entirely housed or possessed by celebrities and concomitantly lacked by fans. As different versions of potentially 'powerless elites', the question here is how – and to what degree – fan and celebrity cultural identities can overlap and interact rather than belonging to wholly separable domains.

With this in mind, I will firstly consider how media fans can become celebrated and niche-mediated figures of recognition within their own subcultures, and then I will move on to consider how fans can become celebrities by virtue of moving across into the category of media professionals/producers working on the very text which they are fans of. Each of these types of hybridized fan-celebrity provides a way of challenging the otherwise 'restrictive categories' of pure celebrity and fan, where media production and consumption are neatly carved apart, and where symbolic inequalities are assumed and perpetuated between these supposedly monolithic cultural identities. And each type of hybridized fan-celebrity also allows for a more careful examination of how power relationships and differentials may not simply operate between 'powerful' celebrities and 'disempowered' fans represented as a flattened mass or sameness of consumers. This depiction, though significant in some ways, masks the extent to which hierarchies and symbolic inequalities can also be present within fan cultures, with fan-celebrity being one such marker of intra-subcultural symbolic inequality.

Subcultural celebrity as name recognition: Big Name Fans

The conceptual separation of celebrities and fans has, in large part, been due to the fact that celebrity has been assumed, in academic analyses, to connote a culturally ubiquitous and mass-mediated recognition. This has meant that forms of social recognition and cultural celebration which do not fall into these typifications have not generally been accorded the status of celebrity. However, such emphases have rendered invisible the way in which celebrity status can also be attained via niche-mediation within a subculture. Here, certain subcultural participants can become known to a wide range of distant others via mediation, despite the fact that these subcultural celebrities may still be unknown by the public at large. Elsewhere I have argued that it is important to restore subcultural celebrity to theoretical visibility:

Although ... previous work on celebrity has considered how audience subcultures interpret and recognize their idols in distinctive ways, such work has still tended to focus on culturally ubiquitous celebrities who are read differently by audience subcultures. Academic work has not, to date, focused significantly on the *restricted celebrity status* that might be created by audience subcultures. Cult TV and its fan cultures offer one cultural site where this type of celebrity is generated and sustained (Hills 2003a: 61).

Celebrity is a relevant term here precisely because this type of recognition and status is not simply a matter of 'renown' within a 'social network' (see Rojek, 2001: 12; and Hills, 2003a: 60) against which mediated celebrity can be contrasted. Mechanisms of subcultural and niche mediation play a role in constructing and sustaining specific individuals as widely known within their subculture, where this recognition can – just like more generalized celebrity – be non-reciprocal, i.e. the subcultural celebrity is known to a far wider circle of fan-consumers than he or she in turn socially knows.

As Lauri Mullens has pointed out, this 'phenomenon of "Big Name Fans" demonstrates a kind of hierarchy within fandom itself' (2005: 9). 'Big Name Fans' is one of the fan-cultural or subcultural terms for fans who have attained a wide degree of recognition in the community, and so who are known to others via subcultural mediation without personally knowing all those other subcultural participants. Tulloch and Jenkins (1995: 150) partly recognize the existence of this fan hierarchy by dubbing some fans 'executive fans': 'in the absence of power over either production of the series or over the wider viewing public, these senior fans do have *discursive* power in establishing the "informed" exegesis for their subculture of fans'. Yet, while observing that 'editors of fanzines can have an important agenda-setting function' (1995: 150), Tulloch and Jenkins do not link this to any theorization of celebrity. The opinions and niche-mediated writings of Big Name Fans or executive fans may 'matter within the subculture', but their discursive power is not seen as indicating any subculturally celebrated status (1995: 150). Nor, somewhat strangely, is the position of the executive fan viewed as one which internally differentiates and stratifies fan subculture: rather, it appears to be highlighted as a supposed representation of, and stand in for, the generalizable lot of fans viewed as a monolithic powerless elite. By contrast, Andrea MacDonald (1998) sets out to catalogue the variety of ways in which Big Name Fan subcultural status can be achieved. For MacDonald this includes:

[1] hierarchy of knowledge ...
[2] hierarchy of fandom level/quality ...
[3] hierarchy of access ...

[4] hierarchy of leaders ... [and]

[5] hierarchy of venue (1998: 137–8).

The first hierarchy regards 'knowledge about ... the fictional universe' (1998: 137), and so indicates a fan's immersion in diegetic information. (Although MacDonald is specifically referring to fandoms based around fictional/diegetic texts here, a similar hierarchy could also be said to operate around 'real life' fandoms, such as the factual, historical knowledge character- izing many sports fandoms.) The last hierarchy, meanwhile, corresponds broadly to Tulloch and Jenkins' discussion of fanzine editors' agenda-setting, since it regards who has gate-keeping control over a venue of discussion, whether this is a face-to-face meeting at a fans' home, or an online discussion group. Hierarchy [2] indicates the extent to which a fan takes part in socially organized subcultural activities such as convention-going. And hierarchy [3] concerns whether or not 'fans have direct access to actors, producers of the show, production personnel, and in some rare cases, actual shootings of episodes' (1998: 137). This indicates some degree of permeability, however limited, between fan culture and celebrity media professionals. It indicates that by virtue of their relative 'insider' social contacts and knowledge, specific fans can become celebrities within their subculture. Of MacDonald's list, hierarchy [4] seems somewhat tautological and perhaps the most problematic of the set, since it suggests that there is a pecking order among fan group 'leaders', ranging from those who run/organize local fan groups to those who run larger national or even international fan clubs (1998: 138). This appears to simply state that there is a hierarchy within socially organized groups of fans, and thus is neither clearly differentiated from [5] nor based on any further variable, as are all the other specified forms of fan hierarchy.

MacDonald also notes that 'fans may occupy multiple positions simulta- neously' (1998: 138) but doesn't consider exactly how these positions in different hierarchies may work to reinforce one another. Nor does she fully consider the role of subcultural and commercial niche media in cementing the 'recognition or authority' communally accorded to Big Name Fans (1998: 139) – i.e. it is by editing/contributing to a fan club zine, other fanzine, or even a commercially available fan magazine (Hunt, 2003) that fans can get their names known and their identities mediated/circulated as those of subcultural celebri- ties. It is also through working for commercial fan magazines, or running websites recognized by industry professionals (see Murray, 2004), that fans can get access to set visits. The range of interlocking hierarchies identified by MacDonald (1998) can thus be argued to underpin fans' subcultural celebrity.

Further to this, fans can also achieve different types of subcultural celebrity, becoming niche-mediated and so known to factions of fans for their fan-fiction writing, their costuming, their replica-prop-building, or their specific archival research into a given show. Fans' subcultural celebrity can therefore be minutely specialized: while some fans may become known for their administrative roles within the institutions of fandom, others can forge niche-media reputations as experts in specific areas: as literary analysts of character, or as fan-historians. Although this communal construction and dissemination of knowledge can certainly be interpreted as a type of 'collective intelligence', with fans pooling their interpretive resources (see Jenkins, 2002), it is not an exchange among pure equals, given that specific fans attain subcultural celebrity via the niche-mediation of their skilled interpretations/specialist information.

Although neither Tulloch and Jenkins (1995) nor MacDonald (1998) relate fan hierarchies to subcultural celebrity status, Kirsten Pullen's more recent work regarding online fandom has begun to note the conceptual and empirical spread of celebrity beyond its more usual parameters:

> Celebrities from all forms of media [now] engage in interactive, online discussions with their fans, especially when promoting a new film, special television programme, [or] new season ... For example, the website for the US entertainment channel E! features weekly chats with stars ... These chats are conducted by E!'s online columnists, who also participate in weekly chats with their fans. As this example demonstrates, not only has access to celebrities increased, but the number of 'celebrities' whom one can access has increased as well (2004: 84).

Pullen's final invocation of 'celebrities' here has an uneasy set of scare quotes around it, as if the term is somehow not fully or clearly merited. This ambiguity appears to stem from the fact that Pullen is commenting on two different types of celebrities: the first mention in the above quote corresponds to ubiquitous celebrities – or what academic work has always termed celebrities in the past – whereas the second group is made up of 'E!'s online columnists', i.e. professional journalists who cannot be argued to fit into the conventional mould of ubiquitous celebrity. It is perhaps as a result of this uncertainty (the latter 'celebrities' are known to a specific audience only, and are journalists rather than actors/film stars/TV and film producers) that Pullen casts some conceptual doubt over the proper use of the term. And yet the wider scope of and for celebrity that is gestured to in her account also fits with how we can describe media fans' subcultural celebrity. Here, much like the recognition accorded to E!'s columnists by their niche audience, cult TV fans can also interact online with 'proper' celebrities – i.e. media producers/actors/professionals working on their favoured shows – as well as with 'celebrities' in the guise of other fans who are recognized as subcultural authorities.

The nature of fame is somewhat reconfigured heresince, as Graeme Turner has noted in a related context, 'the construction of fame within these small networks tends to remain within these networks ... celebrity takes on new functions and meanings ... as it is effectively turned into a demotic strategy of identity formation' (2004: 20). This process is evident on the forums of cult TV fan websites such as Outpost Gallifrey (www.gallifreyone.com), a *Doctor Who* site founded by J. Shaun Lyon. Here, there are dedicated sections where fans can pose questions to specific Big Name Fans – those who have become celebrities within the subcultural fan community – and there is also a range of more contingent threads which thank, recognize and applaud specific fans who possess status in terms of MacDonald's hierarchies of access and venue, including Shaun Lyon himself (as in 'To Shaun Lyon with Thanks', Darren Rodway, 25 March 2005, 05:07 p.m.).

The contribution made to this fan community by a range of 'noteworthy individuals' is thus affirmed (see Baym, 2000: 171), as they are celebrated by other fans, and their communal pre-eminence re-iterated. Another example of this on Outpost Gallifrey is a thread entitled simply 'Who loves Andrew Pixley?' (Inflatable Dalek, 10 March 2005), which runs to 133 replies affirming the work of Pixley, a fan-historian and *Doctor Who* archivist who has frequently contributed reference works on the series' production history to *Doctor Who Magazine*:

> Tireless devotion to our cause and a regular poster here of the highest intelligence, courtesy, taste and modesty. (Okdel, 10 March 2005, 05:25 p.m.)

> He comes across as an *unbelievably* nice bloke online, and his archives are an amazing piece of work – I really hope they can be issued as some sort of book! (Matthew Tate, 10 March 2005, 05:36 p.m.)

There is a discernible hierarchy of subcultural celebrity here: beyond what MacDonald identifies as a hierarchy of access, there is also a *hierarchy of canon*, where fans attain a greater degree of subcultural celebrity the closer they come to contributing to what is generally accepted to constitute the canon of *Doctor Who* texts. Some fans attain relatively weak subcultural celebrity by editing fanzines, running fan clubs or founding websites, but those individuals who write for official BBC-licensed publications such as assorted ranges of *Doctor Who* books or *Doctor Who Magazine* accrue higher status in the fan community, while those who have actually ended up working on the TV series itself – the apex of canonicity – earn the highest subcultural celebrity status. The ultimate in *Doctor Who* fan-celebrity subcultural recognition thus belongs to an elite group of fans who have written for and produced the 2005 BBC Wales-produced TV series, people such as writers Paul Cornell, Rob Shearman, Steven Moffat and executive producer

Russell T. Davies. Far from being a 'powerless elite', these fans combine the
symbolic and discursive power of subcultural celebrity status with industry
power – unusually, they can determine the direction taken by the show that they
are fans of. However, in relation to this move from fan to professional media
producer, it is worth noting that *Doctor Who* fandom is, when compared to many
other media fandoms, unusually male-dominated (see Pugh, 2005:7). The fact
that the vast majority of *Doctor Who* fans who accrue subcultural celebrity status
are men is thus no accident, while the permeability between *Who* fandom and
Who media-professionalism may also be enhanced by this fandom's specifically
male-centric status. By contrast, movements from the predominantly female *Star
Trek* fandom into media-professionalism have been far less marked, implying that
female fans may be taken less seriously as potential professionals by still male-
dominated media industries.

The overarching hierarchy of subcultural celebrity corresponds, in a sense,
with differentiations in textuality identified by John Fiske. Fiske distinguishes
between what he terms primary, secondary and tertiary texts:

> Vertical intertextuality is that between a primary text, such as a televi-
> sion program or series, and other texts of a different type that refer
> explicitly to it. These may be secondary texts such as ... publicity, jour-
> nalistic features, or criticism, or tertiary texts produced by the viewers
> themselves in the form of letters to the press or ... gossip and conversa-
> tion (1987: 108).

What cult TV fans' subcultural celebrity indicates is that although some fans can
distinguish themselves via what MacDonald (1998) calls their 'fan level' – i.e.
attending conventions or organizing fan clubs – this generally restricts such fans to
tertiary textual productivity in Fiske's terms. It is fans who cross over into
secondary textual production who begin to carry more developed and sustained
levels of subcultural celebrity. This celebrity status can be earned by writing for
Doctor Who Magazine like the aforementioned Andrew Pixley, penning journalistic
reviews of the programme for other commercially available magazines/newspa-
pers, or publishing criticism of the programme, even academic criticism. To take a
further example, Professor John Tulloch – co-author of scholarly titles *Doctor Who:
The Unfolding Text* (Tulloch and Alvarado, 1983) and *Science Fiction Audiences*
(Tulloch and Jenkins, 1995) – was accorded subcultural celebrity recognition and
status when he appeared in news coverage as a survivor of the 7 July 2005 suicide
bombings in London:

> Was quite shocked to hear his name on the news. In fact just a couple of
> months ago I was browsing through Science Fiction Audiences in a

library as I was working on an essay on Doctor Who. Hope he gets better soon (Theta Sigma, 11 July 2005, 01:44 a.m.).

Yes, I was quite shocked about seeing John Tulloch there as well – I regard The Unfolding Text as being the most in-depth analysis of Doctor Who's roots that I've seen. Hope he recovers well (Cyril Washbrook, 11 July 2005, 11:37 p.m.).

Though Tulloch's initial appearance in mainstream news was clearly contingent on his accidental involvement in the 7/7 bombings, the way that online *Who* fans then awarded him recognition was far from accidental, since it drew on the prior subcultural prestige which Tulloch had accrued as the author of studies of *Doctor Who*. Such subcultural recognition is not at all the same thing as 'renown' in Chris Rojek's (2001) terms, since Rojek defines renown as 'the informal attribution of distinction on an individual within a given social network … [which] depends on reciprocal personal … contact' (2001: 12). By contrast, the celebrity status conferred on a range of fans by their subcultural peers, although limited to a specific 'social network', does not hinge on 'reciprocal personal' contact, though it can sometimes involve this. Instead, fans-turned-subcultural-celebrities are – like ubiquitous celebrities – 'distanced … by … some medium of communication' from their own subcultural readers (Rojek 2002: 12). Fan-produced secondary texts thus begin to carry niche-mediated name recognition and to construct niche-mediated reputations for their writers. Perhaps surprisingly, however, subcultural celebrities' faces frequently tend not to be recognizable to other fans operating solely at the level of tertiary textual productivity. Celebrity is not, in this case, based on the mediation of physical likeness, belying the slippage between 'recognition' and *facial* recognition which some academics have attributed to celebrity:

> What, then, is a celebrity? There are many possible answers to the question, but this is surely the most basic, the most fundamental, and the most irreducible: a celebrity is someone who is recognized by more people than they themselves recognize. To be more specific, we might posit that a celebrity is someone whose *face* is widely recognized (Gilbert, 2004: 87).

Subcultural celebrity certainly meets Jeremy Gilbert's 'irreducible' account of celebrity by involving non-mutual subcultural recognition, but this does not appear to inherently involve faciality. Instead, it most frequently hinges on the writer's name as a pure signifier – one reason why fans were uncertain whether the 'John Tulloch' featured in mainstream news reports of the 7/7 bombings was indeed 'their' John Tulloch:

It does appear that 'our' John Tulloch was in fact hospitalized. He has now been released ... Oddly enough, he is also the author of 'Risk and Everyday Life' as part of his studies on perceptions of risk and crime (Esperantisto, 16 July 2005, 02:55 p.m.).

The general absence of mediated likenesses for fans working at the level of secondary textuality is one major difference, of course, between this and what is typically theorized as celebrity in scholarly work. Subcultural celebrity, we can suggest, is typically typographic rather than iconic, being primarily carried through name-recognition rather than through iconicity. The one area where this difference does not generally hold – and thus where subcultural celebrity moves closest to the iconic nature of mass-mediated and ubiquitous celebrity – is in relation to fans who become producers of primary texts. Fans would be highly likely to recognize this class of professionalized fans thanks to the frequent circulation of their likenesses in secondary, fan-niche-targeted texts, even if the people concerned would probably still not be recognized by the non-fan, general audience for *Doctor Who*:

[A]ctors are on the frontline ... 'the Chris [Eccleston] and Billie [Piper] show'. ... You're much more protected as a writer ... Really your name is only known in the industry [and by fans – MH]. Ask most of this restaurant who Russell T. Davies is ...? Not a clue! And that's brilliant. That's the way it should be, really (Davies, in Cook, 2005: 33).

Given the highly distinctive position of *Doctor Who* fans who have crossed over into the media industry as producers/writers of the primary text itself, I will now go on to consider their subcultural celebrity in more detail. Fans who attain subcultural celebrity via the production of tertiary and secondary texts demonstrate that fan cultures cannot be thought of only as 'powerless elites' (Tulloch and Jenkins, 1995) inherently subordinated to the 'extra-ordinary' status of media professionals (see Couldry, 2003: 85). Specific fans can also take on (niche-)mediated symbolic power within their own communal networks, carrying a type of demotic and restricted celebrity status by virtue of fan-cultural recognition for their expertise and authority. However, it is fans turned primary media producers who most centrally enact and potentially challenge 'the idea of an invisible, but symbolically significant, barrier between ordinary world and media world' (Couldry, 2003: 85). Whereas fans operating at the level of tertiary texts can build a metaphorical 'career' within fan culture (see Crawford, 2004: 38–49), fans who crossover into secondary and especially primary textual productivity enter the literal or 'professional stage of [fan] career development' by making 'at least a partial amount of their income from their involvement in their ... enthusiasm' (Crawford 2004:

48). And fans who become primary textual producers are, of course, directly positioned within the TV industry itself, as well as playing roles in the subculture of media fandom.

Subcultural celebrity and textual poachers turned textual gamekeepers: primary producer-fans

In *Textual Poachers* (1992), Henry Jenkins uses the image and figure of the poacher as a model for fan activity, suggesting that fans poach meaning selectively from media texts over which they have no control and power. This approach to fandom – one which pits fan-consumers against media producers as two reified categories – has undoubtedly become extremely influential, but it has recently been challenged in a variety of fan studies work (see e.g. Hills, 2002; Sandvoss, 2005). Alan McKee has most significantly deconstructed the binaries of production and consumption, and power relations, implied in such work on fan poaching:

> From my analysis of *Doctor Who*, it seems that the distinction between the cultural production of fans and that of television producers is not nearly so distinct as these [prior academic] accounts might suggest ... And ultimately, there can be no firm boundary set ... between the fan and the producer (2004: 171).

McKee points out that 'there are hierarchies of cultural status and earning power within fandom, just as there is in the media' (2004: 172; see also Bacon-Smith, 2000). His argument takes in the fact that supposedly 'powerless' fans can be the very people who go on to produce canonical *Doctor Who*, even working directly on the television series itself (2004: 174). McKee cites the example of Gary Russell, interviewed as an executive fan in Tulloch and Jenkins (1995), who later ran a production company 'licensed by the BBC to produce a new series of *Doctor Who* (in audio format)' (2004: 172). And another of McKee's examples (2004: 181) of 'professionalized fan' cultural production, Russell T. Davies, is in fact currently executive producer on the BBC TV series of *Doctor Who* (2005–): 'In short, fans produce the television program, edit and write the official novels, edit and write the official magazine' (McKee 2004: 174). This situation may well not be reproduced in relation to other 'younger' media fandoms – it is partly a product of *Doctor Who* fans having grown up with the show they love, being inspired by it to work in the media industry – but it does nevertheless issue an empirical and theoretical challenge to rigid binaries of powerful producers versus powerless consumers.

Although McKee doesn't explicitly develop such a line of argument, his account also challenges other consumption/production-related binaries such as that of fans versus celebrities. More than simply being a Big Name Fan or 'BNF', Russell T. Davies is accorded supreme subcultural celebrity status amongst fans for bringing *Doctor Who* back to TV screens for the first time since 1996, and overseeing a highly successful reinvention of the show. Unlike the 'TV celebrities' who are represented as the show's 'star' actor and actress, Davies's likeness may well not be familiar to the 'general public' (as he himself argues in Cook, 2005), but it is nevertheless repeatedly mediated and circulated in subcultural media (e.g. *Doctor Who Magazine*). Furthermore, online fans posting to Outpost Gallifrey conventionally refer to Davies simply as 'RTD', implying the 'non-reciprocal intimacy at a distance' which has been said to characterize fans' relations with mediated celebrities (Thompson 1995: 219). Discussions of 'RTD' and his work tend to be among the dominant topics for online fans (for example, as of 31/7/05 just one Outpost Gallifrey thread entitled 'My personal view on Doctor Who 2005 and RTD' started by Ian Levine – a fan who had himself worked as a consultant on the classic series – ran to some 4,935 postings). Davies himself has not been known to contribute to such debate, preserving a symbolic boundary of sorts between his professional identity and fan debate. At the same time, Davies has contributed a 'Production Notes' column to *Doctor Who Magazine* since issue number 341 (31 March 2004) repeatedly expressing his credentials as a fan, and constructing a niche-mediated identity as such:

> You'll be able to read about it [new series news – MH] here first, in the pages of *DWM*. Because I love this comic. I really do. I've bought it since the very first issue. There was one newsagent's in Swansea ... which would get the original *Doctor Who Weekly* [forerunner of *DWM* – MH] on a Wednesday instead of a Thursday. Every Wednesday, I'd cross town to get there (Davies, 2004: 50).

It should be noted that this identity construction is, however, not open to reciprocal fan communication. Unlike other 'professionalized fans' (Hills, 2002) working on the primary text of *Doctor Who* 2005 – e.g. scriptwriters Rob Shearman and Paul Cornell, who respond to Outpost Gallifrey posters' queries in its dedicated 'Ask the Authors' section – Davies is less accessible to rank-and-file fans. He writes about his fandom in subcultural media such as *DWM*, but to date he has studiously avoided making himself personally available to the fan community through events such as online chats. As a fan who is also in charge of making *Doctor Who*, and furthermore an acclaimed media industry professional, Davies's bridging of fan and primary-text producer identities is unusual. It represents a possibility to powerfully collapse together the 'media world' and the 'ordinary world' of the fan-consumer (Couldry, 2003), and though Davies plays with these distinctions in his columns for *Doctor Who Magazine*, blending 'insider' industry knowledge with knowledge of fan trivia (Hunt, 2003), the two worlds are also kept symbolically apart through his relative inaccessibility to 'ordinary' fans.

Subcultural celebrity reaches its apotheosis, it would seem, where it most clearly replicates the symbolic inequalities theorized in relation to ubiquitous celebrity. That is, while *Doctor Who* fan audience discussion, speculation and interpretation of 'RTD's' work is rife, the man himself only enters into the subcultural arena of contemporary fandom under highly controlled and stage-managed conditions, thus preserving a sense that his 'professional' identity is set apart from the profane world of fandom. Rather than Davies being able to unproblematically unite fan and producer roles, it appears that these cultural identities can only co-exist somewhat uneasily and liminally, given the very different institutional 'imagined subjectivities' (Hills, 2002) and forms of exper- tise which mark out each subcultural world.

Furthermore, Davies's fandom may not inevitably or necessarily be recognized as a source of value within his professional role as a writer/executive producer for the BBC, despite his professional role according him high status within fandom. For example, Davies omitted material from his original pitch for the 2005 series of *Doctor Who* which later became highly significant to and for fans: this was the back-story of the Time War and the figure of the 'Bad Wolf'. Regarding this omission, Davies notes that the pitch 'document was designed to be straightforward and easy to read for the Big Bosses' (2005a: 47). However, the material left out in the 'professional' media-insider's document concerned *Doctor Who* continuity as well as Davies's familiarity with the Big Finish audio range. In other words, in the name of 'straightforwardness' (and this does thus appear to be a somewhat disingenuous or at least reductive claim) Davies mini- mized his 'fan' identity in material which had to work to construct his 'profes- sional' identity, therefore distancing himself from the textual continuity so beloved by *Who* fan culture: 'The fiction of the Doctor has got forty years of back-story. Which we'll ignore. Except for the good bits' (2005a: 42). Davies may be eager to display his credentials as a fan in material written directly for the fan market (e.g. his *DWM* column), but he is seemingly far less fannish in his dealings with other media professionals and 'Big Bosses'. Other fans working on the primary text of *Doctor Who*, such as Paul Cornell, the writer of an episode entitled 'Father's Day', have claimed that their fan identity does not come into conflict with their 'professional' self:

> I don't think an association with *Doctor Who* has affected how I'm seen by professionals, because all professionals care about is the work – there isn't a fannish stigma there, really. Amongst the *Doctor Who* fan community, I'm either 'Local boy makes good', or more often, 'He's not a proper writer, is he? He's one of us ... ' (Cornell, in Darlington, 2005: 55).

However, it should be noted that rather than indicating fan-producer hybrid identities are unproblematic, this claim attributes tensions between recognition as a fan and as 'a proper writer' to the fan community rather than to 'media professionals'. Furthermore, the interviewer had not explicitly raised the issue of 'fan stigma' within media-professional circles. I would suggest that Cornell's deflection actually lends credence (via its very defensiveness) to the very thing he is at pains to deny or culturally re-locate: both other fans and media professionals may not view writers as 'proper' if they are too close to fandom.

Any such asymmetry – whereby media professionals attempt to set themselves against the 'imagined other' of the negatively-stereotyped fan audience – suggests that the subcultural capital (Thornton, 1995) accrued by the likes of Cornell and Davies (i.e. their hierarchical positions within given subcultures) can carry two distinct and non-aligned sets of 'relevant beholders': namely other fans and media industry professionals. The forms of knowledge valued by one subculture (fans) may not be shared by the other (media industry/producers). Codes of professional conduct will also inevitably inhibit what production information can be shared in the subcultural arena of fandom. Davies's status in fan culture may be enhanced and elevated by his position as a media professional working on *Doctor Who*'s primary text – after all, he did not enjoy such a centrality to the fan culture when he had only written the secondary text or 'media tie-in' *Damaged Goods* (1996) for Virgin Publishing – but his status as a media producer does not similarly rely on his fandom. Davies's structural position as a 'textual poacher' turned 'textual gamekeeper' thus involves him in attempting to manage the distinct subcultural hierarchies and separate recognitions of knowledge/status which belong to industry and fandom. By participating too freely or widely in fan discussions and fan activities, Davies could potentially damage the status which he possesses as a media professional, risking 'unprofessional' and excessively 'fannish' action:

> *Doctor Who* is now one of those ratings-busting, Top 10, high impact programmes … It makes it difficult to write this column [in *DWM*]. Partly because you're all so used to programmes being archived … that it's hard to realize that this is a primetime show currently in production for BBC One. It demands that we have to be professional. For example, I would no sooner discuss an actor's contract than I would run naked through the street (and you really don't want that) (Davies, 2005b: 66).

A 'boundary reproduction' (Couldry, 2003: 86) of 'media' versus 'fan' world is thus constructed by the incommensurable nature of those different subcultural capitals which are simultaneously carried by the fan-primary-producer (see also Lancaster, 2001: 1–33, on the producer-fan of US science-fiction TV series

Babylon 5, J. M. Straczynski). Whereas Big Name Fans are not generally or always restricted by powerfully normative codes of 'media professionalism' (which construct an 'us' versus 'them' moral dualism of the 'professional' versus their 'audience'), fans working on the primary text – and those closer to it by virtue of working on officially-licensed publications such as *Doctor Who Magazine* – have to much more carefully police the ways in which they articulate fan and producer identities. The end result of these cultural processes of identity management is that what could constitute a much more significant challenge to the categories of 'fan' and 'producer' tends to be blunted: producer/consumer symbolic inequalities are partly re-installed. Despite this, it remains important to take heed of Alan McKee's (2004) argument to the effect that producer/consumer binaries are complicated by cases such as Davies's.

Given that fan/producer and ordinary/extraordinary binaries are partly re-installed around the figure of 'RTD', it could be suggested that this type of professionalized fan works to support classical ideologies of fame, i.e. that anyone can 'make it', and be touched by fame's caress. However, any such ideological reading – presupposing that other *Doctor Who* fans would view Davies *et al.* as a legitimation of their own desires/abilities to turn pro or 'make it' in the media industry – significantly reduces the complexity of subcultural celebrity. Rather than simply endorsing or legitimating conventional, culturally ubiquitous, distant and iconic celebrity, subcultural celebrity (in its differing manifestations and levels) acts to qualify and modify such celebrity, making names as important as physical likenesses, and linking these names to fan-cultural notions of work which merits value/recognition. Whereas it remains possible for mass-mediated celebrity to be more-or-less purely 'manufactured', subcultural celebrity is necessarily linked to subculturally-valorized achievements, whether these are writing fan fiction which only circulates within the fan culture, writing academic studies which perhaps circulate slightly more widely in terms of niche-mediation, or producing a specific, beloved TV series for primetime, international consumption.

In this chapter I have argued that we cannot simply contrast fandom to celebrity, using these terms to prop up and reinforce a media producer/consumer binary (Marshall, 2004). Rather than fans being 'ordinary' and disempowered consumers of 'extra-ordinary' media professionals who attain celebrity status by virtue of their mediation (and/or their work in the 'media world'), I have suggested that fan culture sustains its own specific network of subcultural celebrities. By displaying textual productivity at different levels – creating tertiary, secondary and, in the case of *Doctor Who* fandom, primary texts – fans can succeed in niche-mediating their names and iconic likenesses, acquiring restricted celebrity status. I have argued that this fan-celebrity hybridization is distinct from the 'renown' that can be accrued by social actors within specific settings (Rojek, 2001) since fan-celebrities are not directly known by other fans, but instead typically acquire fan-cultural reputations and recognition via the subcultural, niche mediation of their names and their work. Cult TV fans who become producers of primary TV texts perhaps move closest to prior, general academic definitions of televisual 'celebrity' (see Holmes, 2004), since their names and likenesses tend to circulate in mass-media publicity and intertexts via 'non-reciprocal intimacy at a distance' (Thompson, 1995). Even here, though, it can be suggested that television celebrity is conferred most centrally on actors ('the Chris and Billie show') rather than upon production personnel such as writers, who can thus retain multiple, incommensurable forms of subcultural capital (Thornton, 1995) within both industry and fan subcultures.

Considering the mechanisms of celebrity and (online) niche-mediation which operate within fan cultures can allow us to analyse how '[d]iscourses of celebrity invade all kinds of [cultural] sites today' (Turner, 2004: 15), moving far beyond the domains which have classically been associated with such discourses. Celebrity culture, we might conclude, is no longer entirely co-terminous with the production and consumption of mass-mediated/ubiquitous 'star' texts and intertexts, for it is also produced and consumed intra-subculturally via the fan audience phenomenon of Big Name Fans and in relation to vari-ously 'professionalized fans' (Hills, 2002). And since fan cultures can generate 'their' celebrities rather than merely interpreting pre-existent mass-mediated celebrity texts in distinctive ways, to consider media fandom simply as a 'power-less elite' misses its own subcultural stratifications, and its own hierarchies of subcultural celebrity, in which not all fans are similarly 'elite' nor equally 'pow-erless'. Despite issuing this challenge to influential work in fan studies (Jenkins, 1992; Tulloch and Jenkins, 1995), I have also argued that it is important to consider how the symbolic inequalities sustained by fan versus celebrity and 'ordinary world' versus 'media world' binaries (Alberoni, 1972; Marshall, 1997; Couldry, 2003) are also partly re-enacted and recuperated, especially in the case of what I have termed here (and in Hills, 2002: 36) textual poachers turned textual gamekeepers.

Bibliography

Alberoni, Francesco (1972) 'The Powerless "Elite": Theory and Sociological Research on the Phenomenon of the Stars', in Denis McQuail (ed.), *Sociology of Mass Communications*, Harmondsworth: Penguin, pp. 75–98.

Bacon-Smith, Camille (2000) *Science Fiction Culture*, Philadelphia: University of Pennsylvania Press.

Barbas, Samantha (2001) *Movie Crazy: Fans, Stars and the Cult of Celebrity*, New York: Palgrave.

Baym, Nancy K. (2000) *Tune In, Log On: Soaps, Fandom and Online Community*, London: Sage.

Braudy, Leo (1986) *The Frenzy of Renown: Fame and Its History*, Oxford: Oxford University Press.

Cook, Benjamin (2005) 'A Long Game: The Russell T Davies Interview, Part One', *Doctor Who Magazine* 359: 31–7.

Couldry, Nick (2003) *Media Rituals: A Critical Approach*, London and New York: Routledge.

Crawford, Garry (2004) *Consuming Sport: Fans, Sport and Culture*, London and New York: Routledge.

Darlington, David (2005) 'Script Doctors: Paul Cornell', *Doctor Who Magazine* 352: 55–8.

Davies, Russell T. (1996) *Damaged Goods*, London: Virgin Publishing.

—— (2004) 'Production Notes #1: The Sound of Silence', *Doctor Who Magazine* 341: 50.

—— (2005a) 'Pitch Perfect', *Doctor Who Magazine Special Edition: The Series One Companion*: 40–9.

—— (2005b) 'Production Notes', *Doctor Who Magazine* 357: 66.

Fiske, John (1987) *Television Culture*, London: Methuen.

Gilbert, Jeremy (2004) 'Small Faces: The Tyranny of Celebrity in Post-Oedipal Culture', *Mediactive* 2: 86–109.

Giles, David (2000) *Illusions of Immortality: A Psychology of Fame and Celebrity*, London: Macmillan.

Hills, Matt (2002) *Fan Cultures*, London and New York: Routledge.

—— (2003a) 'Recognition in the Eyes of the Relevant Beholder: Representing "Subcultural Celebrity" and Cult TV Fan Cultures', *Mediactive* 2: 59–73.

—— (2003b) 'Putting Away Childish Things: Jar Jar Binks and the "Virtual Star" as an Object of Fan Loathing', in Thomas Austin and Martin Barker (eds), *Contemporary Hollywood Stardom*, London: Arnold, pp. 74–89.

—— (2005) *How To Do Things With Cultural Theory*, London: Hodder Arnold.

Holmes, David (2005) *Communication Theory: Media, Technology and Society*, London: Sage.

Holmes, Su (2004) '"All You've Got To Worry About is the Task, Having a Cup of Tea, and Doing a Bit of Sunbathing": Approaching Celebrity in *Big Brother*', in Su Holmes and Deborah Jermyn (eds), *Understanding Reality Television*, London and New York: Routledge, pp.111–35.

Hunt, Nathan (2003) 'The Importance of Trivia: Ownership, Exclusion and Authority in Science Fiction Fandom', in Mark Jancovich, Antonio Lázaro Reboll, Julian Stringer and Andy Willis (eds), *Defining Cult Movies*, Manchester: Manchester University Press, pp. 185–201.

Jenkins, Henry (1992) *Textual Poachers*, New York and London: Routledge.

—— (2002) 'Interactive Audiences?', in Dan Harries (ed.), *The New Media Book*, London: BFI Publishing, pp. 157–70.

Lancaster, Kurt (2001) *Fan Performances in a Media Universe: Interacting with Babylon 5*, Austin: University of Texas Press.

Littler, Jo (2004) 'Making Fame Ordinary: Intimacy, Reflexivity and "Keeping it Real"', *Mediactive* 2: 8–25.

MacDonald, Andrea (1998) 'Uncertain Utopia: Science Fiction Media Fandom and Computer Mediated Communication', in Cheryl Harris and Alison Alexander (eds), *Theorizing Fandom: Fans, Subculture and Identity*, New Jersey: Hampton Press, pp. 131–52.

McKee, Alan (2004) 'How to Tell the Difference between Production and Consumption: A Case Study in *Doctor Who* Fandom', in Sara Gwenllian-Jones and Roberta E. Pearson (eds), *Cult Television*, Minneapolis: University of Minnesota Press, pp. 167–85.

Marshall, P. David (1997) *Celebrity and Power: Fame in Contemporary Culture*, Minneapolis and London: University of Minnesota Press.

—— (2004) *New Media Cultures*, London: Arnold.

Mullens, Lauri (2005) 'Editor's Introduction', *Spectator* 25/1: 5–10.

Murray, Simone (2004) '"Celebrating the Story the Way It Is": Cultural Studies, Corporate Media and the Contested Utility of Fandom', *Continuum* 18/1: 7–25.

Pugh, Sheenagh (2005) *The Democratic Genre: Fan Fiction in a Literary Context*, Bridgend: Seren.

Pullen, Kirsten (2004) 'Everybody's Gotta Love Somebody, Sometime: Online Fan Community', in David Gauntlett and Ross Horsley (eds), *Web.Studies*, 2nd edn, London: Arnold, pp. 80–91.

Rojek, Chris (2001) *Celebrity*, London: Reaktion Books.

Sandvoss, Cornel (2005) *Fans: The Mirror of Consumption*, Cambridge: Polity Press.

Stacey, Jackie (1994) *Star Gazing: Hollywood Cinema and Female Spectatorship*, London: Routledge.

Staiger, Janet (2005) *Media Reception Studies*, New York and London: New York University Press.

Thompson, John B. (1995) *Media and Modernity*, Cambridge: Polity Press.

Thornton, Sarah (1995) *Club Cultures*, Cambridge: Polity Press.

Tulloch, John and Alvarado, Manuel (1983) *Doctor Who: The Unfolding Text*, London: Macmillan.

Tulloch, John and Jenkins, Henry (1995) *Science Fiction Audiences: Watching Doctor Who and Star Trek*, London and New York: Routledge.

Turner, Graeme (2004) *Understanding Celebrity*, London: Sage.

Part II

Fame Body

Introduction

What defines a film star or a glamorous celebrity? What is it about them, at least in mythic terms, that attracts attention, commands identification, and lights up the screen? In filmic terms the star is often defined as a potent synthesis between an incredible face and a perfect body. The star's face, when captured in cinematic close-up, supposedly reveals their absolute beauty and acts as a metaphorical doorway into their inner being. The face of Greta Garbo, for example, is:

> Offered to one's gaze a sort of Platonic Idea of the human creature ... The name given to her, *the Divine*, probably aimed to convey less a superlative state of beauty than the essence of her corporeal person, descended from a heaven where all things are formed and perfected in the clearest light (Barthes, 1985: 650–1).

The star's body is also to be read as fleshed perfection, an exemplary form of femininity, masculinity or sexual desirability. For example, the female star's long legs, slender wrists, ample bust, thin neck, and flat stomach are idealized signifiers for the perfect woman. The female star's perfect body is photographed so that it is to-be-looked-at although, historically at least, it has been the adorable clothes that cover up (*cling to*) parts of the star's body – the fetishized garments and jewellery – which have made it such a potent, and problematic, form of human embodiment (Mulvey, 1975). A number of female stars seem to self-consciously revel in their desired/desirable bodies, offering it up as a symbol of their worth. As Richard Dyer writes of Monroe's sex-object status in 1950s America:

> Unthreatening, vulnerable, Monroe always seemed to be available, on offer ... many observers saw her career in terms of a series of moments in which she offered herself to the gaze of men ... She was the playboy playmate who wanted to be one (2004: 227).

The body of the film star also functions narratively: their encoded bodies often help to define the characters they play (vamp, femme fatale, romantic lead, twisted killer, masculine hero); and they energize plot and story through their movement and action (Jeffords, 1994). Arnold Schwarzenegger's hard body, for example, became a recurring narrative device for wreaking havoc and punishing criminals.

Celebrities are often represented in a similar way. Their handsome or beautiful faces adorn billboard posters, magazine covers and advertisements. Their idealized bodies are attached to consumer brands such as sports goods and body lotions, and are put on display at public engagements, photo-shoots, and through the media coverage which comments on and constructs the corporeal perfection they encapsulate. In fact, certain celebrities, such as supermodels and famous male models, are solely embodied performers: desirable and desired because of the look, size and shape of their bodies. In the 1980s, for example, the supermodel Elle Macpherson was re-named 'The Body' by fashion magazines and the tabloid press.

One can actually argue that the star or celebrity body has become increasingly central to the way famous people are represented and consumed. Seemingly, now much less about capturing the transcendental face in mesmerizing close-up, the body of the star or celebrity becomes the primary site on which ideological enunciation and identification takes place (Negra, 2001). The body of the star or celebrity circulates in intertextual fantasy environments whereby fans/consumers are asked to like (love), and be physically like, the famed figure in question. While there have always been ancillary media texts promoting the ideals of the famous person, this identification/emulation centred on consumption practices. Fans were sold the idea that they could feel a little of what it was like to be a star or celebrity through the purchase of the perfume, chocolate, clothes and cigarettes with which their idols were associated (Gaines and Herzog, 1991; Stacey, 1994). Today, fans/consumers are increasingly asked to *become* the precise figure of the star or celebrity in and through their *modified* bodies. Women's magazines, for example, constantly construct desiring narratives around the beautiful body of the female star, with diet, fitness and cosmetic surgery advice central to the 'imagined' transformation of the self (although these wish-fulfilment narratives can also be see as empowering and liberating – a position taken up by Rebecca Feasey in this section). The growth in the number of men and women who have cosmetic surgery to change their appearance to one that resembles (embodies) their favourite star or celebrity, speaks to an age where the identificatory processes of fame are played out on the body.

However, it is the naked, stripped or unzipped body of the star or celebrity that arguably suggests a definite shift in the way famous people are represented. No longer covered up or teasingly glimpsed at, and no longer always ideal and perfect, the nude or partially dressed star or celebrity is found across an increasing range of media sites. For example, famous flesh is 'unofficially' paraded in so-called 'skin' magazines and 'officially' sanctioned in glamorous photo-shoots. Tabloid newspapers and gossip magazines capture the star or celebrity falling out of a dress or a suit, topless/bottomless on a beach, or with cellulite marks or plastic surgery scars in clear view. Indeed, celebrity magazines such as *heat* and *Now* seem to relish the process of 'deconstructing' the (usually female) celebrity, claiming to offer 'the province of the cellulite bottom, the rogue nipple' (Llewellyn-Smith, 2002: 120), and to capture celebrities 'off-guard, unkempt, unready, unsanitized' (ibid.). The obsessive interest in 'Who's Had What Done?' (*heat*), has also increasingly come to direct an almost forensic-like gaze, as items such as 'Surgery Spy' scrutinize famous flesh – often with the aid of 'expert' opinion – in a bid to distinguish the modified (parts of the) body from the (holistic) 'natural' beauty. No longer simply the province of the 'heavenly body' (Dyer, 2002), then, the celebrity self is to be prodded, probed and exposed in such a way that revels in the *processes of corporeal fabrication,* rather than the finished product itself. On the internet, official star and celebrity websites offer fans photo galleries and video clips that reveal them at their most intimate, while 'unofficial' (and often pornographic) sites depict the famous naked and engaged in lewd acts. In recent years, Rob Lowe, Pamela Anderson, Colin Farrell and Cameron Diaz have all appeared on the internet either in homemade sex films they didn't want released, or in 'glamour' photographs made before they were famous.

The famous body, then, is now increasingly shown to be less than ideal, physically imperfect, and morally reprehensible. And fans/consumers rush to such sites, to buy/see such images, because they supposedly allow access to famous people as they 'really' are – literally caught in the flesh – and this authenticity, as suggested elsewhere in this collection, roots or makes meaningful the fan/star/celebrity relationship. It also allows the fan/consumer to see right into the sex or beauty that the star or celebrity image was built on, offering them 'the ultimate sign of availability – the unlicensed display of their naked bodies' (Turner, 2004: 125).

In this formulation, the body of the male porn star may well be the best approximation of contemporary stardom. Stars principally because of their perfect toned bodies and the size of their penis, onscreen they appear naked, fully erect and aroused. Such porn stars are polygamous, sexually active and transgressive: gender, or marital status, isn't (and shouldn't be, according to the porn narrative) a bar to their bad-boy behaviour. The watching fan/consumer is meant to be either in a similar state of arousal, or is supposedly playing out the sex games that she/he is watching the porn star perform on screen. As such, the star/fan/consumer body is in near perfect alignment, experiencing together the shared sins of the flesh.

However, in wider political terms, the famous body is often the medium through which dominant ideological messages about gender, race, class and sexuality are transmitted. The body of the star or celebrity is often implicated in the construction of hegemonic notions of masculinity and femininity; in stereotypical ideas about racial difference and Otherness; and in normative assertions about sexual desire and class relations. The famous body emits signs, it is a cultural text, a 'symbol of society' (Douglas, 2002: 373). As such, it is involved in sustaining, and giving authority to, the unequal power relationships that exist between people in the wider world. For example, when the discourses of fame and race coalesce in the body of the star or celebrity, a supercharged representation emerges which often Others them. The famous black body, for example, is regularly hypersexualized – too fleshy and too sexual – so that the script of their fame (even if it is meant to be based on merit) reads in terms of their 'strange' and inferior racial difference. Of course, such a powerfully constructed representation may rupture the discourse in which it is constructed – an argument offered by Ramona Coleman in this section in relation to the black sporting body of Serena Williams.

The essays in this section all take the body to be central to the way in which celebrities and stars communicate and can be read. Through a fascinating range of case studies, and across a number of media sites, the famous body is made sense of in terms of idealization, fabrication, sexuality, identification and emulation, and racialization. The story of the famous body that emerges is a provocative one, and contrasting and sometimes competing arguments are made.

Summaries

The essay that opens this section offers a historical context for how the famous body has come to have such cultural importance in the modern age. In his essay 'Spectacular male bodies and Jazz Age celebrity culture', David Magill argues that 'to understand the contemporary obsession with the body, we must examine celebrity culture's historical reliance on idealized corporeal images, as well as the technologies used to produce them – the methods used to write these fictions on (or as) the celebrity body. Such examinations reveal how celebrity culture provides a vantage point for the dramatization of our own corporeal tensions.' The starting point for Magill's analysis is the white male celebrity body in Jazz Age America. Magill contends that the idealized bodies of Bernarr McFadden, Charles Atlas, Rudolph Valentino and Lon Chaney functioned, albeit in different ways, to provide white American men with a 'panacea for postwar disillusion'. According to Magill, the need for psychic and physical healing emerged due to the wide-scale ruination of the male body during the Great War. White men 'faced their own fragile physicality and found it psychically troubling'. Identification with celebrities who were famous for their fit, healthy and beautiful bodies, or for bodies that were proven to be repairable or reconstituted, as was the case with Lon Chaney's horror body, enabled white men to deal with these latent corporeal fears and anxieties. For example, the health and fitness guru Bernarr MacFadden, founder of the extremely popular magazine *Physical Culture*, came to stand for a restored hard body ideal. In addition, 'MacFadden's rejuvenation plan and his life story combine to rearticulate white manhood's connection to national identity through the body'. Magill concludes his essay by suggesting that the Jazz Age celebrity body provides a 'historical and cultural antecedent' to the famous body today, since these bodies also attempt to assuage latent white male anxieties over the worth of their masculinity.

While the academic study of pornography has garnered greater attention over the last ten years (led by Linda Williams's ground-breaking *Hard Core*, 1990), there has been little work on the relationship between gay pornography and stardom. Given the centrality of the body to both areas, it is timely that in John Mercer's essay, 'Seeing is believing: constructions of stardom and the gay porn star in US gay video pornography', the gay porn star is explored in terms of muscularity, sexual prowess, and the sexual desire they elicit or produce. Mercer suggests that the gay porn star 'must be defined in relation to an abundance of sexualized physical attributes. The gay porn star exists critically at the level of surface, of appearances.' For Mercer, this is one of the key differences between the porn star and the Hollywood star: while the porn star is solely about the sexed flesh they possess (interiority and psychic truth are redundant), the Hollywood star, at least historically, is defined by their charisma and transcendental energies. The gay porn star 'exists almost exclusively *within* the fleshy world of the pornographic text and the accompanying promotional materials that refer to the star's performance in such texts. As a result of this, the gay porn star signifies at the level of textual or "onscreen" enunciation.' Mercer's essay, then, revisits star theory through the physical agency of the porn star's body, and its central role in grounding identification and idealization through corporeal signifiers.

Naked celebrity flesh is also central to the analysis that Adam Knee makes of 'celebrity skin' magazines such as *Celebrity Skin* and *Celebrity Sleuth*. In fact, in his essay, 'Celebrity skins: the illicit textuality of the celebrity nude magazine', Knee suggests that 'their sensationalized pictorials of film and television stars, models, pop singers, and other public figures … are in some cases presented alongside pictorials of porn film stars. In effect, one could argue, these magazines render *all* stars as porn stars.' However, Knee's more general position is that these celebrity nude magazines cater for a range of 'fundamentally voyeuristic' impulses that define much of the desire for famous people. More precisely, it is in the *apparently* illicit nature of these 'authentic' images where desire and attraction become perfectly aligned. As Knee contends, 'the image can be utterly unclear, unposed, unglamorous – as long as there is a seemingly unauthorized glimmer of skin. The actor's bare body is positioned here as a crucial site of authenticity, as that which reveals the truths hidden by publicist-controlled facial iconography and clothing.' In this context, the body takes its place as the 'ultimate *visually verifiable* realm of the private, the physical adjunct of the individual's sexual secrets – even if this is tempered by our awareness that body imagery can itself be manipulated both by more long-standing photographic techniques (such as airbrushing) and by newer digital technologies'. Knee explores how there is a fervent drive to present these images as snatched and unauthorized (and as escaping publicist control), primarily because it is integral to their claim to authenticity. But closer inspection reveals that, far from being 'stolen' and illicit they are carefully constructed and controlled images that get us no nearer to knowing the real person (body) behind the representation. Knee concludes his essay by making a fascinating link between 'trash' magazines and para-cinema, suggesting that readers and viewers are interested in exploring and appropriating the marginal, or what he refers to as the 'dregs' of media culture.

The idea that fans are critically active 'readers' of the stars and celebrities they consume is taken up in Rebecca Feasey's essay, 'Get a famous body: star styles and celebrity gossip in *heat* magazine'. Feasey argues that female readers of celebrity-centred magazines such as the UK's *heat* are presented with empowering ideas about what it is like to be a woman in contemporary society. *heat* 'can be read as an empowering post-feminist text that validates feminine meanings and competences for the female reader'. Feasey suggests that one way in which this affirmation of the feminine self takes place is through the way stars and celebrities are shown to be physically flawed, or through the effort they are shown to have to put in to create the 'perfect' body that is there to be admired. As indicated above, readers of *heat* get to see 'film stars, supermodels and television personalities' looking ugly, suffering from spots and cellulite, and subject to gruelling regimes of dieting. According to Feasey, this making 'ordinary' of the extraordinary female may 'liberate the reader from feeling inadequate for failing to create her own celebrity body'. Feasey also draws attention to the way *heat*'s commitment to celebrity gossip validates gossip as a 'valuable feminine discourse'. *heat* allows female readers not only to take part in gossip but to understand gossip as a positive, gender-affirming discursive practice.

If Feasey's essay assesses the positive values that the celebrity body can bring to female readers, Coleman's analysis of the black sporting body of Serena Williams is much more ambivalent. In her essay 'Droppin' it like it's hot: the sporting body of Serena Williams', Coleman argues that Williams's body is racially marked and yet 'also dramatizes a counter-hegemonic subjectivity that struggles for agency and autonomy'. According to Coleman, Williams's body is clearly subject to, and the object of, a racist discourse: she is forced to take on two of the prevailing racial stereotypes found in dominant culture. Williams 'is imaged as hard bodied *and* all-butt, as both "bad-buck" and "Jezebel". Williams, then, is excessively racially marked: her über-black body is doubly abnormal, and as such needs to be fetishized to render it/her "safe".' However, Coleman also makes the argument that Williams's athletic prowess, and her empowered sporting and media performances can work against the grain of the racist imagination, and that they possibly open up 'positive spaces of racial becoming'. In fact, Coleman contends that Williams's sporting and economic success enables her to be a 'positive and transformative image of/for black womanhood'. Nonetheless, Coleman concludes by finally arguing that Williams remains caught up in the ideological and economic wheels of late capitalism in so far as she 'has very little control over the meanings ascribed to her, or the goods that are bought and sold on her name. She is product, brand, caught in the belly of capitalism, its slave rather than its Kingpin.'

Chapter 7

Spectacular male bodies and Jazz Age celebrity culture

David Magill

The circulation of body images sits at the core of contemporary celebrity culture, and a host of medical and technological interventions produce and maintain these images. Plastic surgery aims to create the idealized visual body form, while personal trainers promote dietary and physical endurance regimes to further define that muscular, toned, flawless fiction. Similarly, digital photography enables the visual artist to pixellate the body and erase its flaws in ever more seamless representations of corporeal perfection. Yet while these various technologies have enabled individuals to achieve new heights in body production and maintenance, the desires that fuel such goals are coterminous with the rise of celebrity culture as an industry, as well as modernism as a cultural movement. The rise of celebrity culture in the 1920s incorporated these desires as part of its definition. To understand the contemporary obsession with the body, we must examine celebrity culture's historical reliance on idealized corporeal images, as well as the technologies used to produce them – the methods used to write these fictions on (or as) the celebrity body. Such examinations reveal how celebrity culture provides a vantage point for the dramatization of our own corporeal tensions.

This essay examines the particular set of images that coalesce around the white male body in the Jazz Age by reading a variety of celebrities across multiple media, such as Bernarr MacFadden, Rudolph Valentino and Lon Chaney. While each figure's celebrity takes shape in relation to their individual field and background, what connects them is a particular focus on the male body as part of their celebrity. These men constructed idealized images of themselves, and these constructions provided particular configurations of the male body as a panacea for postwar disillusion. Strongly encouraged to identify with these stars, white men could potentially find ease from corporeal tensions through a temporary psychological alliance with the celebrity image. In other words, celebrity culture produces a form of imaginary fraternalism for white males, assuaging their anxieties through willing subjection to the celebrity's fictional self-image. This mechanism both mourned and resurrected male bodies across a wide variety of cultural arenas such as film, advertising, and physical culture. Examining such celebratory presentations in the context of Jazz Age male bodily discourses reveals the power of celebrity culture to perform a particularized form of white masculinity, elucidating the spectacular bodily and psychic practices by which these men managed their corporeal fears and frailties.

Star culture and the masculine body ideal

Celebrity culture rose to new heights in the 1920s, though its origins come earlier in the century. Joshua Gamson notes how 'Attention getting and image management were common but not systematically practised until the early twentieth century' (1994: 22). As leisure culture became more central to American life, celebrities became more prominent for their embodiment of that lifestyle. Movie manufacturers capitalized on the burgeoning interest in celebrities, producing fan magazines and promoting films as star vehicles in order to create demand for specific individuals and profit for film companies. Citing the rise of the star as a cultural figure in 1914, Richard Dyer notes: 'The star phenomenon consists of everything that is publicly available about stars . . . star images are always extensive, multimedia, intertextual', though the films have a privileged place in that textual mélange (Dyer, 1998: 2–3). The public became infatuated with film stars, wanting to know about their private lives to reconcile with onscreen personae. Gamson notes that the resulting creations marked the stars' equality with everyday persons: 'Such ordinariness promoted a greater sense of connection and intimacy between the famous and their admirers' (1994: 29). Private and professional become two separate spheres articulated in tandem relationship to create a celebrity image for consumption. While 'the publicity system was clearly visible and commonly noted' (Gamson, 1994: 33), the psychology of celebrity suggested a distinction that required emulation by subjection. That is to say, celebrity culture at once stressed the equality of the star and fan and promoted the unique individuality of the celebrity in both personality and body. Tim Armstrong traces this corporeal logic through 1920s advertising, arguing that advertising disperses and zones the body through the 'cosmetic visibility in bodily parts' (1998: 100). This dispersal is accompanied by a reconstitution: 'the bodily part is knitted into a system of virtual prosthetics, implying a "whole" body which can only be achieved by technology; a whole which is constantly deferred' (1998: 100). These ads reproduce the anxieties regarding the body as incomplete, needing reconstitution and expecting it in the future. In fact, 'it is fragmentation and the promise of a restored integrity, like that in war, which renders the commoditization of the body possible' (Armstrong, 1998: 98). Men in particular desired this rebuilding in the form of a newly armoured, impenetrable body because of contemporary corporeal tensions. Faced with wholesale disfiguration as a result of the Great War's bodily ravages and technological interventions, it is suggested that men sought to re-constitute their bodies as a central strategy for coping with corporeal identity and its attendant fears.

Invaders visible and invisible: 1920s bodily anxieties

Klaus Theweleit argues in *Male Fantasies* that fascist masculinity is an armoured organization of the physical and psychic self against the continual threat of disintegration from without. In particular, he examines the German *Freikorps* novels and memoirs of the 1920s, revealing their constant fear of the feminine (portrayed in images of flood and filth that also racially distinguished the *Freikorps* members as specifically white), and their constant desire to maintain their bodily and psychic integrity through strict, often violent, boundary maintenance. As a result, these men portrayed their bodies as machines and followed regimens designed to keep their bodies hard, and therefore masculine. While his theories pertain specifically to the German fascist soldier, Theweleit recognizes that fascism is an extreme example of the polarization of gender that takes place more generally in Western culture. In addition to this, his discussion of the German soldiers' identities reflects the abjection of racialized traits that US white supremacists also exhibit in similarly virulent fashion. As a result, his arguments can apply, in a less strict fashion, to my discussion of white males in the United States. Though they may not always take such drastic measures to ensure their body and ego maintenance, 1920s American white men faced similar anxieties about their bodies and instituted comparable organizing practices to 'armour' white masculine identity.

To assume corporeality is to accept mortality; the Great War brought home that axiom with anxious clarity. Many young white men valorized in patriotic ideology returned from the war mangled by bullets or gassed into disability, missing limbs or arriving as corpses. The war wound could be a badge of honour, but these wounds could produce psychic as well as physical trauma. Photographs of injured soldiers in popular media revealed the permeability of the white male body. Parades and other ceremonies honouring the fallen and the returned made visible the veteran regardless of his physical state. Such public displays provided compelling evidence of the white male body's frailty even as it was celebrated as the essence of '100% Americanism'. Not all soldiers were white, of course, but the overwhelming image in the national ideology was a young white male fighting for American freedom.

Some penetrations of the male body were not as visible as machine gun bullets. The use of mustard gas in the war sent many veterans home with internal maladies ranging from pulmonary and abdominal distress to impotence and sterility.

While mustard gas did not remove limbs or leave wounds, its marks were clear in victims' dissipated manliness. The penetration of the male body in such cases occurs on a cellular level, invisible except through secondary symptoms such as respiratory problems or tuberculosis. The maladies caused by gas attack made visible the body's weakness against invisible invaders. Influenza provides another extreme example of 1920s male anxieties. The epidemic ravaged the United States and Europe, killing millions. While it did not separate by gender, masculine anxiety regarding bodily borders would suggest that male fear of the disease took a different shape. Invisible yet deadly, its ability to defeat masculine armour on a cellular level caused physical and emotional trauma for men who saw their bodies falling apart. Other men came home shell-shocked, mentally destroyed by the horrors they had experienced. Gilbert and Gubar relate: 'Paradoxically, the war to which so many men had gone in the hope of becoming heroes ended up emasculating them, confining them as closely as any Victorian woman had been confined' (1988: 318). They cite doctors who diagnosed shell shock as similar to hysterical disorders, a peacetime female malady. Shell shock is a masculine disease of anxiety; the inability to cope was seen by some as an indication of lack (of virility, of manliness, of bravery).

Not all bodily penetrations caused such dire physical consequences. Medical advances in the early twentieth century allowed doctors to peer inside the body safely for the first time. Doctors could avail themselves of such helpful devices as the stethoscope, ophthalmoscope and the X-ray machine. These devices, however helpful, represented one more means by which the male could be 'invaded'. Such technologies directly opposed a masculine aesthetic of impenetrability on a psychic and physical level. Masculinist modernism could thus be accurately characterized as the tension between the drive for intervention and the defence against penetration.

In addition, male bodily trauma could metaphorically signify for a larger anxiety regarding white men's dominance in political and economic realms, particularly since 1920s writers such as Lothrop Stoddard, Madison Grant and Waldo Frank imagined the nation as a male body. As a result, the health of the nation as a political sphere required the health of the male body in a rhetorical equivalence. The Great War, however, brought the connections between national citizenship and white manhood into sharp relief through the visibility of the damaged male body produced in the national interests of war. Further, less tangible penetrations of the body politic in the form of the women's suffrage movement, minority rights agitation and immigration influx threatened male power as well. White masculinity faced a variety of challenges to its dominance in the 1920s, and those challenges shaped the corporeal crisis in particular ways. Male bodies fragmented in the pursuit of US goals and displayed as symbols of patriotic fervour exposed the dissimulation of US identity as a white masculine formation. The male body in popular discourse, then, was a contested and frag-mented image; celebrity culture provided an avenue by which to confront those anxieties and re-form the body whole.

Men faced their own fragile physicality and found it psychically troubling. Of course, these anxieties were not new to the 1920s. They continue forward from the pre-war decades in the structured movement and physical culture reforms of the Progressive era and the anxieties of all war-torn eras. Yet the 1920s stands out because of their connection to late-nineteenth- and early-twentieth-century body movements and to the racial conflicts within the country that were resolved by corporeal means. White men eager to restore their power in the postwar United States required strategies for defending the male body.

Hard bodies on display

One strategy for countering the evidence of masculine corporeal frailty was to display a bodily ideal, and it seems reasonable to suggest that celebrity culture became a central space for such displays. These productions allowed audiences to identify with the bodies displayed and claim those in juxtaposi-tion with the nation. One might expect a fetishized male figure to arise in the decade as a synecdoche for the ideal male. Celebrity culture, however, produces no one figure. Instead, it provides a variety of individual configura-tions drawing upon a larger set of 'masculine' characteristics, thus articu-lating individualism in collective identity structures. As the decade was a time of intense flux, these ideals were particularly under negotiation, in move-ment. The plastic age produced a plethora of possibilities for that role model, but as quickly as one 'star' rose, he fell in the darkness of innuendo and fickle public response. Our historical narrative of the period privileges certain actors in careers marked by longevity, yet this approach neglects the vast chaos of the emergent star system and the constantly shifting visions of partic-ular actors at the time. Significantly, the most virile figure in the period and the one whose star never dimmed was the fictional Leyendecker Arrow Collar or Shirt Man. Richard Martin argues:

> Leyendecker distinguished an American Adonis in his consummately condensed image of WASP (white, Anglo-Saxon, Protestant) mascu-linity and style. He did so in keen awareness that in his lifetime many who sought the endemic American character in letters and in the visual arts believed in America as a masculinized version, an artistic bent always virile, always distinct from effete European aestheticism (1996: 454).

The Arrow Adonis reflected a vision of the United States as a white masculine domain, and because he was not real, he was a fantastic image of perfect masculinity. Emannuel Cooper notes:

> Leyendecker created the ultimate masculine image whether it was within typical male occupations ... or merely smart men about town. Without exception, all are broad-shouldered and powerful, the epitome of health, strength, and social standing. Power is conveyed in all parts of the body and the modelling around the genitals always carries a suggestion of the form beneath (1994: 132).

By embodying a generalized masculine vigour, the Arrow shirt man could be transplanted into various situations or images, appealing to a wider variety of men and linking them all in an identificatory fraternalism that reduced competitive anxieties.

Leyendecker's ads produce a fantasy of male fraternal equivalence as well as an ideal masculine body image dependent on the discourses of bodybuilding and health proffered by such magnates as Bernarr MacFadden and Charles Atlas (discussed below). The celebrities of the period, caught up in a public desire for the 'real', faced ever growing pressure to remain perfect. Only a fictional character, nothing more than a series of pictures with no real body behind it, could remain unscathed. Of course, the public treated even Leyendecker's creation as 'real'; Martin reports that in the figure's 1920s heyday, 17,000 fan letters were received each month, including marriage proposals and erotic suggestions. But the Arrow Adonis resonated with men and women searching for the ideal man.

Competing health discourses also arose across the early twentieth century, from Fletcherism to bodybuilding, to create that ideal corporeal identity and institute a desire for it. Though earlier movements were focused on females, the Jazz Age saw a wresting of physical fitness away from females through a re-gendering of its ideals as masculine. Advice manuals and hygiene guides sold briskly, and their ideas spread by word of mouth across the United States. These discourses were, in part, perhaps a reaction against medicine's new ability to probe the male body by promoting a healthiness that would prevent a need for doctors. A reduction in doctor's visits would mean that the male body could remain solid, impenetrable. While women could and did adopt these doctrines, the production of such ideals by men and for men suggests the tensions they displace. Perhaps the most influential celebrity health figure in the early twentieth century was Bernarr MacFadden, founder of the magazine *Physical Culture*. MacFadden rose to prominence at the turn of the century, espousing a regimen of diet and exercise that would harden the body and restore virility. By the end of World War I, MacFadden was the United States' leading physical fitness guru.

Biographies by Clement Wood and Fulton Oursler appeared during the 1920s detailing his rise to success and his masculine virility. Wood, for example, describes MacFadden as 'the restorer, the rebuilder, the guardian of the living and necessary foundation of all human existence' (1929: 2). MacFadden published magazines on all topics, gave talks across the nation, founded Physical Culture schools, and wrote books detailing his methods for increasing masculine vitality, health and strength. He touted himself as an expert on masculinity and presented his vision for attaining such an ideal to an American public in need of a restored manly body.

MacFadden's vision became so popular with 1920s men because it restored the hard body ideal fractured by the war and further damaged by the encroachments of 'civilization'. In addition, MacFadden's rejuvenation plan and his life story combine to rearticulate white manhood's connection to national identity through the body. Wood describes MacFadden's life as 'American in a high sense' (1929: 4), while Fulton Oursler notes how 'MacFadden's career was built on strictly American lines' (1929: 42). Both biographers, as well as MacFadden himself, marketed his life and his body as ideals by linking them to discourses of '100% Americanism', making himself exemplary of national identity. MacFadden touted the natural effects of his regimen as counteracting the debilitating effects of civilization. As such, he tapped into notions of the weak civilized body and advocated a return to a more 'primitive', manly state. His arguments thus echo 1920s white supremacist tracts such as Madison Grant's *The Passing of the Great Race*, which he promoted vigorously in *Physical Culture*.

MacFadden's programme linked virile manhood to the creation of a hard masculine body. He advocated bodybuilding for improved musculature through a series of publicity photos and tours highlighting his own physique. He even wrestled the champions of three weight classes and won all matches. His writings further demonstrate his plan for the hard body by accessing anxieties regarding white manhood. In *Manhood and Marriage*, he writes:

> To be a male and not a man, to wear the clothes indicative of the male sex and realize that you are masquerading – a hypocrite, a pretender – is indeed a torturous experience. But remember that if you really are a man in every sense of the word, then you are in possession of all the forces that go with superior virility – for virility is nothing more than the physical expression of manly qualities (1916: 8).

MacFadden simultaneously argues for a biological and cultural notion of manhood. One can masquerade as a man, but one is always also a man inside; white men's anxieties can thus be resolved through physical management. MacFadden's popularity in the postwar era arose from his ability to assuage masculine anxieties regarding identity and corporeal form. Harvey Green notes: 'MacFadden's extraordinary success lay in his ability to perceive the needs and evoke the dreams of his readers, nearly all of whom were middle-class white men' (1986: 250). While he was certainly a well-known figure before the war, his books became bestsellers and his publishing company flourished as the war continued and ended.

By the 1920s, MacFadden was an extremely important figure, influencing over 25 million people during the course of his career by espousing and embodying physical doctrines of hard virile bodies and reconciling the contradictions of masculine identity. In addition, he professed a healthy sexual desire and maintained regular intercourse as part of his regimen, denying the 'spermatic economy' advocated by other health experts. His carefully constructed and exquisitely performed public persona served as an exemplar of white manhood.

Another physical culture guru who came into fame during the 1920s was Charles Atlas, perhaps the most famous American bodybuilder of the twentieth century. His popularity also stemmed from a fantasy of hardened white masculinity that he advertised, among other places, in MacFadden's *Physical Culture*. Atlas's advertisements accessed masculine anxieties regarding strength, success and virility. His advertisements, creating fantasies that any man would become strong and manly, defeat the bully and get the girl, produced tensions about the male body even as they promised to alleviate them. Atlas's popularity suggests that many men found his ads convincing. Both Atlas and MacFadden became popular in the 1920s in part because their public persona presented a male body free from concern. These men represented a reconstituted white masculine body that cemented identities through physical spectacle. Men bought into their fantasy because of a desire for the hard body promised by MacFadden and Atlas. Postwar disillusion and corporeal anxieties brought these two men increased fame and fortune. As a result, they inhabit the celebrity status also achieved by cinema's stars, another arena where a publicized male figure spectacularized the male body.

Cinema provided another space for narrativizing the reconstruction of the white male body. Tim Armstrong notes: 'Film can be seen . . . as a visual illusion which exploits the limits of perception, but which also offers the cinematic body as recompense for the fragmented body of technology' (1998: 5). Although an individual film can address masculine tensions on a limited basis, the star figure provides a more dynamic space for examining the ongoing negotiations of white masculine identity. Richard Dyer states: 'Stars articulate these ideas of personhood, in large measure shoring up the notion of the individual but also at times registering the doubts and anxieties attendant upon it' (1986: 10). An important part of such work, according to Dyer, is the star's way of making sense of the body, of *lived* experience. Their personae suggest means of registering and resolving corporeal anxieties.

Douglas Fairbanks, for example, was one extremely popular star in the Jazz Age. His ascendance came in part from a congruence between his onscreen characters and his public persona. In each case, Fairbanks demonstrated a bodily vigour that produced a revitalized white manhood. Fairbanks, in film, interview or public appearance, constantly proved his own virility through action. He would do acrobatic stunts, turn flips, run around the room, or balance himself on a chair while talking to interviewers, mirroring the physical capabilities of his onscreen characters in such films as *The Mark of Zorro* (1920), *The Three Musketeers* (1921), *Robin Hood* (1922) and *The Black Pirate* (1926). In each film, his characters are expert swordsmen, strong fighters and stunning acrobats. His performance of identity mirrored a masculine ideal defined by what a body could do, assuring white men that their bodies were as strong as ever.

Rudolph Valentino also produced an idealized masculine form, although his celebrity production involved challenges to whiteness that make him a more ambiguous figure. Valentino popularized the figure of the Lothario in a series of desert films, such as *The Sheik*, that kept constantly on display another hard male body for public consumption. These texts titillate readers with plots of a 'miscegenative' desire threatening the prerogatives of white masculinity, then block those threats by plotting ways for white manhood to sojourn among and even assimilate to primitivity, emerging triumphantly virile and polished white. *The Sheik* was Rudolph Valentino's first film, and made him a star overnight. Billie Melman states: 'The first filmed version of *The Sheik* (1921) was seen by 125 million viewers, the majority of them – to judge from the contemporary press reports – women' (1988: 90). Perhaps one reason for Valentino's success lies in the fact that the film does not portray Diana's rape; it does show the Sheik's desire for her, but does not portray the violence the Sheik inflicts on Diana in the novel. Though *Son of the Sheik* does suggest a rape, the curtain closes before the camera visually records any physical contact. As a result, with the violence expurgated, the film maintains the illusion of a hypermasculine yet sensitive lover. In addition, as Melman notes:

> The silent film with its emphasis upon expressive performance emulated and stylized the image of the oriental lover … The first production of *The Sheik* cunningly exploited a variety of sexual symbols: the sheik's smouldering cigarette, among the disarrayed objects on Diana's dressing table on the morning that follows the rape; close-ups of Valentino's ludicrously enlarged eyes and of his muscular arms (1988, 103).

Each of these symbols enhances the Sheik's masculinity cumulatively through phallic signification and physical attribution. Thus, the film presents Valentino as emblematic of primitive manhood, an identity that is both empowering and exoticized. He becomes the object of womanly desire even as his character subjects others to his whims.

The Sheik and its sequel promulgate a racial layering of manhood through Valentino's characters. Valentino's Sheik is darker than the anaemic white men tainted by civilization, signifying his superior manhood through access to primitivism. Yet he is much lighter than the primitive Arabs he rules, avowing his racial superiority. Finally, the Sheik's race in the film is a matter of contingency, reflecting his ability to masquerade visually. The director lightened Valentino through the use of make-up and lighting effects, while the 'Arabs' in the film are darkened almost to blackness, heightening the racial contrast. Valentino is also costumed almost exclusively in bright white robes throughout *The Sheik*, while the Arab's dingy or even blackened clothes mark their racial inferiority. As a result, the Sheik becomes a superior white man visually long before the narrative reveals his identity. Combined with the removal of all violence against Diana as avatar of white womanhood, Valentino's visual presentation marks him as white and channels desire toward him in the film. The Sheik lightens and darkens before our eyes as he racially cross-dresses and then asserts his whiteness, chameleon-like. In all cases, however, he evokes superior manhood for the public, and women flocked to see the films with Valentino's smouldering eyes and naked muscular arms and chest on display. In both *The Sheik* and *The Son of the Sheik*, he appears *sans* shirt, baring his chest to display a muscled body. Publicity stills and other photographs also depicted his hard body. While, as Miriam Hansen (1991) argues, this display could be seen as opening Valentino's body to the feminizing gaze, it could also be perceived that Valentino's postures and his own look deflect the erotic masculinized gaze and destabilize homoerotic notions through a projected image of strength and corporeal hardness. Furthermore, the plots of both films attest to Valentino's physical invulnerability. He demonstrates his superior strength in physical combat with rivals and enemies as well as in sexual conflict with his latest conquest and future wife. Indeed, the central means by which he conquers his unwilling bride is to rape her until she relents. Even when he appears mortally wounded in *The Sheik*, his body seems untouched and he eventually recovers.

The Sheik enacts the injury (significantly gained in a war with a neighbour sheik) and recovery of the white male body. The film's narrative assuages bodily anxieties by enacting a tale of corporeal resurrection that the studio supported with ad campaigns designed to mark Valentino as hypermasculine against criticisms raised in the press about his sexuality and ethnicity. Miriam Hansen further notes that 'A more aggressive line of defense was Valentino's participation in the cult of physical fitness' (1991: 265). Such an association, as noted above, would have marked Valentino as masculine in a particularly embodied form. In addition, it would give him access to a whiteness of a different colour. Yet, as Hansen meticulously details,

Valentino's offscreen image caused consternation in white men, accentuating the bodily crisis of Jazz Age white men and foregrounding the performative nature of the idealized male body. Valentino represents an ambivalent figure that the studio marketed to appeal to white women in a manner that highlighted its construction offscreen, thus placing into view the mechanisms of white masculine identity. Therefore, Valentino could perform a bodily resurrection appealing to white men because of these associations while also representing a threat to that ideal. In both cases, his celebrity arises from the same bodily complex; in contrast to Hansen's argument, Valentino's films drew on a primitive manhood through the cinematic techniques delineated above, labelling him an emblem of re-constituted white manhood, even as his offscreen figure generated controversy because of that background. His 'off-white' conception of manhood, accenting white masculinity's need for an armoured body, also highlights its social construction. Valentino's feminization in the contemporary press circled around his body and persona being too 'soft'; that attack reveals white manhood's anxious development of its hardness as well as its accessibility to non-whites. Valentino's films presented a racialized hierarchy of masculinity dependent not only on binaristic distinctions of black and white but also on levels of distinction within whiteness that reveal the white male body's fictions. Thus, race and gender intertwine, mutually determining one another in a complex layering of racial features. These layers were delineated in part by one's ability to access a primeval heritage; the men who successfully incorporate the primitive become even more virile and more 'white'. Fairbanks and Valentino thus pursue a male body ideal that occurs synchronously with notions of a revitalized Jazz Age white manhood.

Perhaps the most interesting white male body of postwar cinema, however, belonged to Lon Chaney. Gaylyn Studlar has argued that we should read Chaney's career through the cultural lens of the freak show. She states that while we might consider the historical trauma thesis I argue here, and see Chaney's depiction of monstrous bodies as 'a symptomatic instance of the anxiety surrounding masculinity and the male body', she finds it 'too easy an explanation, especially when one considers that the flu epidemics of 1918–19 took many more American lives than the war and created tremendous national anxiety' (1996: 210). These seemingly separate spheres, however, can be reconciled via Theweleit's armoured male body. Chaney's popularity is a defence against both war's bullets and disease's germs; sympathetic identification with his characters assuages anxiety over the body's penetration. Chaney's films continually show a disabled or defective male body made whole by the movie's end. They rehearse the refurbishment of white male bodies and the alleviation of corporeal tensions in the postwar era. Chaney's early star status, then, stems not from his 'Man of a Thousand Faces' reputation, which came later, but from what we might call his 'Man of a Thousand Bodies' phase.

Chaney's films continually reject the beautiful and active bodies of Fairbanks and Valentino, presenting instead a series of damaged or monstrous bodies in their place. As Studlar notes, 'his monstrosities of masculinity are almost never attributed to the supernatural, but to nature, to the tragic results of human disaster, or to his characters' assumptions of masquerades of mutilation and self-stigmatizaton' (1996: 210). His films first produce then come to terms with such bodies, healing or removing them from public view in order to restore the normative white male body. Not coincidentally, Chaney rose to stardom in the silent film era, a period that further focused cinematic attention on the body as vehicle of communication. The body, then, becomes the cinematic template for meaning and, by extension, the ideologies that attend to such narrations.

Consider, for example, *The Shock* (1923). Lon Chaney portrays Wilse Dilling, dangerous criminal and 'mystery, even to Chinatown'. The introductory shot of his character depicts an ordinary man, drinking tea and smoking a cigarette. But his discreet communication with his Chinese partner through Morse code suggests that there is more to him than meets the eye, a supposition supported when he stands only through the use of crutches. Dilling uses his body as a signifier of meaning, a pattern that the film suggests we must extend to Chaney. His gait further reveals the twisted feet that prevent him from walking, as he lurches from place to place with evident difficulty. Dilling, working for the gangster Queen Ann, is sent to the town of Fallbrook to spy on a bank leader, where he meets Gertrude Hadley, the bank president's daughter and symbol of regenerate white womanhood. Through her faith in God and human nature, she reforms Wilse Dilling so that he foils Queen Ann's plots against Mr Hadley and Gertrude through the power of 'thought' and 'will', the mechanisms which Gertrude earlier assures Dilling can save him. And his spiritual transformation at the hands of Gertrude mirrors his physical transformation by the movie's end. Dilling, fearful for Gertrude's life at the hands of Queen Ann's mobsters, falls to his knees and prays for divine intervention. An earthquake answers his prayers in an incredible *deus ex machina* that not only forces the henchmen to flee but also destroys Queen Ann and plummets Dilling into the basement of her Mandarin House. After weeks of convalescence, he reveals to Gertrude that the accident has cured his deformity and restored his body in time for their marriage. *The Shock* presents Chaney's body as healed, restored to its normal configuration by a miracle of faith. The plot uses spiritual recovery as a means of introducing the restored male body so desired by 1920s audiences, while suggesting that the body innocently mirrors the inner change even as the body itself is displayed as the primary means for transmitting ideals. Thus, *The Shock* presents the typical Chaney pattern of physical renewal that both individually resurrects the male body and collectively restores the body politic.

Other films follow this pattern, marking Chaney as a lead figure in the consolidation of body anxieties. In *The Unknown* (1927), for example, Chaney's character Alonzo passes as armless, depicting a body configuration often seen on war veterans but here reduced to circus performer. Alonzo can restore his arms, however, by removing his bindings. As a result, Cheney's onscreen figure represents the body's healing process; damage becomes a sleight-of-hand that can be erased in a moment. Chaney's star figure resonates with what Robyn Wiegman (1999) calls whiteness's paradox of particularity. Chaney displays his wounds as a means of claiming injury in a politics that assigns special status to white masculinity while restoring its normative invisibility. In *The Penalty* (1920), Chaney plays Blizzard, a man whose legs have been amputated as a child to cure a blow to the head. Blizzard leads a life of manic abandon and crime, but in the end, the same doctor operates on his brain and cures him while also restoring Blizzard's legs. *Flesh and Blood* (1922) tells the story of a man who effects the disguise of a cripple to escape his unjust imprisonment and re-capture. He can revert to his natural form, however, as he does at movie's end. In each film, the male body is damaged and restored in a narrative of masculine anxiety performed and then assuaged. Chaney's popularity, I argue, stems from his ability to contort and restore his body.

Even in films where his body is not 'fixable', such as in *The Hunchback of Notre Dame* (1923) and *The Phantom of the Opera* (1925), Chaney's star figure intercedes. The main character dies or is removed from view, disappearing the disabled body from the screen. Then, Chaney's offscreen images work to reassure men that even those bodies are repairable. In *The Phantom of the Opera*, Chaney's figure disappears, never to be seen again; in fact, only a beautiful woman can bring him out of hiding in the first place. The film thus figures the damaged body as abject and completes the process through cinematic plottings that make clear this body is unnatural in its configurations and its desires. Chaney's 1920s films thus present a series of disfigured male bodies refigured through intervention and contortion. *Outside the Law* (1920) presents an interesting variation on this theme, as Lon Chaney figures body politics by playing a dual role: he simultaneously plays dangerous rake 'Black Mike' Sylva and gentle Confucian student Ah Wing. While the former role presented Chaney as a normal white male, the latter role required prosthetic teeth and facial contortion to change Chaney's features to Oriental. The dual roles simultaneously play up the malleability of the body even as it normalizes those bodies through a Chaney transformation striking in its completeness. *Outside the Law* creates a comparative matrix; audiences know Chaney plays both roles, making explicit the prosthetic nature of Chaney's Orientalist disguise and thus naturalizing the white male body of his 'normal' character by comparison.

This matrix also appears in his film *Shadows* (1922), where Chaney plays Yen Sin, a disfigured Chinese sailor become laundryman. Over the course of the film,

Yen Sin facilitates the marriage of Reverend Malden and Sympathy Gibbs, helping to uncover the blackmail plot perpetrated on the Reverend in order to restore the Malden family as well as the larger church family over which he presides. Chaney's character restores the community while also serving as implicit contrast to the Reverend; while Yen Sin cannot stand straight or speak correctly, the Reverend is the picture of health and vigour. Chaney's portrayal thus directs the audience's identification; his star power works to connote authority even though he is not the object of adulation in the particular film. Studlar notes:

> These patterns of interest would seem to follow the gender-related trends of viewing established in the 1920s when both studio promotion (such as pressbooks), reviewers, and exhibitor reports seemed to agree that Chaney's stardom was supported, by and large, by the spectatorship of men and boys (1996: 207).

One possible reason for his popularity among men would seem to arise from his ability to assuage their corporeal tensions through sympathetic identifications. One might also argue that men could gain a measure of manhood from their superior gaze at his feminized (because injured) male body. The repeated refurbishment of such bodies in his films, however, suggests that some viewers may have identified with the masculine anxieties produced in Chaney's cinematic bodies and found pleasure in their resurrection.

The body's end?

In a period where race and gender identity were in flux, and white masculine power was threatened by a variety of sources, the male body becomes one textual space of negotiation for the complex anxieties and desires of the Jazz Age. Facing the evidence of bodily and psychic fragmentation, white men turned to a variety of strategies in hopes of reconstituting their corporeal identities through synecdochal acts that obscured the damaged body from view.

The anxious display of hardened or reconstituted male bodies both reflects the opportunities white men had to represent their own bodies and reveals the constant anxieties that led these men to obsess on those physical forms. The celebrity culture of the 1920s, then, proves a historical and cultural antecedent to contemporary body issues. Though their technologies were not as advanced, Jazz Age celebrities sculpted their own bodies to meet the needs of the plastic age.

Bibliography

Armstrong, Tim (1998) *Modernism, Technology, and the Body: A Cultural Study*, Cambridge: Cambridge University Press.

Cooper, Emmanuel (1994) *The Sexual Perspective: Homosexuality and Art in the Last 100 Years in the West*, 2nd edn, New York: Routledge.

deCordova, Richard (1990) *Picture Personalities: The Emergence of the Star System in America*, Urbana: University of Illinois Press.

Dyer, Richard (1986) *Heavenly Bodies*, London: Macmillan Books.

—— (1998) *Stars*, London: BFI.

Gallop, Jane (1988) *Thinking Through the Body*, New York: Columbia University Press.

Gamson, Joshua (1994) *Claims to Fame: Celebrity in Contemporary America*, Berkeley: University of California Press.

Gilbert, Sandra and Gubar, Susan (1988) *No Man's Land: The Place of the Woman Writer in the Twentieth Century*, 3 vols, New Haven: Yale UP.

Green, Harvey (1986) *Fit for America: Health, Fitness, Sport, and American Society*, New York: Pantheon Books.

Hansen, Miriam (1991) *Babel and Babylon: Spectatorship in American Silent Film*, Cambridge: Harvard University Press.

MacFadden, Bernarr (1916) *Manhood and Marriage*, New York: Physical Culture.

Martin, Richard (1996) 'J. C. Leyendecker and the Homoerotic Invention of Men's Fashion Icons, 1910–1930', *Prospects: An Annual of American Cultural Studies* 21: 453–70.

Melman, Billie (1988) *Women and the Popular Imagination in the Twenties: Flappers and Nymphs*, New York: St Martin's.

Oursler, Fulton (1929) *The True Story of Bernarr MacFadden*, New York: Copeland Books.

Studlar, Gaylyn (1996) *This Mad Masquerade: Stardom and Masculinity in the Jazz Age*, New York: Columbia University Press.

Theweleit, Klaus (1989) *Male Fantasies*, 2 vols, Minneapolis: University of Minnesota Press.

Wiegman, Robyn (1999) 'Whiteness Studies and the Paradox of Particularity', *Boundary 2*, 26/3: 115–50.

Wood, Clement (1929) *Bernarr MacFadden*, New York: Copeland Books.

Chapter 8
Seeing is believing

Constructions of stardom and the gay porn star in US gay video pornography

John Mercer

This chapter deals with a specific strand of fame, the star in gay video pornography. Contrary to the views expressed by Andrea Dworkin (1991: 56) and others, pornography cannot be regarded as a monolithic entity, whether we are speaking of its modes of address, its aesthetic form, or its agendas and effects. Definitions of what constitutes pornography change across national boundaries, cultures and historical periods, and differing pornographies emerge that address themselves to differing audiences. Just as pornography is not a uniform phenomenon, so gay pornography is equally diverse. My focus in this chapter is based on an analysis of specific aspects of commercial American gay video pornography, and I should explain the reasons for choosing this focus. France, Germany, several Latin American countries and the UK, all have their own indigenous gay porn industries. However, the American gay porn industry is by the far the largest producer of widely available pornographic texts. While statistical data concerning the size of the porn industry are notoriously unreliable, the dominance of American porn is suggested by its proliferation on the internet, the large number of influential American producers (on a global scale), as well as the ubiquity of the American gay porn aesthetic across the world.

My research is primarily concerned with the iconography and formal and stylistic conventions of gay pornography and the emergence of a range of generic and idealized types that I call prototypes. Prototypes are neither entirely stereotypical nor archetypical; they are conventionalized but constantly subject to revision. Prototypes are repetitive but never identical; they exist primarily in the world of the gay text but their influence is widely felt. I suggest here that the prototypes of gay pornography contribute to the construction of what can be understood as a mythology and typology of gay desire.[1]

The gay porn star is muscular, generically handsome, well endowed and Caucasian, and he is typically identified through the hyperbolic marketing discourses of the gay porn industry. Indeed, it is these discourses which call him into being. It should also be noted that I am talking here about the gay pornography of a specific historical epoch that may already be at an end. Between approximately 1985 and the end of the 1990s, the gay pornographic video market was dominated by a small number of established major production companies, namely HIS Video, Catalina, Vivid and – perhaps the most prominent – Falcon Studios. During a period when the home video market for gay porn flourished, this small group of companies dominated the production of gay pornography and established distribution networks, positioning themselves as the primary manufacturers of mainstream, hardcore, video pornography.[2]

This historical moment is of considerable significance for both gay men and the gay pornography industry. The advent of AIDS had inevitable and well-documented consequences for the gay community, but it also had a considerable impact on the traditional venues for the exhibition of gay pornography, especially in the major, urban, gay centres. During the mid 1980s, pornographic cinemas and bathhouses were shut down in the climate of panic and uncertainty that resulted from the early identification of AIDS as the so-called 'gay plague'. Consequently, the pornography industry needed to diversify into alternative means for the distribution of its material. The same period saw the concomitant rise in popularity of home video technology and as John Burger (1995) notes, the gay pornography industry would aggressively capitalize on this new, privatized form of consumption. These new conditions of production and consumption facilitated the emergence of the gay porn star phenomenon that I am identifying here. As Burger observes: 'When gay video became big business, the filmmakers became money moguls, and the concept of porn stars developed into a full-blown star system' (1995: 24).

In many respects, the rapid growth of the gay pornography industry during the 1980s has its parallel in the emergence of the studio system during the Classic Hollywood Cinema period. The dominance of a small group of studios, a high level of institutional control over the marketplace, the hiring of contracted performers and directors and the emergence of a star system – maintained through the control of jealously guarded, exclusive performers – were characteristic of both the heyday of Hollywood and the gay porn industry in mid 1980s San Francisco. These factors alone, however, do not account for the emergence of the gay porn star. Wider cultural factors also play a role here. The growing interest in health, fitness and the rise of 'body culture', both within the gay subculture and more generally, informs the presentation of the kind of muscular athleticism epitomized by the gay porn star. In the climate of fear that prevailed as a result of the AIDS crisis not only being healthy but also *looking* healthy had an increased, although illusory, value for many gay men. Second, the 1980s also saw the rise of the muscular, male action star, as noted by Paul McDonald (2004), Yvonne Tasker (1993) and Susan Jeffords (1994). McDonald notes:

> Emerging during the 1980s, the muscular heroes of American cinema belonged to a culture for which the disciplinary regime of physical development worked as a metaphor for the striving and enterprise which motivated the Reagan years and the 'yuppie' revolution (2004: 181–2).

Ironically, it is the very iconography that has become so closely associated with the oppressive conservatism of the Reagan years and of the reassertion of a version of strident heterosexuality, that the gay porn star references and eroticizes.

By the end of the 1990s, and with the advent of the internet, the market for gay pornography had begun to fracture. Increasing numbers of smaller companies emerged during this transitional period, producing videos catering to niche markets as the worldwide promotion of gay pornography increased. The market dominance of the major gay porn studios declined, along – to some extent – with the ubiquity of the specific types promoted by these studios. While it is still true that contemporary gay pornography deals in 'types', the dominance of the type exemplified by the gay porn star of the mid 1980s to late 1990s has perhaps been supplanted by a more diverse range of iconographies and physical ideals.

Just as gay pornography is a diverse generic category, so stardom is equally not a uniform phenomenon. This paper observes the specific ways in which the gay porn star compares to, yet differs from, the Hollywood film star. As scholars in film studies have previously noted (Dyer, 1979; Ellis, 1992; McDonald, 2004), the star in the Hollywood star system is deployed both as a highly effective way of organizing the market for cinema and as an exemplar of dominant ideals in wider culture. Similarly, in gay pornographic video, the star is deployed as a means to ensure repeat purchase and to act as an indicator of the qualities that are considered of value within the pornographic text and, by extrapolation, within wider gay culture.

In the context of the mid 1980s, with the burgeoning pornography industry and the emergence of the AIDS crisis, hypermasculine and muscular males, frequently prodigiously endowed, became exemplars of what it meant to be desirable in gay pornography. Those who exhibited an abundance of these characteristics became those who were sold to consumers as gay porn stars. Examples of idealized homoerotic types abound in gay pornographic videos and the gay porn star is constructed through a hyperbolic discourse which foregrounds the idealized qualities which are prized within the gay pornographic text. Perhaps the best examples of such physical characteristics and iconography are offered by promotional, box cover images for gay pornographic videos. These act as both as an advertisement for the product they accompany, and as a distillation of the 'flavour' of the material that the film will deal with. These promotional images are instrumental in presenting the prototypes that gay pornography uses, and the images themselves manipulate a set of generic expectations through the use of a homoerotic vernacular. Unlike mainstream cinema, a producer cannot (for the most part) assume any prior level of familiarity with the text itself, as the mainstream channels for promoting cinema or video are not available to the porn industry. Indeed, the interplay between the on/offscreen persona that is regarded as central to discourses surrounding the Hollywood film star is largely, if not entirely, absent in the case of the gay porn star. This is one of the key differences between these two articulations of stardom. Unlike the film star, the gay porn star exists almost exclusively *within* the fleshy world of the pornographic text and the accompanying promotional materials that refer to the star's performance in such texts. As result of this, the gay porn star signifies at the level of textual or 'onscreen' enunciation.

For consumers, the video/DVD box cover frequently acts as the first point of contact with the pornographic star. Through these images (and subsequently in the films that the images promote), prototypic ideals are vividly articulated.[3] For example, in the cover image for *Idol Worship* (1991, Ric Bradshaw, HIS Video/ VCA) the protagonist, Ryan Idol, is presented as the principal focus of the image and as the subject and the star of the text. Ryan Idol is presented as tanned, muscular, smooth-bodied and generically handsome. The title of the video and the inclusion of the star's name in red, boxed copy, with the addition of an autograph in the bottom right-hand corner of the image, emphasize the notion of both stardom and desire: Ryan Idol is a star and Ryan Idol is a figure to be worshipped. The video itself is set upon a naval submarine. This location is suggested by the use of accompanying nautical props, including a background of control panels and dials, and a red glow that illuminates Idol's smooth, muscular body. Additionally, this suggests that Idol is both an object of erotic desire and a dangerous playmate. Idol is pictured straddling the captain's seat of this phallic sea vessel, his captain's cap at his hip. He is presented, then, as in charge both of *his* ship and *his* sexuality. This sense of self-assuredness is further exaggerated by Idol's posture, which emphasizes his broad shoulders and developed pectoral muscles. His static pose is reminiscent of the classical sculpture of civic figures of antiquity. In this context, however, the signs of hegemonic masculinity represented by such rhetorical strategies are radically subverted. A mode of signification that was designed to inspire awe, respect, civic pride and even fear, has been co-opted into the service of homosexual desire. Just as Idol's commanding posture broadens his shoulders, his clenched fist, placed well into the groin, emphasizes his narrow hips. With his left arm, Idol leans on the back of the seat which, emerging from between his legs, metonymically stands in for his penis. This contrived nonchalance further emphasizes both the sense that Idol demands the viewer's gaze and that he is in charge of that gaze. This is further reinforced by Idol's own gaze at the viewer: direct, aggressive and yet not provocative, his gaze incites desire.

In the cover image for *The Matinee Idol* (1995, Gino Colbert, HIS Video/VCA) Ken Ryker is similarly presented as an ideal of eroticized manhood. Like Idol, Ryker is smooth, tanned, heavily muscled and handsome. The video concerns the story of a Hollywood star whose forays into the world of gay pornography are exposed. Originally conceived as a vehicle for Ryan Idol, the title of the video yet again plays on the name of the star as a figure of adulation, while simultaneously drawing on references to Hollywood cinema's history. It evokes matinee idols such as Tab Hunter and Rock Hudson, generically handsome film stars who were sold as sex symbols to the suburban housewives of Eisenhower's America but were also the objects of desire for gay men during the repressive 1950s (and the site of a contradictory, camp appreciation). In the image for the video, Ryker is similarly, although rather more explicitly, presented as beefcake. Ryker seems to be engulfed by an enormous pile of popcorn that emerges from a bucket held at his shoulder and which runs suggestively down his smooth, taut torso. The image wittily draws on intertexual references: 1950s physique photography, popcorn, associated with popular cinema audiences, and the pseudo-classical art/fashion photography of Herb Ritts or Bruce Weber. Rather than a bronzed Adonis holding a Grecian urn full of water, we are presented with the gay porn star holding a bucket of popcorn. Running water, a familiar Freudian metaphor for sexuality, is replaced by a product of popular culture. Popcorn in this specific context acts as a metaphor for Ryker's own edibility and as a metaphor for semen. His raised arms exaggerate both the width of his biceps and the narrow tautness of his waist, effectively elongating his body. Contrapposto is also deployed as a rhetorical strategy in the presentation of Ryker as a prototype. Unlike the static, statuesque pose of Idol in the previous image, the use of contrapposto is frequently suggestive of both dynamism and eroticism in Western art. His twisted torso, raised arms and the flow of popcorn over his chest, produces an image that suggests both movement and sensuality. As in the case of the previous image, Ryker's gaze is direct and controlling; this is a body and a style of presentation that the audience is supposed to respond to as a form of sexual invitation.

So far, I have suggested that the gay porn star is prototypical as a result of a process of manufacture, that the gay porn star is presented as an idealized figure through the use of a range of homoerotic iconography, and that the concept of the gay porn star is broader than the specific instance of a particular star's presence. I have identified instances of commonality and difference between the gay porn star and the Hollywood film star. Perhaps the predominant difference between these two articulations of stardom occurs, however, at the level of discourse. Unlike the often mythic construction of the film star, the manufacture of the gay porn star is scarcely denied. In commentaries with porn directors and other industry professionals, the acknowledgement and indeed validation of star manufacture is a recurrent feature. In popular debate around the film star, the same processes are made to appear natural and 'invisible' through the dual discourses of authenticity and charisma (both qualities that are absent in the prototypical gay porn star, as I will explore). At the same time, the discursive constructions of film stars (as part of broader celebrity culture) are not static. Gamson (1994), like Braudy (1986) before him, challenges the axiom that fame is a phenomenon of modern, mass culture and notes that popular debate surrounding celebrity predates the emergence of the culture industries that facilitated its rapid growth. In this respect, Gamson notes that popular explanations of fame have always been framed by two recurrent – and often apparently competing – discourses, what he refers to as 'fame as rise to greatness and fame as artificial production' (1994: 16). With respect to Hollywood stardom, the explanation of fame has often rested on discourses that emphasize the star's natural, innate or 'special' qualities, including the possession of such metaphysical traits as charisma and authenticity. As Gamson argues:

> The narratives about and explanations of fame that were developed in the earlier part of the century have remained commonplace, even dominant. 'Call it star quality, star power, even star magic,' a 1991 *USA Today* article suggested, sounding exactly like articles from six decades earlier. 'Those who possess star quality have it onstage and off … star quality can be spotted and nurtured … Star quality is real and shining – and here to stay' (1994: 44).

In contrast, in the gay porn industry the notion of fame as artificial production is the dominant discourse surrounding the gay porn star. In gay porn the processes by which the star is constructed appear transparent. Moreover, the fact that porn stars are constructed is openly acknowledged, even *celebrated*, by porn producers. As Matt Sterling observes of his creation of the gay porn star, Jeff Stryker:

> Jeff wanted to be a porno star but he had no idea how to do it. We changed his image … we showed him how to dress differently and how to comb his hair and we had his teeth fixed. And in addition to that we decided to create an image (*The Advocate*, September 1989: 29).

Similarly, John Travis (another director associated with the circulation of gay porn stars) notes 'the work and effort that needs to be done to create a talent, promoting them properly and creating an aura and mystique around them' (*Skinflicks*, May 1997: 54). Although this does suggest the desire to associate the gay porn star with mythic (and mystifying) connotations, such remarks in no way conceal the efficacy of the porn star as a marketing device or the rigorous deployment of the generic iconography surrounding them. In a similar vein, a special edition of *Men* magazine, celebrating the thirtieth anniversary of Falcon Studios, features an interview with the then artistic director John Rutherford:

> What makes a superstar? Their look, their sexual being on screen ... Studios have to promote them properly. We've made icons. Falcon has created them, moulded them and recorded them on tape. It's not just the man, but the choice of co-stars, the production values and photography (2002: 85).

Perhaps one of the most potent symbolic expressions of the porn star's manufactured status is offered by his name. In porn, as elsewhere in the entertainment industry, performers change their names. This in itself is not remarkable. What is notable in gay porn is that stars recurrently adopt names that are characteristically prototypic (that is generic, highly manufactured and in most cases connotatively sexual). This is of course also true of porn performers who have not been identified as stars. However, in the case of the porn star, along with the various iconographic signifiers of stardom, the adoption of a prototypic name emphasizes the generic qualities I am identifying here. Names such as Troy Punk, Joe Sport, Jason Adonis, Race Jensen, Matt Rush and Chase Hunter clearly signify at a sexual and physical level.

The 'naming' convention involves the adoption of an exaggeratedly masculine appellation. This usually means selecting a Christian name that is monosyllabic, strident, connotative of an Americanized, sporty, outdoors ideal of masculinity (Matt, Joe, Chase). The origin of the sexual frisson offered by such names is based in the copy accompanying the photographs of models in *Physique Pictorial* during the 1950s and 1960s. The models, discovered by Bob Mizer, were usually identified as ex-marines and manual labourers – men whose admirable physique was gained through hard work rather than narcissism.

This mundane virility is usually counterbalanced by a degree of exoticism afforded by a rather more fanciful surname, usually providing connotations of sexual prowess, potency or desirability. An interesting case here is the surname of the most celebrated gay porn star, Jeff Stryker, who is discussed later in this chapter. Stryker, unlike Hunter, Rush or even Adonis, has no specific metaphorical correlation.[4] Stryker seems connotatively suggestive of physicality and, more specifically, of active aggression (to strike out). The substitution of the letter 'i' for the letter 'y' is enigmatic – connotative of some degree of exoticism, mystique and perhaps even sophistication.

With this in mind, the generic quality of the name Ken Ryker becomes even more striking as any connotations that such a name has are entirely predicated on a familiarity with the generic referent; Jeff Stryker. Ryker's name is in this sense intertextual. Further evidence of the prototype's proliferation in gay pornography is provided by the recurrence of these generic names. The seminal work of Jean Baudrillard (1994), and in particular his theorization of simulation and the simulacrum, has been a significant influence in the development of the concept of prototype that I am proposing. Baudrillard argued that 'out of the crisis of representation the hyperreal has had to be connected to repetition. First in relation to a reproduction of reality but, as reproducibility is established as dominant it ceased to require this support' (Gane, 1991: 102). As in Baudrillard's concept of the hyperreal, the generic prototypes of gay porn refer intertextually to themselves, to a constructed machine of desire.

Race is also an issue here, not merely in the naming of gay porn stars but also in the rhetoric of gay porn star signification. The gay porn star is constructed as a distinctively Caucasian, even Teutonic phenomenon. Indeed, any indicators of ethnicity that is other than white and American is almost completely absent. In the case of Matt Rush this is especially interesting as this contemporary Falcon Studios exclusive performer is of mixed race parentage. While in some small respect it may be regarded as a progressive step for Falcon to promote a mixed race performer as a gay porn star, the overwhelming absence of ethnic diversity in the performers promoted as stars previously by Falcon, or any of the other major producers, mitigates against such a reading. The issue of race and eroticism in gay pornography is one that requires a more detailed discussion than can be allowed in the context of this chapter (see Fung, 1991, and Mercer, 1991). It is also a subject which requires further investigation.

Typage in gay porn

The types in gay porn and their presentation as prototypic constructions are significant for several reasons. One of the key significances is that not only does gay video pornography construct ideals of desirability but it also markets those ideals. Gay porn tells us what the object of our desire as gay men should be and, by inference, the type of gay man we might be. The types that populate the world of gay pornographic video are organized according to a variety of criteria. With the absence of gender difference as a technique to organize and categorize behaviour, performance and role in gay pornography, a plethora of codified types emerge. The pre-eminent form of categorization concerns itself with sexual performance and sexual role: performers who are assigned the 'active' Top role in sexual encounters and those who are categorized as 'passive' Bottoms. This assignation of roles is based on predetermined assumptions about the nature of gay sexual practice and normative conduct, assumptions that are based largely on the agendas and perspectives of the producers of gay pornography. The model Jason Di Biasio (known in the industry as Jackson Phillips), offers an insight into the importance of the categorization of sexual roles in gay pornography:

> Gay porn is produced, for the most part, by men in their 50s & 60s who grew up in an era of far more rigid roles. Hence they carry that dichotomy into the projects they produce. Tops get serviced by bottoms, twinks get plowed by muscle guys, hairy men fuck smooth boys. There's not a lot of variation from those basic themes in most gay porn (1999).[5]

For Baudrillard, the binarism inherent in the active/passive dichotomy is an inevitable product of incorporating sexuality into the realm of the symbolic:

> The more it is functionalised the more sexuality takes on a structural form (like the products of an industry or the language of communication). It reverts to the great oppositions (male/female) in whose disjunctions it is imprisoned, and crystallises around the exercise of a particular sexual *model*, attested to by a particular sexual organ (1993:115).

Though Baudrillard discusses sexuality here in an abstract sense, his comments have a direct relevance to the models of sexuality and sexual desire that are produced by gay pornography. This is indeed the product of an industry and a form of communication. It makes use of oppositions, crystallizes itself around a particular sexual model and – in the case of the gay porn star – around a particular sexual organ.

It is often an a priori assumption in commercial gay video pornography that to get fucked or to perform oral sex is to adopt the role of a passive Bottom, and that to fuck a man or to receive oral sex is what it means to be a Top. This is not to suggest that these roles are eternally fixed nor that they are not transgressed, but this is one of the guiding principles in the categorization of gay porn types: the performance of specific sexual acts determines the signification of specific prototypes. At the same time, these established forms of performance, presentation and conduct have regularly been played with and problematized, resulting in the categorization of new roles and forms of conduct.

The gay porn star as the Classic Top is the most recurrently deployed prototype of gay pornography. As such, it is the type that most explicitly exhibits the characteristics of prototypic construction. The Classic Top is idealized, a manufactured construct of the gay porn industry. His deployment emphasizes the repetitive and generic status of his iconographic characteristic. The starting point for a discussion of the characteristics of the prototypical Classic Top must inevitably include a discussion of Jeff Stryker. Stryker was to be the first gay porn performer to be aggressively marketed as a gay porn 'star' and the combination of both his physical characteristics and his performative qualities were to significantly inform the development of the prototypical Classic Top. As I have already noted, Stryker was discovered by the directors John Travis and Matt Sterling in the mid 1980s and first appeared in *Bigger Than Life* in 1986. But it was to be the video *Powertool* that was to establish his status as porn star. *Powertool* is still widely touted as the best-selling gay porn video of all time.

In the promotional image for *Powertool* (1987, John Travis, Catalina) perhaps the most iconic image of the gay porn star, we see Stryker as powerfully muscled, with a gleaming, hairless body. Slightly unusually, he is not positioned frontally, but the reason for this structured posture becomes apparent when we move further down the frame. His position affords (along with tight-fitting white jogging shorts, a raised left leg and a black backdrop), pronounced visibility to the extremely large bulge in his shorts, which in fact appears to extend halfway down his leg. The raised position of the left leg gives the appearance of it being shorter in length – thus becoming evocative of an erect member. In a sexual invitation, the thumb of his right hand pulls down the back of his shorts. The title *Powertool*, with its connotations of machinery and masculine virility and its obvious play on the word 'tool' (as well as the subheading 'Seeing is believing'), anchors the image and leaves us in no doubt as to what we are supposed to be looking at. Further emphasis is offered by the formal qualities of the image with Stryker's form being elaborately structured into a triangular composition. His face, knee and penis, the three most directly sexualized signifiers in the image, are positioned at the axes of the triangle.

Stryker's star signification is emphatically reiterated within the texts themselves, both through narrative and performance. In his video appearances, Jeff is recurrently distanced – both diegetically and rhetorically. Nowhere is this more evident than in *Powertool*, which stands as the breakthrough point in his porn career. Throughout the video we see Stryker positioned as the object of the viewers' gaze. The video deals with Stryker's sexual experiences as a prison inmate, confined for thirty days for an unspecified offence. In the second scene he is ordered to strip by a prison guard and made to present his genitals for the voyeuristic gaze of the camera. His sexual performance throughout might best be described as willing, if somewhat indifferent. This was to become a characteristic of Stryker's performance: he is recurrently presented in videos in somewhat disengaged sexual scenarios. A good example here is in the third scene of *Powertool* where Jeff watches two prisoners in a cell opposite engage in vigorous sex. Stryker masturbates throughout this sequence, caressing his own body and forcing his enormous penis through the bars of the cell. However, there is a clear sense that it is not the sexual encounter opposite that is turning Jeff on so much as himself. This sense of narcissism is emphasized by Stryker's orgasm, which is placed some time after the end of the cellmate's encounter. The combination of camerawork focusing on Jeff's body, the increased tempo of the music and Stryker's own performance, identify his climax as an autonomous entity, generated by and *for* himself.

These elements of solipsism and narcissism are characteristic of most of Stryker's video appearances. Solipsism is further emphasized by his entirely active sexual role-play. According to Matt Sterling, the director attributed with the discovery of Stryker, this is a central aspect of his persona: 'he held back on video a lot of the things that people wanted him to do, partially on my advice … he was not willing to get fucked. He hasn't even done it in his own movies' (*The Advocate*, 1989: 30).

Similar examples of this self-absorbed performativity abound in gay pornography. For example, a notable vignette entitled *The Power of Suggestion*, from Colt Studios' *Minute Man 10* (1992, unattributed, Buckshot Productions), features Ray Dragon masturbating to his own reflection while listening to an erotic answering machine message. More startling is the opening scene of *Perfect Fit* (2004, Steven Scarborough, Hot House Entertainment). This commences with gay porn star Aiden Shaw masturbating in a sex club in front of an enormous back-projected film, displaying him engaged in a variety of sexual encounters.

A significant, and far from subtle or ambiguous point that needs to be made at this stage, is the significance of 'being hung'. The pre-eminent unitary currency of gay pornography is the large penis and it is therefore the case that performers who are hailed as Tops should be in possession of this valuable commodity. The simple rubric that underpins this notion is that that the larger the member, the more effectively a performer can fulfil the requirements of the Top role. This is exemplified by Jeff Stryker: his signification as both the classic porn Top and as a porn star is based on a hyperbolic discourse surrounding his sexual organ. This strategy of privileging 'hung' performers can be seen to have been adopted by commercial production companies based on the success that Catalina experienced with Stryker, and it is a pattern that repeats itself to this day. Falcon Studios were to follow the lead set by Catalina in promoting a succession of 'hung' prototypical Classic Tops such as Rex Chandler. In his first star vehicle for Falcon, *Manrammer* (1989, Steven Scarborough, Falcon Studios), Chandler is presented as the idealized Classic Top. His body is smooth, sculpted and muscular, his looks conforming to the generic, blond, handsome features that were to become the defining characteristics of the 'Falcon look'. The video's subheading *A Battle of Size*, and Chandler's provocative posture for the pack shot, tease the viewer with the expectation that his sexual organ will be revealed. Both work to emphasize that within the discourse of the Classic Top, size does indeed matter.

It might be argued that the representation of the porn star as Classic Top, and the ubiquity of this specific mode of representation, seems to privilege the 'active' role in gay sex. Richard Dyer has argued that gay porn narrative is structured, like heterosexual pornography, around the desire to fuck:

> the narrative is never organised around the desire to be fucked, but around the desire to ejaculate (whether or not following on from anal intercourse). Thus although at the level of public representation gay men may be thought of as deviant and disruptive of masculine norms because we assert the pleasure of being fucked and the eroticism of the anus (Hocquenghem 1978), in our pornography this takes a back seat (1989: 128).

Mark Simpson agrees with this assertion, suggesting that 'since Dyer made this assertion in 1985, the portrayal of anal sex seems to have become even more constructed as the "desire to achieve the goal of a visual climax" – the desire, that is, of the fucker' (1994: 134). Tom Waugh however challenges this assertion:

> This may be true of many or even most theatrical films (though I think this requires further research – certainly lots of individual sequences I remember contradict this); however passive penetration fantasies are extremely common as narrative principles in many non-commercial films and anecdotes (1993: 314–5).

I would also like to dispute this assertion. Dyer (and by appropriation of his position, Simpson also) uses Linda Williams's reading of heterosexual pornography as a model to analyse the narrative structures of gay porn. While I also consider Williams's work to be of value in the exploration of pornography (her approach has informed the model adopted in this study), it does not engage significantly with gay pornography. (This is a limitation that Williams herself suggests she would redress if she were rewriting *Hard Core*, and it has been considered in the more recent collection *Porn Studies*: Williams, 2004.) Gay porn simultaneously offers prototypical constructions both as a point of identification and as figures of desire. We are positioned as both *wanting*, as well as *wanting to be*, the porn star/prototypical Top. Furthermore, there are abundant examples of mainstream commercial videos in which the desire to be fucked clearly motivates the narrative. Rather than thinking that this is a position that is absent in gay pornography, I would argue that it is an extremely common narrative construction. A fine example, which demonstrates both a narrative structured around this desire and the porn star as prototypical Classic Top in operation, is provided by the video *Basic Plumbing II* (1998, John Rutherford, Jocks). The video deals with the antics of a firm of urban plumbers staffed by a team of prototypical Classic Tops who become the objects of desire for a succession of Classic porn Bottoms. The first scene of the video revolves around Classic Bottom Christopher Scott, who calls upon the gay porn star Mike Branson to unblock his kitchen sink. Through the contrivance of getting wet while performing his manual work, Branson reveals his sculpted torso which acts as the catalyst for a sexual exchange between the couple. Branson is objectified throughout the sequence and we are encouraged to position ourselves in the scene with Scott, both admiring and desiring this ideal figure of manhood. The scene ends with Branson leaving and Scott deciding to re-block his sink in order to call out a second plumber. In between these self-enclosed sexual scenes the video includes a running narrative concerning the desire of Brennan Foster, the blond Classic Bottom, for the owner of 'Basic Plumbing', the muscular and handsome Top, Chase Hunter. Foster loiters outside the firm's offices and, using the ruse of a car breakdown, is invited back to Hunter's apartment where the two engage in a lengthy sexual encounter. Foster (and by inference the audience) is placed in a position of worship in relation to the sculpted, statuesque porn star, Hunter. The rhetoric of the sequence, through the use of low camera angles, encourages the viewer to occupy the same point of view as the Bottom (Foster). The scene suggests that we should imagine what it would be like to engage in a hot sexual encounter with a man like Hunter. This viewpoint, emphasized by the narrative of the sequence which is concerned with Foster's desire to engage in sex with Hunter, demonstrates the familiar shifting position of identification that gay porn frequently deploys in sex sequences. But it is ostensibly concerned with identifying Hunter – the Classic Top and porn star – as the object of our desire, and Foster – the Classic Bottom – as our figure of identification.

The emphasis on exteriority and physicality is illustrated by the strategies deployed in the construction of the ideal homoerotic body; the body that the audience is positioned to read as inscribed with desire and the body that the gay porn star exemplifies. Feminist analysis of both classic cinema and heterosexual pornography has repeatedly identified the rhetorical devices deployed that fragment the female body. Laura Mulvey (1975) argues that the close-up of the female in Classic Hollywood cinema is deployed as a device that disrupts narrative flow. For Mulvey, it is through such techniques that the female is positioned as *other*. Annette Kuhn (1985) similarly argues that women are reduced to their body parts in heterosexual pornography. Both critics observe the visual devices that fragment the female body as essentially disruptive and dehumanizing; through these devices women are objectified. Similar techniques are employed in the presentation of the erotic male body in gay pornography. However, I would argue that the fragmentation of the male body in gay pornography *constructs* the homoerotic narrative: it is in fact *central* to it. The devices of fragmentation in gay porn are deployed in the service of creating a way of looking at the eroticized male body, they effectively invent the gay male erotic gaze. These representational strategies are used with such relentless regularity in the presentation of the gay porn star that examples are too numerous to mention. One particularly notable example is offered during the opening scenes of *Big River* (1995, John Rutherford, Falcon Studios). Ken Ryker plays 'Big Ryker', a mysterious woodsman who is admired fleetingly by the protagonist Christian Fox prior to their final meeting and sexual encounter. In these early sequences, Ryker is pictured chopping logs and engaged in other suitably macho woodland pursuits. These sequences of the silent and mysterious 'Big Ryker' are edited through a series of close-ups which focus on various parts of Ryker's body: his chest, back, arms, upper torso, together with slow cross-fades that reconstruct Ryker's already impressive physique. In the sequence, Ryker, the gay porn star, becomes the sum of his over-determined parts.

The formal and aesthetic strategies and conventions that have been discussed so far lead on to the final and fundamental feature of the gay porn star. As discussed, in relation to the Hollywood star, the notion of authenticity is tied to the discourse of charisma – a quality which Dyer identifies as 'a fantasy of personality' (1998).[6] Charisma can be regarded as operating as a veil which mystifies the industrial processes of filmmaking. The gay porn star is distinguished by an absence of charisma. This observation should not be regarded as evaluative but as an acknowledgement of the differing textual qualities and priorities at stake in the gay pornographic text. Pornography is constructed around a discourse that might be described as the fantasy of the visible: exteriority rather than interiority is what is at stake in the construction of the gay porn star. Therefore the porn star's value and signification must be defined in relation to an abundance of sexualized physical attributes. The gay porn star exists critically at the level of surface, of appearances. What constitutes the gay porn star is the exemplary nature of these visible characteristics. Any sense of interiority, psychic depth or charisma would in fact detract from the function of the gay porn star as a machine of desire. The gay porn star, then, is psychically absent and physically present, existing as a highly manufactured and unobtainable ideal.

Notes

1 A more detailed discussion and exploration of the concept of prototype is offered in J. Mercer (2003), 'Homosexual Prototypes: Repetition and the Construction of the Generic in the Iconography of Gay Pornography', in J. Still (ed.), *Men's Bodies*: Edinburgh: Edinburgh University Press.

2 Gay pornography remains a significantly under-researched area of cultural production. The work of Richard Dyer (1994) has played an important part in identifying some of the issues at stake in the study of gay pornography, and Tom Waugh's comprehensive historical study *Hard*

to Imagine: Gay Male Eroticism in Photography and Film from Their Beginnings to Stonewall (1998) is particularly notable. Beginning with the earliest examples of nude photography and ending with pornographic film and gay cinema of the late 1960s, Waugh's study stands as the most comprehensive historical overview of the development of homoerotic representation. Scholarly work on contemporary gay pornography, however, is still rare. An example is John Burger's *One Handed Histories: The Eroto-Politics of Gay Male Video Pornography* (1995). Burger's slim study, to some extent, attempts to follow on from the point at which Waugh's study ends and focuses on the emergence of home video gay porn. More recently, the *Journal of Homosexuality* has devoted a special issue (2004) to the study of contemporary gay pornography from a variety of perspectives that has been co-published simultaneously as *Eclectic View on Gay Male Pornography: Pornucopia* (Harrington Park Press).

3 A variety of factors mitigate against the reproduction of the images referred to in this chapter, ranging across copyright clearance (porn producers are notoriously difficult to negotiate with in this regard) and the potential offence these images may cause. Interested parties, however, will soon discover that the most cursory internet search will generate any number of sites featuring the images in question.

4 During the mid 1960s the magazines *Physique Pictorial*, *Adonis* and *Young Physique* featured photo shoots of a model using the name Jim Stryker photographed by Champion Studios. It is of course a possibility that the surname Stryker was adopted in homage to this particularly popular model.

5 I am indebted to Jason DiBiasio who, over the course of several years, kindly consented to correspond with me concerning his experiences and perspectives as a performer in the gay pornography industry. The comments cited here are extracted from correspondence that took place during 1999.

6 I would like to take this opportunity to extend my thanks to Richard Dyer who has given his time on several occasions to discuss some of the issues explored here, and who suggested that an article on contemporary gay porn stars might be of value. The comments here emerged out of a conversation that took place in 1998.

Bibliography

Baudrillard, Jean (1993) *Symbolic Exchange and Death*, London: Sage.

—— (1994) *Simulacra and Simulation*, Ann Arbor: University of Michigan Press.

Braudy, Leo (1986) *The Frenzy of Renown: Fame and its History*, Oxford: Oxford University Press.

Burger, John (1995) *One Handed Histories: The Eroto-Politics of Gay Male Video Pornography*, New York: Harrington Park Press.

Dworkin, Andrea (1991) 'Against the Male Flood: Censorship, Pornography and Equality', in Robert Baird and Stuart Rosenbaum (eds), *Pornography, Private Right or Public Menace?*, New York: Prometheus, pp. 56–60.

Dyer, Richard (1979) *Stars*, London: BFI.

—— (1989) 'A Conversation about Pornography', in Simon Shephert and Mick Wallis (eds), *Coming on Strong: Gay Politics and Culture*, London: Unwin, pp. 198–212.

—— (1991) 'A Star is Born and the Construction of Authenticity', in Christine Gledhill (ed.), *Stardom. Industry of Desire*, London: Routledge, pp.132–9.

—— (1991) 'Charisma', in Christine Gledhill (ed.), *Stardom. Industry of Desire*, London: Routledge, pp. 57–59.

—— (1992) *Only Entertainment*, London: Routledge.

—— (1994) 'Idol Thoughts: Orgasm and Self Reflexivity in Gay Pornography', *Critical Review* 36/1: 49–62.

Ellis, John (1992) *Visible Fictions: Cinema, Television, Video*, London: Routledge.

Fung, Richard (1991) 'Looking for my Penis: The Eroticized Asian in Gay Video Porn', in Bad Object Choices (eds), *How do I Look? Queer Film and Video*, Seattle: Bay Press, pp. 145–60.

Gamson, Joshua (1994) *Claims to Fame: Celebrity in Contemporary America*, Berkeley: University of California Press.

Gane, Mike (1991) *Baudrillard's Bestiary*, London: Routledge.

Gledhill, Christine (ed.) (1991) *Stardom: Industry of Desire*, London: Routledge.

Jeffords, Susan (1994) *Hard Bodies: Hollywood Masculinity in the Reagan Era*, New York: Rutgers University Press.

Kuhn, Annette (1985) *The Power of the Image: Essays on Representation and Sexuality*, London: Routledge.

McDonald, Paul (2004) 'Reconceptualising Stardom', in Richard Dyer (ed.), *Stars*, London: BFI, pp. 177–200.

Mercer, John (2003) 'Homosexual Prototypes: Repetition and the Construction of the Generic in the Iconography of Gay Pornography' in Judith Still (ed.), *Men's Bodies*, Edinburgh: Edinburgh University Press, pp. 280–90.

Mercer, Kobena (1991) 'Skin Head Sex Thing: Racial Difference and the Homosexual Imaginary', in Bad Object Choices (eds), *How do I Look? Queer Film and Video*, Seattle: Bay Press, pp. 169–210.

Mulvey, Laura (1975) 'Visual Pleasure and Narrative Cinema', *Screen* 16/3: 6–18.

Simpson, Mark (1994) *Male Impersonators*, London: Cassell.

Tasker, Yvonne (1993) *Spectacular Bodies: Gender, Genre and the Action Cinema*, London: Routledge.

Waugh, Thomas (1993) 'Men's Pornography: Gay vs. Straight' in M. Gever, J. Greyson and P. Parmar (eds), *Queer Looks*, London: Routledge, pp. 307–27.

—— (1998) *Hard to Imagine: Gay Male Eroticism in Photography and Film from Their Beginnings to Stonewall*, New York: Columbia University Press.

Williams, Linda (1989) *Hard Core: Power, Pleasure and the 'Frenzy of the Visible'*, Berkeley: University of California Press.

—— (ed.) (2004) *Porn Studies*, New York: Duke University Press.

Chapter 9

Celebrity skins

The illicit textuality of the celebrity nude magazine

Adam Knee

The inspiration for this essay came quite literally from the trash heap of popular culture. I was dashing out of my apartment building on Manhattan's lower east side, late to teach a seminar on 'Stars in Popular Culture', when an image of bare flesh amidst the garbage barrels caught my eye. Closer inspection revealed that a neighbour had tossed out a pile of skin magazines – not your garden-variety pornography, but publications featuring nude images of popular stars. They were culled from a variety of sources evidently in the public domain, then reformatted so as to appeal most strongly to the reader's celebrity fascination. It took a moment for the propitiousness of my find to fully dawn on me: a common (in various senses of that term) artefact, which vividly and succinctly expressed many key principles regarding the circulation of celebrity in popular culture, had just fallen into my lap. Here, in a lurid nutshell, were the broad cultural tendencies I had been trying to demonstrate to my class. I eagerly scooped up this provocative refuse and went on my way, later to share my neighbour's trash and new thoughts with my students.

I relate this story not because it provides an excuse for my familiarity with the arguably prurient texts examined here (although happily it does happen to do that) but because it highlights, for want of better words, the trashy, off-cast nature of this particular kind of star discourse – its seeming illicitness and marginality. Indeed, my finding the magazines in the trash certainly served to pique, rather than dull my interest in the material – augmenting its taboo aura. These publications have in fact much invested in cultivating their associations with 'trash' – in its connotations of both the discarded and the disreputable. Thus, while their images of unclothed celebrities do not generally follow the conventions of, or reach the explicit extremes of, most commercially available pornography, these magazines nevertheless go out of their way to package themselves as such. They are produced by publishers which also produce more conventional skin magazines, are displayed with such magazines at newsstands, and in the case of *Celebrity Skin*, contain some of the same sexually explicit advertising (for phone sex services, pornographic videos, and the like) as do the other magazines. Moreover, their sensationalized pictorials of film and television stars, models, pop singers and other public figures (Maria Shriver, Hilary Clinton and Diana, Princess of Wales, for example), are in some cases presented along-side pictorials of porn film stars. In effect, one could argue, these magazines render *all* stars as porn stars.

These texts, most centrally *Celebrity Skin* and *Celebrity Sleuth*, are well worth examining more closely, not so much because they have a broad popularity (although the existence of several imitative magazines and countless related websites, as well as celebrity nude sections in more typical skin magazines, would attest to this) but because, in their seeming illicitness, they manage to illuminate some highly significant underlying principles of more mainstream star culture. Of course, it is hardly a revelation that lurid information about stars piques our interest. This fact is readily evident from the profusion of star-scandal tabloids (e.g. the *National Enquirer*) in supermarket checkout aisles, as well as from the emphasis on personal details of stars' lives in more mainstream publications such as *People* magazine and its imitators (on the rise since the 1970s) and in 'infotainment' television programmes such as *Entertainment Tonight*. Even 'hard news' outlets such as CNN regularly carry items on the most prominent star and celebrity scandals or gossip. I will be making the case here, however, that in the distinctive form of their discourse and, most crucially, their unique emphasis on the bodies of the famous, the relatively marginalized celebrity nude magazines provide a significant means of understanding the basic nature of our fascination with celebrities. These texts also bear examination in relation to the more specific phenomenon of 'trash cinema'. I will argue that celebrity nude monthlies and trash cinema are linked in a number of important ways, both of them existing at the disreputable periphery of Hollywood spectatorship, but paradoxically also pointing to the very centre of that spectatorship, illustrative of the fundamental dynamics of cinematic pleasure.

Titillating tidbits

In his book *Claims to Fame*, Joshua Gamson (1994) describes contemporary celebrity as involving a process of negotiation, a struggle for image control, among stars, publicists, and journalists. The audience is aware of the highly planned and constructed nature of such star imagery, but it enjoys watching the processes of industry hype at the same time as it desires a glimpse of 'authentic' aspects of the star's existence. Thus, the battles for discursive control

> are part of a war in an economy of information – specifically an economy of tidbits. Bits of personality information, either written,

spoken, or photographed, are the primary currency circulating and fought over between those seeking exposure and those providing it. The celebrity is divided up into pieces and those pieces move between parties, are exchanged, invested, cashed in (Gamson, 1994: 94).

Part of what is so interesting about magazines such as *Celebrity Skin*, *Celebrity Sleuth*, and *Celeb Confidential* is the distinctive way they position themselves within this 'economy of tidbits'. What these publications do through a range of strategies is to reframe industry-authorized tidbits as unauthorized. They recast what are often widely available images in such a way that they appear to reveal aspects of the 'authentic', to unmask the 'true' nature of the celebrity, to communicate to us what it is that does – or does not – make these particular human beings different from the rest of us (see also Adrienne Lai's essay in this collection). The magazines thereby offer a particularly concrete illustration of what Richard Dyer has termed a 'rhetoric of authenticity' operating in media texts – that is, the active construction of the star's authenticity 'by the use of markers that indicate lack of control, lack of premeditation, and privacy' (1991: 137).

The peculiar placement of these monthlies within the celebrity economy of information is probably most akin to tabloids – publications which can give stars free and sometimes commercially beneficial publicity but which are 'structured on an *institutional divorce* from those in the entertainment industry trying to control publicity [original emphasis]' (Gamson, 1994: 97). Significantly, however, the skin magazine's divorce from the usual star-making machinery is distinct from the tabloid's in that it makes use of at least as much studio or publicist-provided imagery as of imagery acquired elsewhere. Where magazines such as *Celebrity Sleuth* primarily break the rules, again, is in a refiguring of readily available material as *un*-authorized, uncontrolled, and hence, more 'authentic' than formally sanctioned publicity.

The magazines consist primarily of two- to four-page spreads focusing on individual celebrities. In turn, groups of such spreads are in many cases organized around a loose theme, such as 'Cable Queens', 'The 25 Sexiest Women', 'Hollywood Bra-Busters', or 'At Your Request'.[1] These spreads are invariably dominated by photographic material, most of which features the given star in various skin-revealing images. These images are accompanied by differing amounts of text which generally offer biographical information on the star, comment on the star's connection to the particular theme at hand, and highlight any particular personal or sexually-oriented rumours in circulation.

De-authorizing the image

The effect of de-authorization is achieved through a range of textual strategies within these layouts. One key strategy shared by these magazines is to vary the textual nature of the differing images used in any given layout and to highlight these variations, thereby implying the absence of a single controlling vision, such as that of a publicist or production company PR department. Posed celebrity portraits and official production stills sit alongside stills lifted from videotapes and (to a far lesser degree) photos purchased from tabloid photographers and auxiliary publicity materials such as movie posters and video cassette boxes. More recently these materials have been joined by images from websites and (in the case of *Celebrity Sleuth*) reproduced pages from tabloids and covers from magazines. Black and white images sit alongside colour ones, fine-grained photographs alongside video freeze-frames (blown up to such a degree that the scan lines are highly prominent), and carefully composed stills alongside blurry and uncentred action shots.

One might assume that this diversity of textual registers is merely a function of the range of sources from which the imagery is culled, but in fact the publications clearly make efforts to ensure that there is a sense of disjuncture among the photos displayed. Layouts tend to highlight contrasts not only through sharp juxtapositions among kinds of imagery, but through variations in image dimensions and relative size; it is rare that one finds a matrix of equally-sized photographs. This variation in size and format, sometimes in conjunction with variations in the degree of freeze-frame enlargement (and graininess), allows the publications to make images from the same or similar sources appear graphically disparate. Significantly, this process is facilitated by the effacement, to varying degrees, of information about photo sources. For example, two stills from the same film might appear to be a film still next to a candid shot. The now-defunct *Celeb Confidential* often seemed to dispense with photo identification altogether, while *Celebrity Skin* and *Celebrity Sleuth* make the retrieval of such identification cumbersome by burying very general source information in single dense blocks of text alongside large mosaics of disparate images.

A typical example from a 1996 *Celebrity Sleuth* (which tends to have more pages in a given spread than does *Celebrity Skin*), will serve to illustrate these tendencies more concretely. A four-page section on Uma Thurman opens with two paragraphs of text, in a single quarter-page column, giving a brief overview of the actor's career (40–3). The remainder of the first page is devoted to a layout of nine photographs of widely varying dimensions (with both portrait and landscape orientations), and an explanatory paragraph is inserted in the mosaic about three-quarters of the way up from the bottom. The photo spread continues on the facing page in an arrangement which mirrors that of the first page, with three-quarters of the space devoted to a mosaic of six images of varying sizes (and one more paragraph of text, here at the bottom). The remaining right-hand one-quarter column is devoted to a sidebar on a green background containing some additional biographical data and three paragraph-long items about the performer (one, for example, about her 'discovery' by Terry Gilliam, another about a brief marriage to Gary Oldman). This is followed by an additional two-page spread of seven photos of Thurman, once more of varying dimensions and qualities, with an explanatory block of text on each page.

The two explanatory paragraphs placed among the photographs on the first two pages do not, it should be noted, fully identify the sources of the images. One would need to read through the columns of text at either side of the spread, as well as the explanatory paragraphs, in order to ascertain where the images came from. Instead, these obstacles to identification clearly prompt the reader to scan the two-page array of adjoining photographs (largely uninterrupted by text), thus avoiding the work necessary to learn where each shot comes from.

The fifteen images on these two pages include colour press photographs of Thurman at a number of media premieres and ceremonies, either alone or with other celebrities and family members, a black-and-white snapshot of her mother with former husband Timothy Leary, and stills from several of Thurman's films (cropped in varying aspects to suit the magazine's purposes). Some of them are high-quality colour or black-and-white images, others are blurry shots lifted from videos, with scanlines more or less prominent depending on the degree of enlargement. One film still is of Thurman with Glenn Close, while another features the famous Twist scene from *Pulp Fiction* (1994). Two stills are from a masturbation scene in *Even Cowgirls Get the Blues* (1993) (one of them cropped to focus solely on Thurman's hand reaching into her panties), two feature Thurman's bared breasts, and another shows her cleavage as she leans forward. One of the breast shots is cropped to show nothing but breasts, and it is blown up to such a degree that the video image visibly breaks down into little dots of colour on a white background. Again, the disparateness of the images erases the overall sense of producer/publicist authorization in what is being presented, even if many of the individual images are in fact part of official press packets. This adds to the sensation of peering in on Thurman's privacy.

The additional photos on the following two pages amplify this sensation considerably: most of them are grainy colour shots of the actress relaxing topless (and evidently unaware of photographers) on a Caribbean beach. Mixed in with these are an obviously posed black-and-white glamour shot of Thurman at a beach in a long tee-shirt, and a black-and-white paparazzi shot of the young woman 'stark-ass naked' (as the caption describes it), evidently taken from a tabloid publication and enlarged so that the image begins to break up into small dots.

A further example from a 2004 issue of *Celebrity Skin* should serve to suggest the consistency of representational strategies of these magazines, both over time and across titles. A relatively chaste one-page entry on Kirsten Dunst in a section of the magazine titled 'Young, Hot & Nude' is divided into two columns, one just over two inches wide, the other five inches wide (22). The narrower column, on the left side of the page, is headed with the 'Young, Hot & Nude' title, beneath which appears a photo of Dunst from head to waist – possibly at a public event – attired in a metallic gold tank top with a matching scarf. Below the photo are two boxes of unequal size, the one in the middle containing some text, the one at the bottom featuring a photo of Dunst in a bikini top, which is cropped just below her breasts. The text box, following a format appearing throughout the issue, offers a date of birth, the URL for a fan website, and a one-sentence description of the woman's star imagery ('wholesome good looks, combined with a killer bod'), which includes mention of her films.

Two of the film titles are followed by parenthetical indications, suggesting that they are the sources for some of the photos which appear in the wider column at right. We can therefore learn, if we happen to take the time to read, that the top row of four similar images (themselves, characteristically, in two different sizes) of Dunst shown head to thigh in a bikini are from the film *Get Over It* (2001). That the bikini matches the one in the first column clarifies the source of that image as well. We are also told that the images at bottom are from *Crazy/Beautiful* (2001). Since the evidently amorous pose and form-fitting shorts of one of the images on the very bottom row match those of the single image on the second row from the bottom, we assume that both of those rows are composed of stills from that film. This leaves the images in a fourth row – three shots of Dunst from head to waist that are different from the others in being slightly out of focus (perhaps because of the speed of her movement). They are also different in appearing to capture an accidental flash of skin: the side of one of Dunst's breasts is revealed as she dances or gestures (or perhaps even tries to change her top). The image could conceivably be from a film, but this is not specified, again giving the sense that it may be an unauthorized 'find'.

This particular mode of employing star imagery from a wide range of sources, not all fully identified, has some interesting commonalities with that described by Chuck Wolfe in a study of *Newsweek*'s representation of Jimmy Stewart during the World War II era. Wolfe describes how *Newsweek* employs various techniques to adjust the meaning of Stewart's star image in relation to *It's a Wonderful Life* (1946). *Newsweek* attempts 'to situate the film within the news events of the day, to find a context within which to make it legible for its readers' (1991: 105). Wolfe goes on to suggest that news magazines in general:

> bring unity to a flow of disparate events, to juxtapose fragments in such a way that they are given coherent social meaning in a familiar package. Their general practice of not specifying sources – where and how images were obtained, who or what is transmitting the news – aims at a homogeneous style whereby potentially cacophonous 'voices' are flattened out into a single 'voice' which speaks with authority (ibid.).

The magazines I am discussing here likewise try to bring contemporary contexts (those of the star discourse) to bear upon specific isolated star images, and likewise obfuscate photographic sources in part to achieve this end. A key difference, however, is that while *Newsweek* effaces photo sources to ensure a seamless (and semi-fictional) narrative, *Celebrity Skin* and the like efface sources to do in effect exactly the opposite: they work to *create* seams in their (also semi-fictional) narratives even where none existed, to structure their source materials as being diverse, unmediated, 'cacophonous', to remove any sense of authority.

The work of de-authorization in these layouts is achieved not only through the highlighting of disparateness, however, but also through the creation of unexpected unities, the association of approved materials with unsanctioned photos, the obfuscation of ontological distinctions among more fully 'fictional' images (that is, stills from fictional films), semi-fictional images (press photos from publicist-staged film premieres),[2] and more 'real' personal snapshots or images captured by paparazzi. In the Thurman spread, for example, there is nothing present to immediately distinguish the press photos of the actress from the adjoining film stills. Likewise, nothing distinguishes the distorted motion picture stills of Thurman's breasts from the similarly unclear paparazzi photos of her sunbathing on the following pages. The downplaying of distinctions among different kinds of imagery serves to imply, through association, that all of the photographs present may be equally revelatory.

These magazines want to imply that they are selling us publicity-savvy readers the 'reality' behind the surface star image and so must distance themselves from their often legitimate (and hence controlled, relatively univocal) sources. To paraphrase Dyer, they work to construct their images as uncontrolled, unpremeditated, and private. Here inside this ostensibly unregulated hodgepodge, we can find (to quote *Celebrity Skin*'s subheading) 'the photos the stars don't want you to see'. A heavy emphasis on video freeze-frames augments this sense of unauthorized image capture, of celebrity voyeurism, even though the film sources are in public release. It is as if these 'celebrity sleuths' have found, hidden within the illusory temporal flow of cinema, the star's static video reality – grainy, muddy, and distorted by scan lines, but revelatory nonetheless. These stills bespeak 'authenticity' both in that their sometimes degraded image quality marks them as 'trash', as that which has been discarded and not originally intended for public consumption, and in that they have been wrested from their original, highly controlled (and temporally regulated) narrative and cinematographic frameworks. As one reader of *Celebrity Sleuth* explains, in a letter describing a brief glimpse of one of Sigourney Weaver's breasts in *Ghostbusters* (1984), 'sometimes these *unintentional* flashes have an appeal that intentional, blatant exposures do not' (1996: 2).

From this standpoint, it appears that the work done by these ostensibly disreputable, non-mainstream publications in fact plays to, and extends, certain fundamental psychic processes of spectatorial gratification which have been identified in the field of film studies. In Christian Metz's classic formulation, a key part of what distinguishes cinematic voyeurism and renders it so distinctively intense is that it is in effect an *unauthorised* scopophilia', that, despite the perceptual richness of the cinematic signifier, the object of visual desire is spatially and ontologically removed from the spectator and seemingly unaware of the spectator's presence (1982: 61–6). Following Metz, John Ellis describes such processes at work in the more specific instance of spectator–star relations:

> The play between the possibility and impossibility of the star as an object of desire is intensified by the photo effect of presence–absence … Introduced here is a whole new dimension of the star: not just the star-in-movement, but also the incidental aspects of that movement. The star's performance in film reveals to the viewer all those small gestures, particular aspects of movement and expression, unexpected similarities to acquaintances or even to self … In other words, what the film performance permits is moments of pure voyeurism for the spectator, the sense of overlooking something which is not designed for the onlooker but passively allows itself to be seen (1982: 99).

As the above account has begun to suggest, the magazines discussed here highlight this particular kind of fundamental voyeuristic dynamic and, through their distinctive textual strategies, work to foster and further exploit these celebrity desires. The narrative flow is suspended to allow us to scrutinize aspects of the star that have previously been hidden by the conventional consumption of the film text.

The naked and the dead

In some respects, however, the foregoing analysis may beat around the bush. Clearly, the magazine images' sense of illicitness and authenticity arises not only from the aesthetics of de-authorization described earlier, but from their distinctive content as well. To restate the obvious, the overwhelming emphasis – which constitutes the magazines' most overt selling point – is celebrity nudity. In some cases this nudity is little different from what one might see in relatively soft-core, relatively mainstream skin magazines. The unclothed star is flatteringly photographed in a professionally lit, evenly composed, retouched image. This is particularly so for pictorials of stars from the cable or porn industries, where the layout sometimes includes photos which were evidently taken for and have presumably appeared in more conventional skin magazines as well; it is clearly the case, for example, in a spread on 1980s porn star Ginger Lynn Allen in *Celebrity Skin* (19/59, May 1997: 88–9) or in a spread on British adult film actress Sarah Young in *Celebrity Sleuth* (10/7, 1997: 76–9). However, what is interesting about the other kinds of images in these celebrity magazines is that they often place little emphasis on the star's face, traditionally *the* central site for star iconography. The focus, rather, is on photographically displaying the star's bare skin by any means necessary – even in a scarcely legible freeze-frame, even if the star's face is completely hidden and there is no clear means of identification. (See also John Mercer's essay in this collection which makes a similar point in relation to the body of the porn star.)

Richard deCordova's work on the evolution of star discourses in the first decades of Hollywood cinema may provide one avenue for understanding this particular kind of preoccupation. DeCordova convincingly argues that the evolution of the star focused on exposing progressively more about film performers, the 'private truths' behind their screen images. With the star scandals of the 1920s, it becomes eminently clear that the 'ultimate truth' being sought out, the source of the most profound audience fascination, is that of sexuality. (Indeed, Linda Williams (1990) has suggested that the very invention of cinema is bound up with the human fascination with the observation of the body – a fascination given most direct expression in pornography.) As deCordova explains: 'The star system, and arguably twentieth century culture in general, depends on an interpretive schema that equates identity with the private and furthermore accords the sexual the status of the most private, and thus the most truthful, locus of identity' (1990: 140). I would propose that this picture might need to be adjusted somewhat for the postmodern audience in that it is increasingly savvy about and wary of media manipulation and hence more profoundly sceptical of any representations of the private. Sexuality may remain the ultimate source of fascination, but its representations can no longer be trusted; portrayals of 'the sexual' are now a priori suspect. In this context, the body takes its place as the ultimate *visually verifiable* realm of the private, the physical adjunct of the individual's sexual secrets – even if this is tempered by our awareness that body imagery can itself be manipulated both by more long-standing photographic techniques (such as airbrushing) and by newer digital technologies.

It is not surprising then that, as we have seen in these magazines, the revelation of the body is structured as important enough that usual technical considerations fall by the wayside. The image can be utterly unclear, unposed, unglamorous – as long as there is a seemingly unauthorized glimmer of skin.[3] The actor's bare body is positioned here as a crucial site of authenticity, as that which reveals the truths hidden by publicist-controlled facial iconography and clothing. This perspective is evident as well in photos where a star's skirt has been inadvertently left open to view or where a breast has strayed from a loose-fitting outfit. There is a strong sense that the body is significant not only for its erotic value but as an arena of potentially revelatory non-control, which can provide singular insight into what a celebrity is literally made of. This might partially explain the fascination with images of dying or dead or autopsied celebrities, where control over the body is completely lost – a fascination demonstrated, for example, in the reported photographing and circulation of images of a mortally injured Princess Diana. In that particular case, the supposed accident-scene photographs would have captured the celebrity at a moment where she was wholly unable to manage her image, her body literally opened up for the paparazzi (and us) to view.

This signifying value of the body counters the classical formulation of the reve-latory function of the facial close-up as articulated, for example, by Bela Balazs. Writing from the romantic perspective that stars are charismatic beings, Balazs suggests that 'In the silent film facial expression, isolated from its surroundings, seemed to penetrate to a strange new dimension of the soul' (1970: 65). With the reification of this face, however, soulful truths must be sought out in the excess that is the body. The potentially revelatory capabilities of high quality image technology concordantly become secondary to *any* indexical representation of bare skin, no matter how degraded. The blurry, authentic torso takes prece-dence over the clear, constructed face.

Low-tech pleasures

Indeed, it is in some way the low-tech status of the magazines which endows them with their relatively strong feeling of indexical authority. For example, in comparison with these magazines, celebrity-nude websites might appear to have a diminished existential bond to the star bodies presented, and the gratifications they provide are therefore qualitatively, if not also quantitatively, different. The internet's lessened sense of indexicality is connected in considerable part to its ostensible fluidity, its fugitive nature in several respects. Where the magazine images have a palpable, stable, physical reality – a colour reproduction on a glossy page – the internet image is driven by temporary electrical impulses on a computer monitor, and many of the available online images (though by no means all) have a low resolution (and hence lack the evident saturation of a quality magazine image). The greater interactivity of the computer-based medium of course also requires greater fluidity; the editor-determined photographic mosaic of the magazine gives way to the varied point-and-click options of the website. The internet image, moreover, is delivered digitally. We therefore tend to make the metonymic assumption that the source image might have itself been previ-ously digitized, that the candid celebrity nude shot might be a simulated one (as in fact many in circulation are). Of course, this could just as well be true of a magazine image (it is now standard procedure to 'Photoshop' images going into print), but the relative 'solidity' of the medium, the photo's physical delivery on a printed page, nevertheless seems to reassure us, reinforcing a sense of indexicality.

Such reassurance is furthered in that the magazine also seems more palpably rooted in terms of legal, business and production regimes. The 'publishers' of a given website may or may not in fact be a grounded legal enterprise, but magazine publishers at the very least need access to an infrastructure for extensive layout and design work, delivery of paper stock and ink and chemicals, printing of the publication and physical distribution. *Celebrity Skin* and *Celebrity Sleuth* in fact have each been in print for some time (the former dating back to 1979, the latter to 1987), and are part of established business enterprises with numerous legal and business ties. (*Skin* is published by the company that produces the better known men's magazine *High Society*.) There is thus a literal 'paper trail' for all they do, and one assumes that these publications would potentially have more to lose by presenting a simulated image as real, both because there would be immediate hard evidence of this (the actual magazine in question) and because an entire established business could be held liable. And the publications are indeed aware that they are selling this strong sense of reliability: *Celebrity Sleuth*'s website proudly declares in bold type, 'We offer a money back guarantee if you can find any "fakes" in issues you order!'

On the other hand, a nude celebrity website may not be part of such an established and physically-based network and may simply exist one day and be gone the next; we are therefore less likely to trust the veracity of the images presented on such websites, some of which openly indicate that they cannot vouch for the authenticity of all photos and that some images may have been picked up 'floating around' on the internet. The better known celebrity nude websites not surprisingly go out of their way to assure prospective customers of the authenticity of their material. '100% Real! No Fakes!' Mr Skin's website promises, while The Celeb Club's online advertising emphasizes again and again that they are a longstanding, respected enterprise, and devotes an entire page of their online tour to discussing their honesty. A further striking commonality between the two aforementioned websites is their emphasis on voluminous databases of film clips and stills fully accessible by subscribers – as though the sites must fetishize the electronic 'presence' of massive quantities of searchable data in order to disavow the physical 'absence' of the printed page of old.

Another defining characteristic of these nude celebrity texts (one which is quite obvious but nonetheless significant) is that the bare skin to which I have referred is primarily female. There is occasional male nudity in the magazines, but it usually occurs in photographs emphasizing a female nude, the subject of a given spread. One regular exception is *Celebrity Skin*'s 'Grin and Bear It' section, which features paparazzi and other press photos of accidental exposures of skin or other embarrassing public moments; many issues include one or more male stars within this section. In some cases, sections *are* organized around male celebrities, but feature nude images primarily not of them, but of women associated with them.[4] Certainly this is dictated in part by the generic tendencies of skin magazines (and websites) more broadly; the gender inequities of pornography, whatever their socioeconomic and psychoanalytic causes, are repeated here. But I would also note that the overwhelming emphasis on female star nudity conforms with the distinctive, and degraded, status of the female celebrity, in Hollywood culture in particular. As is often noted within the industry, while male celebrities can succeed on a distinctive personality and/or skills alone, female celebrities are generally assumed to need first to conform to conventions of sexual attractiveness and physical beauty in order to succeed. Even then, the assumption is that such success will inevitably be short-lived compared with that of a male celebrity of similar stature, and the salaries she can command reflect this. I would suggest that while the preponderance of female nudes in these magazines is largely a function of their positioning as pornography for heterosexual males, it also bears a relation to the high commercial valuation and paradoxically low cultural status of the female body in Hollywood.

Taking out the trash

It should be clear by this point that part of what distinguishes these magazines is that they work to reinforce and highlight rather than disguise the disreputable, voyeuristic side of filmic spectatorship. To the degree that this is so (and as my various refuse analogies would further suggest), such publications and their readers particularly bear comparison to what has been called 'trash cinema' (or more recently, 'paracinema') and its adherents. Trash cinema is generally understood as encompassing various kinds of cinematic texts and practices which have been 'discarded' by others for being below or beyond widely accepted standards of morality, social value, cinematic technique or narrative comprehensibility. In one of the most significant academic discussions of this phenomenon, Jeffrey Sconce emphasizes the practices integral to this formulation, contending that: 'Paracinema is ... less a distinct group of films than a particular reading protocol, a counter-aesthetic turned subcultural sensibility devoted to all manner of cultural detritus' (1995: 372). Sconce emphasizes that this reading strategy is a distinctly oppositional one, aiming to confront reigning cultural parameters of 'good taste'. The paracinematic reader does this in part by looking for 'excess' (the distinctively trashy elements, as it were) in the film text and then interpreting such elements not in terms of an abstract formal system (a traditional 'art cinema' reading strategy) but as socially and culturally significant – pointing, for example, to the social and industrial deviance of the director. Thus, Sconce argues, the paracinematic strategy allows the reader to 'see through' surface levels of the text to the original marginalized context of production (ibid.: 389).[5]

The reader of the nude celebrity magazine is likewise, in a somewhat more literal sense, trying to 'see through' film and star texts by way of an alternate reading strategy, one that, as I've explained, creates or amplifies certain cracks in the star discourse and exploits these for voyeuristic gratification. One would be hard-pressed to call this reading strategy an oppositional or confrontational one, nor I think could we describe a subculture of celebrity skin magazine readers as having the cohesiveness of the paracinematic subculture. Yet I think the comparison of these reading strategies may be illuminating. The celebrity-nude magazine reader is, like the paracinematic reader, interested in exploring cinematic dregs. However, for the magazine reader, these are to be found not in marginalized texts but primarily in mainstream ones, and it is here, precisely, that the gratification lies. To extend the analogy, these are the dregs which are left after the consumption of what might be a perfectly respectable cup of Hollywood tea, an excess which is always present but not ordinarily the focus of attention. The magazines in effect work to bring these dregs to the surface for closer reader scrutiny and gratification, or – should the text be too 'clean' – to attempt to 'dig up dirt' of some sort, to *generate* an excess even where none previously existed.[6]

What the magazine audience practises, then, is not so much an oppositional reading strategy as an ancillary one (and a largely closeted and atomized one at that), a supplementary means of gaining increased pleasure from film and star texts which does not really negate (and in fact arguably illuminates) more typical, publicly practised reading strategies. It is more a way of leering at, and rendering intermittently lewd, rather than undermining or destroying, Hollywood texts with a broad popularity. This tone of grinning lewdness is possibly most evident in the textual address of *Celebrity Sleuth*, a commentary which perhaps suggests more than anything else the sexually punning, tongue-in-cheek articulations of an announcer at a burlesque show. For example, in the 'stacked' issue on 'treasured chests', a photo caption declares, 'Let's hope the *dual talents* of Heather Graham keep audiences laughing for a long, *lung* time' (2000: 91). In a spread on Helen Hunt, the organ complains, 'the closest [*Twister* (1996)] ever comes to depicting *graphic* sex is to show a few houses getting *blown*' (10/3, 1997: 18). The back cover of the magazine is usually reserved for a backside view of a clothed actress, with a caption along the lines of 'DAISY FUENTES Ass-erts: "They Couldn't Get Me to Put My Clothes Back On at the END of the Day!"' (1998). While Fuentes likely had not anticipated the ends for which her image would be used when she turned around to smile at the photographer, the lewd captioning could hardly be construed as a radical deconstruction of her star image. The aforementioned Mr Skin website concretizes this kind of implied burlesque-show narrator in the form of its eponymous figurehead, drawn as an immaculately coiffed 1950s bachelor, whose witticisms appear throughout the website and whose grinning visage is superimposed on the corners of video clips.

To bring this essay to its own end, then, *Celebrity Skin* and other similar publications highlight through their textual strategies a number of distinctive facets of our celebrity culture, in particular a fascination with getting at the 'authentic' aspects of stars' existences and the association of this authenticity with the unregulated body. Employing a lewd, tongue-in-cheek humour, the magazines cultivate and cater to a voyeuristic desire for the 'dregs' of star imagery, a desire which may in fact go to the heart (or get to the bottom) of our interest in celebrities.

In fostering this desire and simultaneously functioning as pornography, these star texts are in some respects more exploitative than most. Performers' private lives are deeply scrutinized, while their images are used for highly sexualized purposes – purposes they might well have not intended. Their skins become the chief currency in an eroticized economy of information in which they do not wield primary control and which bears them no direct returns. But at the same time, I would mention in closing, the texts are not without their more progressive dimensions. First, they constitute star counter-discourses to some degree in that, as noted, they largely bypass the usual industrial regulation of celebrity information, subverting in some (perhaps minor) measure the aims of the starmaking machinery and opening up a different perspective on the star. And second, I think it is important to note that these texts do reassert, on some level, the material, physical, human reality of the celebrity. Dyer, deCordova and Gamson all take some note of the fact that the living star is not merely a set of discourses but also a person, a worker, a body.[7] In reinscribing and privileging this body, albeit in an exploitative fashion, these magazines force us to take note, at least briefly, of the material reality of the performer that provides the foundation for the star.

Notes

1 A brief note on method: I did not use a 'scientific sampling' here (back issues of these magazines are not held in academic libraries), nor was it necessary for my particular purposes specifically, to analyse some tendencies in the rhetoric of these magazines. That said, I did procure a substantial sample of magazines for each of two years, seven years apart. I looked at seven of the eighteen issues published in 1997 (that is, nine each of *Celebrity Skin* and *Celebrity Sleuth*), and nine of the eighteen published in 2004, along with various additional issues from 1996–2004.

2 See Gamson (1994), chapter 3, for an account of the 'semifictional' event in celebrity marketing.

3 This presupposes, of course, that the image is photographic in nature. All of the constructions of authenticity discussed here are premised, in part, on the assumption of the image's indexical link to the person originally photographed (famously emphasized in the writings of André Bazin). See Dyer's discussion of this precondition in 'A Star is Born' (1991), pp. 135–6.

4 For example, *Celebrity Sleuth* 10/2 (1996) offers a 'Trophy Wives' section; while *Celebrity Skin* 19/63 (November 1997) includes a 'Stern Girls' segment comprised of photos of models and actresses associated with Howard Stern; and *Celebrity Sleuth* 15/1 (2002) focuses on women connected with male celebrities in sections titled '"Talk" is Cheap', 'Stud's Muffins', and 'Support Ho's'.

5 Sconce here cites Fiske's account of how various kinds of knowledge increase (to quote Fiske) 'the power of the fan to "see through" to the production processes normally hidden by the text' (1992: 43).

6 The choice of terminology here should suggest a comparison with work in cultural studies that argues that various kinds of popular texts – those in electronic media in particular – are by nature messy and 'dirty' in the sense of having a semiotic excess beyond complete institutional control; see, for example, John Hartley (1983), 'Encouraging Signs: Television and the Power of Dirt, Speech and Other Scandalous Categories', *Australian Journal of Cultural Studies* 1/2: 62–82.

7 See, for example, Dyer, 'A Star is Born', pp. 135–7, and *Heavenly Bodies: Film Stars and Society* (New York: St Martin's Press, 1986), introduction; deCordova, pp. 110–11; and Gamson, p. 58.

Bibliography

Balazs, Bela (1970) *Theory of the Film: Character and Growth of a New Art*, trans. Edith Bone, New York: Dover.

Celeb Club web page (accessed 18 March 2005).

Celebrity Skin (1997) 19/59 (May).

Celebrity Skin (1997) 19/63 (November).

Celebrity Skin (2004) 28/133 (October).

Celebrity Sleuth (1996) 10/2.

Celebrity Sleuth (1997) 10/3.

Celebrity Sleuth (1997) 10/7.

Celebrity Sleuth (1998) 11/2.

Celebrity Sleuth (2000) 13/4.

Celebrity Sleuth (2002) 15/1.

Celebrity Sleuth web page (accessed 18 March 2005).

deCordova, Richard (1990) *Picture Personalities: The Emergence of the Star System in America*, Urbana: University of Illinois Press.

Dyer, Richard(1986) *Heavenly Bodies: Film Stars and Society*, New York: St Martin's Press, pp.135–7.

—— (1991) 'A Star is Born and the Construction of Authenticity', in Christine Gledhill (ed.), *Stardom: Industry of Desire*, London: Routledge, pp. 132–40

Ellis, John (1982) *Visible Fictions*, London: Routledge.

Fiske, John (1992) 'The Cultural Economy of Fandom', in Lisa A. Lewis (ed.), *The Adoring Audience: Fan Culture and Popular Media*, London: Routledge, pp. 30–49.

Gamson, Joshua (1994) *Claims to Fame: Celebrity in Contemporary America*, Berkeley: University of California Press.

Hartley, John (1983) 'Encouraging Signs: Television and the Power of Dirt, Speech and Other Scandalous Categories', *Australian Journal of Cultural Studies* 1/2: 62–82.

Metz, Christian (1982) *Psychoanalysis and Cinema: The Imaginary Signifier*, trans. Ben Brewster, London: Macmillan.

Mr Skin web page (accessed 18 March 2005).

Sconce, Jeffrey (1995) 'Trashing the Academy: Taste, Excess, and an Emerging Politics of Cinematic Style', *Screen* 36/4 (Winter): 371–93.

Williams, Linda (1990) *Hard Core: Power, Pleasure and the 'Frenzy of the Visible'*, Berkeley: University of California Press.

Wolfe, Charles (1991) 'The Return of Jimmy Stewart: The Publicity Photogroph as Text, in Christine Gledhill (ed.), *Stardom: Industry of Desire*, London: Routledge.

Chapter 10

Get a famous body

Star styles and celebrity gossip in *heat* magazine

Rebecca Feasey

Introduction

Extant literature in the field of star studies has routinely focused on the contrast that is seen to exist between the work of the actor on screen and the offscreen lifestyle of the performer. According to Richard Dyer, the disparity exists between the glamorous film world and the surprisingly ordinary domestic life of the Hollywood star (Dyer, 2004: 35). Although this dual nature of film stardom remains relevant today, it is often suggested that interest in – and information about – any given star focuses on what happens outside the sphere of their work, rather than on the skill or craft of performance. For example, while Richard deCordova states that the star system only developed when 'picture personalities' outgrew the textuality of their pictures (deCordova, 1990: 98), Christine Gledhill suggests that actors only become stars when their offscreen lifestyle overshadows their acting ability (Gledhill, 1991: xiv). Although this duality of image is clearly evident in the sphere of film stardom, it can also be seen to exist in relation to other sports and entertainment industries. In this way, both contemporary film stars and other celebrity figures are 'highly visible through the media; and their private lives attract greater public interest than their profes-sional lives' (Turner, 2004: 3).

Although public figures ranging from Brad Pitt to David Beckham can be understood as contemporary figures whose public life seems to take on more importance than their professional careers, it is worth noting that it is women rather than men who 'are particularly likely to be seen as celebrities whose working life is of less interest and worth than their personal life' (Geraghty, 2000: 187). For example, Christine Geraghty notes that 'Liz Hurley's work as a model and actress [has] contributed less to her celebrity status than Versace dresses and an errant boyfriend' (ibid.: 187). However, while existing work suggests that the media routinely 'write vacuous nonsense about famous women – their appearance, their fluctuating weight, their dress sense' (Gritten, 2002: 33), I would argue that such celebrity reporting can be seen not simply as a trivial or tyrannical comment which privileges appearance over talent, or attractiveness over ability, but rather as a potentially empowering discourse for the female reader.

This chapter will focus on *heat* magazine in its role as 'the bible of contemporary celebrity culture' (Llewellyn-Smith, 2002: 114), and consider the ways in which this particular title can be read as an empowering post-feminist text that validates feminine meanings and competences for the female reader. I am using the term post-feminist here to point to those contemporary discourses of gender within the field of media and cultural studies which suggest that shopping and consumption can be understood as a 'means to self-expression and control' (Curran, 2000: 239).

Celebrity gossip and reader's lifestyle

heat magazine was first launched in February 1999 as a film and television weekly aimed at contemporary young women, or more precisely, at the '18–34 year old fashion-conscious shopaholic' (Emap, 2005b: online). However, even though Emap, a company famed for publishing such successful titles as *FHM*, *Arena* and *New Woman*, had spent close to £4 million on the launch of this particular magazine, *heat* was failing to entice or excite its target demographic. In fact, the circulation figures were so low that the magazine would have closed if it had not repositioned itself (Media Week, 2001: online). In May 2000 *heat* was transformed in both tone and content so as to include star fashions, celebrity features and 'unapproved' gossip. This change of focus brought what has been described as 'Lazarus like' sale increases (Media Week, 2001: online) and helped to situate the title as a market leader in the celebrity gossip sector. In fact, despite heavy competition from other glossy gossip weeklies, *heat* currently sells over 540,000 copies every week (Emap, 2005c: online). According to the Audit Bureau of Circulation, the magazine 'continues to be Emap's biggest consumer magazine in the UK, worth over £40m in newsstand revenues alone' (ibid.).

heat is part fashion bible, part gossip magazine, and part television listings guide. However, for the purpose of this particular chapter, I am going to focus on those star fashions and celebrity gossip features that attract the target reader. After all, *heat* carved out a niche among young female readers based precisely on the publication's dedication to star scandals and celebrity coverage (see also Holmes, 2005: 21–38).[1] The presentation of celebrity gossip is so important to *heat* that the magazine's own profile highlights the significance of stylish stars and celebrity reporting to its weekly content, stating that it is 'packed with exclusive interviews, up-to-date gossip and photos of our favourite stars' (Emap, 2005a: online). What is most interesting here is the fact that that those images of fashion and style that are regularly presented in the magazine are the very same images that are being discussed in recent work on contemporary feminism (Brunsdon, 1987: 81–104; Hollows, 2000: 190–204; Read, 2000: 3–21). As such, it is relevant to employ a post-feminist reading of the celebrity-obsessed and style-conscious text in question. However, before I introduce such a reading, it is necessary to situate this work within existing literature on women's glossy magazines and gossip publications respectively.

Reading women's magazines

Much feminist work on glossy women's magazines has focused on why women should not read such populist gendered texts. For example, while Susan Douglas is 'outraged [by the] unattainable standards of wealth and beauty' (Douglas, 1995: 9) presented here, Naomi Wolf challenges these texts for their role in the growth of what she sees as the destructive beauty and plastic surgery industries (Wolf, 1991). If one considers that glossy magazines traditionally focus on 'shopping, sex and cellulite' (Craig, 1998: 26, cited in Gough-Yates, 2003: 132), then one might suggest that feminist concerns about such publications are pertinent to a discussion of *heat* magazine in its role as a gossip publication dedicated to star styles and celebrity reporting. Furthermore, a consideration of existing women's magazines becomes even more relevant when we find that such publications have recently increased their focus on the sphere of celebrity. In this same way, existing work on weekly gossip publications routinely configures these texts as a problem for the female reader. It has been suggested that if women's magazines are derided for their role in the oppression of the modern woman, then the reader of gossip magazines is introduced as a 'woman untouched by feminism, their main concerns being marriage and parenthood' (Bird, 1992: 76).

Women's glossies and female-defined gossip publications have been dismissed for their role in the subjugation of women, and as such, one might look to dismiss *heat* magazine for its own focus on fashion, beauty and entertainment news. However, before I condemn *heat* in line with existing debates surrounding the role and responsibility of women's magazines, it is worth noting that not all feminist media scholars have set out to censure the reading of such seemingly superficial texts. For example, Anna Gough-Yates explains the appeal of the glossy magazine formula based on the fact that such magazines are 'in touch with women's lives' (Gough-Yates, 2003: 138). By this, Gough-Yates means that the magazines put the 'emphasis on women's sexual confidence and independence' (Gough-Yates, 2003: 137). Likewise, gossip publications can also be applauded for validating feminine meanings and competences. For example, while Elizabeth

Bird reclaims gossip publications for their focus on the personal (Bird, 1992: 160), Mary Ellen Brown supports the discourse of gossip for its ability to cater 'to women's interest in each other's lives' (Brown, 1994: 31). With this in mind, this chapter will consider the ways in which a post-feminist reading of *heat* can be seen to validate the magazine based on its commitment to the famous body through fashion, beauty and celebrity reporting.[2] However, before I begin to examine the ways in which discourses of style, shopping, or star scandals can be taken up as positive frames of reference for the reader, it is necessary for me to introduce the tone, content and style of the magazine in question.

'Star Style': the pleasures and paradoxes of consumption

heat regularly presents a range of features on star style and celebrity fashions – be it designer casual wear, vintage clothing or glamorous red-carpet gowns. In this way, one might suggest that that the reader can look to the gossip publication as a quick, easy and entertaining way to browse contemporary styles and fashion trends on a seemingly endless array of beautiful stars and glamorous celebrities. However, rather than dedicate its star style pages to the exclusive, vintage, or couture of celebrity clothing and expect the 'fashion-conscious' (Emap, 2005b: online) reader to live somewhat vicariously through such exquisite yet often unattainable clothing, it is worth noting that the magazine encourages the female reader to both try on and buy such feminine fashions.

In the 'Steal Her Style' feature one celebrity is picked out for her fashionable ensemble which is then recreated from high-street stores so that the reader can choose to 'try on' the look of today's fashionable stars. Moreover, although *heat* encourages the reader to look at stylish celebrities as possible models of fashionable femininity to try on from week to week, the magazine also encourages the reader to consume such feminine fashions. For example, 'Steal Her Style' tells the reader how to recreate the star style of Angelina Jolie for the 'total cost of £146.99' (2–8 October 2004: 54), how to emulate Kylie's look for the 'total cost of £355.50' (23–29 October 2004: 56) and how to transform your wardrobe à la Cat Deeley for the 'total cost of £336.29' (22–28 January 2005: 52). Furthermore, features such as 'That's so a Good Look' and 'Now Buy it!' go further to encourage female spending. While 'That's so a Good Look' is a photospread of celebrity figures from the world of film, television, music and modelling who are all immaculately dressed according to the week's chosen fashion theme, be it 'Floral Prints' (17–23 July 2004: 52), 'Wrap Dresses' (11–17 September 2004: 60) or 'Flat Shoes' (12–18 February 2005: 44), 'Now Buy it!' offers the reader not only one possible high-street alternative but a range of inexpensive substitutes to those designer trends favoured by the stars.

Although one might suggest that *heat*'s dedication to budget fashion shopping could be understood as part of the wider domestic and spendthrift economy as presented in the women's magazine sector, it is clear that this particular title makes no attempt to advise the reader on their food, transport or social spending beyond the fashion sphere. However, before condemning the title for encouraging such spending, one needs to consider the pleasures at stake for the female reader who can earn and enjoy a sense of celebrity membership through such commodity consumption. After all, we rarely buy clothes and fashion accessories because we need them, but rather because we would

> like to project a certain image of ourselves … to align ourselves with like-minded others, to remind ourselves who we are and who we'd like to be … in short, our motivation is much more to do with aspirations and wants than needs (Cashmore, 2002: 133).

However, in the 'Steal Her Style' fashion feature, what is particularly interesting here is the way in which the magazine applauds star styles based entirely on the appearance of a particular personality, irrespective of the women's success or failures in their chosen careers as actress, entertainer or presenter. My point is that *heat* makes no distinction between a Hollywood star, a successful film and television actress, an international singing phenomenon, a respected designer, a national television presenter or IT girl in her role as a fashion icon. Rather, *heat* seems to be providing evidence of the fact that fame is a process, a consequence of the way in which individuals are treated by the media. According to David Giles,

> the brutal reality of the modern age is that all famous people are treated like celebrities by the mass media, whether they be a great political figure, a worthy campaigner, an artist … , a serial killer or … one of the participants in a … reality TV programme. The newspapers and television programs responsible for their publicity do not draw any meaningful distinction between how they are publicised (Giles, 2000: 5).

At a time when research into the field of stardom and celebrity is looking to break down the more obvious career distinctions between film actors, television performers, musicians and other public figures in favour of defining broader categories of celebrity via accident, achievement or lineage (Monaco, 1978; Gamson, 1994; Rojek, 2001), so too *heat* pays scant attention to career distinctions or divisions in the celebrity sphere. Instead, the publication is concerned to disclose specific types of consumer knowledge in terms of 'what to buy, where from, how to wear it and what to wear it with' (Skeggs, 1997: 103), rather than trying to offer a commentary on the nature of celebrity by discriminating between singer, stylist or socialite. One might even go as far as to suggest that the magazine is operating like a conventional manufacturing industry in that it produces a steady supply of standardized, formulaic, interchangeable 'fashionable' faces for the reader to emulate and admire.

If contemporary feminist theorists are to consider the ways in which *heat* magazine encourages the female reader to become an enthusiastic consumer of fashion styles, it is worth noting that there exists a long-standing and negative link between feminism, fashion and female consumerism. However, while a dedication to feminine fashion and beauty practices has been seen as a problem by the second-wave, it is worth considering the ways in which those feminine dress codes and the role of female consumerism encouraged by *heat* magazine can be understood as part of the contemporary feminist agenda. After all, the emphasis on feminine fashions and beauty practices is one way in which feminist concerns have entered into mainstream popular forms (Brunsdon, 1987: 81–104; Read, 2000: 3–21).[3] In her research on post-feminism and shopping films, Charlotte Brunsdon highlights differences between 1970s feminism and contemporary feminism in relation to ideas about consumption, femininity and identity:

> 1970s feminism, in both Britain and the USA, arose partly out of the New Left and Civil Rights and anti-war movement, and generally involved women with access to higher education [and] was anti-consumption. Ideas of identity ... were marked by notions of sincerity, expression, truth-telling. 1990s feminism, in contrast, partly through the 1980s feminist defence of 'women's genres' such as fashion, soap opera and women's magazines, is permissive and even enthusiastic about consumption. Wearing lipstick is no longer wicked, and notions of identity have moved away from a rational/moral axis and are much more profoundly informed by ideas of performance, style and desire (Brunsdon, 1997: 85).

One might suggest that the contemporary feminist views fashionable femininity, as evidenced in *heat* magazine, as a sign of the female consumer being in control not only of her wardrobe but also of her sexuality and social situation (Crane, 2003: 315; Roach and Eicher, 1965: 187). For example, while Joanne Entwistle's research on fashion and dress finds that a dedication to style and consumerism is a positive way of coping with the trials and tribulations of contemporary society (Entwistle, 2000: 139), Susan Douglas' work on commercial advertising argues that today's advertisers assure women that 'control comes from cosmetics' and the other accoutrements of contemporary femininity (Curran, 2000: 239). In this same way, Sarah Berry challenges the long-standing and negative link between feminine fashions and female oppression by stating that consumer fashion has the power to be subversive; after all, features such as 'Steal

Her Style' and 'Now Buy it!' encourage what have been termed 'fantasies of self-transformation' (Berry, 2000: 185).

I have suggested that *heat* magazine's dedication to surface appearance and celebrity fashions can be understood as a site of post-feminist empowerment within the field of media and cultural studies. But it is also worth noting that the magazine is post-feminist in the more popular understanding of the term, in the sense that it addresses conventionally feminine concerns of clothes and beauty culture, and is centrally occupied with questions of femininity (Moseley, 2002: 7). For example, according to *The F-Word*, an online journal committed to 'encouraging a new sense of community among UK feminists' (Redfern, 2004: online), feminine fashions, beauty practices and female consumerism can be championed as part of the contemporary feminist project. *The F-Word* suggests that fashion is a source of power for young women in contemporary society:

> Young feminists have reclaimed everything traditionally feminine, including a love of dressing up and fashion. Feminism has reclaimed the girlie look. Nail painting is a pleasure, not selling out the sisterhood. The babydoll look is an ironic riot grrrl comment. Lippy is no more than something to express yourself, to make yourself loud and proud. Feminists can take enjoyment in fashion now (Redfern, 2001: online).

If one considers that contemporary feminism is enthusiastic about the role of feminine fashions and female consumerism, and that *heat* magazine regularly presents these selfsame notions of style and shopping, then one might suggest that the celebrity gossip publication positions its fashion-conscious female reader as a contemporary feminist. One might even go as far as arguing that *heat* magazine not only defines its readers in terms of the post-feminist agenda but actually helped to bring this empowered image of woman into being. Either way, the glossy pages of *heat* provide a space where women's dedication to surface appearance and attractiveness can be recognized as a valuable, and more importantly, as an available cultural force.

Star style and the fashion faux pas

According to Graeme Turner's work on mass market celebrity magazines, we are told that '*OK*, *heat* and *Hello!* woo their readers by offering positive pictures and gossip features about celebrities' (Turner, 2004: 73). In this way, such titles are seen as 'promotional outlets for carefully managed and produced publicity' (Gamson, 1994: 105). However, although I have argued that *heat* provides the reader with a fashionable shop window in which star styles are on display, it is worth noting that the magazine does not only present contemporary celebrities as flawless models of fashionable femininity but that it is keen to expose a range of celebrity fashion faux pas. The reader is routinely told that celebrity fashion disasters or successes don't go unnoticed or unrewarded in the magazine (22–28 January 2005: 20–1). For example, in a feature entitled 'Golden Globe Outfit Awards 2005', *heat*'s prizes are made up of both 'the good' outfits and 'the bad' in the celebrity sphere (29 January–4 February 2005: 4–5).

heat can be seen as an arbiter of fashion tastes, dictating which star styles to try on and which celebrity fashions to avoid. Taking its cue from American couturier Richard Blackwell and his infamous 'worst dressed' lists, *heat* regularly presents a feature entitled 'What Were You Thinking'. 'What Were You Thinking', as the name suggests, is an item committed to exposing those fashion faux pas of the entertainment world; be it Rachel Stevens' 'sparkle encrusted all-in-one' (24–30 July 2004: 76), Winona Ryder's 'shapeless sack' (4–10 September 2004: 68) or Teri Hatcher's 'highlighter-pen pink leisure wear' (5–11 February 2005: 68). The point here is simply that those outfits that are not flattering to the eye are deemed fashion mistakes while those that create an aesthetically pleasing image are applauded. However, unlike Blackwell's annual poll, *heat* does not draw the line at mocking what it sees as style disasters or fashion mistakes, but rather, seems to take particular pleasure in revealing those physical imperfections that the celebrity has unwittingly exposed to the camera.

A range of short features entitled 'Scandal!', 'Look Closer', 'Spotted' and '100% Unapproved: Stars Making Utter Fools of Themselves' form a mock pull-out section of the magazine, and it is this particular section that is testament to *heat*'s zealous reportage of unapproved celebrity exposure. According to Su Holmes's recent work on the construction, circulation and consumption of fame in *heat* magazine, such unapproved features are 'based upon the "capturing" of the celebrity through a more explicitly unflattering lens. This may simply be an unforgiving facial expression, pose or situation ... or images displaying everything from a protruding stomach ... to spots' (Holmes, 2005: 26). The pleasure of such candid photography lies in the exposure of celebrities' physical imperfections, as if the discovery of 'Kylie's dimples' (15–21 January 2005: 65), 'Paris' peek-a-boo padding' (29 January–4 February 2005: 65) or 'Tara's Scary Bumps' (12–18 February 2005: 65) somehow penetrates the fashionable façade in favour of revealing a more realistic or authentic presentation of the celebrity body in question. Journalist Caspar Llewellyn-Smith makes this point when he states that the guiding principle of celebrity gossip magazines is to show famous figures 'off-guard, unkempt, unready and unsanitized' (Llewellyn-Smith, 2002: 120, cited in Holmes, 2005: 23). *heat*'s dedication to unflattering and unapproved celebrity images provides evidence of a shift in fashion reporting as the magazine seems to be playing with the conventions and modalities of existing fashion titles such as *Vogue* (1892–) and *Harpers & Queen* (1929–). After all, *heat* both resists and subverts those carefully choreographed images and post-produced photo-shoots that allow today's celebrities to appear picture-perfect. In this way, the magazine can be seen to encourage the reader to negotiate those managed and manicured images routinely seen in established fashion publications.

heat demonstrates that today's film stars, supermodels and television personalities should not simply be admired as flawless fashion icons. Instead, the magazine makes it clear that such celebrities should be seen as ordinary women with extraordinary wardrobes. After all, the very nature of stardom itself is based on the combination of 'the spectacular with the everyday, the special with the ordinary' (Dyer, 2004: 35). One reader's letter highlights this particular duality of image when she says 'Stars without make-up, Great, I can see celebs as normal people, just like you and me' (23–29 October 2004). Such reader responses are revealing as they can be seen to challenge existing work on star–audience relationships as notions of 'worship' (Stacey, 1994: 142–3) and 'transcendence' (Stacey, 1994: 145–51) are replaced by a less exalted form of fascination.

I am not suggesting that the reader does not find pleasure in the seemingly flawless fashions and perfect physiques that the celebrity often presents, but rather that *heat's* focus on spots, cellulite and ill-concealed (or ill-conceived) padding encourages the reader to negotiate such images. For example, when the magazine tells the reader that 'Welsh wonder [Charlotte Church] has got the voice of an Angel and the body of a cherub' (29 January–4 February 2005: 12) the magazine does not mock the singer for her weight gain but rather thanks her for proving that celebrities can and indeed do face 'the same body worries as we do' (ibid.: 9–10). In this same way an interview with Geri Halliwell ends with the reporter looking at the singer's cellulite. Once again the magazine does not ridicule the woman for her unruly body but rather presents this physical imperfection as 'a reassuring sight' (27 November–3 December 2004: 4) to be shared with the magazine's readership. Furthermore, although *heat* regularly exposes celebrity imperfections to the reader, the magazine also goes to great lengths to reveal the ways in which celebrities construct and maintain their impeccable physiques through diet, exercise and cosmetic surgery.

'Get a Famous Body': constructing celebrity

There exists a long history of glamorous film stars sharing their body-shaping secrets with the star-struck female reader. For example, as far back as 1921, the movie fan magazine *Photoplay* 'ran a series titled "How I keep in Condition" with monthly instalments by such stars as Corinne Griffith and Marion Davies' (Addison, 2000: 21). Therefore, while *heat's* regular features on body-shaping are nothing new to the world of celebrity reporting, I would suggest that the tone of such features has undergone a dramatic transformation.

Although one might suggest that *heat*'s dedication to 'the art of body mainte-nance' (Coward, 1985: 21) is tyrannical in its unrealistic and unattainable presen-tation of the perfect body (Douglas, 1995: 260), it is worth noting that *heat* foregrounds diet, exercise and cosmetic surgery in order to both construct and undermine what constitutes the female star's body. With this in mind, I would suggest that the magazine regularly features articles on celebrity health and beauty practices as evidence of the time, money and energy that celebrities spend in order to present themselves as flawless figures. Therefore, rather than assume that the reader could or should follow such beauty or health advice, such tips can act as a reminder of the stringent health regimes faced by today's stars as they strive to both create and maintain the perfect body. The reader is told that celeb-rities such as Beyoncé Knowles and Elizabeth Hurley are not effortlessly thin women; rather, these performers have to work at constructing and maintaining their perfect physique through a calculated and controlled diet (1–7 January 2005: 14; 26 February–4 March 2005: 41).

In the same way, the magazine's focus on celebrity fitness does not simply concentrate on naturally lithe and slender images of contemporary celebrities but rather takes great care to reveal the 'before' and 'after' of such exercise regimes. For example, in a feature entitled 'Amazing Body Makeovers' (8–14 January 2005: 4–10) the reader is presented with dramatic transformations including what they term 'tubby to trim' (ibid.: 4), 'pot belly to washboard' (ibid.: 10) and 'boxy to foxy' (ibid.: 7). The magazine goes to great lengths to remind us that each and every transformation has been and will continue to be hard work for the celebrity in question. For example, the reader is informed that soap star Nikki Sanderson has to run and swim regularly to maintain her physique (ibid.: 4), that pop singer Kimberley Walsh has to spend hours working out in the gym (ibid.: 10) while actress Lindsay Lohan has had to 'work damn hard' (ibid.: 7) in order to stay in shape.

Although it has previously been suggested that 'with exercise refined to a science in late nineties culture, the star's body has become the object for mass display and emulation as once were the costumes that adorned it' (Epstein, 2000: 191), my point here is simply that contemporary stars are not presented as effortless beauties or with naturally perfect figures but rather as women having to make sacrifices in order to appear well toned and perfectly coiffed for public interaction. Therefore, although a reader may well want to emulate the physiques of such famous figures and choose to purchase a personality's work-out book or exercise video, or some celebrity-endorsed exercise equipment, the same reader may not be prepared either to survive on 'Liz Hurley's watercress wonder' (1–7 January 2005: 13) or 'work like a squaddie' (8–14 January 2005: 7) to achieve the celebrity body. Plea-sure lies in the knowledge that these celebrity figures have to diet and exercise to maintain such seemingly effortless appearances.

Sean Redmond has made a similar point concerning the ways in which British women's magazine adverts draw attention to the amount of work that goes into being thin. Redmond argues that even though the reader is made aware of the ways in which the women in these adverts are seen to 'go to work on their bodies in ever more extreme ways' (Redmond, 2003: 175), such images still wield tremendous ideological power in terms of coercing the reader to take part in the 'tyranny of slenderness' (Redmond, 2003: 181) that he sees operating in such images. However, unlike Redmond, I would suggest that such reporting in *heat* magazine does not pressurize the reader to work towards an idealized celebrity physique but rather may liberate the reader from feeling inadequate for failing to create her own celebrity body. This negotiation is hinted at in a feature on Elizabeth Hurley's new swimwear range:

> We don't know about you, but most of us here at *heat* Towers are still trying to fight the flab from Christmas and the New Year ... So you can imagine our dismay when we spotted these pictures of Liz Hurley ... looking frankly amazing as she posed for a photo shoot for her new ... swimwear range. But then she does eat just one big meal a day and snacks on raisins. How dull. Maybe we'll keep our curves after all (26 February–4 March 2005: 41).[4]

Although the feature is somewhat flippant in tone, it nevertheless exposes and dismisses the hidden labour and labourers necessary to maintain the celebrity body. Moreover, it is worth noting that the magazine can be seen to offer a more serious commentary on the recent trend for dramatic weight loss in the celebrity sphere. A feature entitled 'you are *too* thin!' condemns excessive dieting and food deprivation, foregrounding the hidden health risks rather than the surface beauty of such calorie counting (6–12 November 2004: 87). The article offers words of caution and advice to the reader in order to discourage her from emulating this particular celebrity trend, and the accompanying photo-spread goes further to reinforce this notion, with 'before' and 'after' pictures of celebrities that reveal how women such as Nicole Kidman, Sophie Dahl and Saffron Burrows, once seen by the magazine as radiant, now look fragile and gaunt. More recently the magazine has applauded stars such as Britney Spears and Courtney Love for putting weight on their previously slender frames. Although the phrase 'stars pile on the pounds' (19–25 February 2005: 16–17) might initially appear derogatory, the article makes it clear that it commends these women for transcending rigid diet regimes and excessive exercise programmes in favour of challenging those stereotypes of physical perfection that have been said to encourage eating disorders and cosmetic surgery as part of what feminist theorists have termed the beauty myth.

With this in mind, the magazine can also be seen to question the role of cosmetic surgery in contemporary society. *heat* makes it clear that 'having plastic surgery isn't always the miracle makeover stars hope for' (27 November–3 December 2004: 82) and, as such, implies that such surgery will not necessary be the miracle makeover that the reader may crave. The magazine goes to great lengths to point out cases where the disfiguring telltale signs of surgery such as 'bulging bottom lips' (27 November–3 December 2004: 85), 'liposuction dents' (27 November–3 December 2004: 85) and 'misshapen breasts' (27 November–3 December 2004: 86) are clearly evident on a host of celebrity bodies. The point here is that *heat* clearly offers its own ideological agenda concerning weight loss and plastic surgery as 'the new celebrity obsession' (12–18 February 2005). At a time when glossy women's monthlies are looking to surgery as a 'perfectly natural, affordable, routine procedure' (Douglas, 1995: 266), *heat* continues to look to both dramatic weight loss and the surgeon's knife as a warning to the female readership. Therefore, while *heat* routinely encourages the reader to emulate fashion trends from the world of celebrity, the magazine makes it clear that fun from fashion is key. The point here is that the reader should play with fashion trends and find pleasure in their health and beauty regime rather than feel societal pressure to take such drastic and potentially harmful steps to create a particular look. *heat*'s stance here is clearly respected by the female reader as the letters page routinely commends the magazine for its attitude to the female body and their presentation of the ideal physique:

> Regarding your feature on skinny celebs, one word springs to mind: fan-blooming-tastic. The article was a real eye-opener. Sophie Dahl was once a beautiful and curvaceous young woman – now she just looks ill. Seems to me they need to learn a lesson from Geri Halliwell – she's got her curves and her confidence back and she looks a lot sexier (13–19 November 2004).

Likewise:

> You decided to celebrate the curvier lady in your Stars Pile on the Pounds story. It was a really nice piece and very positive. I think these teeny-weeny Twiglet-limbed celebrities look so much better with curves, and I thought it was lovely the way you celebrated this (26 February–4 March 2005: 16).

'Everyone's Talking About' and
the role of celebrity gossip

I have suggested that *heat* draws on fashion, diet and surgery scares as a way of both constructing and undermining what constitutes the ideal celebrity body, however, it is also worth considering the tone with which the magazine chooses to 'expose' the diet tips, exercise regimes and style secrets of the stars. What I mean by this is that the magazine draws on women's discourses of gossip in order to present such celebrity stories to its readership.

Gossip magazines, like other traditionally female orientated texts such as soap opera, romance literature and shopping films, have been routinely derided as formulaic and sensational cultural forms (Brown, 1994: 115; Brunsdon, 1997: 81–82; Wilkes, 2003: 1). However, before condemning *heat* magazine for its presentation of star rumours and celebrity hearsay, it is necessary to note that an apparently trivial genre can be associated with a notion of empowerment for its users. For example, while soap opera fans find pleasure in challenging the ephemeral meaning codes associated with their popular text of choice (Hobson, 1982: 109–10), fans of romance fiction find satisfaction in the knowledge that men disapprove of their taste and in 'their defiant assertion of their right to plea-sure in the face of masculine disapproval' (Radway, 1984: 90–1). Mary Ellen Brown's work on oral culture makes this point when she states that 'women and other subordinated groups do, in fact, get pleasure out of the very things that dominant culture designs to give them pleasure' (Brown, 1994: 5). From this estimation, then, it is worth considering the ways in which *heat*'s commitment to celebrity gossip can be read as a valuable feminine discourse (see also Sofia Johansson's essay in this collection).

In terms of celebrity exposés and entertainment revelations, *heat* presents a range of regular celebrity-photo features such as 'Everyone's Talking About', 'Breaking News', 'LA Confidential: eavesdropping at Hollywood power lunches', 'Scandal', 'Fast Gossip', 'On or Off?' and 'The Week in Pictures'. In brief, 'Every-one's Talking About', as the title suggests, picks up on the most explosive enter-tainment news story of the week, be it 'Celebrity Big Brother' (8–14 January 2005: 3), 'Jude and Sienna's engagement' (15–21 January 2005: 3) or 'Kerry's Brave Face' (29 January–4 February 2005: 3). 'Breaking News' takes a more in-depth look at a particular celebrity figure such as Kerry Katona (8–14 January 2005: 14–15), a celebrity couple such as Brian McFadden and Delta Goodrem (15–21 January 2005: 14–16) or feuding celebrities such as George Michael and Elton John (18–31 December 2004: 26–7). 'LA Confidential' exposes the latest entertainment news from the big screen, while 'Scandal' reveals 'shocking' celeb-rity truths including unseen school pictures and early audition photos. 'Fast Gossip' aims to provide a short, snappy overview of the week's entertainment news and celebrity reporting, and 'On or Off?' is a short feature that speculates on the love lives of today's stars. 'The Week in Pictures' fills out several pages of the magazine by looking at full-page photo-spreads of celebrities drunk and disorderly ('Had a Few Too Many, Nadine?', 5–11 February 2005: 38), in court ('Michael Jackson's First Week in Court', 12–18 February 2005: 34–35) and in bad disguises ('Britney's Dodgy Wig', 19–25 February 2005: 42).

Such star scandals and celebrity reporting situate the magazine firmly within the gossip sector, and as such, the title can be read as a positive feminine discourse. After all, in her audience research project concerning the pleasures and paradoxes of supermarket tabloids, S. Elizabeth Bird found that gossip serves a powerful discursive function in women's culture. Bird argues that women routinely use gossip publications to negotiate their personal world. The reader is told that those lonely women who miss the social network of 'real' gossipers often turn to the tabloids to 'fill in the role of missing friends' (Bird, 1992: 149; Giles, 2000: 148). From this estimation then, *heat*'s dedication to celebrity gossip can be seen to support a discursive network among women by provoking 'fantasies of belonging, of imagined communities' (Hermes, 1997: 141). Joke Hermes offers a persuasive argument concerning this 'extended family repertoire' as it is structured in the celebrity gossip magazine:

> In the case of both spoken and printed gossip a sense of community may be established. While spoken gossip is built on learning about the other speaker through what she or he says about 'third persons who are not present', written gossip tends to create closeness or familiar faces in a wider world by helping the reader to bring celebrities into her or his circle of family, friends and acquaintances (Hermes, 1997: 121).

However, rather than blithely assume that gossip magazines simply take the place of real friendship networks, it is worth noting that they can also provide a 'cultural medium', which presents a connection between the lives of women who have otherwise been isolated from each other (Jones, 1980: 197). After all, feminist media studies repeatedly comments on the ways in which female readers use such gossip publications as a 'focal point for discussion' (Bird, 1992: 150). According to Graeme Turner's work on the social functions of celebrity, 'gossip is … an important social process through which relationships, identity, and social and cultural norms are debated, evaluated, modified and shared' (Turner, 2004: 24). After all,

> Celebrities are like neighbours whom nearly everyone knows, in nearly every social setting, and 'stuff' about them is easier to find and share than information about friends and colleagues. More important[ly],

celebrity gossip is a much *freer* realm, much more game-like than acquaintance gossip: there are no repercussions and there is no account-ability (Gamson, 1994: 176–7).

Moreover, Hermes examines the pleasures on offer in the cultural consumption of women's magazines, concluding that the notion of emotional learning and connected knowledge is of importance to the female reader (Hermes, 1991: 137). The point here is that it is only after reading *heat*'s 'breaking news' or 'scandal' that one can participate in debates over it.

Conclusion

In the late 1990s, Joke Hermes introduced her research on women's magazines by stating that she felt uncomfortable with existing feminist work on such gendered texts due to the fact that such work routinely showed '*concern* rather than *respect* for those who read women's magazines' (Hermes, 1997: 1). With this in mind this chapter has examined the manner in which *heat* magazine can be read as an empowering media text that validates feminine meanings and compe-tences for the reader.

In light of this reading of *heat*, it would be interesting to examine the relation-ship between the editorial content as it has been considered here and the signifi-cance of advertising as it is presented throughout the magazine. After all, 'no magazine can make a profit on its cover price alone' (Winship, 1987: 38) and 'the primary source of profit for magazines is advertising' (Crane, 2003: 316). Even though women's magazines are routinely derided for presenting a vast array of hair, fashion and beauty promotions that insist that women 'be passive, anorexic spectacles whose only function is to attract men' (Douglas, 1995: 271–2), I would suggest that the advertising in *heat* magazine offers an altogether more positive representation of contemporary women. After all, if one considers that 'editorial content must supplement and reinforce advertising' (Crane, 2003: 316) then it is relevant to remind ourselves of the ways in which *heat* can be understood as an empowering female-defined text that applauds an interest in celebrity and champions a dedication to consumption.

Notes

1 Those glossy weekly magazines that are aimed at the 18–34-year-old male reader such as *Zoo* (2004–) and *Nuts* (2004–) seem to distinguish themselves from women's titles based precisely on their lack of celebrity coverage and star reporting.

2 My analysis is based on reading a sample of 26 *heat* magazines dated between February 2004 and March 2005.

3 The role played by women's magazines and related media in the construction of a consumer

culture has long been of interest to feminist theorists. Feminist film theorists have examined the relationship between the fashionable film star, the female viewer and the viewer as consumer, arguing that the cinema screen has been experienced as a shop window occupied by marvellous mannequins in which goods and stars are on display for the female spectator (Eckert, 1978, 33; Street, 2001: 8). For example, Jackie Stacey's seminal research on Hollywood cinema and female spectatorship suggests that glamorous female stars of the 1940s and 1950s 'functioned as fashion models for women spectators who watched actresses' star vehicles and associated their own attainment of ideal femininity with the consumption of clothes' (Stacey, 1994: 196–7, cited in Studlar, 2000: 159).

4 I have suggested that the reader takes pleasure in the fact that seemingly flawless celebrities have to work at their appearance, and nowhere is this more evident than in *heat*'s 'fitness, fashion and beauty' DVD release entitled *heat: Get That Celeb Look!* (Emap, 2003). The DVD sets out to reveal the style secrets, beauty regimes and exercise programmes of some of today's most emulated celebrities. For example, the section entitled 'getting the body' informs the viewer that: 'we show you how to get a peachy posterior like Kylie Minogue's, a toned tum like Britney Spears' and legs like Cameron Diaz'. In the same way, the section devoted to 'getting the beauty' tells the viewer 'how to transform your hair à la Rachel Stevens or get your face as flawless as Jennifer Lopez ... We reveal the lotions and potions the stars swear by and show you all the tips and tricks you need to make the right impression.' Last, but not least, in the section on 'getting the style', the reader is told why some clothes work and some don't on the fashion elite. What is interesting here is that throughout the 90-minute makeover, the style, beauty and fitness experts repeatedly inform the viewer that the painful stomach exercises, time-consuming hair-straightening sessions and arduous wardrobe try-ons are those selfsame painful, time-consuming and arduous activities that the celebrities themselves have to endure in order to maintain their perfect body, flawless hair and fashion-conscious reputation.

Bibliography

Addison, Heather (2000) 'Hollywood, Consumer Culture, and the Rise of Body Shaping', in David Desser and Garth Jowett (eds), *Hollywood Goes Shopping*, Minneapolis and London: University of Minnesota Press, pp. 3–33.

Berry, Sarah (2000) *Screen Style: Fashion and Femininity in 1930s Hollywood*, Minneapolis and London: University of Minnesota Press.

Bird, S. Elizabeth (1992) *For Enquiring Minds: A Cultural Study of Supermarket Tabloids*, Knoxville: University of Tennessee Press.

Brown, Mary Ellen (1994) *Soap Opera and Women's Talk: The Pleasure of Resistance*, London: Sage.

Brunsdon, Charlotte (1997) *Screen Tastes: Soap Opera to Satellite Dishes*, London and New York: Routledge.

Cashmore, Ellis (2002) *Beckham*, Cambridge: Polity.

Coward, Rosalind (1985) *Female Desires: How They Are Sought, Bought and Packaged*, New York: Grove Press.

Craig, Olga (1998) 'Men on Top', *Sunday Telegraph* 7 June: 26.

Crane, Diane (2003) 'Gender and Hegemony in Fashion Magazines: Women's Interpretations of Fashion Photographs', in Gail Dines and Jean M. Humez (eds), *Gender, Race, and Class in Media: A Text Reader*, 2nd edn, London: Sage, pp. 314–38.

Curran, Angela (2000) 'Consuming Doubts: Gender, Class, and Consumption in *Ruby in Paradise* and *Clueless*', in David Desser and Garth Jowett (eds), *Hollywood Goes Shopping*, Minneapolis and London: University of Minnesota Press, pp. 222–52.

deCordova, Richard (1990) *Picture Personalities: The Emergence of the Star System in America*, Urbana: University of Illinois Press.

Douglas, Susan (1995) *Where the Girls Are: Growing Up Female with the Mass Media*, New York: Times Books.

Dyer, Richard (2004) *Stars*, 2nd edn, London: BFI.

Eckert, Charles (1991) 'The Carole Lombard in Macy's Window', in Christine Gledhill (ed.), *Stardom: Industry of Desire*, London: Routledge, pp. 30–9.

Emap (2003) *heat: Get That Celeb Look!*, DVD.

Emap (2005a) '*heat* Editorial', Emap Advertising, available at www.emapadvertising.com/magazines/portfolio.asp?ID=13, accessed 25 January 2005.

Emap (2005b) '*heat* Reader's Lifestyle', Emap Advertising, aavailable at www.emapadvertising.com/magazines/portfolio.asp?ID=13, accessed 25 January 2005.

Emap (2005c) 'ABC Release Reveals Across the Board Success for Emap's Magazines', Emap Press Office, available at www.emap.com/nav?page=emap.news.story&resource=1149997, accessed 25 January 2005.

Entwistle, Joanne (2000) *The Fashioned Body: Fashion, Dress and Modern Social Theory*, Cambridge: Polity Press.

Epstein, Rebecca (2000) 'Sharon Stone in a Gap Turtleneck', in David Desser and Garth Jowett (eds), *Hollywood Goes Shopping*, Minneapolis and London: University of Minnesota Press, pp. 179–204.

Gamson, Joshua (1994) *Claims to Fame: Celebrity in Contemporary America*, London and Berkeley: University of California Press.

Geraghty, Christine (2000) 'Re-Examining Stardom: Questions of Texts, Bodies and Performance', in Christine Gledhill and Linda Williams (eds), *Re-Inventing Film Studies*, London and New York: Oxford University Press, pp. 183–202.

Giles, David (2000) *Illusions of Immortality: A Psychology of Fame and Celebrity*, London: Macmillan.

Gledhill, Christine (1991) 'Introduction', in Christine Gledhill (ed.), *Stardom: Industry of Desire*, London: Routledge, pp. xiii–xx.

Gough-Yates, Anna (2003) *Understanding Women's Magazines: Publishing, Markets and Readerships*, London and New York: Routledge.

Gritten, David (2002) *Fame: Stripping Celebrity Bare*, London: Allen Lane.

Hermes, Joke (1997) *Reading Women's Magazines*, Cambridge: Polity Press.

Hobson, Dorothy (1982) *Crossroads: The Drama of a Soap Opera*, London: Methuen.

Hollows, Joanne (2000) *Feminism, Femininity and Popular Culture*, Manchester and New York: Manchester University Press.

Holmes, Su (2005) '"Off-guard, Unkempt, Unready"?: Deconstructing Contemporary Celebrity in *heat* Magazine', *Continuum: Journal of Media and Cultural Studies* 19/1: 21–38.

Jones, Dorothy (1980) 'Gossip: Notes on Women's Oral Culture', *Women's Studies International Quarterly* 3: 193–8.

Llewellyn-Smith, Caspar (2002) *Poplife: A Journey by Sofa*, London: Sceptre.

Media Week (2001) 'The Man Who Made *heat* Magazine Hot', available at mediaweek.co.uk/articles/2001/3/QuantumArticle-2001-03-210000000.793077175927, accessed 25 January 2005.

Monaco, James (ed.) (1978) *Celebrity: The Media as Image Makers*, New York: Delta.

Moseley, Rachel (2002) *Growing up with Audrey Hepburn: Text, Audience, Resonance*, Manchester and New York: Manchester University Press.

Radway, Janice (1984) *Reading the Romance: Women, Patriarchy and Popular Literature*, Chapel Hill: University of North Carolina Press.

Read, Jacinda (2000) *The New Avengers: Feminism, Femininity and the Rape-revenge Cycle*, Manchester and New York: Manchester University Press.

Redfern, Catherine (2001) 'Confessions of a Failed Fashionista', *The F-Word*, November, available online at www.thefword.org.uk/features/2001/11/confessions_of_a_failed_fashionist, accessed 25 January 2005.

—— (2004) 'About the F-Word', *The F-Word*, August, available online at www.thefword.org.uk/general/about_the_fword, accessed 25 January 2005.

Redmond, Sean (2003) 'Thin White Women in Advertising: *Deathly Corporeality*', *Journal of Consumer Culture* 3/2: 170–90.

Rich, Adrienne (1983) 'Compulsory Heterosexuality and Lesbian Existence', in Ann Snitow *et al. Powers of Desire: The Politics of Sexuality*, New York: Monthly Review Press, pp. 177–205.

Roach, Mary Ellen. and Eicher, Joanne Bubolz (eds) (1965) *Dress, Adornment and the Social Order*, New York: John Wiley and Sons.

Rojek, Chris (2001) *Celebrity*, London: Reaktion.

Skeggs, Beverly (1997) *Formations of Class and Gender*, London: Sage.

Stacey, Jackie (1994) *Star Gazing: Hollywood Cinema and Female Spectatorship*, London and New York: Routledge.

Street, Sarah (2001) *Costume and Cinema: Dress Codes in Popular Film*, London and New York: Wallflower.

Studlar, Gaylyn (2000) 'Chi-Chi Cinderella: Audrey Hepburn as Couture Countermodel', in David Desser and Garth Jowett (eds), *Hollywood Goes Shopping*, Minneapolis and London: University of Minnesota Press, pp. 159–78.

Turner, Graeme (2004) *Understanding Celebrity*, London: Sage.

Wilkes, Roger (2003) *Scandal: A Scurrilous History of Gossip*, London: Atlantic Books.

Winship, Janice (1987) *Inside Women's Magazines*, London: Pandora.

Wolf, Naomi (1991) *The Beauty Myth: How Images of Beauty are Used Against Women*, London: Vintage.

Chapter 11
'Droppin' it like it's hot'
The sporting body of Serena Williams

Ramona Coleman-Bell

From their awesome athleticism to their 'charismatic' personalities, black female athletes are proving quite valuable to the sports industry – as the success of tennis player Serena Williams has made clear. Some would say that Serena is 'droppin' it like it's hot', a popular phrase in hip-hop vernacular that delineates anyone who has a 'hot' property to promote, trade, circulate and sell. From tennis championships and endorsement deals to entertainment endeavours, Serena Williams's image has become the site of a highly lucrative celebrityhood. There is no doubt that her rise to public visibility is in part the result of her hard work on the tennis courts, yet her continued celebrity success is attributed to more than her awesome athleticism. By charting the circulation and impact of Williams's celebrity status, I aim to situate her image within the context of discursive constructions of the black female body in contemporary American society. I ultimately offer a contradictory reading of Williams's circulation: it is marked by a racist ideology and (to borrow from Stuart Hall, 1997) a racialized regime of representation, while it also dramatizes a counterhegemonic subjectivity that struggles for agency and autonomy.

Serena Williams's entrance into superstardom began when she emerged from the shadow of her older sister, Venus Williams, to become a professional tennis player in 1995 – one year after her older sibling. By 1998, Serena was ranked number 21 by the World Tennis Association (WTA). Sharing the spotlight with her sister in 1998 at the Australian Open, Serena Williams shocked the tennis world when she defeated second seed Lindsay Davenport. At the time, Davenport was ranked number nine. By July 2002, Williams's superb athleticism had catapulted her to number one in the world, and her victory titles are many. To mention only some of her wins, in 1999 at the age of 17, she upset number one Martina Hingis to capture her first grand slam single, and at the 2000 Olympics, Serena and Venus won the gold medal for the doubles. She then held all four grand slam titles at once – winning the French Open,

Wimbledon and the US Open in 2002, and the Australian Open in 2003 – and her wins became known as the 'Serena Slam'.

As a result of this success, some of her entertainment endeavours have included appearances on television shows such as *Oprah*, *My Wife and Kids* and *Law and Order: SVU*. She has also appeared in films such as *Black Knight* and in several rap videos. In terms of magazines, her fashion photo spreads, featured articles, and front cover appearances are numerous, including publications *ESPN Magazine*, *Jet*, *Black Woman*, *Essence* and *Vogue, Sports Illustrated Swimsuit Edition, 2003, 2004*. In 2003, Serena launched her own line of designer fashion called 'Aneres' (Serena spelt backwards). The endorsement deals have also been both numerous and lucrative, including contracts with Avon cosmetics, McDonald's, Puma, Nike, Wrigley's, Close-up toothpaste and the 'Got Milk' campaign. At 22, she reportedly signed a record-breaking contract with Nike that was worth at least $60 million over the next eight years.

As Andrews and Jackson assert, sport is one of the cultural arenas which still pivots on meritocratic ideologies of fame:

> In true neo-liberal fashion, the ascent to sport celebrityhood is habitually reduced to individual qualities such as innate talent, dedication, and good fortune, thus positioning the sport star as a deserved benefactor of his/her devotion to succeed within the popular imaginary (2001: 8).

As an unranked African American tennis player, Williams's dedication on the courts soon became a media sensation as she began beating top-ranked players in a white-dominated sport. She was instantly positioned as a 'deserved benefactor' as mediated narratives focused on her unconventional training on the dilapidated courts of Compton, California. This nascent representation of Williams 'succeeding' despite an impoverished background can clearly be understood in terms of the specific mechanics of star construction, most notably through the currency of the success myth which suggests that 'American society is sufficiently open for anyone to get to the top, regardless of rank' (Dyer, 1998: 42). According to the mythology here, Williams has been blessed with natural talent and 'specialness' and it is these essential qualities that enable her to succeed in America where individual merit is rewarded regardless of class, race or gender background.

The black sporting body in American culture

As this suggests, Williams's celebrityhood is a part of a complex cultural narrative when it comes to the relationship between athleticism, African American identity and national belonging. The 'famous' black sporting body has been variously used as a means to signify racial difference (otherness), and to provide the evidential material out of which meritocratic success can be proven. The black sporting body is brought into racist discourse either to prove that all black people are physical creatures, that their vast black mass *essentially* connects them to primitive impulses, excessive desire and 'mindless' behaviour (all body and no brain); or to herald the athletic power of the body so that all Americans can be proud of 'it'. In this respect, Andrews (2001) identifies Michael Jordan as an inclusive black sport star whose super-heroic body brings inferred 'success' to all Americans. However, the successful black sporting body is often one where the blackness of the body is effaced or 'made safe', in what might be termed a paradoxical process of splitting. The absent/present paradox of the black sporting body allows Michael Jordan's black body to be championed by all Americans because he/it is both black and All-American. that is simultaneously raced and de-raced.

Critiquing the construction of national belonging has its roots in W. E. B. Dubois' notion of a 'double consciousness' (Dubois, 1903). In describing the situation of African Americans at the turn of the twentieth century, Dubois highlighted the duality of the Negro experience whereby one constantly saw the self through the eyes of others. Dubois identifies, then, the notion of being externally defined and racially objectified by hegemonic ideologies scripted from a white-centric perspective. By virtue of their visual difference, black Americans were the targets of an ideological warfare involving the construction of their bodies as naturally wanton, criminal, sexual, irrational and primitive. Nonetheless, this putting into vision of racial difference also ensured that black Americans had a space in which to define themselves, and with which to wrestle with the dominant ideology that sought to objectify them. Racist hegemony brings into discourse that which it seeks to discredit, marginalize, make 'strange', but in doing so, it necessarily opens up a (counter)space where such forms of otherness can gather together and resist the ideology on offer. Black power emerges in and through the very political system that is trying to disempower and disenfranchise black people. I would like to argue that this ideological warfare continues to be waged today, in all cultural spaces, and that Williams's unruly black sporting body is an exemplary case study to explore this process.

The significance of Williams's celebrity is due in part to the lack of positive images of black womanhood in America's imaginary. Dominant discourses about womanhood have for the most part rendered African American women invisible, while at the same time, they have manipulated constructions of the black female body, offering what Patricia Hill Collins conceives as 'controlling images' of black womanhood (Collins, 2000). Images such as the hypersexualized Jezebel, the desexualized mammy, the leeching welfare queen and the emasculating Sapphire have been designed to make 'racism, sexism, poverty and other forms of social injustice appear to be natural, normal, and inevitable parts of everyday life' (Collins, 2000: 70). If these kinds of images are mapped onto the history of the black female body, what happens when an 'empowered' black female sporting celebrity enters this space? In relation to Williams's black body, the answer is an ambivalent or contradictory one.

Heywood and Dworkin contend that black female bodies are still constructed outside the norms of white, middle-class beauty ideals. For them, the black female body is still constructed as 'threatening', 'scary', 'angry' and 'frightening' (Heywood and Dworkin, 2003: 155). On one level, it is clear that Williams's sporting black body signifies in this way. Williams's athletic, muscled body enters into a cultural space that immediately defines her as *a black body* that is excessive, overtly masculine, and yet at the same time overtly female. Williams is imaged as hard-bodied *and* all-butt, as both 'bad-buck' *and* 'Jezebel'. Williams, then, is excessively racially marked: her über-black body is doubly abnormal, and as such needs to be fetishized to render it/her 'safe'. Take for instance the response to Williams when she wore a form-fitting black lycra catsuit at the 2002 US Open. Some carped that her choice of attire 'cheapened her game' (Boeck, 2002: 10c), while others argued that she had 'gone too far' for the sport, and responded with disdain (O'Neil, 2002: 12d). The attention given to Williams's catsuit is rooted in the wider historical imaginary of the black female body in the American public consciousness. The catsuit accentuates every curve in Williams's body, and images of her in such form-fitting gear often draw attention both to her breasts and her butt. In fact, many of the images of Williams's body that have circulated via magazines and internet sites have focused on her extremely fit, curvaceous physique. The catsuit, with its connotations of the feline huntress, and the repetition of sexualized and racialized iconography, works to draw attention to, and then displace, the fascination with Williams's hyper-encoded sexuality. As Hall writes:

> Fetishism, then, is a strategy for having-it-both-ways: for both representing and not-representing the tabooed, dangerous or forbidden object of pleasure and desire. It provides us with what Mercer calls an 'alibi'. We have seen how, in the case of 'The Hottentot Venus', not only is the gaze displaced from the genitalia to the buttocks; but also, this allows the observers to go on looking while disavowing the sexual nature of the gaze (1997: 268).

Unlike the responses to representations displaying the body of Anna Kournikova, the attention given to Williams in this respect becomes marked by a more contradictory ambivalence, even deviance. Williams's body becomes the site for currents of fascination, celebration, the grotesque and desire. Moreover, talk of Williams's catsuit is indicative of the ways in which her clothes, hair, jewellery and body have been discussed in ways that escape her white counterparts. Indeed, various websites contain discussions about Williams's physique – and particularly her butt. In fact, I remember receiving an image of Williams in her black catsuit via email, and the way the camera angle captured her body position mirrored the sexualization of Saartjie Bartman. Sander Gilman documents the plight of Saartjie Bartman, an African woman who was publicly displayed like an exotic animal, so that whites could observe her buttocks and genitalia. Gilman observes that in the nineteenth century 'the black female was widely perceived as not only [exhibiting] a "primitive" sexual appetite but also [as displaying] the external signs of this temperament – "primitive" genitalia' (Gilman, 1985: 232). Thus, for nineteenth-century sensibilities, the black female body became a signifier of deviant sexuality, and the discursive traces of this are still clear in the representation of Williams's Hottentot body.

The media concentration on Williams's buttocks seems to confirm the way that race, gender and sexual deviancy and desire are aligned. Williams's sporting prowess is encoded as a form of sexual excess: she doesn't just play sport, she *is* sport. The representation of Williams's black sporting body is loaded with carnal connotations so that she becomes a compliant whore for the white imagination that she is centrally 'packaged' for. bell hooks suggests that this is a recurring trope in the racist imagination:

> Although contemporary thinking about black female bodies does not attempt to read the body as a sign of 'natural' racial inferiority, the fascination with black 'butts' continues. In the sexual iconography of the traditional black pornographic imagination, the protruding butt is seen as an indication of a heightened sexuality (hooks, 1992: 63).

Nonetheless, as hooks also points out, 'black butts' can function as 'unruly and outrageous' signifiers, or as overly empowered motifs that resist the dominant reading that accompanies them (ibid.: 63). In some instances (such as rap videos), the representation of the female black butt becomes playfully self-reflexive and a positive way to imagine the difference between the 'dull dish' of white culture and the life-enhancing vitality of black culture. Black female butts revel in their flesh while white women simply cannot, or dare not. In this respect, Williams's body is 'not a silenced body' (ibid.: 63) but one that loudly resists the racialized grammar that seeks to define it in negative terms. This argument gathers force when one considers the way that Williams seems to consciously celebrate her body: her flamboyant play, her 'risky' attire, and her confidence in fielding questions about her identity. Each of these open up resistant and potentially positive spaces of racial becoming. Williams challenges the repressed and conservative status quo of traditional professional women's tennis. Her colourful clothes stand in opposition to the white attire that has historically been worn by tennis players.

Williams's high-octane and physical/masculine performances on court challenge the discourse that women should play tennis gracefully, delightfully (*beautifully*). Williams's black, athletic body stands in stark contrast to the white, often blonde, 'soft' tennis players who historically have dominated the game. Williams's colourful, physical, self-reflexive performance demands of the audience that they recognize her blackness on her terms, without recourse to a double consciousness.[1]

Williams's black sporting body also resists such forms of fetishization because of the representational power that her celebrity affords her. Williams's dominant performances on and off court allow her to signify or function as an empowered black woman, one who is in a position to transform ways of seeing black womanhood in America's public sphere. Williams's sporting and economic success enables her to be a positive and transformative image of/for black womanhood. But William's black celebrityhood is also 'positive' in another sense: she draws attention to the softness, dullness and the emptiness that sits at the centre of white culture. William's black sporting body annihilates the myth that white people are superior. At the same time, predicated as this is on the 'power' of the body, this in part returns us to the racial stereotypes which naturalize the terms through which the black body can be elevated and celebrated.

The commodification of the black female sporting body

These contradictions also structure the commodification of Williams and her circulation within the wider commercial framework of advertising texts and product promotion. Williams's success comes at a time when multinational consumer and service-driven corporations are recognizing new markets to address. These include so-called 'brown America', and the buying power of independent female consumers. As a result, black female stars and celebrities have a premium value in the marketplace so that a talented and attractive black female athlete such as Serena Williams becomes a highly marketable capitalist brand. The commodification of the black female sporting body is key here: it becomes a site where the services of dieting, fashion, and leisure and fitness can be played out. In fact, precisely because of their historical circulation, one can argue that the contemporary commodification of the black female sporting body is eerily reminiscent of descriptions of black female slaves on the auction block, bought and sold on the basis of their size, weight, strength and beauty. For example, when voted the most marketable athlete in the USA, those in the sports marketing system intriguingly described the branding of Serena Williams thus:

The Bonham Group Chair ... added of Serena, 'Sexy, sassy, strong. If she stays healthy, she has marketing legs. Extra Points for her ability to appeal to multicultural audiences.' Drotman Communications Founder Doug Drotman said Serena has 'the ability to reach different target audiences – black, white, young, old, rich and poor.' ESPN's Michele Tafoya added, 'Serena continues to dominate a sport that gets plenty of exposure. Add to that her smile, good looks, flair for fashion and her controversial family, and you've got an interesting and highly marketable commodity' (Glase, 2003).

Bonham's description of Williams as 'sexy, sassy, strong', along with the suggestion that 'if she stays healthy, she has marketing legs', indeed sounds as if Williams is on the (endorsement) auction block. Lisa Collins contends that the histories of various markets for black female bodies, or what she calls 'economies of the flesh', have affected the creation and reception of images of black women in Western Europe and America (2002: 91).

In analysing commercial advertising images of athletes such as Ben Johnson, Florence Griffith-Joyner and Jackie Joyner-Kersee, Stuart Hall (1997) illustrates how little has changed in terms of the representation of racial, ethnic and gender difference in popular culture. For Hall, black athletes are fetishized and sexualized in these adverts. The same can be said for the way the Williams sisters are used to endorse and promote products. For instance, in a Wrigley's Doublemint advert in the 1990s, the Williams sisters became the updated version of the Doublemint twins. The Williams sisters are depicted as fully engulfed by green spearmint leaves that reveal only small headshots of each. While positioned in the centre of the advert, Serena Williams's lips appear to be in a pucker – as if blowing a kiss to the camera. Williams's lips are heavily sexualized (vulva-like), and given the tag line of 'double your pleasure' that accompanies the advert, the impression is that Williams is implicated in this giving of immense pleasure. In commenting on the three-year, $7 million contract to endorse Wrigley's Doublemint Gum, Spencer acknowledges the complexity of African American women athletes in the imagery of advertising:

> On the one hand, the accompanying tag line may be a double entendre in suggesting that consumers 'double [their] … pleasure'. On the other hand, the ad could be read as a reflection of progress, given that African American female athletes once faced double jeopardy in the marketing arena by virtue of being female and Black (Spencer, 2003: 41).

The McDonald's adverts similarly offer a racially loaded representation of Williams. In November 2002, the Williams sisters joined McDonald's in an unprecedented three-year advertising agreement beginning with the introduction of

McDonald's National Dollar Menu. In their first televised commercial in America, Venus and Serena negotiate a dramatic rooftop liaison with the Hamburglar (who informs the sisters that he will be selling the Big 'N' Tasty Sandwich for only one dollar). The Williams sisters are first introduced to the viewer from inside a platinum E-class Mercedes Benz sedan. When the tinted window rolls down, we see Serena Williams's long, straight, blonde glam-diva-like criminal character sitting in the car. Next we see her colluding with the Hamburglar to promote McDonald's dollar menu. In the McDonald's press release, the Big 'N' Tasty Sandwich commercial is described as a 'mysterious adventure' (McDonald's Press Release, 2002). Once again, then, Williams has been placed in an advert that locates her as deviant, criminal, sexually dangerous and 'mysterious'. Her blonde hair works to 'sully' white identity and essentially connect blackness to leaky borders and boundaries (the advert allows Williams to try on whiteness, and as such re-enacts white culture's great 'racial' fear of becoming, of having one's racial identity taken over by, the Other). Carole Vance describes this framework as 'simultaneously a domain of restriction, repression and danger as well as a domain of exploration, pleasure, and agency' (Vance, 1995: 72). bell hooks expands on this in terms of the commodification of black female sexuality in the advertising arena:

> It is within the commercial realm of advertising that the drama of Otherness finds expression. Encounters with Otherness are clearly marked as more exciting, more intense, and more threatening. The lure is the combination of pleasure and danger. In the cultural marketplace the Other is coded as having the capacity to be more alive, as holding the secret that will allow those who venture to dare to break with cultural anhedonia (hooks, 1992: 26).

While the McDonald's commercial may appear to be harmless, a 'bit of fun', the advert seamlessly grafts the combination of pleasure and danger onto the body of the black celebrity. The commercial also resonates with wider stereotypes of class and gender in the inner-city context, as two glamorously dressed black females mysteriously search for a 'good deal', almost as if they are getting black market Big 'N' Tasty sandwiches from the infamous Hamburglar (with whom they collude). The Williams sisters become ghetto hoes, badass girls with nothing to lose, and are therefore connected to racist discourses that have all urban black people as coming from the delinquency of the 'hood'.

However, at the same time it is important to note that there are also advertisements which seem to work against the grain of racist ideology where Williams is concerned. For instance, in the Close-Up toothpaste advert a de-sexualized Williams appears as the 'light' that lights up America. Photographed sitting at a table, with one hand resting comfortably on her tennis racket and the other hand raised up close to her face, she holds a tube of Close-Up toothpaste next to her smiling face. At the centre of the advert, then, is Williams's beaming and magnetic smile, a smile that is meant to connect with all Americans. In this advert Williams is represented as something of the girl next door, and a black body that is confident and empowered – a black body that comes to stand for a multi-racial, *inclusive* American society. In fact, Serena Williams was featured in a national Close-Up campaign that included three collectible boxes – each with a different picture of Williams on the front. While these images can be argued to de-race and pacify Williams (so that she becomes just like a white girl in the advert), the residues and echoes of her unruly and independent celebrity status electrify this advert, upsetting the usual binaries that black stars find themselves in. In a sense, Williams's appearance in such domestic and everyday adverts invites blackness into the American household, where, given the evidence of demographic profiling, it is increasingly welcomed.

Susan Birrell and Mary G. McDonald argue that the critical analysis of sporting celebrities offers 'unique points of access to the constitutive meanings and power relations to the larger worlds we inhabit' (Birrell and McDonald, 2000: 3). On a related point, Marshall suggests that ideas about individualism, social identity and difference, consumption and success are wrapped up in commodification of the celebrity (1997: 51). The economic and ideological machinery of late capitalism is dependent on the celebrity turn – this is not a space for representational freedom but of greater social control and manipulation. In this sense, Serena Williams has very little control over the meanings ascribed to her, or the goods that are bought and sold on her name. She is product, brand, caught in the belly of capitalism, its slave rather than its Kingpin. While Williams's celebrity persona displays moments of resistance and opposition, and while it is possible that she can be read against the grain of racist culture, Williams's power to be free from racist discourse is finally limited.

Conclusion

Serena Williams's celebrity image speaks to the ways in which black womanhood has been contested, negotiated and redefined. On the tennis courts, Williams's agency and autonomy is quite apparent, but this is much more contested and complex in the wider construction of her celebrity image, especially in the world of advertisements where she is regularly fetishized. Nonetheless, in seeking to explore the multiple meanings of Serena Williams's celebrity status, one is also hoping to discover much about the way race and gender play out in contemporary American society.

Overall, Williams's celebrityhood reveals that a racist ideology still operates in US society wherein African American women are included in the American project under particular conditions; yet Williams's sporting body serves as counterdiscourse that transforms images of African American womanhood wherein black is once again beautiful.

To this end, how African American women collectively benefit from the power of Williams's celebrity remains to be explored. Does the increased visibility of Serena Williams in advertisements for McDonald's, Avon, Puma, Nike and Wrigley help to change the popular imagination of the construction of black womanhood? Since Williams's entrance into the public sphere, her insistence on agency and autonomy attempts to transform the ways in which race and gender have been socially constructed because of her refusal to be externally defined. At the same time, images of Serena fall back on stereotypical images of black womanhood. Nonetheless, despite the complexity of Williams's celebrityhood, one thing is certain: the literal presence of her black female sporting body across a wide range of media texts displaces the white female body from its position as dominant identity. This shifting of power relations is played out in a 2004 Olympics Nike advert where white female bodies are imaged morphing into the black female body of Serena Williams. Is Serena the embodiment of the 'new woman' in American culture? Is there a new super-iconic role model in town which young women wish to emulate? If so, move over, Marilyn and Madonna: Serena is coming, and she is changing the face of America as she keeps on 'droppin' it like it's hot'.

Notes

1 There are, of course, a number of examples of white tennis players who have challenged gender norms. For example, Martina Navratilova's foreign, masculine, lesbian body was initially placed in a power- saturated binary with 'golden girl' Chris Evert Lloyd. However, it is the racial specificity here which increases the division – the 'difference' – so that Williams's corporeal presence has to be acknowledged.

Bibliography

Andrews, David (2001) 'The Fact(s) of Michael Jordan's Blackness: Excavating a Floating Racial Signifier', in David L. Andrews (ed.), *Michael Jordan, Inc.: Corporate Sport, Media Culture, and Late Modern America*, Albany: State University of New York Press, pp.107–52.

Andrews, David L. and Jackson, Steven J. (eds) (2001) *Sport Stars: The Cultural Politics of Sporting Celebrity*, London: Routledge.

Birrell, Susan and McDonald, Mary G. (2000) 'Reading Sport, Articulating Power Lines: An Introduction', in Susan Birrell and Mary G. McDonald (eds), *Reading Sport: Critical Essays on Power and Representation*, Boston: Northeastern University Press, pp. 3–13.

Boeck, Greg (2002) *USA Today*, August 28: 10c.

Cahn, Susan K. (1994) *Coming on Strong: Gender and Sexuality in Twentieth-Century Women's Sport*, New York: The Free Press, pp. 3–13.

Collins, Lisa (2002) 'Economies of the Flesh: Representing the Black Female Body in Art', in Kimberly Wallace-Sanders (ed.), *Skin Deep, Spirit Strong: The Black Female Body in American Culture*, Ann Arbor: University of Michigan Press, pp. 99–127.

Collins, Patricia Hill (2000) *Black Feminist Thought: Knowledge, Consciousness, and the Politics of Empowerment*, New York: Routledge.

Daniels, Donna (2000) 'Gazing at the New Black Woman Athlete: How Do We See the New Women Athletes of Color? Donna Daniels Gazes at Venus and Serena Williams', *Colorlines* 3/1: 25–6.

Dubois, W. E. B. (1903) *The Souls of Black Folk*, New York: Oxford University Press (1993).

Dyer, Richard (1998) *Stars*, 2nd edn, London: BFI.

Gilman, Sander (1985) 'Black Bodies, White Bodies: Toward an Iconography of Female Sexuality in Late Nineteenth-Century Art, Medicine, and Literature'. *Critical Inquiry* 12 (Autumn): 204–38.

Glase, Tim (2003) 'Serena Williams Voted the Most Marketable Female Athlete', *The Sports Business Daily*, available at www.realsportsmag.com/about/press/sept03_sportsbizdaily.pdf, accessed 5 December 2004.

Hall, Stuart (1997) 'The Spectacle of the "Other"', in Stuart Hall (ed.), *Representation: Cultural Representations and Signifying Practices*, London, Thousand Oaks, New Delhi: Sage Publications, pp. 223–90.

Heywood, Leslie and Dworkin, Shari L. (2003) *Built to Win: The Female Athlete as Cultural Icon*, Minneapolis: University of Minnesota Press.

hooks, bell (1992) *Black Looks: Race and Representation*, Boston: South End Press.

McDonald Mary G. and Andrews, David L. (2001) 'Michael Jordan: Corporate Sport and Postmodern Celebrityhood', in David L. Andrews and Steven J. Jackson (eds), *Sports Stars: The Cultural Politics of Sporting Celebrity*, London and New York: Routledge Press, pp. 20–35.

Marshall, P. David (1997) *Celebrity and Power: Fame in Contemporary Culture*, Minneapolis and London: University of Minnesota Press.

O'Neil, Dana Pennett (2002) *Philadelphia Daily News*, August 31

Spencer, Nancy E. (2004) 'Sister Act VI: Venus and Serena Williams at Indian Wells: "Sincere Fictions" and White Racism', *Journal of Sport and Social Issues* 28/2: 115–35.

Vance, Carol (1984) 'Pleasure and Danger: Towards a Politics of Sexuality', in Carole S. Vance (ed.), *Pleasure and Danger: Exploring Female Sexuality*, Boston: Routledge & Kegan Paul, pp. 1–2.

Part III

Fame Simulation

Introduction

On one level, it appears that at no other time in the history of stardom and celebrification have we been offered the chance to get so 'close' to the famous person. Their 'authentic' selves are uncovered or exposed in tabloid newspapers and popular magazines. The real person 'behind' the fabricated personality is increasingly revealed to fans in confessional moments, or in the rawest of biographical storytelling (Littler, 2004). Stars and celebrities are given greater psychological depth and verisimilitude by fans in slash fiction and through internet fan websites that circulate 'true' stories about them. And such online arenas put the famous person under the discursive control of fans who can write their own star or celebrity scripts in ways that increase or intensify their relationships with the famous. While 'authenticity' has always been a key signifier that brings the famous person into being, the affective and emotional connectivity that exists in the present culture of fame seems qualitatively and quantitatively different.

And yet, on another level, stars and celebrities have never seemed so manufactured, media-produced and simulated. Increasingly, the self-reflexive and ironic media commentary on the fame game draws attention to the artifice that sits at the centre of stardom and celebrification (Gamson, 1994). The famous person exists *only* at the level of representation, cut free from any existential potentiality or possibility. Stars and celebrities originate in sites that are virtual, digital or animated, so that at the material, cerebral or corporeal level they are literally hyperreal and technological. The fakery of fame, then, is found not just in the media myths and promotional material but in the 'new' ways that stars and celebrities are given a cultural presence. In this respect, Barbara Creed has explored the impact that digital film and special effects have and will have on stardom:

> Now it is possible to create computer-generated objects, things and people that do not have referents in the real world but exist solely in the digital domain of the computer ... Central to these changes is the possibility of creating a virtual actor, of replacing the film star, the carbon-

based actor who from the first decades of the cinema has been synonymous with cinema itself. In the future, living actors may compete with
digital images for the major roles in the latest blockbuster or romantic
comedy (2002: 130).

In the present, real stars and computer figures do merge or converge. For
example, the Tomb Raider film franchise melds the digital gaming image of Lara
Croft to the star image of Angelina Jolie, so that their convergence onscreen is a
hyperreal one, with the trajectory of the relationship dependent on a digital
conception. Lara Croft is 'an agile cipher, a vehicular android, a smooth-seamed
femme-bot' (Carr, 2002: 178), and Jolie embodies this – *becomes* this – in the
play of the film. Digitally animated films such as *Star Wars: Episode I: The Phantom
Menace* (Lucas, 1999) created stars that were solely computer-generated (Jar Jar
Binks, for example), while *Polar Express* (Zemeckis, 2004) re-created a digital
version of Tom Hanks to author (star in) the film. Animated cartoons, such as
The Simpsons and *South Park*, are perhaps the prime examples of hyperreal fame:
they are cartoon stars who nonetheless are marketed as 'real' stars and consumed
by fans as possessing star quality and genuine authenticity. In fact, because the
cartoon character and cartoon star are absolutely fused (for example, the character Bart Simpson *is* the star Bart Simpson), there is a greater degree of 'truth'
about the fame that emerges. Their authenticity resides in the fact that they are
what they are (famous cartoon characters).

This constant search for truth – even if it is a search for the 'lies' that hide
behind the idealized mask of stardom and celebrification – is intensified in an age
where new media technologies and new media formats have increased the range
and nature of surveillance. Digital audio, video and stills photography, for
example, have enabled bugging, filming, capturing the star or celebrity, to esca-
late to a stage where one can argue that there is no longer a 'private' realm that
the famous person can retreat to, or a 'mask' that cannot be shown to be just
that. Alternatively, such panoptic devices can be argued to be the very things that
show how 'real' the star or celebrity is. There is, then, a constant push-and-pull
between authenticity and simulation, played out in an age where vision and
representation machines see into everything.

Celebrity reality TV may well be the format that best explores the very nature
of fame simulation (an area explored by Su Holmes in Part I). New and has-been
stars and celebrities attempt to woo viewers into believing that their fame is,
was, or will be justified, not least because they are (were) 'authentic' and true-
to-life people. Their goal is not to be voted off the show because the longer they
stay the more validated their personae become, and the more famous they will be
when the show finishes. They are clearly constructed famous people (shows such
as *I'm A Celebrity … Get Me out of Here!* sometimes mock and draw attention to

the 'game' the stars or celebrities are playing so that they don't get voted off). But they are also evidently 'real'. The technological logic of the format suggests they have to be, because the 24-hour surveillance regime that is in place must in the end capture who they really are – the mask will slip, or their 'talent' will show through.

New media technologies have enabled fame to be re-constituted, and to circulate in a web of inter- and hypertextual media sites that extends the places and spaces where it can be consumed. The internet, in particular, has given fans a greater ability to speak about, pay homage to, and re-create their idols outside, and some-times in opposition to, the official discourses circulated in the media. (Although a great number of these supposedly unauthorized sites are either supported or care-fully monitored by the producer/studio in question.) Nevertheless, this technolog-ical shift has had particular significance for marginalized fans who can Other their idols or use them as a springboard to talk about their own identities and desires (Turner, 2004). 'Shipping' (short for 'relationshipping') is one online phenomenon whereby fans can re-construct or re-write the relationship that their stars have onscreen. In the *Harry Potter* Webverse, for example, fans have paired Rupert Gint/Ron Weasley with Tom Felton/Draco Malfoy ('fire and ice') in a homoerotically charged coupling.[1] The internet, then, as certain authors aim to explore in this section, can enable the consumption of fame to exist in transgressive spaces of identification and desire, potentially radicalizing its cultural impact. The very liquid or malleable nature of fame means that it can be appropriated or re-simulated again, again and again.

The gallery space has also been transformed by the video presence of the star or celebrity. While famous people have regularly featured in the work of artists, such as Pop Art painters and Andy Warhol in particular, digital art/technology has enabled the star or celebrity to enter the gallery on more 'concrete' terms. Given the supposed intimacy that characterizes the relationship between viewer and artwork in the gallery space, the video installation art that heralds the star or celebrity seems to offer the viewer that rhetoric of authenticity. One can get so very close to the piece of art in question and, consequently, the star or celebrity who is the object/subject of the work on display. And yet, at the same time, the engagement remains a simulated one: this is never the famous person in the flesh but a representation of their star or celebrity being. The use of the gallery space to represent the famous person also speaks to the way in which the borders and boundaries between high and low, elite and popular art are no longer secure, tenable or helpful. The seeing into things extends even to here. Stars and celebri-ties can be found (out) anywhere.

In this section, Fame Simulation, there is a concern with the way the production, representation and consumption of stars and celebrities have been transformed by new media technologies and new media formats. These developments have thrown into question, or have heightened, the relationship between the authentic and the manufactured, the real and the simulated. However, the section is also concerned with exploring the way 'old' media technologies and 'old' media formats (such as television cartoons or photography) have been changed by postmodern sensibilities. In this respect, the section explores the ways in which the search for the 'real' and the 'phoney' in the star or celebrity self is constantly subject to renegotiation, shaped by changing technological and cultural contexts.

Summaries

Adrienne Lai's 'Glitter and grain: aura and authenticity in the celebrity photographs of Juergen Teller' probes the technological mediation of celebrities by exploring what has become a prevalent mode of *aesthetic* representation in contemporary celebrity culture: the shift away from the contrived 'gloss of "the ideal" towards the more mundane territory of "the real"'. Lai is interested in the fact that, rather than drawing on the rhetoric of the 'stolen' snap (as with the paparazzi shot), the images she explores are produced as a result of 'official, star-sanctioned photo shoots'. Lai's focus here is the work of the German photographer, Juergen Teller. Featuring celebrities from Björk and Kate Moss to Winona Ryder, Teller produces images which are the antithesis of the carefully constructed, mythologized pictures of fame glamour. Lai considers how these images are a further site which negotiate discourses of democratization in the celebrity image, not simply in their depiction of the celebrity but also in the context of their exhibition. As she describes it, 'Teller's books, images of Björk … co-mingle with shots of an anonymous girl in a park and a frozen dead dog in a garbage can'. Yet, similarly to other authors in this collection, Lai is critical of this shift, foregrounding its potential to elide the 'vast hierarchical divisions' between celebrities and ordinary people, leading her to suggest that 'one must wonder to what (and whose) ends this expansion of the ordinary is used'.

In 'The mockery of cartoon celebrity: *The Simpsons* and the fragmented individual', Suzanne Rintoul adopts a postmodern perspective in exploring the phenomenon of cartoon celebrity. Although work has more recently explored the concept of the digital/virtual star (Hills, 2003; Flanagan, 1999), there is also of course a long history of characters which become famous through animated worlds. Constituting a topic in their own right, such figures pose interesting theoretical and methodological questions for the study of stardom and celebrity. For example, while cartoon characters exist across the intertextual web of merchandizing and promotion, the negotiation of their 'authenticity' cannot be anchored to a 'real' offscreen existence. But as Rintoul explores here, this in many ways fosters the ideal context for *The Simpsons*' heightened commentary on the simulated nature of celebrity. In studying the series' articulation of a 'hyper-

hyperreal form of fame', Rintoul considers how *The Simpsons* offers a self-reflexive and often critical discourse on celebrity culture, and asks: 'How ... does one begin to make sense of the enormous success of a show that mocks its own audience's relationship to stars and celebrities?' Rintoul argues that the series assumes a viewer/fan who possesses a form of 'double consciousness' – offering a superior position from which to critique the 'naïve' and narcissistic fascination with fame, while simultaneously implicating the viewer within this regime. From this perspective, *The Simpsons* exposes 'the frightening degree to which the contemporary culture industries animate the real and celebrate the virtual, leaving a kind of nothing space in-between'.

As with Adrienne Lai's discussion of the work of Juergen Teller, Catherine Fowler's essay examines the (often neglected) cross-over between art and celebrity culture. In 'Spending time with (a) celebrity: Sam Taylor-Wood's video portrait of David Beckham', Fowler examines Taylor-Wood's *David* (2004), which was commissioned by the National Portrait Gallery in 2004. While the image of David Beckham is part of the everyday fabric of celebrity culture on a global scale, Fowler examines how the video portrait offered a particular form of *access* to his image. The opportunity to witness the sleeping Beckham appears as the ultimate attempt to negotiate authenticity in the celebrity image. With his professional achievements and personal life the site of constant media scrutiny in the public domain, Fowler interprets the video portrait as a bid to capture Beckham at his most 'private': alone and in a state of apparently vulnerable, passive submission, this appears to be the 'guarantor of the as yet uncelebrated'. As with the rhetoric of all celebrity construction, and its basis in a dialectic of absence/presence, this offer of intimate access is of course based entirely upon technologies of mediation. But Fowler considers how this duality is shaped by the temporal specificity of the portrait, and its exhibition within the gallery space, concluding that it 'is the time-based and gallery-situated nature of *David* that creates the binary experience of watching: from an initial impression of unforced intimacy and the private zone, to a gradual realisation of the pose that destroys intimacy and reminds one of the public context of this image'.

As indicated above, the advent of the internet clearly offered a burgeoning space for the proliferation of fan cultures, the impact and significance of which is still being debated and understood. But more than this, the internet has rapidly come to offer an important *resource* for the study of fan cultures, offering access to a profusion of fan interactions, cultures and communities. In this section, Kristina Busse and Judith Franco (see also Matt Hills in Part I) aim to contribute to a dialogue about how the internet shapes – and indeed enables – particular fan engagements with celebrity culture.

Kristina Busse's "'I'm jealous of the fake me": postmodern subjectivity and identity construction in boy band fan fiction' explores the phenomenon of 'Real

People Fiction' (RPF) in which fans envision imaginary versions of 'real' celebrities in narrative form. Drawing on empirical research and focusing on the boy band *NSYNC, Busse explores the phenomenon of 'popslash'. Popslash writers use pop stars to fashion fictional narratives which manipulate public information to question, and often undermine, the media images on which their stories are based. As Busse expands, 'popslashers address complicated notions of reality and performance as the fictional depictions question the truth of public accounts of the stars and their worlds'. Largely written by women and often focusing on romantic and sexually explicit material, Busse emphasizes the high degree of *self-reflexivity* which characterizes the writing process. The narratives are prompted by an understanding of the highly constructed nature of the star text, while at the same time they suggest a desire to locate an 'authentic', 'core' individual. In this respect, Busse's essay offers a further perspective on how stars work through discourses on selfhood and identity (Dyer, 1998; Marshall, 1997). The writers of popslash explicitly confront the issue of performativity, not simply in re-crafting the celebrities they explore but also in 'writing' themselves.

Judith Franco's 'Langsters online: k.d. lang and the creation of internet fan communities' further expands on how the circulation of celebrities on the internet function to perform 'identity work' for audiences, particularly, but not exclusively, with respect to lesbian fans of k.d. lang. Franco bases her discussion around two key internet communities, Chief's site (2001) and Kennedyflairs (2002), both of which were formed as alternative spaces to the official Artist Direct site. Participants in both communities conceive of themselves as occupying a particular group identity that extends its interactions beyond cyberspace. In exploring these sites, Franco argues that k.d. lang functions as a relatively 'open' celebrity text which has the potential to unite both straight and lesbian women, while such fan cultures can also foster the sense of a 'private' space for the articulation of lesbian identity and desire. Yet, like Matt Hills (Part I), Franco brings out the concept of *stratification* within fan cultures. The smaller Chief's site is more hierarchical than Kennedyflairs (with conversations 'dominated by a relatively small number of highly educated individuals'), and Franco foregrounds how 'individual members and subgroups compete over "ownership" of their fan object', not only in terms of sexual investment and desire but also 'segmenting and fragmenting the fan community along the lines of ideological/political and cultural/national differences'. In this respect, Franco's study complements Busse's investigation of how the internet operates as a cultural site for the performance of fan desire, but within a different sexual and political context.

Notes

1 www.the-leaky-cauldron.org

Chapter 12
Glitter and grain
Aura and authenticity in the celebrity photographs of Juergen Teller

Adrienne Lai

The sight of immediate reality has become an orchid in the land of technology.
(Benjamin, 1968: 219)

Throughout most of the twentieth century, the celebrity (or more specifically the 'star')[1] has been linked to notions of the ideal. The celebrity or star is an individual who has acquired fame and fortune because of some extraordinary quality, variously identified as natural talent, charisma, beauty, or athleticism (although 'luck' is also argued to play a part in the celebrification process). Originating with the promotional activities of American movie studios in the early 1900s, the transformation of a performer into a 'star' – circulating a combination of the individual's private identity with his or her onscreen/stage roles – is a mechanism central to the entertainment industry and the creation of contemporary celebrity culture in Western industrialized societies. The mass media, and in particular, the medium of photography, have played a central role in the dissemination of a star image. Accordingly, official star photographs are constructed to portray the celebrity in a positive or flattering manner. They are generally used to induce the consumer's desire for the celebrity and his or her products – in essence, they function as an advertisement. Since much is invested in these images, their creation can be quite painstaking, with the smallest detail managed, massaged and retouched in order to create the appropriate illusion.

However, as the public becomes more aware of the numerous levels of trickery and fiction involved in the creation of the images it consumes, it can become sceptical – even hostile – toward the idealized depiction of a celebrity. In response to sociocultural shifts and the emergence of an increasingly media-literate audience, the iconography of celebrity photography has begun to move away from the contrived gloss of 'the ideal' towards the more mundane territory of 'the real'. Unflattering photographs of celebrities are not new – paparazzi photographs have been a staple of tabloid magazines and newspapers for some time – but now a great number of these images are produced as a result of *offi-cial*, star-sanctioned photo shoots.

A noteworthy source in the production of these 'real' images is Juergen Teller, a German photographer who became prominent in the fashion industry in the 1990s.[2] He is currently recognized in the contemporary art world for work that chronicles the ordinary and the day-to-day, including capturing the famous 'caught unawares', or as 'they really are'. This essay will focus on Teller's photo-graphs of celebrities, examining the visual language employed and the significance of his images as they circulate in the wider context of celebrity culture. His photographs offer casual – and in some cases, utterly unphotogenic – pictures of well-known individuals, often running in complete contradiction to the tradi-tional aesthetic conventions of celebrity portraiture. While Teller's images do in part function as deconstructions of celebrity mythology, they also work in support of the interests of the entertainment industry. It may seem ironic that photographs depicting stars as banal and unremarkable are industry-sanctioned. However, they respond to the contemporary moment, where a steady diet of reality TV, infotainment and media self-reflexivity is making audiences more sophisticated and more cynical about the images they consume.

Celebrity photography: a brief overview

For centuries, portraiture has been used as a significant means of generating interest in, and desire for, the celebrity. In *The Frenzy of Renown* (1986), Leo Braudy investigates histories of fame, tracing the lineage of the phenomenon back to Roman times. Braudy notes the role that technologies of mechanical reproduc-tion – from metal mould-making to printing – have played in the production of fame, and how they have fostered an increasing focus on the individual's face (1986: 265–312). With the development of photography, via an image that presented a faithful depiction of one's physical likeness, the means of spreading the scope of one's portrait was made available to a wider audience.

The subsequent availability of the technology of photography meant that a larger segment of the population had access to the means of making reproducible portraits. The popularity of the medium amongst amateur photographers and the widening availability of the technology contributed to a proliferation of images, representing an ever-increasing range of the social spectrum. This growing inclu-siveness may have contributed to changes in the visual codes used to represent individuals in portraiture. Braudy suggests that in photography, the conventions around the representation of prominent and powerful figures become more relaxed. Describing a Matthew Brady photograph of Abraham Lincoln (circa 1861–65), Braudy sees 'a homely face on an oversized body wearing rumpled clothes, with perhaps a domestic shawl over his shoulders' (1986: 495). This was a portrait devoid of the usual symbols or accoutrements of glory and prestige. In their study of nineteenth-century photography, Peter Hamilton and Roger Hargreaves note similar uses of the photographic portrait by the elite in Europe in the 1850s and 1860s. In the *carte de visite* portraits of Napoleon III of France and Queen Victoria and Prince Albert of Britain, these royal figures chose to be photographed in plain, everyday clothing instead of robes and jewels (Hamilton and Hargreaves, 2001: 45). This was so they could 'represen[t] themselves as "middle class" figures' (ibid.: 13). In these historical instances, photographic portraits have been very deliberately staged in order to elicit particular responses toward the depicted subjects. Whereas these heads of state used a visual vocabulary of commonness to identify with (and thereby appeal to) a mass audience, the images used by the entertainment industry tend to endow their subjects – usually performers who do not necessarily come from elite backgrounds – with a sense of polish.

To these ends, contemporary celebrity portrait photography has become extremely controlled, with technological developments in the areas of make-up, lighting, film, and physical and digital retouching offering the possibility of mastery over every aspect of the photographic frame. A typical magazine shoot does not just involve the labour of a photographer and the celebrity subject, but also that of a make-up artist, a hairdresser, a stylist, a publicist, an art director, one or more photographer's assistants and a retoucher. This tremendous allocation of resources is due to an increase in the symbolic and material 'value' of the celebrity. As Naomi Klein has observed, what is being depicted here is not just an individual, but a brand as well (2000: 49). Because the contemporary celebrity is often tied to a series of products, millions of dollars can hinge on the celebrity's image. Celebrity portraits are designed to embody the celebrity's brand, usually with the evocation of idealized qualities such as glamour, beauty, strength and talent. Because of the industry it supports, the photographs of celebrities that accompany magazine profiles, advertisements or other types of publicity are strictly controlled, and more often than not contribute to an iconography of glory.

The paragon of photographic Hollywood mythology is arguably the Hollywood Issue of the American magazine *Vanity Fair* (editor Graydon Carter has been quoted as calling *Vanity Fair* 'the High Sierra of the Public Image', see Gritten, 2002: 153). In this annual thematic issue, the magazine produces a photographic portfolio of the year's 'hottest' and most renowned actors. Backed by large budgets and shot by high-profile photographers such as Annie Leibovitz, Patrick Demarchelier and Mark Seliger, the images are often epic productions, with elaborate sets and costumes. They strive to capture the 'essence' of their famous subjects by situating them within the context of classic archetypes. (The magazine also produces an annual Music Issue, with a similarly structured portfolio.) For example, in *Vanity Fair*'s 2005 Hollywood Issue, famous actors are categorized by headings such as 'The Captivator' (Leonardo DiCaprio), 'The Thoroughbred' (Annette Bening), and 'The Strong Silent Type' (Javier Bardem), with accompanying romanticized imagery.[3] Even when an archetype denotes commonness, such as 'The Everywoman' (Joan Allen), the visual interpretation is pure fantasy: the 48-year-old actress is depicted lying in the grass, sexily sucking on an ice cube she's lifted from her drink, her long blonde hair highlighted by the sun, and her face smooth and wrinkle-free. The traditional iconography of celebrity portraiture, as exemplified by *Vanity Fair*, never ceases to idealize its subjects; it is situated firmly at the 'mythology' end of the celebrity photography spectrum.

The construction of the celebrity's image is a process whose aim is to build up mythical status, or something akin to what Walter Benjamin describes as 'aura' or 'cult value'. Benjamin defines 'aura' as the 'unique phenomenon of a distance however close it may be' (1968: 222), and attributes this sense of reverence to 'cult value', the reverence an object or image commands by virtue of its origins in ritual or religious use (ibid.: 225). For Benjamin, mechanically reproduced images, such as photographs or films, do not possess the same sense of presence or aura as original works (such as paintings or live theatre). However, he notes that

> The film responds to the shrivelling of the [actor's] aura with an artificial build-up of the 'personality' outside the studio. The cult of the movie star, fostered by the money of the film industry, preserves not the unique aura of the person but the 'spell of the personality', the phoney spell of a commodity (1968: 231).

Here, Benjamin describes the result of the publicist's work: the hype and aggrandizement that is produced the by film industry in the reconstruction of an actor's aura or cult value. The linkage of this cult value to that associated with ritual and religion is cogent. The phenomenon of fandom, involving 'the cult of the movie star', contains aspects of devotion, ritual and ecstasy that are comparable to the practice of religion. Chris Rojek (2001) has examined the various similarities between celebrity culture and organized religion, noting that they sometimes use identical devices to attract and interact with their devotees. These strategies include the use of 'elevation and magic' (Rojek, 2001: 96) and the production of elaborate spectacles (such as the Pope's world tours: Rojek, 2001: 97) in order to elicit a sense of awe and admiration from the public. The reverential, flattering, and sometimes even spectacular approaches taken in most 'official', star-sanctioned photographs adhere to these strategies for building up a star's cult value.

At the opposite end of the spectrum from this idealizing iconography lie the photographs produced by the paparazzi. Paparazzi photography is a hybrid genre that combines aspects of photojournalism, documentary, celebrity (editorial/ promotional) photography, and surveillance photography (Squiers, 2000: 271). Unlike the official portraits made with the celebrity's permission and input, the paparazzi images are made 'on the fly', usually catching the celebrity unaware and unprepared to be photographed. These photographs are characterized by their informal, unposed, candid, grainy and often unflattering depiction of the celebrity in his or her day-to-day activities; they stand as unmediated representations of the celebrity's 'real', or 'private', daily life. Although a print market for sensationalistic celebrity photographs has existed since the 1920s, it has grown into a huge industry, with numerous weekly magazines and tabloids fuelling the demand for candid photographs of the stars. Unlike more upmarket magazines such as *Vanity Fair*, magazines such as *heat*, *Now*, and *Closer*, have little regard for the image the celebrity is trying to promote (see also Rebecca Feasey's essay in this collection). In fact, they generally contradict the mythology of the celebrity's cultivated image by spreading gossip, looking for scandals, or publishing images that are purposefully unflattering. (For example, they aim to illustrate how terrible a female celebrity looks without make-up or to point out her cellulite.) The aim of most tabloids is to procure 'the dirt', to provide the reader with an 'inside' look at the celebrity's life, and the photographs similarly undertake this voyeuristic scrutiny.

Some argue that it is precisely this sense of transgression – the voyeuristic, illicit nature – that gives paparazzi images their value and credence. Allan Sekula refers to this as the 'theory of the higher truth of the stolen image', the presumption that candid, unguarded images are more natural, and thus more truthful, reflecting more of the subject's 'inner being' (1984: 29). This notion of the camera as a tool of penetration and revelation applies to all photography, but is particularly cogent in the celebrity context, where artifice and image dominate. As Sekula notes, 'The image of a celebrity is an institutional edifice ... The paparazzo's task is to penetrate that wall' (1984: 29). This produces an adversarial relationship between the paparazzo and the celebrity, with the star trying to defend his/her private realm against the photographer who assumes photojournalistic pretences in attempting to uncover the 'real story'.

However, due to the publicity and media exposure they provide, celebrities must negotiate some sort of working relationship with the paparazzi and tabloid press, providing them with material while still attempting to maintain some separation of their public and private lives. While many celebrities do scorn the paparazzi for aggressive tactics or undue encroachment on their everyday lives (see Squiers, 2000, and Halbfinger and Weiner, 2005), many also develop coping strategies. These include the fabrication of 'street faces', facades maintained in expectation of constant surveillance by the paparazzi (Sekula, 1984: 29), preemptively selling the rights to photos of their intimate moments (such as weddings) to tabloid magazines and even leaking real or staged photos to the media. The celebrity's need to participate in the economy of tabloid images – and not to restrict their depiction in the media to glossily produced images – speaks to the currency of the 'real'. Photography, portraiture, and the paparazzi are all structures that promise to provide more insightful answers to the question, 'What is so-and-so really like?' (see also Dyer, 2004: 2).

'Really': the celebrity photography of Juergen Teller

The prospect of capturing a truly unguarded moment from a celebrity subject would seem almost impossible, since he/she is highly skilled in assuming a constructed persona for the camera. The celebrity, with his/her inherent interest in cultivating a particular image for the sake of the brand, usually maintains strict control of a photography session through the negotiations of his/her publicist. The positive light favoured by most publicists makes for a fairly homogeneous range of depictions; against this field, the celebrity portraits of Juergen Teller stand out sharply. Casual, unstyled, average-looking, sometimes almost ugly, the photographs made by Teller seem in aesthetic terms more closely related to amateur snapshots than to the often stylized and codified portraits of the rich and famous. Teller's images present a flip side to the grand, glorifying *Vanity Fair*-style productions, showing stars sitting in apartments or hotel rooms, slumped on sofas: they juxtapose their extraordinary subjects with ordinary settings. Not only do these images turn up amidst interviews and profiles in magazines but they can also be found in fine art books, gallery exhibitions and print advertisements.

The trajectory of Teller's career testifies to his work's fluidity between contexts, media and genres. Teller worked for avant-garde fashion magazines *i-D*, *The Face*, *Purple*, and *Index* in the 1990s, helping to push the boundaries of the acceptable visual conventions in fashion photography. He has subsequently shifted his focus from fashion to the art world, garnering recognition for independent projects and gallery exhibitions. (In 2003, Teller won the Citibank Prize, an international award for photography.) His work can be described as an investigation of the everyday; his books and exhibitions combine images of still lives (decorative tchochkes, house plants), landscapes (cave interiors, train tracks) and portraits (friends, family members, and the famous).

In Teller's work, subject matter is treated equally. Photographs in which celebrities appear are not given special consideration in how they are made, formatted or displayed. In his monographs and exhibitions, there is no separation between the commercial work and the personal work, so that the images and 'spaces' of celebrity/fashion can be found alongside family/everyday life. For example, in his book *Märchenstüberl* (2002), images of Björk and Stephanie Seymour commingle with shots of an anonymous girl in a park and a frozen dead dog in a garbage can. The same grainy snapshot aesthetic is present in most of his work, irrespective of whether the context is fashion advertising or self-initiated projects involving members of Teller's family.

The lack of affect with which Teller regards his subjects has motivated writers to describe his work as '*primitive straight photography*' (Poschardt, unpaginated: 2003) and as possessing a 'hard-edged, often playful, occasionally brutal realism' (Smith, 2003: 40). These connotations are elicited by the informal approach favoured by Teller. His photographs of the famous take place in private, domestic settings in lieu of stage sets or the photographer's studio, working mostly with 35mm cameras, with minimal or unobtrusive styling and make-up. While other photographers, Richard Avedon in particular, have produced seemingly candid portraits of celebrities, their images still appear to be highly crafted. They are shot in a studio setting, with backdrops and lighting, often using large format cameras[4] and post-production manipulation. In contrast, Teller's images frequently, albeit not necessarily truthfully, connote the aesthetic of the 'snapshot': photographs that are 'spontaneously' snapped, occasionally with an amateur's point-and-shoot camera. Teller's approach produces images which have a sense of straightforward sparseness, almost to the point of grittiness and abjection. His fashion work in the late 1980s and early 1990s was renowned for its 'grunge' aesthetic, where the images were 'pared down, almost nondescript: the girls looked dishevelled and malnourished, the interiors functional rather than decorative' (O'Hagan, 2003). This 'grunge' approach carries over into his celebrity portraits. My first encounter with Juergen Teller's oeuvre was a photo spread of Brad Pitt shot for *Details* magazine (Jan/Feb, 2001). I recall being amazed at such unphotogenic pictures of a renowned Hollywood sex symbol. He appeared on the cover of the magazine leaning back in a chair, legs awkwardly slung open and fists clenched. Pitt seemed to be caught mid-gesture, lit by on-camera flash, and his face is contorted into a half-pucker, half-grimace. Teller's celebrity portraits contradict the normal aesthetics of celebrity photography to the point that they seem almost amateur. They are often grainy, sometimes lit by a harsh, head-on flash, producing overexposed, red-eyed subjects. The result of these raw portrayals is that the imagery is read as a 'truly uncooked approach to the authentic' (Poschardt, unpaginated: 2003). This concept of the 'authentic' is crucial to an understanding of the appeal of Teller's photographs.

Aesthetics of authenticity

In refuting the traditional iconography of celebrity portraiture, with its elaborate set-ups (which speak to wealth and power) and flattering, reverential depictions, Teller seems to remove the mythologizing constructs that have been built up around the renowned individuals he photographs. Teller's images employ very few modes of elevation. He uses 'as little equipment as possible' (Teller, unpaginated: 2003), and he often favours an automatic point-and-shoot camera with built-in flash instead of more specialized professional gear. Despite the fact that the public is accustomed to viewing these subjects in glamorous contexts or at a remove, the celebrities and spaces depicted in Teller's images appear accessible, regular and 'ordinary'. The effect of his photographs is the opposite of Benjamin's definition of 'aura': they produce the unique phenomenon of closeness however distant their subjects may be. In this process of visual levelling – in bringing the stars' images down to earth – Teller's photographs read as authentic representations, documents of 'real' people rather than larger-than-life stars, fabricated personae, the pampered elite or brand embodiments.

The simple, direct approach and valuation of the 'authentic' are characteristics more closely associated with the genre of documentary photography than with celebrity portraiture. While Teller resists simple categorization as a documentary photographer, his work does borrow elements from the visual vocabulary of documentary. He favours a pared down, straightforward approach which corresponds with documentary photography's ambition to provide objective, evidential accounts of events. In addition, Teller also seems to be concerned not 'with the spectacular or the bizarre but the ordinary and the meaningful' (Stott, 1973: 50) in his chronicling of everyday sights, from tyre tracks in mud and household objects to family life. In his work Teller exhibits an ethos present in documentary photography: the tendency to 'dignif[y] the usual and leve[l] the extraordinary' (Stott, 1973: 49). This process takes place on two levels: in the way in which the famous are depicted in the images; and in the exhibition of their portraits alongside images of the plain and mundane.

However, Teller's work also opposes some of the values embodied in documentary photography. His images lack an overt social project and, for the most part, an accompanying journalistic text. His attention to well-known and well-off subjects contradicts documentary photography's occupation with the powerless and voiceless, the 'people "a damn sight realer" than the celebrities that crowd the media' (Stott, 1973: 56). Furthermore, in Teller's images, there is an acknowledged degree of fiction in the subject's presentation of self before the camera: the result of collaboration between photographer and subject, and in the case of some images, input from stylists and clients. The results reflect a tension inherent in photography, the nebulous zone between the 'real' and the 'performed'. Despite this presence of the blurry boundaries between reality and construction in Teller's work, in the eyes of the general public – and those of most critics – his images still appear to be true, unmediated representations of his subjects. For example, Poschardt notes, 'These photographs are not symbols – they do not try and embody something but present what is shown directly, as reality' (2003: unpaginated). For all the various ways in which Teller's photographs are constructed and performed, the overall impression of his images is that they are straightforward, 'authentic' documents.

Authenticity and proximity: the return of the 'real'

A major distinction between Teller's photographs and the 'stolen' images most often found in tabloids is the access and proximity he is granted by his acquiescent subjects. The degree of cooperation and unselfconsciousness present in his subjects gives the impression that the photographs have been made during a casual get-together between friends, not as a result of a commissioned photo shoot. In Teller's *Kate after 25th birthday at Ritz, Paris* (1999), supermodel Kate Moss lies on a bed in a white bathrobe with her hair wet, as if she has just emerged from the shower (see Figure 12.1). She is on top of the shiny white bedspread, her head propped up by a pillow and her hands resting near her hips. Next to her are two stuffed animals, a leopard and a snake (birthday gifts perhaps?). Lying supine, Moss appears tired, as she looks at the photographer, who is positioned at the edge of the bed. There is not the slightest trace of alarm or concern on her face at the camera's presence or the photographer's proximity to this very intimate space and moment. If the image is to be taken at face value, this is the bed of her hotel room after she has returned from a birthday celebration. She has just bathed and is nude but for a bathrobe.

Figure 12.1 Juergen Teller, *Kate after 25th birthday at Ritz*, 1999

These images of celebrities combine feelings of closeness with the illusion of unmitigated experience, with Teller acting as a witness on the viewer's behalf. His photographs seem to be documentary dispatches from celebrities' inner circles – they aim to give the viewer a sense of what it is *really* like to be a part of a social clique that consists of fashion muses (Kate Moss, Kirsten McMenamy), rock stars (Björk, PJ Harvey), contemporary artists (Roni Horn), actors (Arnold Schwarzenegger, Winona Ryder), and indie film directors (Sofia Coppola, Harmony Korine). Teller's photographs attempt to strip away the 'excess' mythology that accompanies such cliques. For instance, in the aforementioned *Kate after 25th birthday at Ritz, Paris*, the photograph fails to depict any evidence of the decadence one would expect from a supermodel's twenty-fifth birthday party. There are no overflowing ashtrays, empty bottles of champagne or lavish gift boxes from Tiffany's. Instead, a bottle of water rests amidst some unremarkable clutter on the bedside table. While the room does exhibit traces of the hotel's elite qualities (the sheen of the sheets, the tapestry-like wall covering behind the bed), the photograph does not convey a sense of spectacular luxury (the bedside table is plain, the chair cluttered; the overexposure produced by the camera's flash washes out details which may have hinted at the quality of the bed linens). Moss appears tired, but she does not exhibit the level of exhaustion that would lead the viewer to infer a night of extravagant partying. Overall, the images give the impression that the stars' lives may not be so far removed from those of ordinary people.

By visually bringing these remote spheres together, the celebrities in Teller's photographs appear more 'real', a quality that seems increasingly valued by a public tired of glib sound bites and reports of the stars' extravagant lifestyles. The ordinary person is perhaps more likely to empathize with media figures that seem 'real' or 'normal' – not those who flaunt their privilege or who appear to be overly slick or rehearsed. This valuation of the 'real' has, in the last few years, manifested itself in the wide popularity of reality TV, which has led to increased representation of the 'ordinary' within mainstream media, and greater opportunities for 'regular folk' to become celebrities. Turner notes that the phenomenon of reality TV, coupled with technological advances allowing wider accessibility of media production, constitutes a 'demotic turn' in which media representations of the 'ordinary' are increasing in frequency and in their fidelity to the lived experience of the everyday (2004: 80–5).

This trend towards the 'real' is evident not only in the 'real' media depictions of ordinary people, but also in attempts by celebrities to portray themselves as 'real'. Increasing numbers of celebrities are using reality TV as a means of giving the general public insight into their private lives, to generate publicity. Initially, 'celebreality TV' (see also Su Holmes's essay in this collection) was more of a desperate attempt for faded or minor celebrities to revive their flagging careers;

Ozzy Osbourne (*The Osbournes*, 2002–4) and Jessica Simpson (*Newlyweds: Nick and Jessica*, 2003–5s) are good examples of this. However, as the genre proved to be a successful formula, more prominent stars began flocking to the format, for example with *Britney and Kevin: Chaotic* (2005) chronicling pop superstar Britney Spears's newlywed life. These series often show their celebrities in less-than-flattering lights, sometimes working in opposition to their cultivated media images. In their respective shows, pop starlet Jessica Simpson is often shown as a stupid, spoiled princess and heavy metal rocker Ozzy Osbourne as a senile, doddering old man. The effect, as in Teller's photographs, is a destruction of the celebrity's manufactured aura. For instance, Osbourne's image as a badass, bat-biting rock star has been obscured in the public's mind by the TV show segments where he's befuddled by the TV remote or dismayed by the constant pooping of the family dogs. However, in showing themselves struggling with mundane tasks, celebrities are re-imaging themselves in the guise of 'real people': bringing themselves down to a level where the audience can empathize with their foibles, and occasionally even feel superior ('I may not be rich and famous, but I can figure out a simple TV remote!').

The importance of being 'real'

In such a situation, the celebrity's openness and willingness to appear vulnerable may be interpreted as honesty or bravery. The positive effects of gaining the public's sympathy and estimation may well more than compensate for the negative effects of an embarrassing or unattractive depiction. This strategy, along with the dictum 'there is no such thing as bad publicity', may well have motivated Winona Ryder to pose for a series of Juergen Teller-shot ads for the Marc Jacobs Spring 2003 campaign. In 2002, Ryder was convicted of shoplifting a number of items, including a Marc Jacobs top. Indeed, Teller's photographs cheekily contain numerous references to the scandal. Although the campaign can be interpreted as a ploy to stir up controversy, in these images Ryder is directly acknowledging and confronting her scandal, instead of attempting to disavow or evade it. The images cannot be interpreted as apologetic; they contain a mixture of signifiers hinting both at Ryder's culpability and innocence. In one shot, Ryder, bed-headed and clad in a bathrobe, grins as she holds up a white sweater, similar to the one she was accused of stealing (see Figure 12.2). Clothing lies strewn about the room, appearing in and out of store boxes (which suggests the items were bought legitimately). Yet, at the same time, a pair of scissors – the implement she was shown using in store surveillance video to cut security tags off the purloined clothing – is placed within arm's reach on a nearby table. Another image shows a head-and-shoulder shot of Ryder, her bathrobe half-slipping off, holding a high-heeled shoe. Lit by stark on-camera flash, the image gives both the

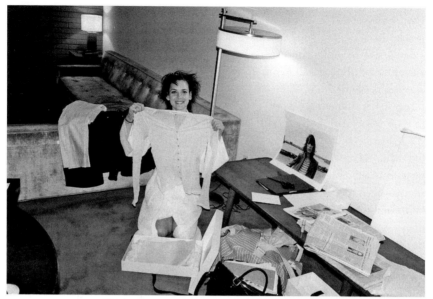

Figure 12.2 Winona Ryder photographed by Juergen Teller for Marc Jacobs' 2003 Spring/
Summer campaign

impression of innocence, a deer caught in headlights (Ryder's eyes seem especially wide and doe-like), and of guilt (the look of surprise and the bright lights
suggest that the camera has caught her red-handed; the frontal, head-and-shoulder view resembles a mug shot). Although somewhat coy, this indication of
Ryder's guilt seems almost refreshing or candid in comparison to the usual sugar-
coated and carefully worded apology offered by a fallen star. If used correctly,
authenticity and directness can be extremely effective public relations tools in
appealing to the public's sense of intimacy and trust.

A star's cooperation with Teller's flaws-and-all depiction is likely to be motivated by the necessity of cultivating the qualities of familiarity, proximity, intimacy
and trust.[5] These qualities are all necessary in the contemporary mechanisms of
what P. David Marshall refers to as the 'affective economy' (1997: 247), the ability
of a celebrity to generate emotionality and intimacy with fans. As the public
becomes more aware of, and hostile to, the manipulations of the media and the
mind-boggling extravagances in which the rich and famous indulge, 'realness', in
terms both of ordinariness and of honesty, holds increasing value. A celebrity's
ability to appear to be just a down-to-earth, regular person, someone the public
wouldn't mind having around, is crucial, since in the current media-saturated environment, the public is practically already living with them.

Because of the depicted proximity and immediacy of the celebrities in Teller's
photographs, they feed into the dimensions of the celebrity–public relationship

described as the 'para-social'. Para-social relations are those that take place at a distance, between individuals who are not in direct contact and who have not met. Turner summarizes the range of interpretations of the para-social relationship, from its characterization as 'disturbed or obsessional behaviour' (2004: 92) to 'an increasingly common feature of everyday life' (2004: 93). This latter point is implied in Chris Rojek's analysis, where he notes the significance of para-social celebrity relations at play in 'the search for recognition and belonging' (2001: 52), particularly in societies where isolation, individualism and depression are prevalent. Para-social interactions with celebrities can be a means of compensating for an absence of actual communities, particularly in advanced capitalist societies, where many day-to-day interactions take place at a distance (via email, teleconferencing, internet chat rooms). By exploiting this void, celebrities cultivate a loyal fan base, an enduring audience for their projects and products.

However, in order for celebrity para-social relations to be perpetuated, the individual must be able to believe that the celebrities are not so distant from those in their social circles. Even in cases of devoted para-social relationships, 'fans are sharply conscious of the gulf between the staged life before them and their own bounded circumstances' (Rojek, 2001:190–1). Images like those made by Teller work to breach this gulf, by bringing the celebrity back into the realm of the real and the everyday (that is, closer to the vernacular of the middle and working classes), and in depicting an intimacy built up via an enduring personal relationship (Teller has photographed Kate Moss over a number of years, capturing key moments such as her twenty-fifth birthday and the later stages of her 2002 pregnancy). A sense of closeness to these celebrities is developed via a series of casual, intimate images whereby they appear to be just hanging out in unremarkable settings, goofing around, or in a moment of tired reflection. Here, banality works as camouflage: because Teller's photographs so closely resemble snapshots of friends and family, it is easy for the viewer to forget that they are actually looking at ingénues in high fashion ad campaigns, paid more for one shoot than many people make in a year.

Conclusion: the rising currency of 'realness'

The importance of a celebrity's ability to appear 'real' has become more and more evident as the public reacts against the deceptive manipulations of those in power, whether they are trying to sell a war in Iraq or *War of the Worlds*.[6] The public's scepticism is no more evident than in the current media blitz and backlash surrounding the whirlwind romance between Tom Cruise and Katie Holmes. A *People* magazine poll reported that 62 per cent of respondents deemed the relationship a publicity stunt (quoted in Brown, 2005, and Rich, 2005), and media commentators describe Cruise and Holmes's engagement as 'a lavishly produced freak show' (Rich, 2005), or 'bad reality TV' (Goldstein, 2005). As *New York Times* editor Frank Rich observes, 'The boundary between reality and fiction has now been blurred to such an extent by show business, the news business and government alike that almost no shows produced by any of them are instantly accepted as truth' (Rich, 2005). Because the Cruise/Holmes romance lacks the appropriate signifiers of authenticity – the majority of photographs of the couple together have been made during prearranged photo-ops (at awards shows, during a press conference to announce their engagement, on the red carpet at movie premieres) – the public refuses to believe it is anything but a crass promotional device.

Juergen Teller seems to offer a counterpoint to these contrivances, his images functioning as visual islands of reality in a sea of PR overproduction. His photographs speak to a contemporary moment that Jean Baudrillard describes as 'an age of simulacra and simulation' (1984: 257), where the real has become extinct, indistinguishable from media fabrications, replicas, artifice. Although Teller seems to simply document his everyday world, it is important to remember his ties to the worlds of fashion and commercial photography, quintessential sectors of simulacra and simulation. In some ways, he does operate like a documentary photographer, standing in as witness on the viewer's behalf to shed light on worlds foreign to most individuals. As a result, he has produced work that disavows the usual Hollywood and fashion world fantasies, with images of stars that seem raw, rough, vulnerable and human. Teller has made considerable contributions to the broadening of the visual vocabulary of fame and fashion, offering alternatives to the ubiquity of gloss and perfect surface. However, these shifts cannot be read as radical critiques of the entertainment industry, as his images have been easily employed in, sometimes even commissioned by, mainstream print media and advertising. The depiction of celebrities as 'real' or 'regular' can be used to hide the vast hierarchical divisions between stars and ordinary people, a masking that is firmly 'in the interests of those who operate this hierarchy in the contemporary context' (Turner, 2004: 83), denying the true reality of economic and material inequality.

Placed within a broader social context, Teller's photographs can be read as evidence of a number of cultural and economic shifts: the demotic turn, the celebrity's need to appear accessible and 'real', and the increased valuation of the authentic in an overly-mediated society. Curiously, his images work simultaneously in the manipulations of the mass media and in their refutation: the desire for the 'authentic', the nostalgia for a sense of intimacy and community, the appreciation of human imperfections over slick fabrications. The photography of Juergen Teller does celebrate the beauty of the everyday, in the moments of aesthetic contemplation of a flock of birds against the sky or the edge of a swimming pool. However, because his work also functions to expand notions of 'the everyday' to include supermodels, rock stars, and multimillionaire actors, one must wonder to what (and whose) ends this expansion of the ordinary is used.

Notes

1 The distinctions between the terms 'star' and 'celebrity' vary according to different theorists, and colloquially they are often used interchangeably. In general, 'celebrity' is used to refer to anyone who has achieved widespread renown, either by merit, accident or notoriety. 'Star' is more frequently used to refer to individuals who have become famous via their activities in the art and entertainment industries, including film, television, music, art, fashion and sports. For the purposes of this essay, my use of the term 'celebrity' will be closely aligned to the concept of the star, with the two terms used interchangeably. This does not take into consideration 'accidental' or 'notorious' celebrities, such as kidnapping victims or serial killers. For more detailed discussions of the categories of 'celebrity' and 'star', see Rojek, pp. 9–24, and Marshall, pp. 4–19.

2 Wolfgang Tillmans, another German-born photographer prominent since the 1990s, also uses a casual aesthetic to photograph celebrities and everyday scenes alike. However, his celebrity portraits constitute a relatively small percentage of his total oeuvre, and their circulation is limited to fine art and editorial contexts, whereas Teller's images are disseminated more widely in commercial magazines and advertising contexts.

3 This categorization mimics the pantheon of social types that are applied to stars and their onscreen characters. Richard Dyer gives an overview of some common star types (1998, pp. 47–59) and suggests that ordinary individuals use these types in the construction, negotiation and performance of their identities. Furthermore, in her 1947 anthropological study of Hollywood, Hortense Powdermaker notes that this system of typing creates a 'standardised product' that can be 'advertised and sold' (1950, pp. 228–9).

4 Large format cameras such as those used by Richard Avedon produce big negatives (usually $4' \times 5'$ or $8' \times 10'$), from which it is possible to make prints with very fine, virtually invisible grain.

5 This is not universally the case. Teller relates an anecdote where he photographed an actress he had long admired; she hated the results, throwing him out of her house. The incident devastated Teller, prompting him to turn towards self-portraiture (see O'Hagan, 2003, and Smee, 2003).

6 Both Brown (2005) and Rich (2005) have used the backlash against the Tom Cruise/Katie Holmes romance and recent White House initiatives such as the war in Iraq as examples of the American public's increasing scepticism towards the news media.

Bibliography

Baudrillard, Jean (1984) 'The Precession of Simulacra' in Brian Wallis (ed.) *Art After Modernism: Rethinking Representation*, New York: The New Museum of Contemporary Art, pp. 253–81.

Benjamin, Walter (1968) 'The Work of Art in the Age of Mechanical Reproduction', in *Illuminations*, New York: Schocken Books, pp. 217–51.

Braudy, Leo (1986) *The Frenzy of Renown: Fame and Its History*, New York and Oxford: Oxford University Press.

Brown, Tina (2005) 'It's Only Publicity Love' available at www.washingtonpost.com/wp-dyn/content/article/2005/05/25/AR2005052502162.html, accessed 9 February 2006.

Dyer, Richard (1998) *Stars*, 2nd edn, London: British Film Institute.

—— (2004) *Heavenly Bodies: Film Stars and Society*, 2nd edn, London: Routledge.

Giles, David (2000) *Illusions of Immortality: A Psychology of Fame and Celebrity*, London, New York: Macmillan Press, St Martin's Press.

Goldstein, Patrick (2005) 'Lovesick Cruise *et al.* is bad reality TV', available at www.calendarlive.com/ movies/goldstein/cl-et-goldstein14jun14,0,2382578.column?coll=cl-goldstein, accessed 9 February 2006.

Gritten, David (2002) *Fame: Stripping Celebrity Bare*, London: Allen Lane.

Halbfinger, David M. and Weiner, Allison Hope (2005) 'As Paparazzi Push Harder, Stars Try to Push Back', *New York Times*, 9 June.

Hamilton, Peter and Hargreaves, Roger (2001) *The Beautiful and the Damned: The Creation of Identity in 19th Century Photography*, London: Lund Humphries in association with the National Portrait Gallery, London.

Klein, Naomi (2000) *No Logo: Taking Aim at the Brand Bullies*, Toronto: Vintage Canada.

Marshall, P. David (1997) *Celebrity and Power: Fame in Contemporary Culture*, Minneapolis and London: University of Minnesota Press.

O'Hagan, Sean (2003) 'Shooting Up', available at observer.guardian.co.uk/magazine/story/ 0,,929861,00.html, accessed 9 February 2006.

Poschardt, Ulf (2003) 'Feeling What You See', in *Juergen Teller, Märchenstüberl*, Göttingen: Steidl.

Powdermaker, Hortense (1950) *Hollywood: The Dream Factory*, Boston: Little Brown and Co.

Rich, Frank (2005) 'Two Top Guns Shoot Blanks', *New York Times*, 26 June.

Rojek, Chris (2001) *Celebrity*, London: Reaktion Books.

Rosler, Martha (1989) 'In, around, and afterthoughts (on documentary photography)', in Richard Bolton (ed.), *The Contest of Meaning: Critical Histories of Photography*, Cambridge, MA: MIT Press, pp. 303–40.

Sekula, Allan (1984) 'Paparazzo Notes', in *Photography Against the Grain: Essay and Photo Works 1973–1983*, Halifax: The Press of the Nova Scotia College of Art and Design, pp. 23–31.

Silverman, Kaja (1996) *The Threshold of the Visible World*, New York and London: Routledge.

Smee, Sebastian (2003) 'Foreign Bodies', *Independent*, September, magazine: 6–10; available online at www.lehmannmaupin.com/files/3e22a0f6.pdf, accessed 13 February 2006.

Smith, Caroline (2003) 'Teller Like It Is', *Photo District News* 23/4: 38–44.

Squiers, Carol (2000) 'Class Struggles: The Invention of Paparazzi Photography and the Death of Diana, Princess of Wales', in Carol Squiers (ed.), *Overexposed: Essays on Contemporary Photography*, New York: The New Press, pp. 269–304.

Stott, William (1973) *Documentary Expression and Thirties America*, Chicago and London: University of Chicago Press.

Teller, Juergen (2003) 'Interview with Juergen Teller, London, February 5, 2002', interview by Ute Eskildsen and Ulrich Pohlmann, in *Juergen Teller, Märchenstüberl*, Göttingen: Steidl.

Turner, Graeme (2004) *Understanding Celebrity*, London: Sage Publications.

Vanity Fair (2005) March: 535.

Chapter 13

The mockery of cartoon celebrity

The Simpsons and the fragmented individual

Suzanne Rintoul

Introduction

The phenomenon of the cartoon star has a long history in film and television. For example, the continuing success of Disney has been predicated on its animated 'stars' – as given on- and offscreen life through film texts which foreground their specialness, through public performances in utopian theme parks, and through the wider mass merchandizing of their iconic images. The super-iconic Mickey Mouse, the first animated character to have his own fan club, is suggested to be one of the world's most reproduced and instantly recognizable images. More generally, star-vehicle cartoons currently make up a great deal of television output – for both adults and children. From *Tom and Jerry* to *The Flintstones*, from *The Powerpuff Girls* to *The Simpsons*, there exists an animated galaxy of stars – an *industry* of cartoon stars – that signifies or enunciates at both textual and commercial levels.

The Simpsons is a striking case in point here. Textually, the show is driven by its star performers – by Bart and Homer Simpson in particular – while commercially it has spawned a vast range of merchandizing including computer games, socks, T-shirts, boxer shorts, DVDs, comic books, board games, Pez dispensers, alarm clocks, watches, satchels, posters, dolls and albums (including *The Simpsons Sing the Blues*). However, *The Simpsons* also adopts a critical perspective on the manufactured nature of fame through its mode of self-critique and ironic doubling. Stardom and celebrification becomes a primary target of mockery on *The Simpsons*, while the 'fame' of its characters is represented as hollow and arbitrary, accidental and ephemeral.

Thematically, *The Simpsons* often directly comments on its own textual and commercial functions so that stardom, merchandizing, the race for television ratings, corporate branding and a wider set of political and economic issues, find themselves regularly lampooned. The show exudes awareness of the ways in which these systems are precisely what facilitate its success and the consequent celebrity of its characters. But *The Simpsons* also implicates the audience in this self-reflexive mockery, since their anticipated desire for stars and celebrities is identified as narcissistic and naive. How then does one begin to make sense of the enormous success of a show that mocks its own audience's relationship to stars and celebrities?

In this essay, I would like to suggest that the cultural and commercial success of *The Simpsons* is predicated on the viewer/fan possessing a kind of double consciousness, or an awareness of being both mocked for participating in celebrity and star fandom, and a vehicle for its augmentation. Fans of *The Simpsons* are simultaneously ridiculed and exalted for being fans of the show. *The Simpsons,* then, offers a unique contribution to star and celebrity studies on a number of levels. The programme critically reflects on the manufactured nature of fame, it self-reflects on the simulated 'fame' that the show produces, and it situates viewers or fans of the show as both 'knowing' commentators on fame and as 'dupes' of the fame industry. *The Simpsons* creates a postmodern viewing position where the fan is marked by a degree of 'fragmentation', situated as both the target and deliverer of social critique.

Cartoon celebrity and celebrity authenticity

One can argue that the animated characters on *The Simpsons* are star and celebrity images without substance. While with 'real' famous people there is always the promise of a private life behind the public façade, with cartoon fame there is no offscreen world to refer to. Furthermore, because the characters in *The Simpsons* are drawn images, and thus entirely simulated, their fame cannot be defined in terms of a 'divine spark' or as having derived from something special inside them. Nonetheless, a 2003 BBC internet poll lists Homer Simpson as 'the greatest American of all time', and fans of the show engage with the characters in the show as if there is something 'real' about them. One can begin to argue, then, that while the stars and celebrities of *The Simpsons* are simulated agents, they are also being read as living individuals who participate in culture and the world at large. As such, they come to epitomize the collapse in distinction between reality and representation. The characters on *The Simpsons* belong to Baudrillard's concept of the *hyperreal*. They constitute 'the generation by models of a real without origin or reality' (Baudrillard, 1994: 1), and they connote the indecipherability of the authentic and its imitation. But *The Simpsons'* characters not only reflect the hyperreal, they ironize it, in what becomes the substitution of 'signs of the real for the real' (ibid.: 2).

While *The Simpsons* is itself known for its highly self-reflexive and ironic perspective on American society, its attitude toward stardom and celebrity is simultaneously part of what Joshua Gamson refers to as the wider adoption of irony and mockery in the construction of celebrity texts. Gamson argues that the media have increasingly chosen to lampoon and defame stars and celebrities, that stars and celebrities have become self-mocking about their status, and that fans/consumers 'read' famous people through ironic and sceptical filters (1994: 19–23). Such free-flowing irony and self-reflexive mockery provides the fan/consumer with the sense that they cannot be fooled by the manipulations of the fame industry, while it simultaneously allows them to participate in it. They are essentially 'part of a system and exempt for derision aimed at it' (ibid.: 52).

The stars and celebrities on *The Simpsons* exemplify the turn to (self-)irony and scepticism. They simultaneously deride viewers for participating in the emptiness of hyperreal stardom and celebrification, while creating the illusion that the viewers are outside, or exempt from, this derision. For example, the viewer's involvement with star or celebrity fakery emerges out of an invitation to identify with a narrative which mocks the machinery of fame and the fans who are 'duped' by it. In the 1994, Season Five, episode 'Bart Gets Famous', the viewer is encouraged to laugh at the ways in which fickle and brainless fans of *The Krusty the Klown Show* initially adore Bart for his quirky one-liner, 'I didn't do it'. The viewer is then asked to understand and identify with Lisa's reading of Bart's transitory fame as 'an obnoxious fad'.

In fact, in the early 1990s a string of Bart's slogans, including 'Cowabunga', 'Don't have a cow, man' and 'Ay Carumba!', were immensely popular. They were printed on T-shirts, recorded on alarm clocks, and imitated by fans of the show in playgrounds and households across North America. Bart became a star of the one-line slogan, and it was these slogans that became central to the mockery of fame taken up in *The Simpsons*. For example, when in 'Bart Gets Famous' Conan O'Brien cuts off Bart's discussion of the rainforest to make him 'do the line', *The Simpsons* is commenting on the de-politicized nature of fame, while simultaneously asking its viewers to laugh at its shallow nature. The comedy is again doubly self-reflexive: the show is referring viewers to its textual and commercial apparatus (the show is 'announcing' to its viewers that the comedy works in part because of Bart's 'starring' one-liners and it is these one-liners that are mass-marketed); and it is asking viewers to see through their own role in consuming (and fuelling the production and circulation of) 'empty' fads. However, because viewers are also supposedly 'in' on the joke, they can imagine that not only are they *exempt* from such derision but they are co-enunciators of this critique. *The Simpsons* allows its viewers to laugh at the show, themselves, and to identify with the politics of the programme even when they are being criticized as 'passive' viewers.

The Simpsons is particularly successful in its deployment of a 'double consciousness' because its animated format functions in terms of splitting. As cartoon characters they hyper-aggrandize their hyperreal status. They are, in effect, *hyper-hyperreal*. Moreover, they also hyper-aggrandize irony about the hyperreality of fame. These markers are important because while there is always an 'offscreen' world to go looking for a human star or celebrity's 'authenticity' or realness, there is no such place, or no other referent, for cartoon stars and celebrities. When Bart or Homer comments on the simulation of (their) fame they do so at least once removed from the usual rhetoric of celebrity discourse. However, they also make their hyper-hyperreal 'form' of fame the more dominant one.

The Simpsons' appearance at the 1990 Emmy Awards to present the award for best actor illustrates the way in which their simulated and ironic star images function to collapse the difference between the real and the mediated, and to draw attention to the fakery of fame. Their presence on the show confirms them as star or celebrity figures and as plastic commentators on the emptiness of celebrification. It undermines the award show's goal – to justify and show-case the 'work' of stars – because they are ironic stars and direct our attention to the fact that all fame is manufactured. In presenting an award, The Simpsons destabilize the notion that stardom finds its origins in charisma and natural talent. In fact, the entry of an animated and ostensibly inauthentic field into a 'real' one implies that neither is distinct from the other. Again, viewers who are 'in' on this implicitly critical message gain a sense that they are, in spite of their role in perpetuating the system by watching the glitz and glamour of an award show, exempt from the devaluation of the star system that emerges out of the convergence of living and animated celebrities. Ultimately, however, one could argue that this sense of clever exemption is ultimately what justifies their desire to keep on watching.

Cartoon celebrity and the fragmented individual

In his empirical audience research on responses to celebrity, Joshua Gamson has found out that three main epistemological frameworks organize reception. *Traditionals* are audience members who believe that stardom emerges out of merit and has a stable point of origin. *Second order traditionals* believe in a meritocracy of fame, but also acknowledge that stars and celebrities are manufactured. In contrast, *Postmodernists* are knowing viewers, aware that stars and celebrities are 'made up' and that success isn't the result of meritocratic drives but of the machinery of fame. In other words, Postmodernists specifically enjoy looking out for the fakery of fame (1994: 146–7). One can usefully employ Gamson's scheme to analyse *The Simpsons*. The show often self-consciously plays out these differing viewing positions through its fame-based storylines.

For example, in Season Twelve's 'New Kids on the Blech', Bart, Milhouse, Nelson and Ralph become famous as members of the manufactured boy band

Party Posse, a parody of pop groups such as *NSYNC and the Backstreet Boys. Even though none of the cartoon band members can sing, they are each given a perfect voice through the use of 'Studio Magic'. As a result they become huge stars. However, the songs the boys sing are actually full of subliminal messages such as 'Yvan eht nioj' or 'Join the Navy', a joke that the 'real' viewers of the show have privileged access to. Fans of Party Posse are examples of Gamson's Traditionals; the Simpson family is an example of Second Order Traditionals; while fans or viewers of *The Simpsons* are Postmodernists. The show, then, ironizes fandom, and draws attention to the 'lie' of fandom, while privileging its real viewers/fans with an omnipotent viewing position.

Nonetheless, the idea of splitting the audience also draws attention to the unstable, insecure nature of modern identity and the way that stars and celebrities wrestle with its fluid nature. As Richard Dyer argues, 'stars articulate a personhood, in large measure shoring up the notion of the individual but also at times registering the doubts and anxieties attendant on it' (1986: 9). *The Simpsons*' emphasis on the viewer who is both implicated in yet exempt from a critique of the game of fame speaks to the individual who is anxious about their identity in the modern world. The show seems to invite such instability or fragmentation since the viewer is caught in a self-reflexive relay that has no root or definite outlet. The viewer/text/star/celebrity relationship is always in flux, or under stress.

Voice and body: 'Stark Raving Dad' and *The Montreal Just for Laughs Festival*

I have so far made the case that the stars and celebrities on *The Simpsons* are hyperreal, animated characters who exist in a virtual reality. However, in one clear sense they do have a human point of origin, through the voices that in part give them life. In fact, one could argue that the human voices enable the 'mystery' of a private life or 'offscreen' world to emerge, but only in and through the performers who provide the lines of dialogue. And yet even here *The Simpsons* critically self-reflects on this relationship between human voice and cartoon body as a form of manufactured fame. This intertextual commentary works to lampoon the show, the show's network, and the show's audience – even if ultimately the mockery of fame that takes place endorses the economic and ideological power of all three agencies. This slippery process involves another type of splitting or double-bluff: making conspicuous what is displaced through the very act of displacement. For example, in Season Three's 'Stark Raving Dad', Homer believes a fat, bald mental patient's claim that he is actually Michael Jackson. Given that the character's 'voice' *sounds* like Michael Jackson, and that Jackson's changing, shifting physical appearance is itself the subject of media discourse, the storyline has a degree of ironic or knowing believability about it. The disjunction between the voice we readily recognize and the cartoon body we do not parallels the corporeal ambiguity that accompanies the 'real' Michael Jackson. This particular episode thematizes the star or celebrity as an unstable sign, as a public version of the fragmented individual, and it implicates the fame industry and the postmodern viewer in the commercial game that is in play here. The show seems to be calling on its viewers to try to figure out if the voice really does belong to Michael Jackson – in fact, it is banking on their desire to want to get behind the mask of fame. But the show, in its knowing and self-reflexive way, is also critical of the fan's desire to search for the authentic or the real. This particular episode, then, is as much about the dissolution of fame as it is about the constructed 'enigma' of Michael Jackson. The setting of the show in an insane asylum is thus a fitting one; it reflects the 'damage' and the madness of fame, and also the split consciousness of the viewer, doubly aware of the fan's inability to resist the ironic play of fame and yet consciously implicated in its enunciation.

The weekly stars of *The Simpsons* are voiced by actors who for the most part remain unidentifiable by the public. However, there is a great deal of fan interest in the human actors who provide the voices and there are opportunities for fans to see the Simpsons in the flesh, most notably at the *2002 Montreal Just for Laughs Festival* where the cast performed live readings that sold out three nights in a row. The title of these shows, *The Simpsons – In The Flesh*, itself suggests a type of splitting involving voice, body and animation. The presence of the human body also draws attention to the unseen cartoon character they now represent: this is a representation that makes it impossible for the audience to imagine that the characters on *The Simpsons* are anything but constructed star images. It is also a representation that returns the fan/viewer to the notion of the fragmented individual. For example, the fact that Bart Simpson is actually voiced by a woman (Nancy Cartwright) and can thus be a woman 'inside', as well as the fact that several characters can be read by one actor, gestures towards the way in which these characters are entirely split (voice/body, human/cartoon, woman/boy) within the context of their construction or manufacture.

The appearances at the *Just for Laughs Festival* can also be understood in terms of how the virtual or simulated becomes the primary referent for public identity and for fame. The embodied actors who *speak* in cartoon voices draw attention to the fact that their own brief moment of 'in-the-flesh' recognition is reliant on animated stars whose indexicality is free of the context of the 'real' person. The human cast of the show experienced a few nights of celebrity by virtue of their relationship to images, not the other way around.

Cartoons and celebrity parody

A great many of *The Simpsons'* comedic moments rely on viewers recognizing ironic and playful references and quotes drawn from popular culture, particularly the culture of stars and celebrities. The parody of fame also takes place through fame-based storylines, and bloated 'stock' characters – such as Krusty the Klown and Troy McClure – who act as commentaries on the negative values of fame and its hyper-hyperreal nature. *The Simpsons'* version of cartoon celebrity parody seems to be an open invitation to question the nature of simulated fame, and also the 'worth' of the show that produces such a bankrupt version of it. But the use of parody also seems to throw into confusion *The Simpsons* own signifying system since, while the practice of simulation involves liquid signifiers, parody is predicated on real world referents. The effect of blending hyperreal signifiers with what are 'real world' parodic targets is the splitting of the cartoon's diegesis – its commentary on fame, and the fragmentation of the viewer (both within and outside the show).

Krusty the Klown is a perfect example of this: he is a star/celebrity amalgam that appeals to both adults and children. He is a children's television show host, and an adult comedian, a parody of the late night television talk show host and the host of a kid's Saturday morning variety show. Krusty resembles a cross between Captain Kangaroo, Johnny Carson and Paul Reubens. The result is a confused and leaky representation that speaks to a viewership that is itself fragmented and not homogeneous. The sense that Krusty is both a rootless or virtual signifier of fame and a reference point for the 'real' stars and celebrities on which he is based is paralleled by the way he is consumed by both a cartoon-world audience and 'real world' viewers – the latter of which enjoy watching him on their 'real' world televisions.

The episodes that feature Krusty use his appearance as a device to collapse the differences between child and adult worlds, and the cartoon and real world. For example, when Krusty's 'live' show presents *The Itchy and Scratchy Show* – identified as the popular children's cartoon short – a high degree of blurring takes place. The representation of Krusty's show as 'real' and *Itchy and Scratchy* as 'fake' or cartoon, when both are similarly animated, draws the viewer's attention to the fact that the difference between the 'real' and cartoon world of Springfield is unstable. Moreover, the identification between real-life viewers of *The Simpsons*'s and the Simpson family as viewers of the Krusty show experientially connects the 'real' viewer to the hyperreal, to what is a space in between reality and representation. In this way, the viewer or fan of *The Simpsons* is divided between two kinds of (non)reality, a decidedly postmodern position to occupy.

Troy McClure is also important to the way *The Simpsons* parodies the machinery of fame. As a hyperreal and parodic *generic* celebrity, McClure provides perhaps the most conspicuous critique of the hollowness of celebrity culture and its hyper-hyperreal nature. For example, in Season Seven's 'A Fish Called Selma', McClure's on- and offscreen personae merge, while the depthless nature of fame is consciously referred to and ridiculed. The episode opens with Homer, Marge, Bart and Lisa watching the film 'The Muppets Go Medieval' starring Troy McClure and Miss Piggy. The show's knowing and satiric appropriation of Jim Henson's muppets nods to a commercial system where 'stars', regardless of talent, energize screen texts. However, the levels of self-reflexivity are much greater than this: the scene involves real viewers watching the Simpson family (the stars of *The Simpsons*) watching a film that stars Troy McClure (who will later 'star' in this episode) and Miss Piggy (a star of *The Muppets*). This constant deferral of signification is taken one stage further when later in the episode, McClure takes Marge's sister Selma to the drive-in theatre where 'The Muppets Go Medieval' is showing. The mise-en-scène here is such that the viewer is positioned in the backseat of McClure's car looking at McClure and Selma as they mimic the actions and words of the muppets on screen. McClure asks Selma, 'Willst thou grant me thy dainty hoof in marriage?' as his onscreen character mutters the same line to Miss Piggy. The placement of a movie screen within the real viewer's television screen further reveals the role of *The Simpsons* in such star and celebrity construction. This scene also places the 'real' viewer in the position previously occupied by the Simpson family at the start of the episode. This complicit real viewer/cartoon viewer positioning once again connects the hyperreal celebrity family with the family at home, gesturing towards the collapse of the real and the imaginary in all its environments.

Nonetheless, in the case of Troy McClure, *The Simpsons* offers an incongruous belief in the power of the real to prevail over the hyperreal. At the end of the episode Selma leaves McClure and their 'sham marriage', and the viewer is left wondering what happens to McClure's career. The epilogue to the episode fills in these details: in news magazine show format, the anchorman reveals that McClure gave up a starring role in the next McBain film – a mainstream Hollywood ultra-macho movie – to star in his own feature called 'The Contrabulous Fabtraption of Professor Horatio Hufnagel'. One is led to assume that it will fail miserably at the box office. In an ironic and final twist, however, the anchor does note that the film is being picked up by Twentieth Century Fox, the same company that produces *The Simpsons*. As such, the show mocks the artistic integrity of the company that facilitates its success, inviting the audience to identify with the joke even though this is the same audience likely to go see a film because of the 'major' star it features. Nonetheless, McClure's 'decision' to star in a 'personal' project can be read as an act of resistance to the rules of the fame game: he gives up a sure-fire blockbuster in favour of a film that seems uniquely 'Troy.' In this sense, McClure speaks to the myth of the tortured artist searching for truth, for realness in a world of fakery and simulation. Of course, in this plastic universe of *The Simpsons*, this is a cartoon star (of one episode) looking for the real in a cartoon world made out of hyper-hyperreality.

Conclusion

The Simpsons revels in its exposition of its problematic relationship to the 'real' or authentic. The show constructs a paradoxically self-deprecating version of star or celebrity to promote itself and to give the show meaning. The show is full of doubling and splitting that renders it textually and ideologically fragmented. *The Simpsons* exposes the frightening degree to which contemporary culture industries animate the real and celebrate the virtual, leaving a kind of nothing space in-between. The parodic and self-reflexive signifying system that constructs and upholds *The Simpsons'* paradigm of fame is, nonetheless, nihilistic – it cares little about the effects of the self-denigration that it wallows in. Postmodern viewers caught up in this game of division and merging are (made to feel) doubly anxious about their fractured identity and the unstable nature of a reality that increasingly resembles a cartoon.

Bibliography

Baudrillard, Jean (1994) *Simulacra and Simulation,* trans. Sheila Faria Glaser, Ann Arbor: University of Michigan Press.

BBC News (2003) 'Your Greatest American', available at news.bbc.co.uk/1/hi/programmes/wtwta/2997144.stm, accessed 10 February 2006.

CBC News (2002) 'Ay Carumba! "Simpsons" give rare reading in Quebec', available at www.cbc.ca/story/canada/national/2002/07/18/simpsons_020718.html, accessed 10 February 2006.

Dyer, Richard (2004) *Heavenly Bodies*, 2nd edn, London: British Film Institute.

Gamson, Joshua (1994) *Claims to Fame: Celebrity in Contemporary America*, Berkeley: University of California Press.

Marshall, David P. (1997) *Celebrity and Power: Fame in Contemporary Culture*, Minneapolis: University of Minnesota Press.

The Simpsons 1F11 'Bart Gets Famous' (1994) Twentieth Century Fox. 3 February.

The Simpsons 3F15: 'A Fish Called Selma' (1996) Twentieth Century Fox. 24 March.

The Simpsons 7F24: 'Stark Raving Dad' (1991) Twentieth Century Fox. 19 September.

The Simpsons 9F03: 'Itchy and Scratchy: The Movie' (1992) Twentieth Century Fox. 3 November.

Chapter 14

Spending time with (a) celebrity

Sam Taylor-Wood's video portrait of David Beckham

Catherine Fowler

I did it for the full 67 minutes, Karen Brant did it for 20 mins, Zoe and her mum from Harrogate only managed 6 minutes – what did we do? We walked, stood, crouched or sat in front of the sleeping body of David Beckham. Like the courtiers who would take turns to watch the king sleeping, we shared some intimate moments with this celebrity legend as he lay as if on the pillow next to us. And each of us was convinced that we had got closer to the 'real' David than anyone else.

In 2004, the National Portrait Gallery in London commissioned artist Sam Taylor-Wood to undertake a video portrait of David Beckham, and the resulting video will be my focus in this chapter. One outstanding quality of *David* is the way in which it seems to address each member of its audience individually: on a 67-minute loop the usually active Beckham is confined to a sumptuous frame in a darkened room where he lies 'sleeping', available for the gaze of his courtiers. Although the image represented in *David* is clearly recognizable as part of Beckham's celebrity sign, in other ways this image surprises. First, the 'hush' that the context inspires is very different from the usual hubbub of 'mass media Beckham'; second, the image is not fixed (in our memory or on the page) and then gone. Instead, it stays, and if we stay with it, it changes.

Through particularities of form (time-based artist's video) and context (the public art gallery), Taylor-Wood's *David* allows us to 'spend time with (a) celebrity'. Clearly, despite the perceived 'pervasiveness of celebrity culture' (Turner, 2004: 15), and the accompanying feeling that the celebrity (of whatever kind) is a 'known' and 'knowable' quantity, we are rarely able to penetrate beyond the mediated boundary that separates that which we are permitted to know from that which is unknown and unknowable. The reasons for this have been well documented by those studying the emergence of both global media and celebrity culture. P. David Marshall contends that this boundary relies on the agreement that the idea of 'intimacy' must always remain 'at the discursive level'. Thus:

> The desire and pleasure [of the relationship between audience and star] are derived from this clear separation of the material reality of the star as living being from the fragments of identity that are manifested in ... interviews, magazines, pinup posters ... and so on (1997: 90).

In a wider context Jean Baudrillard has suggested that '[t]he media present an excess of information and they do so in a manner that precludes response by the recipient' (Poster, 2001: 7). From this perspective, and following Marshall, we can argue that 'the fragments of identity' through which the celebrity is created invite only a *shared acknowledgement* of recognition. In contrast, Taylor-Wood's *David* invites an *individual response*. The image of David Beckham presented in *David* – whilst recognizable from previous encounters with him in newspapers, magazines, pin-up posters and on television – has nothing to do with what might be termed 'low' art mass media versions of celebrity, and everything to do with the high art connotations more frequently attached to the gallery space and often indexed by video art. Whereas the version of celebrity in the former feigns singular address while actually relying on a collective, highly public idolization, that constructed via the latter is presented in the gallery space for the spectator as a highly private image.

The video art of *David* offers a further locus for a 'fragment of identity' not anticipated by Marshall, and one that threatens to disrupt his neat division between 'material reality' and 'mediated image' by placing in-between the problematic 'presence' of the individual spectator. Unlike the media Marshall describes, which are always operating through a past tense, video art unfolds through a present moment, when visitor and work experience each other. That moment of co-presence creates the intimacy that disturbs Marshall's division because, as Chris Townsend has asserted: 'you have to see and feel installation art: its effects, and affect, cannot be mediated in secondary forms' (Townsend, 2004: 14). This notion of 'effects' and 'affect' will be central to my description of the experience of the video portrait of David Beckham.

This chapter uses *David* to explore both the causes and the effects of disrupting the neat division between 'material reality' and 'mediated image'. First, I introduce Taylor-Wood's work and briefly explore her specific interest in and attitude toward celebrity culture, as apparent in her earlier works. I then consider how photographic portraiture has developed in order to fit the celebrity portrait, inserting the sleeping subject in the gallery and *David* in its historical trajectory. Finally, I move to a discussion of the video itself, considering how its form and context produce a slippage between known and unknown and how they crisscross the boundaries between public and private space – both with respect to Beckham himself and the spectator who watches him.

Sam Taylor-Wood and celebrity culture

When one considers Taylor-Wood's background it is easy to see why the National Portrait Gallery offered her this commission. The celebrity culture we find in Taylor-Wood's work connects directly with Andy Warhol's repetitive use of Hollywood stardom in his Pop Art friezes and his factory of B-celebrity non-personalities (the Velvet Underground, Nico, Viva) who feature in his film works. Similarly, Taylor-Wood has surrounded herself with a stable of bright young British actors (Ray Winstone, Saskia Reeves, Oliver Milburn, Dexter Fletcher, Lara Belmont), and has worked with more famous figures: Kylie Minogue (for the short video *Misfit*, 1996), Robert Downey Jnr (who she filmed for her commissioned video of Elton John's 'I've found love' and later used in her own video *Pietà*, 2001), and the Pet Shop Boys (she produced a video to be used within their live concert). She also designed a vast photographic mural to cover the London department store Selfridges while it was undergoing alterations (*15 Seconds*, 2000). Finally, through her work and marriage to White Cube gallery owner Jay Joplin, she has constantly been discussed as part of the group known as the YBAs (Young British Artists). Others in the group are Tracey Emin, Sarah Lucas and Damien Hirst, and all are known for their 'provocative sensationalism often … mediated aesthetically by the high-visual-impact strategies of advertising' (Bush, 2004: 103). While Taylor-Wood's work is less obviously sensational, it certainly goes for 'high-visual-impact', with its frequent use of massive screens, wide-screen photographic canvases, bright colours and striking poses (and poseurs, more of which later). When she is not using British actors, her subjects are surrounded by upper- to middle-class props and settings and are captured in contexts of wealth and leisure (rather than poverty and work).

All of this has meant that Taylor-Wood has frequently been accused of creating a glamorous pseudo-aesthetic with its accompanying accusations of pure surface and sensationalism. Taylor-Wood's reaction to this accusation has been to suggest substance and depth through connections to high art of the past. Examples include assertions that *David* can be connected to Michelangelo's similarly named sculpture, that her Selfridges piece could be seen as 'a contemporary version of the Elgin marble frieze from the Parthenon, peopled with modern-day "gods" to adorn a temple of shopping'(Sam Taylor Wood, quoted in Gall, 2000: 45), and that her use of celebrities can be compared to artists 'from the Renaissance … to Gainsborough', all of whom have 'used important people of their current social situations as subjects' (Carolin, 2002: unpaginated). Furthermore, like many such artists, Taylor-Wood suggests that the intersection between commerce and art, popular culture and high art, has been a subject in her work. As she has asserted many times, her work builds on a solid history of artists who have incorporated recognizable media images as a reflexive act – with the aim of making the viewer reflect on the dominance of the media, and its capitalist capacity for promoting mythic and fantasy narratives.

From photographic portrait to celebrity portrait

Celebrity culture can be said to descend from the development of photography. Early instances of portrait photography (in the 1800s) saw it as 'an art of person: of identity, of civil status, of what we might call, in all senses of the term, the body's formality' (Barthes, 1982: 79), and Barthes has described the ways in which this 'formality' was engendered in the mechanical instruments that allowed the subject to adopt a static position for a long duration. As he explains: '[T]o become an object made one suffer as much as a surgical operation; then a device was invented, a kind of prosthesis invisible to the lens, which supported and maintained the body in its passage to immobility' (ibid.: 13). Even at this early stage the idea of the portrait as conveying an idea of the person to a public (something, then, they are *known* for) is present. However, a key shift takes place in the transition from the portrait to the idea of the celebrity as constructed across photographic media. As Graeme Turner notes:

> Unlike that of, say, public officials, the celebrity's fame does not neces-sarily depend on the position or achievements that gave them their prominence in the first instance. Rather, once they are established, their fame is likely to have outstripped the claims to prominence developed within that initial location (2004: 3).

From the conventions of the portrait, the celebrity photograph would take this interest in the known, but – in keeping with celebrity culture – more emphasis would be placed on the formerly unknown, the private life of those photo-graphed. Using the National Portrait Gallery photographic collection as an example, what is striking in the majority of photographs of contemporary celeb-rities is the way in which they are aware of the camera, either looking straight at it or acknowledging it with a knowing expression. No 'invisible' prosthesis is needed for these subjects to help them to remain still, or in pose for the camera. In fact – leaving the obvious improvements in technology aside – there are few signs of 'work' or time taken to create these portraits. Instead they might be said to express the instant gratification that so many have diagnosed celebrity culture as signifying, in which 'modern celebrity' is often seen as 'a symptom of the worrying cultural shift: towards a culture that privileges the momentary, the visual and the sensational over the enduring, the written, and the rational' (Turner, 2004: 4).

This discussion of how celebrity culture may have shifted the nature of the public portrait and how it engages us as viewers, shapes Taylor-Wood's past work, which has consisted of both large-scale photographic series and video art. Both forms have consistently played around with the perceived boundaries between public and private, ideas of acceptable behaviour, and personal emotions. For example, in her *Five Revolutionary Seconds* series (14 large-scale photos taken with a camera that pans a full 360 degrees; 1995–9), the conventional use of images as evidence of social or subjective reality is challenged. Internal worlds are played out across opulent lofts, and a combination of bodies and subjectivities clash incongruously – such that the idea of the photographic image as a form of proof or a Barthesian 'art of person' is tossed aside. While none of her subjects are 'famous faces', here we see early evidence of the disturbing of the public and private worlds of her figures who we might call pose[u]rs in both senses of the word.

In this series and other photo works, ideas of display and performance are combined with an exploration of intimacy and in particular, the intimate space that surrounds the couple at the moment it is in distress. Rather than ensuring a closeness to 'reality' by reproducing it, she has been particularly concerned with setting up images and scenarios that challenge any desire to identify with a body onscreen, while simultaneously inviting our own bodies to get involved. In *Travesty of a Mockery* (1995), an arguing couple are divided between two screens as they throw crockery and fight in their kitchen. The couple are violent and abusive and the two-screen set-up seems to divide our attention between 'her' space and 'his'. This allows them to largely keep to their territories, up to the point where an object crosses the screen, and suggests an invasion of private space. This onscreen transgression of space suggests similar possibilities offscreen, since the function of the piece is to get the viewer to question the materiality of all space, and in this and several other pieces Taylor-Wood invites our involvement through invading our space of watching.

In *Atlantic* (1997), three screens allow us to see a mid-shot of a restaurant with a close-up of a woman's face on one side, and a man's hands on the third screen. The couple in mid-shot on the central screen can be seen to be arguing or breaking up on the accompanying two screens. Once again, at one point the space of one screen is invaded by an object (here the man's hand touching the woman's face) from a different screen, and our involvement is invited in the way we have to keep turning our heads and bodies in order to map the two end 'close-ups' onto the couple in the middle.

Finally, in *Third Party* (1999), a party has been filmed with six cameras with the view from each placed on the four walls of a black cube. Views are offered of various partygoers, including a husband watching his wife laughing with another man and an older woman (Marianne Faithfull) sitting and smoking. The sixth screen shows a camera that spins round the whole room. The spatial arrangement of *Third Party*, as mapped across six separate screens around a black cube, forces its viewer to constantly turn in space (like the spinning camera). In trying to piece together a highly fragmented narrative, the viewer is encouraged to try and discern what might be happening between the frames (in the offscreen spaces) that are motivating the screen world.

Once these previous works are considered, we can see *David* as the latest of a series of works that negotiate the boundaries between public image and private realities and which use their form to involve the spectator in the conflict. In this case the conflict is between the intimacy (closeness) of being there while Beckham sleeps, and alienation (distance) because of the way this highly constructed subject has been filmed in an eroticized state of being.

Celebrity Beckham

> In the public sphere, a cluster of individuals are given greater presence and a wider scope of activity and agency than are those who make up the rest of the population ... We tend to call these overtly public individuals *celebrities* (Marshall, 1997: ix).

While we can recognize some aspects of David Beckham's celebrity image in Marshall's description above – he is clearly an 'overtly public individual' – it should also be acknowledged that Beckham's precise status as a celebrity is more contested. Having considered some of Taylor-Wood's preoccupations, it seems significant that she chooses to emphasize those aspects that set up this contestation. Beckham's emergence as a talented footballer only slightly superseded his relationship with Victoria 'Posh Spice' Adams. Consequently, his rising celebrity star became both 'deserved' (because of his proven 'natural' talent) and 'constructed' (because of the media hype around his relationship and subsequent marriage). The associations of the second have often overshadowed the first, such as when he was photographed in tabloid sports pages in outfits which were more fitting for the couple's appearances in celebrity magazine fashion photo-shoots (such as the famous sarong).

The active, skilful image of footballer Beckham remains out of frame in *David*. Although there is mention in the text that accompanies the piece that the video was filmed following a training session with Real Madrid, when the player would be presumed to be at his most relaxed, this is really the only reference to Beckham's physical profession. Equally, with the famously skilful feet well and truly out of the picture, focus rests on Beckham's eroticized torso. With his career as a footballer up for constant analysis and criticism, and his family life a series of calculated media spectacles, Beckham's every waking hour would seem to be spent in public. This is perhaps why Taylor-Wood has chosen to film him posing 'asleep' – as an apparent guarantor of the as yet uncelebrated. The decision seems radical: when would we ever get the chance to stay with Beckham while he sleeps? Surely this is the ultimate example of aiming to foster the sense of an 'un-mediated' image, a sense of private vulnerability and of passive submission to the intrusive glare of the lens? Further, the 'availability' of the otherwise married Beckham is suggested once we consider that *David* opened at the beginning of April 2004, some months after Beckham had been accused of having an affair with his PA, Rebecca Loos. Taylor-Wood has managed to capture a portrait of a figure of desire at his most alone (at a time when British newspapers were full of stories of the consequences of his loneliness), while also providing an exploration of presence in the absence of an audience. In the absence of those actions that form the 'fragments of identity' for which he is celebrated – off the football pitch, away from his family, and outside familiar media frames – Beckham assumes an unforeseen presence not for a collective audience but for a spectator. In order to explore the 'presence' of the time-based sleeping subject further, it is worth briefly documenting recent examples. I will consider three: Bill Viola's video installation *Threshold* (1992); Cornelia Parker's 'live' installation *The Maybe* (1995); and Andy Warhol's 6-hour 16mm film *Sleep* (1963), which is mentioned in the text that accompanies *David*.

In Viola's installation *Threshold*, we emerge from a darkened corridor into a chamber where 'we will gradually come to perceive the shadowy images and breathing sleepers projected on to three walls' (Neumaier, 2004: 57). More famously, in *The Maybe* Tilda Swinton and artist Cornelia Parker teamed up, entrapping Swinton in a vitrine for two weeks where she lay in the centre of the Serpentine gallery dozing, tossing and turning, sleeping surrounded by objects that had belonged to historic figures. Viola's piece would seem to be a prelude to the floating, plunging figures we find in his recent installations (such as *Five Angels for the Millennium*, 2001). His sleepers do not move in realistic ways; instead it is as if they are caught in a twilight state, between living and not living, and they assume traces of life that our eyes have to work hard to fully discern. Parker's intentions could be said to be more 'performative'. We are confronted with a large, vivid body laid out as if a corpse, on view. Yet since the act of sleeping is so private and the body so present, one is reluctant to scrutinize Swinton too closely lest she wake up and we are discovered scrutinizing her. If for Viola the sleepers are barely present, and instead they form hulks of slowly moving surfaces into which our gaze can be drawn, for Parker the sleeping body is a challenge to our voyeurism, since at any moment Swinton could wake, stir, and look back at us.

Warhol's *Sleep* seems to want us to be aware of a similar kind of corporeality to that found in Parker's installation. In this film, amateur poet John Giorno (on whom Warhol was partly fixated) invited Warhol to film him sleeping over a couple of weeks. Warhol's camera framed Giorno in several different positions: from the abdomen up, in close-up on his face, and in long-shot across the room. These shots were then edited and repeated to form the 6-hour film. Warhol and Parker confront us with their subjects' bodies such that we cannot ignore the realities of sleep: the loss of pose revealed in involuntary movements, secretions (of sweat, dribble, and tears) or the half-awareness of finding comfort positions for the body. To a certain extent their models could be seen as providing a universalized image of someone sleeping. In contrast, Viola's images are more esoteric and less vivid. Their shadowiness lends to them an abstraction that suggests that the encounter with these images might be like sleep-walking, whereas with Warhol and Parker we are firmly awake.

In *David*, we could say that Beckham exists in between these two examples. He is more visibly present than Viola's figures, but less corporeally real than Swinton. Although he is not actually present (like Swinton), the uninterrupted duration of the video means that the weight of his 'presence' shifts: the more we watch the more we become involved with his body as it makes an increasing impression on the sheets that cover it and the frame that limits it. To explore the transformation of presence that unwinds over time I now turn to the form and context of the video.

Seeing *David*

> I enter the gallery as it opens, 10 o'clock. At first I wander among portraits, not sure where I am going. Then I see the sign: 'David', Rm 417. I gingerly enter the chamber, look to my left, there's the plasma screen, but I am too close in my present position so look to my right and retreat to the far wall – though still only about 10 feet from the screen, I am alone.

The publicity for the opening of *David* describes the piece as an 'intimate' portrait, creating a 'reverential and vulnerable image'. To reach *David* we must walk past photos of similar bright young British things such as Kate Moss and Stella McCartney. Then we turn away from these into the specially created private chamber. It is screened from the outside so that we cannot see the plasma screen or indeed who might be looking at it, until we have actually entered.

The first few minutes of this video show Beckham framed from the top of his head to the bottom of his ribs as he lies on his side facing towards us. He is naked, though blue covers are just perceivable on the right side of the frame, and he wears bracelets around one wrist. Earrings, a cross around his neck and tattoos are all visible, dressing the bare body. The colours are sumptuous: his skin shines against the darkness behind him and the white sheet on which he lies (although the shallow depth of field means that there is not really a behind, only an on-top). The grain of the image is fine and lighting highlights the edges of his body – his shoulder high in the background, his hands folded in the foreground. At the start of the video Beckham is perfectly framed so that all body parts can be seen. His blond hair falls away from his face, and both hands are placed under his chin (fortuitously tilting his face towards us). The background is largely in shadow apart from a blue spot of light just behind his ear.

For the first few minutes he is still, and we feel free to gaze unhindered. We can take in the image as if it were a painting – abstracting lines and colours, shapes and shadows – before registering the media status of the image and its depiction of a ubiquitous sportsman and husband, for once apparently caught off-guard and out of the limelight. Everything about this portrait suggests the private, in Barthes' words, 'that zone of space, of time, where I am not an image, an object' (Barthes, 1982: 15). It suggests this because he is 'alone', because he is 'sleeping' (with its accompanying connotations of authenticity), and because, prior to this, it is an image we could only have imagined, yet never have expected to share. However, very soon our initial, and seemingly unchallenged, look at the still and dormant Beckham is shattered, as from now on *he moves constantly*.

> *He is centrally framed, I have seen this image in reviews. He appears rested and alone. 10.03 the first movement begins, I am shaken from my own stillness as I had fallen in to contemplation of the image, I settle back in to this, then 10.04, 05, 06 his face has moved ever lower, I have to tilt my head to the left to properly view his features. He starts to look like a disembodied head. Through his movements I can now see the impression his body has made on the bedcovers, the first trace of time passing.*

What begins as a painterly still image in front of which we could be left to our own thoughts and desires, suddenly acquires a life and subjectivity of its own.

> *Between 10.06 and 10.13 three people wander in. Like me they are at first unsure about where to position themselves. My scribbling presence in the most favourable corner also seems to put them off staying too long. The angle of Beckham's head still requires a left tilt from the spectator; this means that to stay they would have to sit near me, if they stand they are in my way. In this time Beckham has licked his lips and moved his top (left) arm from its supportive position under his right cheek to a rather awkward position resting on his left hip. We see more of his abdomen, evidence of a taut lean midriff. Once in this position he now rocks from his hips, his whole body facing increasingly toward the bed.*

It is in this moment that the shift from the still photograph to moving (video) image takes place, with a concomitant replacement of the 'blink of an eye' 'perfect' image with an image that moves away from that fixed luminescence. This moving away takes the form of an emergence of corporeality. The body which had been beautifully – flatly – posed begins to acquire dimensions.

> *The three initial visitors have left, I am alone again, but Beckham is no longer restful. He repeats a series of small comfort movements that are in fact increasingly familiar, clichés from all sleepers (including myself). He strives for maximum comfort, but can't seem to decide where to place his hands. He shifts them from under his cheek to down the far side of his body. The second time this happens he scoops his fringe up with one hand, later as he places his top arm back under his cheek he catches his necklace with his thumb and the fluidity of the movement – its seamlessness is broken.*

The effect of Beckham's restless re-adjustment is that even his stillness now seems stage-managed. While asleep we might dribble, snore, twitch and grimace, yet the two dominant resting positions Beckham adopts have clearly been chosen for their acute visual pleasure: the first, in which he begins, with hands tucked under head, allowing his face to be clearly seen; the second, which he moves to, with one hand down the far side of his body, directing the eye to his torso. Though he moves his head, licks his lips, pushes his hand through his hair, along with countless other movements, the impression of a body 'posed' in the sense of 'arranged', aware of and inviting the gaze, never passes. As Dick Hebdige comments: 'to strike a pose is to pose a threat', to 'transform the fact of surveillance into the pleasure of being watched' (Hebdige, 1983: 86).

Following Hebdige we might suggest that this posing on the part of Beckham worries the gaze, disturbing the pleasurable contemplation of the eroticized male body that has thus far existed. Here we can recall the critical attitude that art often adopts towards the mass media and ask: Is it Taylor-Wood's intention to critique the spectator's gleeful, complicit objectification of Beckham, or is it the abundant Beckham she wishes to critique? A brief detour via film theory provides insight here. With his active persona and his confident, decorative masculinity, Beckham might be compared to the 1920s film star Rudolph Valentino. The pleasures of watching Valentino were interwoven through the narratives of his films, as in, for example, *Four Horsemen of the Apocalypse* (1921, Rex Ingram), *The Eagle* (1925, Clarence Brown), and *Son of the Sheik* (1926, George Melford), with their contrived displays of masculine skill in swordsmanship, combat or dancing. Attempting to theorize Valentino's attraction for female fans in relation to Laura Mulvey's (1975) psychoanalytic model of spectatorship, Miriam Hansen suggests that

The figure of the male as erotic object undeniably sets into play fetish-istic and voyeuristic mechanisms, accompanied – most strikingly in the case of Valentino – by a feminization of the actor's persona. These mechanisms, however, cannot be naturalized as easily as they are in the representation of a female body. They are foregrounded as aspects of a theatricality that encompasses both performer and viewer (Hansen, 1991: 260).

The 'feminization' effect to which Valentino is susceptible is also available for Beckham in this video. First, one of the ways in which Valentino neutralized this effect, through the powerful, desiring gaze at the woman, is clearly not possible for Beckham. Not only does he not have the gaze but his sleeping posture ampli-fies the voyeuristic nature of the image: he simply cannot look back. Second, although his body is not 'cut up' in true fetishistic fashion, the adornment of his body with bangles, earrings and a necklace does suggest fetishism (though admit-tedly we might excuse his adornment by calling up the 'metrosexual' and feminized masculinity for which he is known). Reading *David* through Hansen's conception of Valentino, the idea of a complicit theatricality seems highly attrac-tive. On the one hand, we are drawn into the sumptuous image: the time spent with the fidgeting Beckham peels layers and layers from the initial recognizable, public image, to leave a sense of engagement on a personal and intimate level. In the culture of the three-minute celebrity interview, and the snapshot *Hello* life-style-of-the-stars-feature, Sam Taylor-Wood has given us pause, time out, by placing time in the image and making the reward for spending time priceless. Yet on the other hand once the pose is evident, we must decide whether to continue sanctioning the display, or to look away.

This double bind of being complicit with or rejecting the pose must be reconfig-ured in light of the difference between cinema space and gallery space. *David* is not taking place in a cinematic darkened space where we lose our bodies in our private space. Instead, the viewing space for *David* constantly reminds us of our bodies and how we might want to place them in relation to the screen on which he lies. Furthermore, given the small size of the chamber and the placement of the screen, those entering the space are immediately in the way of those already viewing. *David*'s out-of-frame arrangement disturbs the unfolding of a private viewing expe-rience that the in-frame images offer. Even if we settle into the darkest corner the effect is such that we are constantly caught looking. Hansen notes of Valentino's fans, 'the Valentino cult gave public expression to a force specific to relations *among* women' (Hansen, 1991: 260). As Beckham's fans, and in the twilight space of the gallery, we are caught looking at him by other women.

Taylor-Wood's video portrait *David* seems to provide a map of the *actual* distance between celebrity and fan or viewer. On the one hand, the consumption of *David* is driven by its promise to breach the 'tension between the possibility and impossibility of knowing the authentic individual' (Marshall, 1997: 90). On the other hand, the intimacy implied by this promise is continually disturbed by the public space in which this consumption is taking place. We need to remind ourselves here that 'the pleasures and identifications on offer to consumers of certain media products can vary markedly' (Turner, 2004: 8–9). Crucially, it is the time-based and gallery-situated nature of *David* that creates the binary experience of watching: from an initial impression of unforced intimacy and the private zone, to a gradual realization of the pose that destroys intimacy and reminds one of the public context of this image. I witnessed this transformation repeatedly as new women entered the chamber. Finally, although *David* may not actually give us the kind of privacy of the courtier watching the king sleeping, it does allow us to spend more time than we have been used to with a celebrity, and, once the hush has descended, we may find – in-between the posing – that moment in which it feels as if we are getting to know and to respond individually to the new David (Beckham, that is).

Bibliography

Barthes, Roland (1982) *Camera Lucida*, London: Jonathan Cape.

Bush, Kate (2004) 'Young British Art', *Artforum International* 43/2 (October): 103.

Carolin, Clare (2002) 'Interview with Sam Taylor-Wood', in *Sam Taylor-Wood*, Göttingen: Steidl, unpaginated.

Gall, Michaela (2000) 'Frieze-wrapped Art – Sam Taylor-Wood's Mural for Selfridges', *New Statesman*,

Hansen, Miriam (1991) *Babel and Babylon: Spectatorship in American Silent Film*, Cambridge, MA: Harvard University Press.

Hebdige, Dick (1983) 'Posing ... Threats, Striking ... Poses: Youth, Surveillance, and Display', *SubStance* 3/37–38: 84–90.

James, David E. (1989) *Allegories of Cinema: American Film in the 1960s*, Princeton, NJ: Princeton University Press.

Marshall, P. David (1997) *Celebrity and Power: Fame in Contemporary Culture*, Minneapolis: University of Minnesota Press.

Mulvey, Laura (1975) 'Visual Pleasure and Narrative Cinema', *Screen* 16/3 (Autumn): 6–18.

Neumaier, Otta (2004) 'Space time video', in Chris Townsend (ed.), *The Art of Bill Viola*, London: Thames and Hudson, pp. 47–71.

Owens, Craig and Bryson, Scott (1992) *Beyond Recognition: Representation, Power and Culture*, Berkeley: University of California Press.

Poster, Mark (2001) (ed.) *Jean Baudrillard: Selected Writings*, Stanford, CA: Stanford University Press.

Rojek, Chris (2001) *Celebrity*, London: Reaktion.

Townsend, Chris (ed.) (2004) *The Art of Bill Viola*, London: Thames and Hudson.

Turner, Graeme (2004) *Understanding Celebrity*, London: Sage.

Chapter 15

'I'm jealous of the fake me'

Postmodern subjectivity and identity construction in boy band fan fiction

Kristina Busse

It's boyband slash. And man, have I got it bad. Four stories in a week, with more coming. What's more, I hate these bands. I don't go near them. I hadn't even *heard* of *nsync . . . I have feminist-type issues with boybands – they're a multi-media product designed and marketed to stimulate particular emotions in young women, but the mass culture which works tirelessly to generate those emotions also disrespects them, and the industry which profits from them must invalidate them when the band's sales-cycle winds down(Julad 2001).

Over the past few years, thousands of stories have appeared on the internet featuring the members of the male vocal group *NSYNC as their principal characters. *NSYNC, with its members Chris Kirkpatrick, JC Chasez, Joey Fatone, Lance Bass and Justin Timberlake, rose to fame in the late 1990s with chart-topping hits and record-breaking sales; they are a quintessential boy band, adored by pre-teenage girls and derided by almost everyone else. In fact, their star function is such that their public life has become a narrative often unrecognizable to the stars themselves: Justin Timberlake (2003), for example, points out that his life in the media is more interesting and appealing than his actual life, a sentiment exemplified by the quotation that constitutes the title of this essay. However, a large number of the stories circulating on the web differ from such official accounts. As Julad's account above indicates, she became a fan of the group only via the fan narratives. Her fannish obsession with *NSYNC developed out of her engagement with the stories and the fan writing community. Moreover, rather than being a passive consumer, she clearly analyses how she is implicated in the interaction between the commercial presentation of the pop stars and her own fantasies about them.

While popular conceptions of *NSYNC fans tap into historical perceptions of adolescent girl fans from Beatlemania and beyond (Frith and McRobbie, 1990; Ehrenreich *et al.*, 1992; Driscoll, 2002), Julad belongs to a community with a decidedly different fannish lineage, shorthanded by its members as *popslash*. Slash is a term derived from media fan fiction and describes the narrative expansion of media texts and, more specifically, the depiction of relationships between same-sex characters in the fictional world (Bacon-Smith, 1992; Jenkins, 1992; Penley, 1992). While this phenomenon can be traced back to the late 1960s and early *Star Trek* 'zines featuring fan-authored stories, it has become more widespread with the rise of the internet and now includes almost every TV series, many movies and books, as well as any number of celebrities. Popslash writers use pop stars as their protagonists, constructing fictional narratives that supplement and enhance those disseminated by the media. They manipulate public information to question and undermine the very media images that form the source text for their stories. In so doing, popslashers address complicated notions of reality and performance as the fictional depictions question the truth of the public accounts of the stars and their worlds.

As the stories I have chosen to examine indicate, popslash boasts a sizeable number of self-reflexive and theoretically sophisticated texts, which is not surprising considering that many of its writers identify themselves as highly educated adult women. Some, like myself, are academics, and familiarity with recent theories on gender performance and star theory clearly informs the stories, as well as the discourses surrounding them. As recent discussions within fan studies suggest, studying any community of which one is a member is difficult (Doty, 2000; Green *et al.*, 1998; Hills, 2002), but I choose to do so nonetheless. While some would argue that one's position in a given community could lead to a lack of objectivity, I contend that my very subjectivity provides a comprehensive insight difficult to achieve otherwise.

It is of course impossible to clearly define different types of fans, not only because the internet is an anonymous space where everyone can perform any chosen identity, but because various fan positions can be occupied. While it may seem that popslash fans have little in common with boy band or pop fans in general, I would like to suggest that popslashers exemplify an aspect of fan engagement that may be less openly displayed in other fannish testimonies. In other words, insofar as the popslash community shares many qualities with fan behaviour as it is typically described (Jenkins, 1992; Jensen, 1992; Hills, 2002), popslash fans' engagement with the celebrity images suggests a clear – if not always overtly expressed – engagement with the ways stars function for all fans as nodes of signification, desire, and identification (Hansen, 1991; Stacey, 1991).

As popslash stories imagine the split between the 'real' and the public self, they both address and thematize the difficulty of performing the postmodern self, a difficulty exemplified by, but not exclusive to, stars. These stories foreground the way subject positions not only are chosen but are consciously created and shaped by the audience at the same time as they address a desire for an imaginary core identity. The conflicting discourses of authenticity and performance to which they draw attention are concerns which popslashers face not only in the media texts they draw from but in public discourse in general. Popslash fans thus use stars to address issues of 'authentic' identity (Dyer, 1998), at the same time as they recognize the stars' as well as their own postmodern performativity (Lovell, 2003).

In the popular imaginary, the fan is often conceived as an isolated individual who substitutes star or celebrity attachment for actual social interaction (Rojek, 2001; Turner, 2004). Both Turner and Rojek refuse to view this fan/celebrity para-social relation negatively, rejecting the contempt other critics have shown for such an 'illusion of intimacy' (Schickel, 1985). Yet they still ignore the real social relationships that grow up around the para-social ones. In the case of fan fiction, where fans literally write out and share their fantasies, they create a social space of communication and interaction that is about the celebrities, the stories, as well as the women writing them (Ehrenreich et al., 1992; Wald, 2002).

Whether in private, with one's best friend, in organized fan clubs, or at conventions, many fans share and gain 'real' social interaction via their fannishness (Bacon-Smith, 1992; Harris and Alexander, 1998; Hills, 2002). The social community surrounding this often becomes equally central — if not more so — to the fans than the stars themselves. In this way, the stars ultimately function as a conduit through which the fans creatively explore their own identities, desires and sexualities. They create social networks through engagement with each other, as well as with the shared star texts. Rather than replacing real social interaction with para-social ones, popslash exemplifies how the community creates new social networks from which 'real' relationships and friendships evolve.

Boy bands and reality

In their clearly constructed roles, boy bands epitomize issues surrounding identity construction and performativity which are central to all stars (Dyer, 1998; Giles, 2000) and, by extension, all postmodern subjects. In this way, boy bands are a perfect example of the simulacrum, the copy without an original (Baudrillard, 1988; Marshall, 1997: 165–84), and it is this very deliberate construction of the star's persona that appeals to popslashers. Discourses surrounding boy bands consistently criticize the members' supposed lack of talent and authenticity (Wald, 2002). Deliberately marketed as sexual objects toward a female pre-teen audience, the pop stars clearly must confront the issue of constructing one's public self and the effects of being a public figure. They become exemplary for the postmodern subject. As variously (and differently) defined by theorists like Foucault (1970), Derrida (1976), Lacan (1977) or Butler (1990), the postmodern self is built around a notion of performance: its identity shifts among multiple versions of the self, all of which are determined by context. The split between the public and private personae of any star simply exaggerates the performative aspect in which all of us engage on a more general level (Gamson, 1994; Rojek, 2001).

The questions of truth and reality are central in popslash writing, which consciously fictionalizes a reality that itself is already performed and choreographed. Unlike much of the tabloid press, which purports to tell the 'truth', popslashers consciously declare their writing to be fictional and clearly separate their stories from rumors. Of course, this creative process allows the popslasher to construct the star as she wishes: as an object of desire, as someone with whom to identify, or as a recreation of the star's supposedly 'real' self. Moreover, popslashers refuse to follow the cliché of declaring the public performances of pop stars a fiction and the band members fake and fabricated; instead, their stories often reveal deep empathy and sympathy for the stars they depict. Rather than reproducing the star stereotypes often perpetuated by the media, popslash rehumanizes the celebrities by inventing backstories and inner lives. Popslasher Jae W., for example, describes how her fannish engagement and research forced her to 'empathize much more with the people [she's] writing about, and see them as full people' (personal communication, 2003). Popslashers use the available material while inventing what is not and cannot be known, which forces them to simultaneously believe and disavow the 'reality' presented by the media.

Insertion fantasy and identification

This tension between the performed self and the imagined 'real' self drives a variety of fannish desires of intimacy that translate into different narrative fantasies. Following along the lines of identification and desire, I want to distinguish between *insertion* and *observer* fantasy as recurring modes of fannish narratives. In the former, writers may directly insert themselves into the narrative or mould one of the characters to become their representative, while in the latter they voyeuristically fantasize a reality in which the stars remain undisturbed by outside observers. In the insertion fantasy, the text imagines the author entering the story, usually to meet the stars and often to become romantically involved with them; in the observer fantasy, the text envisions the characters in a private unobserved state, allowing deeper insight into the star and the 'real' persons behind the public screen. The observer fantasy thus seems to replace or supplement the desire to be or have the characters with a desire to see or know about them. In other words, the satisfaction in reading and writing these stories is derived from the pleasure of information and insight (Foucault, 1990). Interestingly, this division between having and knowing is mirrored in a similar split in the actual fan–star interaction. Some fans collect objects owned or worn by stars; others simply gather information. For example, one fan may pick up the water glass a star drank from to gain access to his physical embodiment, another will examine his cigarette butt to find out what brand he smokes.

In the most obvious insertion fantasies, the writer explicitly writes herself (or some idealized version or avatar thereof) into the story. The primary logic behind these pieces of fiction revolves around the desire to either become the star or someone close to him in order to be with him. Sarah's 'The Middle of Nowhere' (2000) is an excellent example of an insertion narrative that allows various forms of identification and desire to play out in relation to the principal characters. Justin Timberlake, who wants to temporarily escape the limelight, hides out as a high school student in rural Kansas, where he falls in love with a girl named Maggie. In Maggie, the author creates an identifiable female character, a 'regular' high school girl, thus allowing the reader to imagine an encounter with a nice, everyday guy while simultaneously (as readers of the story) knowing that he is indeed an international pop star. This story represents the ultimate insertion fantasy: Maggie gets to have the real guy, and Justin Timberlake too.

At the same time, the story includes elements of identification with Justin himself. Told from Justin's point of view, the story includes his diary entries, which allow readers to see not only Justin's thoughts but to identify with his feelings. As such, there is a second level of self-insertion: although there certainly may be international male teenage pop stars who write diaries, it seems more likely that this is authorial projection. One early entry clearly establishes the theme of the story: 'It's just like if I could have a break. Even for 24 hours. If I could just find someone with whom I could be Justin. I mean, my parents don't even know Justin anymore.' By removing Justin from the media context and placing him in a regular environment, 'The Middle of Nowhere' fulfils a dominant fan fantasy of meeting the celebrity and beginning a love affair. Considering Dyer's (1998: 49) suggestion of the ordinary/extraordinary paradox, 'The Middle of Nowhere' bridges the paradox of the star being ordinary-yet-special by letting the star occupy both positions simultaneously. At the same time, the story also discusses the issue of public versus 'real' self. Fan logic, of course, demands that 'we' – channelled through Maggie – fall in love with the 'real' Timberlake, not the media construct. Such a distinction presupposes, however, that we can clearly recognize the real thing as distinct from and preferable to the performative. By juxtaposing Justin's celebrity life with his small-town middle America adventure, the story raises not only the question of various selves, but also which of these lives, which of these Justins, is more 'real.'

Fans writing fans

Unlike Sarah's insertion fic, most popslash focuses on and identifies with the celebrities rather than with the fans, often characterizing 'fangirls' stereotypically as obsessive, intrusive and even aggressively physical. When fans appear outside insertion fic fan encounters, their central role is usually to uphold the star's public self, to be the audience for which that self is created and sustained. In general, then, the community identifies with the stars against the fans that they themselves are, or at least against the kind of fans that they do not want to be. Stubbleglitter's 'Smile for the Fans' (2002) envisions the pressure for the star in constantly being chased and touched by fans, yet having to pretend to enjoy it. Her JC is haunted by the fans' overwhelming presence and physical proximity:

> Their fingers are wet. They're always fucking wet, and JC has night-mares about the girls sticking their fingers in their mouths or between their legs before reaching out so he can touch them as he runs along the stage. He cringes every time their slick slimy fingertips slide against his hand, thick with saliva or cum or whatever the hell it is they secrete, smelling heavy and overly sweet like rotting peaches.

The story not only addresses the star's plight of having to pretend to enjoy something he loathes but also disparages the 'excessively' embodied fan who needs to literally touch the object of her affection.

Despite its rather striking tone, and even apparent invocation of a 'monstrous' conception of the female (feminizing) 'mass', the story should not necessarily be read as a form of self-hatred on the part of the fan, or even as pointing to a hatred of other fans. Rather, it can be interpreted as an exaggerated critique of certain (popular) conceptions of fan behaviour that the writer has internalized but wishes to distance herself from. At the same time it is true that the story remains firmly articulated from JC's point of view, thus demanding identification with him rather than the faceless, nameless, objectifying 'mass'. Nevertheless, the emphasis on the anonymous crowd also implies that the threat comes less from individual women, than from the way the music industry presents the stars to them as a commodity.

Media footage and imagination are interestingly merged here as Stubbleglitter relies on JC's public character in her fictional creation of his private one: the disgust pervading the story is one possible extrapolation from the fact that JC usually avoids eye contact during shows, instead performing with his eyes closed. The story concludes in his public persona, the only one we have access to: "'We love our fans,' he smiled into the camera. 'They're what keep us going.'" Stubbleglitter thus conjectures a 'real' self for JC that not only contradicts the one fans are presented with by the popular press but also seriously questions their roles as fans. Jawamonkey and Chris J.'s 'Genuine #1' (2002) directly addresses the relationship between fan and star as well as their respective identity issues. Positing an alternate universe in which non-celebrity Justin encounters Backstreet Boy AJ McLean, the story functions as a self-insertion with a twist: Justin is both regular fan and star, in and outside the story respectively. Interestingly, it is Justin, rather than the story's actual star AJ, who is constantly described as performing a role; he consciously observes and controls his behaviour, going so far as to name and number his smiles according to their intended effects. Shifting the concern of multiple identities and role playing from the celebrity onto the fan (albeit one whom we know in reality to be a celebrity and thereby deserving of AJ) suggests that not only the star but also readers and writers are concerned with issues of how to perform one's identity.

Observer fantasy and identification

The observer fantasy imagines the stars' secret private selves so that its driving force is the emphasis on the gathered facts as a basis to imagine the potential 'truths' they hide. Recognizing 'the real thing' is central to the observer fantasy, because its writers must rely on media footage to create a blueprint of the 'real' star in order to create a fictional extrapolation. Direct self-insertion is impossible here, because the stories fetishize the pop stars' close ties with one another and the fact that any love interest beyond the group must remain an outsider. Slashers, trained in reading between the lines of many TV shows to ferret out homoerotic subtext, carefully trace moments of inconsistency, find cracks in the 'façade' of the official star text, and search for a more genuine 'reality' underneath. The discourse surrounding these stories is often less about a fannish desire for the star in a visceral sense (as in wanting to meet or see him), as it is a fascination with understanding him, stripping away the layers of performance, and catching glimpses of the 'real' self underneath – to know the star better than he knows himself. The attempt to imagine a 'real' self as realistically as possible thus requires extensive research, ranging from concert performances and interviews to articles and personal interaction.

The insertion fantasy faces an obvious paradox: it rests on the premises that only the 'real' self can truly love and be loved while, of course, the fan obviously fantasizes about the star *because* of his star status, not in spite of it. Similarly, the observer fantasy imagines the 'true' self underneath, creating a layered and intricate psychological subject, yet fans are initially interested in these stars *because* they are famous, so the initial attraction is not a complex subjectivity but a simplification of the 'real' person behind the star function. In other words, in both types of story, insertion and observer, fans construct the fantastic life of being a star, as opposed to a fantasy of the stars' realistic life, which is obviously unknowable. The fictional text is built around the public media narrative with the remainder filled by interpolated and extrapolated additions as imagined by the author.

Most stories contain traces of the author's desire and identifications, and popslash in particular offers such a complex source material that interpretive decisions about characterization and interpersonal dynamics are paramount to creating interesting characters. Even though popslashers remain consumers who interact with the imagined and imaginary media construct, they also shape and alter the star to their own specifications, making him more interesting, intelligent or vulnerable, and thus more desirable, identifiable and available. Betty P., for example, describes how she writes her characters 'in a certain way, a little more thoughtful than they probably are, a little more genuine, a little more confused. I write them trying harder to get through life than I think they really are ... I write the way I write because it produces a story that I like and not because I think it mimics reality exactly' (personal communication, 2004). Often the characters are more literate, more sensitive or simply more self-aware than we might extrapolate from the media portrayal, and the particular aspects the fan writer chooses to foreground are indicative of the personality she wants to create or explore. As Betty points out, the popslash readers and writers want to understand, care for and maybe even identify with the characters, and ultimately that desire shapes the fiction more than any particular star quote or media clip does.

Celebrity performance and identity construction

One area in which the fans' desires become clearly visible is in issues of identity, in particular their identity as popslashers. The theme of hiding one's sexuality underlies any story in which the publicly heterosexual members of *NSYNC are having sexual relations with one another. More specifically, popslash requires the celebrities to perform not only their official and private roles but also their (public) straight and (real) queer identities. It may be no surprise that popslashers emotionally engage with stories that revolve around notions of identities and the protection of secret selves, a concern that gets played out most often through anxieties over gender and sexual identity. The number of queer women in online media fandom in general – and popslash in particular – is significant. While not my intention to offer an essentialist (or indeed homogeneous) reading of identity, this may in part explain the central theme of sexuality here. Moreover, popslashers in general confront questions of identity insofar as they are boy band fans who read and/or write homoerotic texts, usually a secret known to few, if any, of their real life friends and family.

It is with this connection between the popslashers' and the stars' identities in mind that I want to look at the way identity is constructed and performed in popslash stories. Often, the fiction tends to emphasize a separation between what fans see and the actual personal lives, since one of popslash's central goals is to imagine the characters behind the supposed façade. Jae W.'s 'Disarm' (2001), for example, thematizes the boundary between public and private as one of the group members suddenly alters his public persona. The narrator notes, 'Of course he wore armor. They all did; it was that or lose themselves to the millions of eyes and fingers and minds that grabbed at them every day ... he had welcomed the safety he felt behind the walls he'd built.' The story posits fans as aggressive antagonists to a star who must protect and safeguard his private self. 'Disarm' traces the difficulties of such a clear split: Justin, for example, is almost unable to access his 'real' self as he 'flash[es] different smiles into the smoky glass ... looking for the smile that was real'; in contrast, JC attempts to present a seemingly vulnerable and weak front as a defence, which is described as 'a brilliant idea, to close yourself so thoroughly by appearing to be so open, to discourage others from hurting you just by seeming so capable of being hurt'. 'Disarm' suggests that the various ways that one constructs one's 'real' self may often endanger that very sense of reality. In fact, the story refuses to end with a romantic relation that would supposedly allow both protagonists to shed their different masks and layers. Instead, it describes how different levels of intimacy and revelation dominate even their personal relationship. In so doing, the story suggests that within personal relations, layers of identity are also taken on and shed, with the implication that such identity transformations characterize the experience of selfhood outside of stardom.

Postmodern critical thought suggests that most subjects enact various, yet closely linked, performative roles depending on context and interlocutor. Stars, however, may be more prone to clearly separating such roles (Rojek, 2001: 11), and popslash often dramatizes this separation. Synecdochic's 'Borderlines' (2003) presents a Justin Timberlake who consciously disassociates personalities and creates a separate identity named Jay as a way to escape his public self: 'They'd built him together ... piece by piece and trait by trait.' The underlying notion here, of course, is that the public self has, on some level, affected or destroyed the 'real' self to a degree where an objective outsider perspective cannot declare him sane. A second personality of a normal boy has to be constructed to safeguard the public Justin; in fact, 'sometimes Justin thinks that Jay is the only thing that's keeping him out of the loony bin' (see also Stephen Harper's essay in this collection on the discursive relationship constructed between 'madness' and fame). This story presents but one interpretation of how much the required public persona and the unceasing spotlight may have affected the emotional development of the fourteen-year-old who joined *NSYNC. In fact, it is no coincidence that most of the stories that directly address the notion of a public persona focus on Timberlake. As the youngest of the group and the one most in the spotlight, popslashers often present him as the one most likely to have had his 'real' self influenced by the public self and by his media image.

Of course, we cannot and will never know any star's 'real' self, because any declaration, any revealing interview, any behind-the-scenes recording, is by default a public statement (Dyer, 1998: 2). Still, the desire to know just how much is real and how much constructed is a driving force in public star discourse and, not surprisingly, in popslash as well. Sandy Keene's 'Your Life Is Now' (2002), for example, addresses the way fans collect information yet always remain on the outside: in the story Justin loses his memory and must piece together his past. Justin has become an outsider to his own life and, mimicking the fans, watches media footage of himself to recapture his identity. Nevertheless, all he can access that way is his public self, which he realizes is not sufficient. In this story, Justin is utterly lost because he cannot distinguish between his private and public selves. He cannot remember one, and he realizes that the other may be purposefully false.

Keene's story describes how the media is evidently crucial to the fans' engagement with the star because it is the principal – if not only – point of access here. Kaneko's 'Becoming' (2003) deals with this interdependence of media and celebrity in a story where JC and Chris are fantastically given the ability to make things come true simply by voicing them: whatever they say out loud to the media becomes reality. Chris jokes about Justin liking gummy bears and JC being afraid of birds, and within a few hours, these likes and dislikes come true. Although the characters initially come upon this ability/curse accidentally, they soon learn to appreciate and fear its effects and begin to manipulate their own behaviour and the real-life changes they effect. By showing how the star may be affected by how the media have constructed him, Kaneko comments on the relationship between public and 'real' selves and how they shape one another.

'Becoming' thematizes the relationship between media, fan and star. Whereas the media and the star are often seen to conspire in creating the star image, in the story under discussion here, the stars themselves become victims of fan and media discourses and only later succeed in taking back limited control of their own image construction. As a result, the story reveals an underlying discomfort that fans may have with their role in making impossible the very thing they want most – the star's 'real' self. 'Becoming' explores, both metaphorically and literally, whether and to what degree fans may be able to manipulate their images and thereby their realities. In so doing, Kaneko criticizes the role of fans, problematizes the relationship between media and celebrity, and addresses fans' desires to control and become who they want to be. In a way, then, 'Becoming' is ultimately about how much anyone can control their behaviour and how they appear to others. Although the relationship between media and star is obviously an extreme case, the issue is nevertheless relevant for fans as well insofar as fans try to separate truth from fabrication and are themselves part of the process that 'makes' the stars they admire. Moreover, fans also create and shape themselves in certain ways, especially on the internet, where individuals create personae that in turn become part of who they are. Thus, while issues of identity construction and performativity may be important to any postmodern subject, they are especially relevant to women who spend much time online with varying degrees of differing personae and who have created strong social ties around these different layers of identity (Turkle, 1997; Baym, 2000; Rheingold, 2000). Popslash allows its readers and writers to explore these issues by playing them out on exemplary star bodies.

Feminism and gender swap

Much of popslash clearly engages with the everyday issues of female fans and the various roles such fans perform. One popular and particularly interesting subgenre of popslash is gender-switching stories, whose central generic trope allows them to addresses various concerns particular to women. These stories deal with issues of identity, sexual identity and sexual orientation by forcing the protagonist to experience the physical and emotional – and, by extension, the social and cultural – realities of possessing a body of the opposite sex. Many popslash gender-switching fics exhibit deeper concerns about how sexual desire is configured in our culture. They explore how a temporary external change may force the stories' protagonists to question how much of their feelings are generated by the person they love and how much is merely a reaction to their biological sex. It is important to realize that gender-switching stories function as a specific fan fiction trope and in no way realistically describe gender dysphoria. In fact, the stories transfer the emphasis from the actual experience of gender switching to its impact. They often focus more on the shifting dynamics within the group than the individual's utter confusion of waking up in the wrong body.

Gender-switching stories thematize a variety of negative experiences often particular to women. These include issues such as greater objectification, a concern with body image, sexual vulnerability (including the larger emphasis on virginity), the risk of pregnancy and the greater danger of sexual violence. The stories displace these issues onto a male character, albeit in a female body. Wald (2002), following Ehrenreich et al. (1992), argues that one of the central appeals of boy bands is their members' ambiguous sexuality with their desirable yet non-threatening bodies that often challenge heteronormative masculinity. The fascination with body imagery in a variety of popslash fics suggest that boy band celebrities, by default, already stand in for many of the bodily concerns of their fans. After all, one of the reasons female slashers may be attracted to boy band characters is the fact that few other males face this same level of scrutiny. Furthermore, considering the fact that women themselves have to perform their 'femaleness', such a displacement onto a male character plays with some of the central issues raised in gender theory (Butler, 1990). Finally, these stories mirror slashers' own identification process across gender. Slash author Cesperanza (personal communication, 2004) suggests that 'the genderswap story parallels two stories: the male celeb[rity]'s taking on of a female role gives him access to his desire for men in much the same way that the female fan's taking on the male role in writing gives her access to her desire for women'. Rather than trying (and failing) to identify with female characters who are found wanting (Doane, 1982), slashers use men as the objects of identification yet mould these men in such a way as to address their own issues.

Helen's 'The Same Inside' (2001), for example, describes how, after Chris changes into a woman, he and Joey fall in love. Once Chris changes back, Joey cannot handle that his 'girlfriend has a fucking cock' and leaves Chris, only to realize that Chris's maleness is less important than the person he is inside, the person Joey fell in love with. This motif of remaining 'the same inside', regardless of apparent gender, permeates the story. Early on, Chris exclaims in frustration, 'I don't *feel* like a girl ... I feel the same inside', only to be rebuffed by Lance's comment, 'Well, girls probably feel the same inside too'. Chris's frustration is immediately turned into a statement on gender equality, thus marking the story as concerned with what it means to be female for women. This emphasis on a consistent core underneath one's gendered body short-circuits the traditional gender binaries and suggests that the person underneath may be more important than the body s/he inhabits, while at the same time addressing concerns of self specific to women. Placed beyond the realities of transgendered individuals to whom bodies indeed make a difference, the story constructs a fantasy of true love outside sex and gender norms. Joey's comment seems to suggest that gendered subject positions are multiple, are often not directly related to biological sex and, ultimately, are not the deciding factor as to whom one loves or desires. Although 'The Same Inside' does acknowledge how both characters change and grow, and how they are affected and influenced by gender stereotypes and social expectations, their ultimate romantic victory suggests that it may be possible to move beyond such notions and limitations. The story combines a constructivist approach to gender, where one's biological sex is ultimately secondary to sexual attraction, with an essentialist understanding of identity that posits a core self that is 'the same inside' regardless of context.

Such competing notions of constructivism and essentialism are not unusual in popslash stories about identity and performativity. A playful belief in postmodern constructedness often exists alongside a desire for authenticity, an authenticity that can be found both in the fan's understanding of the star's success and in her construction of his identity. Fans repeatedly emphasize the stars' innate talents as well as their extraordinary hard work to explain and justify their success. In fact, this narrative illustrates Dyer's adaptation of Max Weber's concept of *charisma* (1998: 30): popslash fans, although perfectly aware of how the system works and how stars are produced and marketed, nevertheless continue to emphasize the stars' abilities and an actual reason for their fame. Similarly, although many of the stories thematize the celebrities as fragmented selves without any core, often a sense remains that underneath, there really, truly may be something that can be recovered or unearthed, most often with the discovery of romantic feelings. Popslash's cynical acknowledgement of our postmodern, constructed selves thus often seems to hide an interest in – if not desire for – a reality beyond the performative, for some central core that makes us special and defines who we are. There thus exists a discrepancy between fans' simple acknowledgement of the constructed nature of stars and the ways in which they actually depict identity and performance in their writing. This is a tension which reflects on the complicated relationship fans display, not only in terms of understanding the stars' identities but also their own.

Conclusion

Even while exploring some of the more unusual identificatory dynamics within popslash, I do not want to argue that popslashers are not 'real' fans; in fact, their written fantasies supplement rather than replace the more typical star–fan interactions. Although their fannish behavior may take on different shapes and outlets than those commonly anticipated by the commercial market surrounding celebrities, popslashers nevertheless are part of that commercial process. As consumers, they spend money on merchandise and concert appearances even as it becomes part of their research; they dismiss certain aspects of fan behaviour while sharing others through their fannish social ties. In other words, fans can engage in fandom while critically analysing it. The emotionally distanced neutrality of some of their stories must be read in relation to their other fannish behaviour and the attention that goes into the writing of these fics. Finally, their often voiced awareness that stars' public selves are constructed must be understood against stories that often foreground the celebrities' inner charisma and work ethic, thus juxtaposing realist and postmodern versions of supposed star–fan interaction.

The central focus in popslash stories on identity and performance, on trying to separate public and private selves, suggests that these are issues that draw the fans both to popslash and to boy bands. In a way, popslashers seem to be identifying with stars, focusing on their constructions of subjectivity, because, as fans, they are similarly constructed by their environment. Boy band members are constantly told who they are supposed to be by their handlers, the media and the fans. Likewise, the audience is told these very particulars about the stars whom they are supposed to desire. In turn, such guidelines on what and how to desire instruct fans on whom they themselves are supposed to be. As a result, the wilful creative (re)writings of media representations and these performative, localized acts of agency still remain dependent on (and thus perhaps contained by) an entertainment industry that generates initial interest in these stars and controls the information fans rely on.

As Julad's epigraph to this essay indicates, many popslashers are well aware of the problems surrounding boy bands' marketing strategies. In fact, the cynicism that surrounds boy band members may indeed appeal particularly to a group of intelligent women who know they ultimately lack agency but attempt to gain it nevertheless, women who are fully aware of the constructedness of their idols, yet love them for that very irreality. Popslashers, well aware that they can never achieve real agency, instead strive for the best any postmodern subject can have: the simultaneous embracing and disavowing of the belief in Justin's realness as much as their own.

Bibliography

Bacon-Smith, Camille (1992) *Enterprising Women: Television Fandom and the Creation of Popular Myth*, Philadelphia: University of Pennsylvania Press.

Baudrillard, Jean (1988) [1981] 'Simulacra and Simulations', in Mark Poster (ed.), *Selected Writings*, Stanford, CA: Stanford University Press.

Baym, Nancy K. (2000) *Tune In, Log On: Soaps, Fandom, and Online Community*, Thousand Oaks: Sage.

Butler, Judith (1990) *Gender Trouble*, New York: Routledge.

Derrida, Jacques (1976) *Of Grammatology*, trans. Gayatri Spivak, Baltimore, MD: The Johns Hopkins University Press.

Doane, Mary Ann (1982) 'Film and the Masquerade: Theorizing the Female Spectator', *Screen* 23/3–4: 74–87.

Doty, Alexander (2000) *Flaming Classics: Queering the Film Canon*, London: Routledge.

Driscoll, Catherine (2002) *Girls: Feminine Adolescence in Popular Culture and Cultural Theory*, New York: Columbia.

Dyer, Richard (1998) *Stars*, London: British Film Institute.

Ehrenreich, Barbara, Hess, Elizabeth, and Jacobs, Gloria (1992) 'Beatlemania: Girls Just Want to Have Fun', in Lisa A. Lewis (ed.), *The Adoring Audience*, London: Routledge, pp. 84–106.

Foucault, Michel (1970) [1966] *The Order of Things*, New York: Random House.

—— (1990) [1976] *History of Sexuality, Vol. I*, New York: Vintage.

Frith, Simon and McRobbie, Angela (1990) [1978] 'Rock and Sexuality', in Simon Frith and Andrew Goodwin (ed.), *On Record: Rock, Pop, and the Written Word*, London: Routledge, pp. 371–89.

Gamson, Joshua (1994) *Claims to Fame: Celebrity in Contemporary America*, Berkeley: University of California Press.

Giles, David (2000) *Illusions of Immortality: A Psychology of Fame and Celebrity*, New York: St Martin's Press.

Hansen, Miriam (1991) 'Pleasure, Ambivalence, Identification: Valentino and Female Spectatorship', in Christine Gledhill (ed.), *Stardom: Industry of Desire,* London: Routledge, pp. 259–82.

Harris, Cheryl, and Alexander, Alison (eds) (1998) *Theorizing Fandom: Fans, Subculture, and Identity*, Cresskill, NJ: Hampton.

Helen (2001) 'The Same Inside', available at www.helenish.net/samep.shtml, accessed 1 May 2005.

Hills, Matthew (2002) *Fan Cultures*, London: Routledge.

Jae W. (2001) 'Disarm', available at www.waxjism.org/jaesepha/disarm.html, accessed 1 May 2005.

Jawamonkey and Chris J. (2002) 'Genuine #1', available at www.mediageek.ca/cj/genuine.html, accessed 1 May 2005.

Jenkins, Henry (1992) *Textual Poachers: Television Fans and Participatory Culture*, New York: Routledge.

Jenkins, Henry, Jenkins, Cynthia, and Green, Shoshanna (1998) '"The Normal Interest in Men Bonking": Selections from The Terra Nostra Underground and Strange Bedfellows', in Cheryl Harris and Alison Alexander (eds), *Theorizing Fandom: Fans, Subculture, and Identity*, Cresskill, NJ: Hampton Press, pp. 9–38.

Jensen, Joli (1992) 'Fandom as Pathology: The Consequences of Characterization', in Lisa Lewis (ed.), *The Adoring Audience: Fan Culture and Popular Media*, London: Routledge.

Kaneko (2003) 'Becoming', available at anyroad.org/kaneko/becoming.html, accessed 1 May 2005.

Keene, Sandy (2002) 'Your Life Is Now', available at suitableforframing.mediawood.net/yourlife.htm, accessed 1 May 2005.

Lacan, Jacques (1977) [1966] *Écrits: A Selection*, trans. Alan Sheridan, New York: Norton.

Lovell, Alan (2003) 'I Went in Search of Deborah Kerr, Jodie Foster, and Julianne Moore but got Waylaid …', in Thomas Austin and Martin Barker (eds), *Contemporary Hollywood Stardom*, London: Arnold, pp. 259–70.

Marshall, P. David (1997) *Celebrity and Power: Fame in Contemporary Culture*, Minneapolis: University of Minnesota Press.

Penley, Constance (1992) 'Feminism, Psychoanalysis, and the Study of Popular Culture', in Lawrence Grossberg, Cary Nelson and Paula A. Treichler (eds), *Cultural Studies*, New York: Routledge, pp. 479–500.

Rheingold, Howard (2000) [1993] *The Virtual Community: Homesteading on the Electronic Frontier*, Cambridge: MIT Press.

Rojek, Chris (2001) *Celebrity*, London: Reaktion Books.

Sarah (2000) 'The Middle of Nowhere', available at railwayshoes.net/sarah/middle/midmain.html, accessed 1 May 2005.

Schickel, Richard (1985) *Intimate Strangers: The Culture of Celebrity*, Garden City, NY: Doubleday.

Stacey, Jackie (1991) 'Feminine Fascinations: Forms of Identification in Star–Audience Relations', in Christine Gledhill (ed.), *Stardom: Industry of Desire*, London: Routledge, pp. 141–63.

Stubbleglitter (2002) 'Smile for the Fans', available at boudicca.com/unaware/smile.html, accessed 1 May 2005.

Synecdochic (2003) 'Borderlines', available at www.kekkai.org/synecdochic/borderlines.html, accessed 1 May 2005.

Timberlake, Justin (2003) Interview, *Total Request Live*, 21 October.

Turkle, Sherry (1997) *Life on the Screen: Identity in the Age of the Internet*, New York: Simon and Schuster.

Turner, Graeme (2004) *Understanding Celebrity*, London: Sage.

Wald, Gayle (2002) '"I Want It That Way": Teenybopper Music and the Girling of Boy Bands', *Genders* 35, available at www.genders.org/g35/g35_wald.html, accessed 1 May 2005.

Chapter 16

Langsters online

k.d. lang and the creation of internet fan communities

Judith Franco

The internet has exploded with communities based on discursive interaction. If online communities initially emerged from the margins of the medium, they now represent one of the great democratic achievements of recent technological development. From the growing body of research in the field, two results of great significance emerge. First, studies of the origin and function of online groups demonstrate the remarkable power of the medium to enable new forms of sociability. Second, research that enquires into the motives for joining and contributing to these groups demonstrates how online participation offers unique opportunities for pursuing identity-related projects that used to be impossible, or even inconceivable (Jones, 2002; Feenberg and Bakardjieva, 2004). In recent years, the internet has also been identified as a new and significant component of fan activity, allowing fans to overcome time and space to engage in communities, and to negotiate their relationship with their favourite celebrities or characters (Watson, 2002; Pullen, 2000, 2004). However, few of such analyses have focused on texts produced and consumed by lesbian fans, despite the fact that 'the celebrity image is especially likely to attract the authorial energies of those in marginal groups for whom recognition, legitimacy and positively evaluated identity are compelling issues' (Coombe, 1992: 378).

I offer here an empirical and textual study which explores how participants negotiate their sexual and cultural identities through online interaction – whether with respect to other members of the group or their favourite celebrity. As an example of a lesbian-dominated, though by no means homogeneous, community, I will be focusing on the most active (in terms of frequency of interaction) Anglo-American fan sites relating to the Canadian singer-songwriter and lesbian icon k.d. lang. The approach I adopt in this study deals with the celebrity as a text which generates meanings and pleasures for its audience. Considering k.d. lang's relative media invisibility over the past five years, the circulation and consumption of the celebrity text is mainly 'a socially based phenomenon generated "from below" at the level of real people who make affective investments in particular media figures' (Rodman, 1996: 12). Lesbian fans in particular turn to online k.d. communities to engage in the identity work that the celebrity can facilitate.

For this study, the public Kennedyflairs bulletin board was read and observed on a regular basis, whereas I have actively participated as a self-proclaimed lesbian feminist 'fan-scholar' in Chief's private community over the past five years. I will draw on my personal experiences with the group dynamic/interaction and conduct a close analysis of the fan text/bulletin boards archives between February 2001 and May 2005. I decided to change the names of all respondents on the private board to ensure anonymity while taking into account the participants' self-presentation/gendered identity reflected in their names/pseudonyms.

This relationship between fan researcher and fan community is clearly complex. In discussing the spectrum of theoretical perspectives on fan culture, Matt Hills identifies a narrative of mutual marginalization that produces a categorical splitting of fan/academic:

> [T]he clash between fandom and academia is less a matter of what fans and academics actually do as subjects, and more a matter of the imagined subjectivities – the different guiding discourses and ideals of subjectivity which are adopted by fans and academics – which are linked to cultural systems of value and community (Hills, 2002: 8).

An alternative approach that can be taken here consists of extending the imagined subjectivity of the academy into the cultural spaces of fandom via discussions of fan knowledge and expertise. Yet as Hills points out, the scholar-fan as a hybrid identity can have problematic consequences for exploring fandom if it involves projecting the values of the academic community onto the fan culture. I approach this study as a fan-scholar, a longtime member of the k.d. lang community who represents fandom from the 'inside', while also retaining a critical awareness of its practices. Drawing on my experience of negotiating fan and academic discourse on k.d. lang boards, I hope to extend the integration of fan and academic identities/subjectivities in this study, while being aware of writing fandom into what might be conceived as academically 'acceptable' norms.

From 1983 until 1992, Canadian singer-songwriter k.d. lang produced unconventional country music and flaunted a disruptive and troubling image that challenged traditional gender codes (Mockus, 1994; Bruzzi, 1997). k.d. lang was never accepted by the Nashville community – she alienated them, for example, with her 1992 'meat stinks' TV commercial for PETA (People for the Ethical Treatment of Animals). The year 1992 marked a radical musical departure in lang's career, when her turn to mellow pop in the album *Ingénue* both firmly established her as an internationally successful musician and encouraged her to come out to the American magazine *The Advocate*. Coming out, 'which rests on the belief that sexuality is a basic, perhaps the basic, dimension of subjectivity' (Gever, 2003: 113), proved to be decisive in k.d. lang's transition from 'alternative' performer/singer to lesbian celebrity. Rojek points out that the discursive regime of celebrity is defined by crossing the boundary between the public and private worlds, preferring the personal, the private or 'veridical' self (Rojek, 2001: 11) as the privileged object of revelation. Since her coming out, k.d.'s media representation has been dominated by references to her lesbian identity, but as Louise Allen points out, it is more importantly the lesbian *identification* with the celebrity which produces her status as lesbian idol (Allen, 1997: 52).

Both in terms of k.d. lang's musical development and style, *Ingénue* has been interpreted as a move into the mainstream – a shift away from playing with performativity, distanciation and irony, and towards a more homogenized, conventionally ambiguous androgyny (Bruzzi, 1997). lang's butch performativity coincided with the commodification of 'lesbian chic' and established her firmly within the 'lesbian celebrity' league, while still attracting a heterosexual audience. Since the mid 1990s she has increasingly abandoned songwriting and cultivated her vocal technique and interpretation skills on albums such as *Drag* (1997), *A Wonderful World* (with Tony Bennett, 2002) and *Hymns of the 49th Parallel* (2004) in an attempt to universalize her appeal.

Private vs. public

Despite lang's dwindling mainstream popularity over the years, predominantly lesbian fans of all generations gather on individual fan websites. These sites were often created as an alternative to the official 'Artist Direct' site, which was perceived to neglect and offend langsters in terms of its paucity of updated information, and lack of monitoring of the (now defunct) bulletin board. Kennedyflairs (2000) and Chief's site (2001) were inaugurated as 'private' spaces, only accessible to members who had already established an offline bond in an attempt to maintain core values and intimacy. As Nessim Watson points out in his case study of the Phish.Net Fan Community: 'A primary purpose of fans coming together around a shared source product is to create a safe space for the expression of fan emotion' (Watson, 2002: 119). In terms of k.d fandom, the creation of private boards was indeed a response to perceived threats – as represented by postings where (racist or lesbophobic) content violated the ethos and values of the community.

In 2002, the Kennedyflairs board was founded and moderated by Shelley, an English heterosexual female fan who introduces herself as 'London based and married with three children'. She invited membership applications from all over the world, and Kennedyflairs became the largest community with a total of 430 members. Chief's board, maintained by an American lesbian fan, remains a privatized enclave of forty longtime fans, with strong offline friendships and romances. Although some members from Chief's board also post to Kennedyflairs, participants in both online communities clearly perceive themselves as belonging to a close-knit group with a distinctive group identity that extends its interactions beyond cyberspace. Numerous members also communicate through private email and meet up before and after k.d. concerts and during the holidays. Even though both websites include original artwork, poems and an archive of images, the cultural production of k.d. lang fans consists mainly of conversation and correspondence with other fans. Indeed, bulletin board discussions (BBS) prove particularly well suited to the kind of interaction and community building that female fans are seeking online. While men may participate in a larger number of online debates through newsgroups or chatrooms, women have been shown to become more intimately involved in fewer but ongoing bulletin board discussions (Clerc, 2000). Clearly, BBS dialogues differ from chatroom or telephone conversations in that they do not necessarily happen in real time. Participants post messages as they would on the physical version of a board to be read by other members of the group when they decide to log on. Asynchronous communication helps respondents to take special care in constructing messages and as such, participants are less likely to engage in heated debates (Bielby et al., 1999). Also, BBS can be monitored and contentious messages deleted, a (self-)regulating practice that aims to avoid conflict and to preserve intimacy on k.d. boards. Henderson and Gilding's (2004) exploration of hyperpersonal communication and trust through a study of online friendships shows that women in particular consider the distinctive characteristics of online communication (such as limited cues and potential asynchronicity) to offer unique opportunities for the development of intimacy through words, undistracted by appearance. k.d. lang fans rely mainly on reciprocal self-disclosure, as well as subcultural gossip, innuendo and speculation about their idol in order to create and sustain an alternative social community (Whatling, 1997: 119).

As the Kennedyflairs' online community expanded, moderator Shelley published a code of conduct which spelt out the 'rules' of the community. Indeed, she set an example by banning five newcomers whose behaviour was deemed inappropriate. Whereas webmaster Shelley is clearly at the top of the group's hierarchy, enforcing site policies, answering questions about k.d. lang and organizing meet-ups, the behavioural norms and hierarchy on Chief's private board are more the result of internal negotiation and struggle. During the formation of the community, heated political and ideological discussions about feminism and lesbianism that were perceived to alienate the two straight participants were eventually worked through, allowing more space for freedom of expression for individual members in terms of political/sexual content and writing 'style' – which ranged from Cockney slang to academic jargon. The early conflicts combined with hyperpersonal communication created and consolidated bonds between (initially hostile or indifferent) individuals who were actively involved in the discussions, thus reinforcing a sense of 'commu-nion' and belonging. Yet they also installed a hierarchy based on knowledge and discursive performance, thus alienating or excluding less vocal women, as well as fans committed to the ideal of a harmonious community. Hence, Chief's board conversations soon became dominated by a relatively small number of highly educated individuals who defined themselves first and foremost in terms of social identity (lawyers, doctors, teachers, students and so on). The fact that some Euro-pean members admitted suffering from the language barrier imposed by the use of English suggests that fans below a certain level of education are excluded from the community. Furthermore, participants whose postings are marked by awkward phrasing, grammatical errors or incoherence tend to be ignored and often migrate to the public, and less hierarchical, Kennedyflairs board. Significantly, the most prominent members and opinion leaders in Chief's private community are not those who have accumulated knowledge about their idol, but are rather the most vocal and educated participants who draw on both official and fan popular capital to differentiate themselves from dominant (heterosexual and/or mainstream) culture in terms of taste and politics (Fiske, 1992).

A comparative analysis of the topics and entries of both bulletin boards reveals that the public/private split has an impact on the dynamic and content of the interaction, as well as the process of community building. The activity on the public Kennedyflairs board has gradually increased over the past two years, peaking in November and December 2004 when 200 new topics were intro-duced and a record number of 3,647 entries were posted. Many of the topics are purely informative, coinciding with k.d. lang's European tour, but there is also a marked increase in discussions not directly related to k.d. – such as coming-out stories that remain contained within a couple of marked lesbian threads. Never-theless, the sharing of personal, emotional and much appreciated 'womyn's coming out stories' or 'a beautiful female history lesson', to quote the contribu-tors' subject lines, can be taken as an indication of growing trust and intimacy among lesbians who express relief and gratitude for being able to share their stories online. Indeed, on mixed boards, coming-out stories allow for an identifi-cation of lesbian members and the construction of a distinctive lesbian (sub)community within the larger fan community.

On Chief's private board, the highest degree of involvement and intimacy can be identified in the early stages of community building as personal information is exchanged in threads unrelated to k.d. which invite members to reveal their cultural origin, national identity, job, height and even bra size. Also, members feel encouraged to post their picture and compile their own photo album or contribute to the butch/femme gallery of role models. Numerous threads are devoted to personal and identity-related issues, such as poetry and song lyrics, tattoos, gay marriage, lesbian parenting, female masculinity and lesbian erotica. But the site also offers a space for flirtation, as well as discussions about politics and mainly lesbian culture, ranging across names and topics such as Jeanette Winterson, Sarah Waters, Judith Halberstam, Ellen Degeneres, Melissa Etheridge, Martina Navratilova, Phranc and the Indigo Girls, and *The L Word*.

Because of its public status and more mixed population in terms of gender and sexual orientation, the Kennedyflairs board is committed to consensus and upholds k.d. as a liberal, humanist role model rather than a lesbian icon, or as one contributor puts it:

> This is the best place to share kd's influence … All people coming together to share their feelings about k.d. and her music, it bridges the gap between those of us who are straight people and those who aren't and makes everybody one as kd would like, very open and non homo-phobic (marymae03, 26 November 2004).

However, the utopian angle is also used by the group's posters as a strategy to delegitimize lesbian interpretations/contributors and k.d.'s lesbian identity. This is demonstrated in a discussion about an interview excerpt from *Boyz* magazine that quotes k.d. lang stating that she fancied boys and thought she was bisexual before she came out. Not only is the quote taken out of its original (textual and historical) context, but it is also introduced as a topic of discussion under the heading 'Attracted to men?', with the intention to question k.d.'s sexuality and 'to stir people up' – as the poster later admits in the thread. One lesbian fan who is clearly invested in k.d. lang as a lesbian idol and role model expresses her frustration:

> Am I the only one bothered by k.d. saying she's bisexual? Of course, it is my issue to deal with but I am rattled a little because when I discov-ered I was a lesbian, there was no one to look up to who was like me … To me, if you are bisexual, you are not a lesbian, which k.d. declared herself when she came out … I know it shouldn't matter but it is confusing to me (h2omole, 28 November 2004).

The numerous replies ignore the poster's emotional reference to lesbian identifi-cation (and betrayal) and pay tribute to utopian values, individualism and spiritu-ality. Typical reply postings read: 'In a more ideal world, we'd all be bisexual', 'You can create your own k.d. lang and enjoy her: homosexual, bisexual or heterosexual – to me it doesn't really matter'; and 'k.d. is a very spiritual person so it wouldn't surprise me if she connects with certain people despite their gender'. Indirectly inflamed by one respondent who fulminates against 'hetero anxiety and the narrow-minded way in which some people find it necessary to put everyone in a box according to their sexual preference(s)', the lesbian poster reluctantly demonstrates a newly-sensed consciousness of the surrounding fan community: 'I figure that the fact that I was so bothered by the bi is something in myself to examine. I love women. I love men, they are fun to be around. I just don't want to be physical with them' (h2omole, 5 November 2004).

Chief's private board, on the other hand, quickly established itself as a privileged white middle-class lesbian community (or as a newly invited member exclaims 'I have joined the elite!'), that uses its idol to work through identity-related issues, but has a hard time sustaining itself because of its protectionism. A side-effect of the hyperpersonal communication characterized by high levels of self-disclosure in words and pictures is the reluctance to expand the community. Over the past three years, membership applications and proposals to invite newcomers into the community were systematically vetoed by long-standing members who expressed concern about a breach of privacy. Furthermore, the ideal of friendship as the cornerstone of the close-knit private community is challenged on a regular basis by the formation and break-up of lesbian couples. Over the years, intense online communication has produced quite a few offline lesbian romances that are negotiated publicly on Chief's board. Since these relationships become a site of emotional investment and idealization, the group dynamic is very dependent on the mediation between on- and offline communication and accountability, especially in the case of break-ups that can cause a crisis of confidence in the community.

Fandom

Online communities offer unique opportunities for fans to interact and form alliances with others who may have different political, social and cultural backgrounds, but the collective sense of identity and community is also challenged by internal differences and struggles over the multiple meanings and identities attributed to the relatively 'open' k.d. lang text. Drawing on Pierre Bourdieu's work on processes of cultural distinction, authors such as Fiske (1992), Thornton (1995) and Tulloch (Tulloch and Jenkins, 1995) have addressed the social hierarchy of fandom, yet Matt Hills argues that Bourdieu's model, premised only on 'distant' mechanisms of cultural distinction, where classes (or fields) defined by their habitus seek to ward off the values of other classes/fields, cannot account convincingly for 'the fine-grained distinctions and moral dualisms' produced by cultural proximity that operate in fan culture (2002: 61) (see also Hills' essay in this collection). Even though long-term commitment and emotional support prevail in the predominantly female and/or lesbian k.d. lang community, particularly in times of crisis (illness, loss of a relative or partner), individual members and subgroups *compete* over 'ownership' of their fan object, segmenting and *fragmenting* the fan community along the lines of ideological/political and cultural/national differences.

As Gill Valentine points out: 'k.d. lang walks a precarious tightrope of ambiguity, attempting neither to lose her heterosexual album-buying public by being labelled a "lesbian artist", nor betray her gay following who are quick to accuse queer celebrities of assimilation or "selling out"' (1995: 477). The ambivalent k.d. text that acknowledges both its marginality and its membership of the dominant culture is often the site of ideological struggle on fan boards, dividing lesbian-identified and heterosexual/bisexual members, while also causing conflicts in the lesbian (sub)community along the lines of oppositional and conformist politics and readings. Reports and conversations about concert experiences in particular, highlight differences and conflicts in the fan community. Gill Valentine argues that k.d. lang's live concerts involve an appropriation and transgression of public/heterosexual space:

> When k.d. lang performs her music publicly at concert venues such as the Hammersmith Odeon or the Albert Hall, these spaces, which are taken for granted as heterosexual, are culturally produced through the meanings given to her/her music as something different, namely as lesbian space. Through appropriating the space of the concert venue, her lesbian audience demonstrates to the few heterosexuals there, how the production of space is dependent on those present. In so doing, the heterosexual audience becomes aware of how 'out of place' it can feel when a space is suddenly taken for granted as a lesbian environment rather than a heterosexual one (1995: 477).

Furthermore, Valentine points out that it is at the concert arena that lang aligns herself most explicitly with a lesbian identity by teasing her fans with lesbian innuendo and a vocal/physical performance that can be readily inscribed with lesbian meaning.

In postings leading up to concerts as well as concert reports, lesbian k.d. fans often pride themselves on obtaining and occupying front row seats and establishing a privileged bond with their idol in terms of eye contact, physical contact and verbal exchange. The appropriation of public/heterosexual space by a lesbian minority on mixed boards often invites hostile reactions from straight fans who feel excluded, as well as disapproval from lesbians who insist on a separation and/or negotiation between a private lesbian self and a public heterosexual self. However, it is interesting that the power struggle between lesbian dissidents and the majority of straight and gay members is displaced onto discussions about 'appropriate' fan behaviour, mobilizing a regulatory discourse that draws implicitly on class- and taste-based values (a controlled distance and reverence for k.d.)

and occasionally, on the articulation of national differences to impose behavioural norms at concerts and on bulletin boards. An incident that divided the Kennedyflairs community was caused by an English lesbian fan who shouted between songs 'k.d., we can see your nipples!' at a live concert in Brussels. The public sexualization of k.d. lang inspired the moderator to launch a thread (using a posting borrowed from another k.d. board) that encouraged fans to vent their anger about inappropriate behaviour during concerts:

> In Brussels on the 11th November (2nd day of the tour) the audience was not much politer than in Utrecht – someone shouted: 'We can see your nipples!', right after she timidly told the audience that she felt as if she were on her first date. She coldly replied that also celebs have nipples [sic]. And that after all, it did NOT feel like a first date. When someone lit a cigarette in front of her and would not kill it, she got upset and sent the person to the foyer. Besides those embarrassing moments, it was a memorable and wonderful concert, but I had the feeling there were no fire works [sic] partly because of those 'welcoming words' (Scottishmini, 20 November 2004).

The omission of k.d.'s name in this post suggests a projection of the author's feelings onto her favourite celebrity. Yet more importantly, the author retreats into a position of moral superiority in order to distinguish herself from the disruptive and 'embarrassing' Dutch and Belgian fans, while also distancing herself in another message from the 'rude English fans' who caused the 'incident'. Replies by other board members who attended the concert provide a different interpretation of the celebrity/fan relationship that valorizes audience participation and collective lesbian consumption of the idol, while also claiming k.d.'s complicity with her lesbian audience:

> Having been a member of various k.d. fan communities for a number of years, including this one, I was the person who made the comment about her 'nipples' and will happily answer any questions ... k.d. was in good spirits from the beginning of the evening and having seen k.d. perform before, I knew that humour (and flirtation) during the show wasn't something that passed her (or anybody) by. If I recall, there was a silence between songs, a point whereby most performers chat to their audience (fans) and vice versa. I shouted to kd 'k.d., we can see your nipples', which we could and she responded well, funny, unoffended and remained unphased by the 'incident' for the remainder of the show (Rie, 22 November 2004).

Here, the respondent foregrounds not simply the history of her engagement as a
fan, but more specifically her implicit understanding of the codes, or 'rules' via
which it operates. There is thus again a vying to display certain kinds of expertise
within the fan culture, as dramatized by the circulation of 'intimate' knowledge
surrounding lang.

In terms of cultural identity, the k.d. lang text is also marked by ambiguity.
Whereas k.d. resides in Los Angeles and has interacted with an American music
tradition throughout her career (country music, interpreting the American songbook in collaboration with Tony Bennett), the celebrity discourse also cultivates
'Canadianness' as a site of otherness and resistance to dominant American
culture. As Lee Parpart points out:

> Canadians, it has often been argued, experience themselves as colo-
> nized, at least historically speaking, in relation to Britain and France,
> and as systematically dominated (or neocolonized) by the United States
> on political, cultural and economic grounds ... Pierre Trudeau famously
> likened Canada to a mouse sleeping next to an elephant, and Canadians
> who have internalized this notion (or simply looked around them) seem
> to instinctively grasp their precarious position relative to the United
> States, while at the same time priding themselves on having produced a
> kinder, gentler society and nursing the idea that a chronic fear of being
> crushed under foot has transformed Canadians into superior observers
> and great comedians (2001: 176).

Thomas Haig (1994) has argued that Canada might even be considered a kind
of 'queer' nation – a marginal site that shares many of the qualities and predica-
ments of gays and lesbians. In any case, 'Canadianness' defines itself more in
terms of its divisions – highlighting individual difference through regionalism,
bilingualism and multiculturalism – than in relation to any metanarrative of
national unity (Howells, 1991). As such, the 'openness' of the k.d. lang text
clearly contributes to the fan communities' international, though mainly
Western/white, group identity. However, the recent affirmation and celebration
of her Canadian identity also produces antagonism amongst fans.

Since k.d. lang is largely the product of an American media environment and
music industry, American fans who represent the majority of board members are
perceived and treated as 'insiders'. They report on their concert experiences and
close encounters with k.d. and distribute tapes with television interviews/perfor-
mances to the culturally isolated and 'deprived' fans. In many respects, American
culture is the culture of reference uniting all participants in the community across
their different national origins, but this cultural hegemony also produces tensions
and conflicts, primarily along an American/European axis. Whereas American

contributors occupy a privileged position in the community in terms of fan knowledge and experience, the boards' cultural and political discourse tends to be monopolized by European participants who align themselves with alternative, national or 'high' culture (from auteurism and world cinema to royalty and national sports stars) while frequently criticizing American popular culture for its 'colonial' appropriation of the cultural Other. Yet it was the presidential campaign and George Bush's re-election on 2 November 2004, coinciding with k.d.'s American tour and promotion of her Canadian Songbook album *Hymns of the 49th Parallel*, that provoked the most heated and emotional discussions on fan boards. This caused a major rift between progressive and conservative participants, especially since the latter's allegiance to the international and lesbian (sub)community was challenged because of Bush's pro-war stance and opposition to gay rights and marriage. This polarization was fuelled by k.d. lang's anti-Bush statements in pictures (a photo depicted k.d. wearing a badge that says 'lick Bush'), at her concerts (she invited the Americans in the audience to move to Canada if Bush was re-elected), and in the interviews posted on fan boards. Under the heading 'Canadian Idol', k.d was asked about her activism in a local American magazine *The Wave*:

> Although I don't believe the stage is a place for political stomping grounds, I believe it is very, very important that we start speaking out and we're not supportive of the Bush administration … And in light of our present-day situation, politically and globally – and I'm not a nationalistic person, that's not what drives me – but I appreciate coming from a country that takes a more neutral and passive role in the world's goings-on (Lanham, 2004).

k.d. lang is increasingly promoted and constructed via national 'otherness' in a bid for authenticity. Lang claims her musical heritage in *Hymns of the 49th Parallel* by paying homage to songwriting compatriots such as Joni Mitchell, Jane Siberry and Leonard Cohen while also inscribing herself in the Canadian Songbook by 'covering' one of her own previously recorded songs 'Simple'. In an essentialist move, the singer attributes the 'purity' and range of her voice to 'the wide, open spaces that surrounded her as a child' (Sturges, 2004). Interviews and reviews in the mainstream press in particular invariably invoke k.d.'s roots ('Canadian-born') and childhood in rural Alberta whereas photographic representations show a casually dressed k.d. merging into her natural surroundings. Significantly, *Hymns of the 49th Parallel* is the first album that withholds k.d. lang's image from the cover, replacing the star with a snowy landscape/representation of the 'Great White North'. Despite the prioritization of national identity over lesbianism in the construction of the celebrity discourse, k.d.'s idealization of Canada as an imagined community opens up a privileged space of alterity that lends legitimacy to critical and oppositional voices on fan boards.

Lesbian identities

Martha Gever argues that:

> [T]he emergence of lesbian celebrities represents the amalgamation of two previously incompatible categories: female celebrity, which involves an ability to project some form of consummate femininity, and identifiable lesbianism, indicated by some kind of display of nonconformity to gender norms by means of stylistic markers associated with masculinity (Gever, 2003: 37).

Indeed, Gever cites k.d. lang as exemplary in terms of this basic configuration and considers the lesbian idol's glamorous, stylized and 'feminized' (though not necessarily conventionally feminine) representation in mainstream media to be representative of Lesbian Chic. Louise Allen (1997) combines an ethnographic approach and textual analysis to explore the relationship between celebrity, image and identity across lesbian culture. Allen argues that k.d. lang and Martina Navratilova 'at once exemplify, but are also separable from an increasing commodification of lesbian sexuality in the media' (1997: 1), because their female masculinity challenges the heterosexist sex/gender relationship which is central to lesbian culture as a site of recognition.

Fan discourse and photographic representations of k.d. lang in online communities reveal an important investment in lesbian masculinity as an empowering site of identity formation and a locus of desire. Jackie, who met k.d. backstage after a live concert, provides a description of her idol that revels in signifiers of masculinity and gender misrecognition, while also invoking traditionally feminine qualities such as compassion and vulnerability:

> I can't help recalling standing beside k.d. in New York and thinking to myself 'this is like talking to a guy'. Part of it is the way she looks at you – very direct – those blue eyes are saying 'I don't tolerate fools gladly'. Not that there isn't any kindness but it's measured and there is absolutely no forced friendliness. I think most of the 'guests' as we were called, were somewhat intimidated … To me k.d. has always been the quintessential butch – strong but vulnerable, confident, compassionate. No one else can wear a suit like k.d., no one else can walk like k.d. No one else has her commanding presence. k.d. in butch mode can make other self-styled butches, e.g. Ellen Degeneres look like total wimps. As

k.d. herself said, somewhat ruefully 'people will always call me sir' (Jackie, 2 July 2001).

On Chief's private board, the celebration of lesbian masculinity extends to the participants. Butch members are often challenged by self-identified femmes to discuss their identity and desire ('What do butches want?') and to post pictures of themselves (or body parts), allowing fans to articulate/perform their identities and express desire in the context of a butch/femme dynamic that subverts heterosexual models of gender (Case, 1992: 297). One of the most prolific and creative threads so far is 'The Battle of the Butches – Lesbian Icons & Ourselves' (Wolfie, 14 November 2003) that invites participants to vote for the 'butchiest' lesbian icon and board member.

However, k.d.'s relative media invisibility over the years, her increasingly subdued performance, use of classical repertoire/ballads and negotiated appearance during her 2004 World Tour (barefoot, wearing a concealing dress/robe designed by Donna Karan), is perceived by many lesbian fans as a disappointing break with the idol's previous, spectacularly masculine or disruptively queer performance during her country and western days and the *Drag* era. P. David Marshall points out that 'style represents a statement of difference from as well as a statement of solidarity with the particular audience. A change in style indicates a reassertion by the performer of his or her own authenticity' (Marshall, 1997: 162). The increasingly 'naturalized' (discursive, vocal and visual) representation and construction of the k.d. lang star text implies an evacuation of gendered and sexual difference (partially displaced onto a more safe national difference/otherness). This is experienced by longtime lesbian fans in particular as a loss (or even a betrayal of k.d.'s lesbian fan base), and invites an outburst of nostalgia on k.d. boards where images and performances from the past are both cultivated and celebrated. However, k.d. fans are mainly invested in a lived-out lesbian identity as a marker of authenticity. While fans do appropriate straight femme stars such as Madonna, Deborah Harry, Gina Gershon and Cindy Crawford in romantic and sexual fantasy scenarios, the status of lesbian icon is reserved for 'real lesbians' as opposed to the commodified versions as exemplified by the Russian duo Tatu and *The L Word*. Despite k.d. lang's attempts to universalize her appeal by playing down her sexuality, lesbian fans continue to celebrate their idol as a heroic and empowering alternative to the media spectacle of lesbian chic.

Conclusion

In her article 'Mannish Girl. k.d. lang – from cowpunk to androgyny', Stella Bruzzi claims that 'The act of spectatorship or fandom can in itself be performative, but the ones who are having their cake and eating it too are, in k.d.

lang's case, all those who are *not* lesbian' (Bruzzi, 1997: 202). Over the past five years k.d. lang's star discourse, both in terms of musical development and visual representation, is indeed marked increasingly by a retreat from performativity and an evacuation or displacement of gendered and sexual difference. Even though this may make her representation more palatable to a heterosexual audience, this mainstreaming move also precipitated her invisibility in the popular media – which thrives on the stylistic markers of lesbian visibility. It implies a sense of loss for longtime lesbian fans who invest in iconic images from the past and lesbian readings to give meaning to their social and sexual identities. Nevertheless, the intense online interaction that extends beyond cyberspace proves that k.d. lang still stands out as being represented by a complex celebrity text which has the potential to unite straight and lesbian women in a community committed to utopian values, while also inspiring the creation and cultivation of a private lesbian, performative space where identity and desire are variously and diversely formed and played out.

Bibliography

Allen, Louise (1997) *The Lesbian Idol: Martina, kd and the Consumption of Lesbian Masculinity*, London: Cassell.

Bielby, Denise D., Harrington, Lee and Bielby, William T. (1999) 'Whose Stories Are They? Fans' Engagement with Soap Opera Narratives in Three Sites of Fan Activity', *Journal of Broadcasting and Electronic Media* 43/1: 35–51.

Bruzzi, Stella (1997) 'Mannish Girl: k.d. lang – from Cowpunk to Androgyny', in Sheila Whiteley (ed.), *Sexing the Groove: Popular Music and Gender*, London and New York: Routledge, pp. 191–206.

Case, Sue-Ellen (1993) 'Toward a Butch–Femme Aesthetic', in Henry Abelove, Michele Barale and David Halperin (eds), *The Lesbian and Gay Studies Reader*, New York: Routledge, pp. 294–306.

Clerc, Susan (2002) 'Estrogen Brigades and "Big Tits" Threads: Media Fandom Online and Off', in David Bell and Barbara Kennedy (eds), *The Cybercultures Reader*, New York: Routledge, pp. 216–29.

Coombe, Rosemary (1992) 'Author/izing the Celebrity: Publicity Rights, Postmodern Politics, and Unauthorized Genders', *Carodza Arts and Entertainment Law Journal* 10: 365–95.

Feenberg, Andrew and Bakardjieva, Maria (2004) 'Virtual Community: No "Killer Implication"', *New Media & Society* 6/1: 37–43.

Fiske, John (1992) 'The Cultural Economy of Fandom', in Lisa Lewis (ed.), *The Adoring Audience. Fan Culture and Popular Media*, London and New York: Routledge, pp. 30–49.

Gever, Martha (2004) *Entertaining Lesbians: Celebrity, Sexuality and Self-Invention*, New York and London: Routledge.

Giddens, Anthony (2000) *The Third Way and its Critics*, Cambridge: Polity.

Haig, Thomas (1994) 'Not Just Some Sexless Queen: A Note on "Kids in the Hall" and the Queerness of Canada', *semiotext(e) canadas* 4/17: 227–9.

Henderson, Samantha and Gilding, Michael (2004) '"I've Never Clicked This Much with Anyone in my Life": Trust and Hyperpersonal Communication in Online Friendships', *New Media & Society* 6/4: 487–506.

Hills, Matt (2002) *Fan Cultures*, London and New York: Routledge.

Howells, Caroll Ann (1991) 'No Transcendental Image: Canadianness in Contemporary Women's Fiction in English', in Cornelius Remie and Jean-Michel Lacroix (eds), *Canada on the Threshold of the 21st Century*, Amsterdam: John Benjamin Publishing, pp. 317–22.

Jones, Steven (2002) *Virtual Culture: Identity & Communication in Cybersociety*, London, Thousand Oaks and New Delhi: Sage Publications.

Lanham, Ton (2004) 'Canadian Idol: k.d. lang Celebrates the Music of the Great White North', *The Wave* 4/17, available online at www.thewavemag.com.

Marshall, P. David (1997) *Celebrity and Power: Fame in Contemporary Culture*, Minneapolis and London: University of Minnesota Press.

Mockus, Martha (1994) 'Queer Thoughts on Country Music and k.d. lang', in Philip Brett, Elizabeth Wood and Gary Thomas (eds), *Queering the Pitch: The New Gay and Lesbian Musicology*, London and New York: Routledge, pp. 257–74.

Parpart, Lee (2001) 'The Nation and the Nude: Colonial Masculinity and the Spectacle of the Male Body in Recent Canadian Cinema(s)', in Peter Lehman (ed.), *Masculinity: Bodies, Movies, Culture*, London and New York: Routledge, pp. 167–92.

Pullen, Kirsten (2000) 'I-love-Xena.com: Creating Online Fan Communities', in David Gauntlett (ed.), *Web Studies: Rewiring Media Studies for the Digital Age*, London: Arnold, pp. 52–61.

—— (2004) 'Everybody's Gotta Love Somebody, Sometime: Online Fan Community', in David Gauntlett and Ross Horsley (eds), *Web Studies*, 2nd edn, London: Arnold, pp. 80–91.

Rodman, Gilbert (1996) *Elvis After Elvis: The Posthumous Career of a Living Legend*, London: Routledge.

Rojek, Chris (2001) *Celebrity*, London: Reaktion Books.

Sturges, Fiona (2004) 'kd lang: Just Hear my Song', *The Independent*, 19 November, available online at enjoyment.independent.co.uk/music/features/article20918.ece2, accessed 14 February 2006.

Thornton, Sarah (1995) *Club Cultures: Music, Media and Subcultural Capital*, Cambridge: Polity Press.

Tulloch, John and Jenkins, Henry (1995) *Science Fiction Audiences: Watching 'Doctor Who' and 'Star Trek'*, London: Routledge.

Valentine, Gill (1995) 'Creating Transgressive Space: The Music of kd lang', *Transactions of the Institute of British Geographers* 20/4: 474–85.

Watson, Nessim (2002) 'Why We Argue About Virtual Community: A Case Study of the Phish.Net Fan Community', in Steven Jones (ed.), *Virtual Culture: Identity and Communication in Cybersociety*, London, Thousand Oaks & New Delhi: Sage Publications, pp. 102–32.

Whatling, Claire (1997) *Screen Dreams: Fantasising Lesbians in Films*, Manchester and New York: Manchester University Press.

Whiteley, Sheila (2000) 'K.d. lang, a certain kind of woman', in Sheila Whiteley (ed.), *Women and Popular Music: Sexuality, Identity and Subjectivity*, London and New York: Routledge, pp. 152–70.

Part IV

Fame Damage

Introduction

> Consumption and success ... are the key notes of the image of stardom,
> but it would be wrong ... to ignore elements that run counter to this.
> Through the star system, failures of the dream are also represented
> (Dyer, 1998: 44).

As Dyer's comment suggests, we have historically understood stardom to be a
meritorious phenomenon, offering a set of promises which are glorious,
aspirational and desirable. In short, it plays out an image in society of the ultimate way to *be* (Braudy, 1986). Yet stardom and celebrity, and indeed public
visibility more generally, clearly offer a more contradictory set of associations
than this implies. 'Fame Damage', the title of this section, is not necessarily
intended to indicate how the consequences of public visibility can inflict 'harm'
on an individual, society or audience (although its impact on the physical and
psychological 'health' of the famous is an issue addressed here). Particularly
where the audience is concerned, social commentators have often expressed
concern about the negative 'effects' of fame, whether with respect to celebrities
as superficial role models for measuring social achievement or success, their role
in circulating unobtainable images of physical perfection, or their apparent cultivation of obsessive – and occasionally murderous – fans. In terms of academic
analysis, to sail too close to this perspective was also difficult for a field aiming to
secure its academic legitimacy. But this section is less intended to denounce the
social 'ills' of celebrity than to explore how decidedly more negative discourses –
from failure, death, mental illness and notoriety, to 'hate' for celebrities – are
also *integral* to the cultural circulation of fame. How do these discourses
contribute to the cultural construction of celebrities, and indeed how they
connect with their audience?

Clearly, the dominant definition of stardom and celebrity still carries attractive
and enticing associations. We only need note, for example, the recent discussion
that media celebrity, such as that bestowed by reality TV, increasingly functions
as a form of self-realization and *validation* for 'ordinary' people (Biressi and

Nunn, 2005: 99). But at the same time, a recurrent emphasis here has also been on 'exploitation' and failure: contestants are often constructed in media discourse as falling victim to powers of a ruthless fame-making machine. Rather than self-affirmation, we encounter cautionary tales about the price of public visibility and the lure of immediate wealth, promises seen as false and hollow when, as one programme put it, 'instant television fame is over in a dream'.[1]

While it is clear that these dystopian inflections do not ultimately destabilize the overall economic and cultural enterprise of celebrity (although they can certainly ruin or harm the economic profitability of a particular celebrity image), we should not underestimate their pervasive presence. At the same time, the extent to which these discourses represent a particularly recent or radical shift is open to debate – as various authors discuss in this section. For example, Leo Braudy reminds us that 'the performer who hits the top only to disintegrate into a psychic mess has been around in various guises since the middle of the nineteenth century' (1986: 577). Braudy emphasizes here how fame was understood as a 'depersonalizing as much as individualizing' phenomenon (ibid.: 578), and this makes clear how the emphasis on identity (as discussed in Chapter 1) is once more apparent. While many critics have insisted that celebrity is inextricably linked to the construction of identity, individualism and selfhood in modern society (Dyer, 1998; Marshall, 1997; Turner, 2004), here we have an image of the self as 'damaged' – used and discarded – by the mechanistic excesses of capitalism. Dyer refers to two examples when he describes how the 'recognition of Hollywood as a destroyer was perhaps most forcibly expressed by the deaths of Marilyn Monroe and Judy Garland, whose ruined lives and possible suicides were laid at the front door of Hollywood's soulless search for profits' (1998: 44). In his discussion of the star scandals in the 1920s, however, Richard deCordova reminds us that the predominantly utopian image of (film) stardom was tarnished well before this time. In the 1920s, the most famous incidents (Mary Pickford's divorce in 1920 and quick remarriage to Douglas Fairbanks, 'Fatty' Arbuckle's alleged murder of Virginia Rappe in 1921, William Desmond Taylor's mysterious murder in 1922, and Wallace Reid's death by drug overdose in 1923) were not isolated events, but pointed to a further discursive *shift* in the cultural construction of stars. Rather than 'success, security and marital bliss', instead 'transgression, betrayal, restlessness and loss entered the dramatic formula' (deCordova, 1990: 121); these representations were the site of an intense struggle where the morality of the cinema was concerned (later playing a role in the institutionalization of film censorship). Yet deCordova positions this less as a radical shift in the representation of the star than more the logical extension of a framework which pivoted on the rhetoric of secrecy, the fascination with locating a 'concealed truth … that resided behind or beyond' the surface of appearance (ibid.: 140). Clearly, there is a difference between celebrity 'misdeeds' and those events or misfortunes which are perceived to be 'caused' by the pressures of fame, yet they all suggest that the glory of public visibility can leave its subjects wanting.

But it is important that in contemporary celebrity coverage, some examples of what was then conceived as the 'darker side' of fame (Grieveson, 2002) would perhaps now appear less shocking. Headlines sprawled across the pages of tabloid newspapers and celebrity magazines which proclaim that a particular celebrity is 'Off to Rehab' are now part of the everyday ebb and flow of celebrity discourse, although the impact of such disclosures will still depend on the nature of what is revealed and the wider context of the celebrity's image. (At the time of writing,[2] the British media were still picking over the revelation that supermodel Kate Moss had developed a serious drug addiction, and charting its disastrous impact on her previously lucrative modelling career and cosmetic contracts.) Even while we acknowledge that this 'darker side' is not an intrinsically new possibility, there is certainly the sense that the more unseemly side of fame has increasingly infiltrated cultural discourse.

As Braudy notes, particularly since the 1960s, the 'hazards [of fame] have become obligatory fare in every celebrity interview' (1986: 8). Braudy refers in particular to the last fifty years, and the post-World War II context is important here, particularly at the level of celebrity production. Not only is it associated with the decentralization of celebrity image control (the decline of the Holly-wood star system, the wider proliferation of media outlets) but also with the ever-increasing fascination with the 'private' lives of celebrities – their circula-tion 'offstage' rather than on. But the emphasis on the decentralization of image construction, with the implication that celebrities are often 'authored' from so many different contexts, would seem to negate their often willing role within these frameworks. Celebrity biographies, as well as the tabloid press and celeb-rity magazines, would now seem strangely empty without celebrity disclosures ranging across the horrors of plastic surgery, eating disorders, and drug and alcohol abuse, not to mention 'confessions' about depression or infidelity. To observe this is not to trivialize the experience of any of these matters (whether associated with celebrities or not) but only to point to their increasing conventionalization within the parameters of celebrity discourse.

The emphasis here may be linked to arguments about changing discourses of selfhood in the late modern period (Giddens, 1991), particularly, perhaps, the significance of confessional and therapeutic cultures. But it can also be connected to what might be called the will to publicly enact and witness destruction amidst the despair and decay of the (post)modern age. There has arguably been a collapse in the belief in the goodness or purity of things and a corresponding increase in irony and scepticism, and in this apocalyptic scenario, fame damage is but an offshoot of the philosophical and political decay that is all around us. From this perspective, despite their particular connection with the world of fame and the role it might play in mapping these narratives, celebrities articulate changing notions of identity and individualism in modern society. As Stephen Harper (on mental illness) and David Schmid (on serial killer fame) explore in this section, celebrities are often the most exemplary models for playing this out.

As this suggests, the emphasis on the 'failures' of celebrities – the failure to sustain a career, to remain monogamous, the failure to stay 'naturally' slim or to 'cope' without addictive stimulation – may also offer a further inflection to the ordinary/extraordinary paradox which has long since structured the circulation of fame (Dyer, 1998). In short, it may work to humanize celebrities, facilitating identification, empathy, and an apparent levelling of ground between celebrity and audience. Alternatively, it may invoke a more antagonistic rhetoric, and as Turner *et al.* suggest, 'as signs of the potential for ordinary people to transcend their condition, celebrities are inspirational, as signs of the inauthenticity and the superficiality of success, they are consoling' (2000: 13). Such narratives still function to *individuate* the celebrity, and as noted, there is of course a history of scandals, problems and disclosures being used to sell celebrities and material about them (deCordova, 1990: 10).[3] But for certain famous names, such narratives are not back-stories, or 'behind-the-scenes' glimpses of the more 'unseemly' side to their celebrity. As David Schmid discusses in this section, serial killers are famous for heinous misdeeds, but are arguably made legible by the same media spotlight that creates media celebrity. Despite the historical currency of more negative discourses on fame, Evans and Wilson describe how the term originally 'meant "good reputation", hence its association with the good and the glorious' (1999: 7). While this idea has been challenged more generally by conceptions of fame as a more ubiquitous – and thus devalued – currency, probing the less utopian aspects of fame (in which it is not presented as either 'good' or 'glorious') now invites urgent debate. The essays in this section aim to contribute to this project.

Summaries

The fascination with the celebrity serial killer haunts the American imagination. The media regularly report on, and help to manufacture, the serial killer persona, while the trade in murderabilia suggests a general fan desire to invest in, know more about, and get closer to the famous killer. And late capitalism is, of course, willing to provide these artefacts and commodities for as long as there is a marketplace for them. These 'idols of destruction' are worshipped and adored like 'regular' stars and celebrities, but the altar on which they are celebrated is predicated on violent dissolution and what might be termed a perverse desire to get nearer to a figure who is all about death. In David Schmid's opening essay, 'Idols of destruction: celebrity and the serial killer', famous serial killers are explored in terms of the 'cultural work they do in contemporary American culture'. Schmid's position is that the celebrity serial killer 'satisfies a double need, both halves of which have grown over the course of the twentieth century: the need for representations of death, and the need for celebrities'. According to Schmid, images of death emerge because real, direct encounters with death are increasingly removed from the public sphere, while the desire for stars and celebrities grows out of a greater sense of social isolation and 'worries about the decline of individuality in modern society'. Schmid suggests that the celebrity serial killer helps resolve latent anxieties, fulfilling a 'cathartic function for their audience', and he goes on to conclude that the celebrity serial killer mirrors 'our own ambivalent response' to violence and death, 'composed of both fear and attraction'.

The 'damage' that fame does to those who are or have been famous can be read in terms of how mental illness is said to befall a great many stars and celebrities. The supposedly essential link between the great and the gifted and a range of psychiatric disorders has a long history in both the arts and sciences – with the 'romance' of maddening genius played out in the biographies of luminary writers, painters, musicians, political thinkers and ground-breaking scientists. As Stephen Harper argues in his essay, 'Madly famous: narratives of mental illness in celebrity culture', this discourse of twinning greatness with madness has found a 'special' place in the representation of famous people who are perceived to be increasingly caught up in its damaging orbit. Harper agues that mental illness narratives are common in celebrity culture because of the way they serve the interests of capitalism at both an ideological and psychic level. According to Harper, 'these narratives facilitate both the elaboration of meritocratic discourse and the communication of psychiatric risk'. Gender is understood to be an important ingredient in the way celebrity madness is communicated and understood, with the appropriation of 'feminine therapeutic discourses' used to reinforce 'the patriarchal definition of genius as a combination of male and female qualities reserved exclusively for men'. Harper goes on to contend that celebrity mental illness provides women with 'a melodramatic affect correlating to a particular female experience of frustration and disempowerment'. For Harper, the therapeutic qualities of emotional investment in the 'rhetoric of personal trauma' may contribute to the trivialization and infantilization of experiences of mental health problems and to the disempowerment of people (especially women) who buy into them.

Death, auto-destruction and stories of mental ill-health are arguably central to the way rock and pop stars are represented in the media and consumed by desiring fans. 'Rock Gods' who break social taboos, who over-indulge in hedonistic pastimes, and who ultimately live fast and die young, are labelled as extra-special and super-iconic by the legion of fans who embrace such heroic mythology. As Sheila Whiteley argues in her essay, 'Celebrity: the killing fields of popular music', 'the association of death with the heroic remains a powerful signifier within rock culture', since it is identified as the ultimate form of excess. Whiteley poetically maps a history of rock debauchery and tragedy, highlighting the way rock stars from Elvis Presley to Kurt Cobain have courted transgression and been blighted by insecurity. Rock's heroes 'are those whose emotions have broken out of prescribed limits, endowing them with a godlike eminence which is curiously enhanced by their often ignoble deaths'. However, as Whiteley also contends, this is not necessarily the case for female rock stars who live excessive lives. Janis Joplin's aggressiveness, for example, 'marked her as uncontrollable, "unnaturally" active, and outspoken on her numerous affairs and drinking habits' and, as such, she lay 'outside the dominant symbolic order'. Female rock transgressors, in fact female rock stars in general, are a part of a music industry that involves the 'structural subordination of women'. Symbolic and political damage is being done to female musicians all the time: this, Whiteley concludes, is the patriarchal logic of the music industry.

Contemporary stars and celebrities are increasingly represented as fallen, fallible figures, as figures of fun and derision, and as pampered individuals who deserve the 'bashing' they increasingly get from the media. The tabloids in particular are perceived to be among the foremost purveyors of this trope of bringing down the star or celebrity, of uncovering the 'truth' behind the manufactured (false) mask that the star or celebrity hides behind. In Sofia Johansson's essay, '"Sometimes you wanna hate celebrities": tabloid readers and celebrity coverage', the role and function of celebrity journalism is examined, alongside a consideration of the pleasures that readers get from reading and gossiping about the tell-tale stories, exposés and 'damaging' paparazzi pictures which fill the pages of the tabloid press. Johansson places her analysis of tabloid celebrity stories in terms of how they contribute to democratic culture, arguing that 'they stimulate debates about fundamental moral and social issues', and contribute to a sense of community belonging for those who partake in celebrity gossip. Through a small-scale study of UK tabloid readers, Johansson suggests that celebrity gossip plays a role 'in the negotiation of social norms', particularly that of morality, and allows readers to take an 'imaginary adventure' in scenarios which 'serve as a welcome change from the mundane nature of everyday life'. However, Johansson's research also draws attention to the 'frustration, resentment and anger' felt by readers because of the way tabloid celebrity stories 'carry the promise of social mobility, yet invoke restrictions of the social structure'. In this context, celebrity-bashing can be read as a 'momentary experience of power and control' whereby the reader is symbolically involved in 'dragging' the famous person down.

Notes

1 *Tonight with Trevor McDonald* (ITV1, 13 February, 2004).

2 October 2005.

3 As deCordova (1990) notes, there are only certain deeds that appear to be 'too individual' for the system to accommodate (such as Arbuckle's alleged murder of Virginia Rappe), although this does not of course prevent the wider economic enterprise of celebrity from capitalizing on such stories.

Chapter 17

Idols of destruction
Celebrity and the serial killer

David Schmid

Selling murder

Online shopping is all the rage these days. The murderabilia industry, which specializes in selling serial killer artefacts, is booming. At Spectre Studios, sculptor David Johnson sells flexible plastic action figures of Ted Bundy, Jeffrey Dahmer and John Wayne Gacy, and plans to produce a figure of Jack the Ripper in the future. Serial Killer Central offers a range of items made by serial killers themselves, including paintings and drawings by Angelo Buono (one of the 'Hillside Stranglers'). For the more discerning consumer, Supernaught.com charges a mere $300 for a brick from Jeffrey Dahmer's apartment building, while a lock of Charles Manson's hair is a real bargain at $995, shipping and handling not included.

The sale of murderabilia is just a small part of the huge serial killer industry that has become a defining feature of American popular culture since the 1970s. A constant stream of movies, magazines, T-shirts, trading cards, videos, DVDs, books, websites, television shows, and a mountain of ephemera, have given the figure of the serial murderer an unparalleled degree of visibility in the contemporary American public sphere. In a culture defined by celebrity, serial killers are among the biggest stars of all, instantly recognized by the vast majority of Americans. Murderabilia, as a limit case in serial killer celebrity, give us an opportunity to confront the consequences of the fame given to serial killers in its most egregious form.

Not surprisingly, murderabilia have been the focus of a sustained critique by the guardians of 'decency' in American culture. On 2 January 2003, the *John Walsh Show*, the daytime television vehicle of the longtime host of *America's Most Wanted*, featured an 'inside look at the world of "murderabilia," which involves the sale of artwork, personal effects and letters from well-known killers' (Serial

Killer Central, 2003). Guests included Andy Kahan, director of the Mayor's
Crime Victim Assistance Office in Houston, Texas; 'Thomas', who was horrified
to find hair samples from 'The Railroad Killer', the individual who killed his
mother, for sale on the internet; Elmer Wayne Henley, a serial killer who sells
his artwork to collectors; and Joe, who runs the website Serial Killer Central and
sells murderabilia from a wide range of killers. Despite the program's stated
intention to 'look at both sides of the issue', the show was little more than a jere-
miad against the murderabilia industry.

The programme's bias was noted by many of those who visited Joe's Serial
Killer Central site and left messages on the message board on the day this edition
of the *John Walsh Show* aired. Although some visitors shared Walsh's perspective,
others sympathized with Joe because of the way he had been treated on the show:
'I as well saw you on the John Walsh show, you [showed] a lot of courage going
on such a one sided show, and it was shit that they wouldn't let you talk, I would
have walked off' (Serial Killer Central, 2003). But whether the comments were
positive or negative, the *John Walsh Show* clearly created a great deal of interest in
the Serial Killer Central site. As one of the messages puts it, 'I think that [if]
anything else he [John Walsh] has put a spark in everyone's curiosity ... I have
noticed that you have more hits on your page today than any others' (ibid.). Even
the most explicit condemnation of serial killer celebrity can find itself implicated
in (and perhaps even unwittingly encouraging the growth of) that celebrity.

Walsh's attack on the murderabilia industry was another skirmish in a
campaign that has been growing steadily since the late 1990s. One of the
campaign's initial targets was the internet trading site eBay, which was criticized
for allowing serial-killer-related products to be sold online. In support of such
criticism, conservative victims' rights and pro-death-penalty organizations such as
Justice For All formed an online petition against eBay (Justice For All, 1999). In
November 2000, *BusinessWeek Online* featured an interview with Andy Kahan in
which he argued that the online sale of murderabilia should be suppressed:

> The internet just opens it all up to millions and millions more potential
> buyers and gives easy access to children. And it sends a negative message
> to society. What does it say about us? We continue to glorify killers and
> continue to put them in the mainstream public. That's not right (Busi-
> ness Week, 2000).

Bowing eventually to public pressure, eBay decided to ban the sale of
murderabilia items in May 2001, forcing the industry underground.

The ongoing debate about the ethics of murderabilia shows how difficult it is
to draw a line between those who condemn and those who participate in that
culture. An ABC News online article on murderabilia inadvertently highlights the

difficulty of distinguishing a 'normal' from an 'abnormal' interest in serial murder by quoting Rick Staton, one of the biggest collectors and dealers of murderabilia in the United States, who emphasizes that the people he sells to are not 'ghouls and creeps [who] crawl out of the woodwork' but rather 'pretty much your average Joe Blow'. Even his family, Staton goes on to say, who profess to be disgusted by what he does, act very differently in practice: 'The minute they step into this room, they are glued to everything in here and they are asking questions and they are genuinely intrigued by it … So it makes me wonder: Am I the one who is so abnormal, or am I pretty normal?' (ABC News, 2001).

The only way to answer Staton's question and to understand the serial killer popular culture industry it concerns is to concentrate on the conditions that allowed for its emergence. Consequently, my focus in this essay is not exclusively on murderabilia or celebrity serial killer case studies; rather, I want to analyse how the concept of 'fame' has evolved in ways that not only allow for the existence of criminal celebrities such as the serial killer but also make the serial killer the exemplary modern celebrity. In doing so, I will also argue that the fame of serial killers is absolutely central to understanding the varieties of cultural work they do in contemporary American culture.

Defining fame: merit or visibility?

Despite recent critical work on its negative social and ideological dimensions (of which this section of the book is part), the hegemonic definition of fame still tends to present it as an inherently positive phenomenon. According to this line of thinking, criminals in general, and serial killers in particular, are still more appropriately described as infamous or notorious rather than famous, as antiheroes rather than heroes. In fact, the iconic status of serial killers in contemporary American culture is compelling evidence of the collapse of the difference between fame and notoriety. Although the idea that fame is the result of meritorious achievement still has some currency, there has also been a sharp decline in the importance of 'merit' as a defining factor in fame. Consequently, in the contemporary public sphere, to be famous and to be notorious are frequently the same thing.

Most writers on the subject agree that we have witnessed a sea change in the nature of fame over the past two hundred years. If in the past the ranks of the famous were peopled overwhelmingly by those recognized for meritorious achievement, today the famous are often the visible, rather than the talented. Although some would argue that merit is still necessary to achieve fame, the ranks of the famous are also peopled by those who simply get the public's attention. In other words, fame today possesses a performative aspect that is quite new (see Braudy, 1986: 549). When fame first became associated with visibility in the early-nineteenth-century United States, the association was seen as positive. According to Braudy, 'to be seen was to be free, to be heroic, to be American' (ibid.: 453). Once fame is characterized *primarily* by visibility rather than achievement, however, it no longer makes sense to distinguish between good and bad forms of fame. In a society where merit is no longer the sole deciding factor in fame, recognition and self-exposure are now believed to be absolute goods in themselves: 'fame promises acceptability, even if one commits the most heinous crime, because thereby people will finally know who you are, and you will be saved from the living death of being unknown' (ibid.: 562). When the essential factor about celebrities is whether they are broadly known, the way is open for notoriety to fill the gap left open by the decline of merit in definitions of fame. Under these circumstances, crime is no longer a bar to celebrity; indeed, it is as close to a guarantee of celebrity as one can find. Thanks to the 'morally neutral' nature of contemporary fame, 'to be notorious or to be infamous may be no more than shortcuts' to fame (Fisher, 1986: 155). Perhaps this is the motive for those crimes committed by obsessed fans. As Mark Chapman found out when he killed John Lennon, by attacking the famous, you become famous.

Given these developments, it is natural to ask whether it is still useful or accurate to distinguish between fame and celebrity. On one level, these categories seem as distinct as ever, fame remaining an honorific category with a long and glorious history, while celebrity seems a much more recent and debased category, usually because of its association with the mass media (Giles, 2000: 3). Braudy, however, argues that we 'might want to make distinctions between fame, renown, honour, reputation, celebrity, and so on – and have a good deal of moral reason to do. But we should also be sensitive to the way those lines have become blurred' (Braudy, 1986: 562). Indeed, some have argued that the supposedly clear dividing line between fame and celebrity has always been unclear. Although the existence of famous serial killers might seem a perversion of the honorable history of fame, Tyler Cowen reminds us that 'many of the supposed "heroes" of the past were liars, frauds, and butchers to varying degrees' (Cowen, 2000: 65). Bearing this in mind, we might best interpret celebrity serial killers as continuous, rather than discontinuous, with the history of fame.

So although it would be a mistake to use the terms 'fame' and 'celebrity' interchangeably, clearly the two categories are closer than they ever have been before. Whether one is a Pulitzer Prize-winning author, a politician, a killer, or a failed contestant on *American Idol*, nowadays everyone must be treated as a celebrity in order to be 'legible' in the contemporary public sphere. Even if you personify the older merit-based definition of fame, the odds are that you will still be packaged/perceived as a 'mediagenic' celebrity because only in that way will your success be acknowledged and understood by the widest possible audience. Obviously, the collapse of the old distinction between fame and celebrity has not been widely celebrated; indeed, the conventional reaction to the 'decline' of fame has been to present it mournfully as evidence of a broader cultural decline in modern America (e.g. Boorstin, 1962). Unlike such commentators, I am not interested in mourning the decline of fame; rather, I want to understand how and why it happened.

Media technologies, fame and violence

Regardless of their motivations, the ability of individuals who desire fame to realize their ambitions is partly dependent upon the media technologies available to them and the ability of those technologies to create and disseminate fame (see Braudy, 1986). Changes in fame over the past two hundred years have as much, if not more, to do with the development of the market economy for fame as with changes in why individuals desire fame. The introduction of each new media technology represents a decisive shift in both the types of fame available in a culture and the ability of that culture to disseminate fame. The introduction of printing, for example, by allowing for the possibility of a geographically dispersed reading public organized and, to some extent, unified by easily repro-ducible books, shattered the 'old contrast between the good fame of the elite, whether spiritual or intellectual or political, versus the bad fame of common report carried by the tongues and ears of the vulgar crowd' (Braudy, 1986: 267–8). Although the 'democratization' of fame Braudy attributes to the introduction of printing can be easily overstated and perhaps should even be dismissed as part of the propagandizing mythology of contemporary fame, his point that devel-oping media technologies (albeit inadvertently) wrested control of fame from the hands of a tiny elite merits careful consideration, especially when we consider the impact of more recent media forms.

If we can agree that the introduction of printing began to erode the distinction between 'good' and 'bad' fame while also helping to recast fame as an increas-ingly visual phenomenon, these developments were massively accelerated by the introduction of photography and film. Although it is true that there was much emphasis on the 'talent' and 'specialness' of the star at the height of the Holly-wood studio system, it is just as true that the establishment of the star as the organizing principle and of the close-up as the defining technique of the film industry represents the apex of the idea that fame is a visible and not just a meri-torious phenomenon. The changing nature of fame orchestrated by developing media technologies was also conducive to making celebrities out of other groups, including criminals.

Throughout American history, criminals have been the target of professional opinion-makers, whether they be newspaper editors, television reporters, or documentary filmmakers, who all seek to make a point about the state of American culture (either pro or con) by making the criminal into an emblematic figure (Kooistra, 1989: 40). Before the rise of the mass media, these opinion-makers had to rely primarily on oral history to promote the renown of criminals. As a result, they could reach only a small audience. As the variety and scale of media technologies evolved, however, the opportunities for publicizing criminals expanded enormously, so that today, 'the exploits of a criminal may be sung on records that will be broadcast by thousands of radio stations, dramatized in movies that will be viewed by millions, reported by a news service that will ensure a worldwide audience' (ibid.: 162). Such developments are one reason why representations of criminality now play a central role in the American mass media.

If the expansion of types of media technologies is an important factor in explaining the changing nature of fame and in giving criminals more opportunities to become famous, however, it would be the most reductive variety of technological determinism to suggest that the availability of media technologies is the only significant factor. In order to develop a better understanding of how criminals in general and serial killers in particular have become such widely known figures in contemporary American culture, I want to emphasize both the influence of how these technologies are used (rather than the bare fact of their mere existence) and also why there is such a high demand for stories of violence and death among the American populace.

Creating the myth of the serial killer

Sensational coverage of crime has always had a prominent place in American popular culture, from the earliest forms of colonial popular literature, through the 'yellow journalism' of the nineteenth century, to the true-crime book and slasher movie of today. The years since 1985, however, have seen a change in how the American mass media represent crime, a change that has important ramifications for the celebrity status of the serial killer. According to David Krajicek, during the late 1980s, newspapers and television news broadcasts lowered their editorial standards in order to compete with tabloid media such as *Hard Copy* and the *National Enquirer*. This tabloidization of the mainstream media, it has been argued, has had an especially damaging impact upon the reporting of crime (for an alternative position on the tabloidization debate see also Sofia Johansson in this collection). Instead of detailed, nuanced stories about the crime problems facing the United States, now the mass media provide their audience with 'raw dispatches about the crime of the moment, the frightening – and often false – trend of the week, the prurient murder of the month, the sensational trial of the year' (Krajicek, 1998: 4). The tendency of crime news to focus on sex and celebrity trivia and to present chaotic and ultimately false images of crime found its logical culmination in the media frenzy surrounding the O. J. Simpson case (Krajicek, 1998: 9, 63).

If increased attention to crimes involving celebrities was one consequence of the tabloidization of the American mass media in the 1980s, another was a newly prominent role for serial killers during this period. The serial killer became a dominant media figure not only because he personified the tabloid sensibility (all scandal, all the time) but also because he exemplified other important features of how the contemporary American mass media represent crime. One such feature, confirmed by numerous studies, is that the media routinely over-report violent crime. Although murder constitutes a tiny fraction of all crimes committed in the United States, murder and other crimes of violence dominate media reporting of crime. As a result, the incidence of lesser crimes is minimized, and the incidence and impact of violent crime are exaggerated enormously (Schlesinger and Tumber, 1994: 184). The combination of tabloidization, the overrepresentation of violent interpersonal crime, and a preference for the grotesque in the construction of crime myths has led to the rise of a media icon that Ray Surette has described as the 'faceless predator criminal' (Surette, 1994: 135), a figure who represents the American public's attempt to embody the seemingly omnipresent and anonymous threat of violent crime.

The rise of the serial killer reflects the media's attempt to give a face to the faceless predator criminal. If a faceless criminal is a productive motif for media-created crime myths, even more public interest can be generated when we can give that myth a specific name, 'serial murder', and then give that name an identifiable cast of characters, such as Ted Bundy, John Wayne Gacy and Jeffrey Dahmer. According to Philip Jenkins, this is exactly what happened to serial murder in the mid 1980s, when the media, along with government agencies, law enforcement officials, and reform groups, worked together to produce a sense of public panic about serial killers. The key elements of this panic were that serial murder was a qualitatively new phenomenon, that it was growing enormously, that there were a large number of serial murderers active at any given time, that serial murder was a distinctively American phenomenon, and that the crime had reached epidemic proportions, claiming four thousand victims a year. Although Jenkins locates the origins of the serial murder panic in a 1984 *New York Times* article, he emphasizes how smoothly different forms of media worked together to disseminate the myth, as well as how the myth established a few 'representative' serial killers as household names:

> The visual media strongly reinforced the concept of a new and appalling menace ... Each of the major news magazines of the '60 Minutes' format had at least one story of this type, while a 'HBO America

Undercover' episode was a documentary focusing on three well-known
serial killers of the last decade: Ted Bundy, Edmund Kemper, and
Henry Lee Lucas. Interviews with all three were featured, as were
harrowing (and controversial) reconstructions, using actors (Jenkins,
1993: 55).

Although Jenkins discusses the consequences of the serial killer panic at length,
including its use as justification for a reorientation of federal crime-fighting funds
toward serial murder and away from other forms of crime, he does not emphasize the fact that the panic made celebrities out of a large number of serial killers.
The fame of serial killers, however, is not limited to the fact that they are culturally omnipresent in contemporary American culture, or that promoting their
fame has become a staple of American popular culture. If, as Braudy argues, the
exemplary twentieth-century famous person 'is especially the person famous for
being himself or playing himself' (Braudy, 1986: 554), then it is not enough to
say that serial killers are famous. Judging by contemporary standards of fame, the
serial killer is the exemplary modern celebrity, widely known and famous for
being himself. This might seem to be a counterintuitive statement, because surely
serial murderers are famous for what they do, not for who they are. In the serial
killer, however, action and identity are fused. Every detail of the murderer's life
story, everything that concerns who he is, contributes to an understanding of
what he has done. The selfhood and murders of the serial killer thus become two
sides of the same coin.

Many commentators on serial murder have been tempted to jump from noting
the existence of famous serial killers to arguing that the desire for fame serves as
a spur to would-be serial killers. In particular, critics of the intense media
coverage of serial murder have pointed out that the certainty of media attention
sends a dangerous message to potential killers. Park Dietz, forensic psychiatrist
and consultant to the FBI's Behavioral Science Unit, has argued that 'the media
help disseminate the message that it's good to be a serial killer ... There are
rewards to such violent behavior – loyal fans, marriage proposals, splashy headlines' (quoted in Davids, 1992: 150). In a similar vein, Joel Black claims that
potential serial killers can be motivated by a desire for celebrity, pointing out
that their capture and subsequent trial give serial killers many opportunities to
promote their renown (Black, 1991: 141–2). While it is impossible to prove the
causal connection that critics such as Dietz and Black argue for, the behaviour of
some serial killers is suggestive in this regard. The communications of David
Berkowitz (aka 'Son of Sam') with the New York Post during his year-long murder
spree in 1976–7 played a pivotal role both in Berkowitz's evolving self-definition
and in his decision to keep killing. Similarly, Ted Bundy's decision to conduct his
own defence during his capital murder trial in Florida, even though it probably

intensified the jury's negative feelings about him, enabled him to assume the starring role in a narrative of his own making. Perhaps the most thought-provoking example of a serial killer's awareness of and desire for fame came in the midst of a series of murders committed in and around Wichita, Kansas, in the mid 1970s, when the killer, who called himself the 'BTK Strangler', wrote to a local newspaper complaining about the lack of attention his exploits had received: 'How many times do I have to kill before I get a name in the paper or some national attention?' (quoted in Braudy, 1986: 3). Despite the suggestiveness of these examples, whether or not would-be serial killers are motivated by a desire for fame is ultimately undecidable; for this reason, I prefer to concentrate on an equally important question about which it may be possible to come to some more definite conclusions: why are so many Americans willing to support the culture industry that has grown up around the celebrity serial killer?

The market for death

The vibrant market in contemporary America for representations of death in general and of serial murder in particular indicates that the famous serial killer effectively and economically satisfies a double need, both halves of which have grown over the course of the twentieth century: the need for representations of death, and the need for celebrities. Where do these needs come from? We have already seen how the expansion of media technologies that began in the nineteenth century contributed to the scale, variety, and speed of dissemination of types of fame. According to Vicki Goldberg (1998), these expanded media technologies also coincided with an increased need for representations of death as the reality of death receded from everyday life. As the average American became less and less likely to be confronted with the brute reality of death in the form of dead bodies thanks to improvements in public health and the increasing sophistication of the funeral industry, Goldberg argues, there was a related increase in representations of death, an increase largely enabled by the development of new media technologies and fuelled by people's desire to find other ways to manage their continuing anxieties about death now that death had been removed from the public sphere.

Aesthetic representations of death are able to assuage such anxieties because they occur in a realm clearly delineated as not life, even as they refer to a basic fact of life we know but often choose not to acknowledge (Bronfen, 1992). As paradoxical as it may seem, exposing ourselves to representations of death, even violent death, helps alleviate our anxiety about being claimed by such violent death. Consuming images of serial murder in carefully controlled settings (one can put down a book, turn off the television, or hide behind one's hands in a movie theatre) might provide an effective way of managing anxieties about death.

Whether or not this is so, the question remains: what does this have to do with a desire for celebrities? How is the need for representations of death and violence related to the need for celebrities?

Both celebrities and representations of death can be potent means of resolving a variety of anxieties, ranging from a fear of death to concerns about what constitutes acceptable social behaviour and worries about the decline of individuality in modern society. Jib Fowles (1992) has argued that the market for celebrities in general, and film stars in particular, arose as a result of the dislocating impact of urbanization on the American population, a process that began in the nineteenth century but reached a critical point in the early years of the twentieth century, just when the film industry had developed to the point where it was able to satisfy the public need for stars. Faced by an unfamiliar and estranging urban environment, the new generation of city dwellers eagerly looked around for models of personality and found them, according to Fowles, on the screen. Even if we accept Fowles' argument that film stars were adopted as models of personality, there is clearly a big difference between asserting that the first generation of Hollywood movie stars resolved anxieties in their audience and arguing that criminals could do the same thing. Wouldn't criminals be more likely to create, rather than resolve, anxieties? The utility of stars, however, was not limited to displaying positive aspects of personality but extended to exorcizing negative emotions. One of the reasons why violence has become such a central part of American entertainment is that 'by aggressing onscreen or onstage, stars perform the important psychological service of helping to vent anger' (Fowles, 1992: 163). In the safety of the movie theatre, or in your front of your television at home, violent stars might encourage you to express hostile feelings without fearing recrimination or consequence.

This variation on the well-established catharsis argument suggests how representations of death and violence performed by famous stars can serve an important triple function for an audience: managing anxieties about death, providing models of personality, and expressing negative emotions. There is no reason to assume that only fictional representations of death and violence resolve anxieties. Although audiences feel less ambivalent about expressing their identification with fictional rather than actual serial killers, representations of real criminals can also serve a cathartic function for their audience, as Paul Kooistra argues in the context of explaining the appeal of the 'heroic criminal': 'narratives about [heroic criminals] serve a critical psychological function for those who read or write such tales ... through such stories we may vicariously release rebellious feelings generated by the restrictions imposed by authority' (Kooistra, 1989: 10). However, as Kooistra acknowledges, this is an incomplete explanation because only certain types of criminals become heroes. Tellingly, Kooistra excludes serial killers from the category of heroic criminal:

While we undoubtedly find psychological release by vicariously experiencing the rebellious deeds of the lawbreakers, we choose to undergo this experience with a very limited number of criminals. We do not imagine ourselves dining with Albert Fish on the bodies of children he molested and then cooked; nor do we admire the handiwork of Edward Gein, who fashioned lampshades from the skin and soup bowls from the skulls of the women he killed ... Certainly these criminals are fascinating, but we do not make heroes of them (Kooistra, 1989: 21).

Clearly, serial killers are not celebrated in the same way as heroic criminals such as Jesse James and Bonnie and Clyde, because they lack the empathic dimensions of these Robin Hood-type outlaws. Consequently it is inadequate to assert that they resolve anxieties and act as models of personality in exactly the same way as representations of other criminals. Yet stating these facts does not help us to determine why the serial killer has become such a dominant figure in American popular culture. What exactly is the appeal of the serial killer?

Producing and consuming mass idols

In terms of changing explanations of fame, it is perhaps tempting to describe the advent of celebrity serial killers as a further decline in the condition of American culture's 'mass idols' (see Lowenthal, 1961). But in order to decide whether or not that is the case we must clarify the serial killer's relationship to consumption.

Returning briefly to the murderabilia industry reminds us that celebrity culture and consumer culture intermingle just as complexly with serial killers as they do with film stars. Throughout the edition of the *John Walsh Show* that attacked murderabilia, the show's eponymous host showed clips of *Collectors*, a documentary about the industry. *Collectors* is distributed by a small company named Abject Films and on their website the film's director, Julian P. Hobbs, discusses some of the multiple connections between serial killing and consumerism. Hobbs points out that the serial killer is connected with consumerism in the most basic sense in that he has become a commodity, 'a merchandising phenomenon that rivals Mickey Mouse. From movies to television, books to on-line, serial killers are packaged and consumed en-masse' (Abject Films, 2003). But, as Hobbs goes on to argue, serial killers themselves can be seen as consumers, which implicates any representations of them in the same consumerist logic: 'Serial killers come into being by fetishizing and collecting artifacts – usually body parts – in turn, the dedicated collector gathers scraps connected with the actual events and so, too, a documentary a collection of images' (Abject Films, 2003). Hobbs implies that no one (not even Hobbs himself) can avoid being involved with consumerism in relation to serial murder, even if one's reasons for getting involved are high-minded.

In spite of the many reasons for the vigorous market in contemporary American culture for representations of death and violence I discussed earlier, consumerism alone is not enough to explain the appeal of the serial killer. Despite the many ways in which the existence of celebrity serial killers is related to consumerism, it is unclear whether serial killers can be described as 'idols of consumption' (Lowenthal, 1961). In particular, what such a designation hides is the uncomfortable fact that many people do not participate in serial killer celebrity culture solely in order to assuage their anxieties about victimization and death. The existence of famous serial killers also depends upon the fact that some people are fascinated with them, even admire them. No examination of the fame of serial killers could be complete without analysing the reasons behind these more 'affirmative' reactions to serial killers. In short, we need to consider why famous serial killers are often regarded as 'idols of destruction'.

Idols of destruction

In the midst of the Washington D.C. sniper shootings in October 2002, Twentieth Century Fox thought it wise to delay the release of their new movie, *Phone Booth*, which tells the story of a pedestrian who answers a public telephone in Times Square only to be told by the sniper on the other end of the line that he will be shot dead if he hangs up. A few days after Jeffrey Dahmer was arrested in Milwaukee in 1991, Paramount Pictures decided to pull all ads for their movie, *Body Parts*. Even though the studio denied that the movie's story bore any resemblance to Dahmer's crimes, they did acknowledge that the body parts littering the posters advertising the film were, under the circumstances, inappropriate. In 1978, an unknown perpetrator (who would later turn out to be Ted Bundy) killed two female students and attacked several others in their sorority house at Florida State University. The local affiliate of NBC had been planning to broadcast a TV movie, *A Stranger in the House*, a few days after the murders. The movie, a thriller about a psychopathic killer of sorority sisters, was quietly withdrawn from the schedule. Jane Caputi has referred to such moments as 'slip[s] of the societal tongue ... moment[s] of brief but unintended clarity' where we get a glimpse of how the 'acceptable' ways in which American culture expresses its fascination with murder might be implicated with unacceptable actual incidents of murder (Caputi, 1987: 51).

Sometimes we get more than a glimpse of America's fascination with murder; indeed, sometimes that fascination is presented as a full-blown media spectacle. At the 1992 Academy Awards, *The Silence of the Lambs* won Oscars in all five major categories: best adapted screenplay, best director, best actor, best actress and best film. Much of the celebration focused on Anthony Hopkins's portrayal of Lecter. Since 1992, the cult around Hannibal Lecter has continued to grow with the appearance of Thomas Harris's sequel, *Hannibal*, Ridley Scott's film adaptation of *Hannibal*, and Brett Ratner's prequel/remake of *Red Dragon*. So identified has Anthony Hopkins become with the role of Hannibal Lecter that the lavish praise that has greeted Hopkins's performances in the role can reasonably be taken as relatively unguarded expressions of fascination with and admiration of Lecter himself, who was recently voted the top movie villain of all time in an internet poll. In an abstract sense, it seems both offensive and ludicrous to claim that American culture is not only repelled but also fascinated by serial killers. One does not have to look very far, however, to find ample confirmation of the claim. One should not, of course, minimize the differences between admiring the fictional character of Hannibal Lecter and admiring a 'real' serial killer, but the difference is one of degree rather than kind. Characters such as Lecter allow for the free expression of feelings of fascination and admiration concerning serial killers that are more carefully concealed in other instances. And yet even this rule has exceptions. As Elliott Leyton has argued:

> No one ever became famous by beating his wife to death in an alley; but virtually all our multiple murderers achieve true and lasting fame … During their trials, they will almost certainly be surrounded by admiring women who impress their affections upon the killer, radiating towards him little but admiration and love (Leyton, 1989: 21–2).

Even during the crimes themselves, some serial killers have felt and been influenced by the public's fascinated interest in them. After his arrest, David Berkowitz commented that:

> I finally had convinced myself that it was good to do it, necessary to do it, and that the public wanted me to do it. The latter part I believe until this day. I believe that many were rooting for me. This was the point at which the papers began to pick up vibes and information that something big was happening out in the streets. Real big! (quoted in Leyton, 1989: 206–7).

It would be easy to dismiss such remarks as the product of a diseased mind, but as Leyton says, 'Son of Sam was not so very wrong when he thought the public was urging him on during his killing spree, for the media chronicled his every deed in a state of mounting excitement' (Leyton, 1989: 21–2).

Is it possible that serial killers are idols of destruction? Are some people attracted to their destructiveness? Perhaps so, but in a very specific way. In his essay 'Critique of Violence', Walter Benjamin argues that the violent destructiveness of criminals inheres not necessarily (or not exclusively) in the deeds they commit but in what their deeds imply about an attack on the very principle of law itself. To support this claim, Benjamin emphasizes 'how often the figure of the "great" criminal, however repellent his ends may have been, has aroused the secret admiration of the public. This cannot result from his deed, but only from the violence to which it bears witness' (Benjamin, 1986: 281). Benjamin then goes on to clarify his point by arguing that 'in the great criminal this violence confronts the law with the threat of declaring a new law, a threat that even today, despite its impotence, in important instances horrifies the public as it did in primeval times' (ibid.: 283). The criminal's rejection of the law is horrifying but also exhilarating, hence what Jacques Derrida calls in 'The Force of Law' the 'shudder of admiration' we feel for the criminal, an admiration Derrida links explicitly to the way the criminal claims a 'primeval' status as 'lawmaker or prophet' (Derrida, 1992: 40). The serial killer both outrages and thrills us by his seeming ability to stand outside the law, to make his own law, in a gesture whose ambivalent destructiveness and creativity mirror our ambivalent response to the killer, composed of both fear and attraction.

To be sure, these are uncomfortable feelings to acknowledge, but what could be more quintessentially American than a complex and ambivalent reaction to a violent criminal? As Stathis Gourgouris has pointed out:

> If American society is paradigmatically founded on the primacy of law [the Bill of Rights], it is also *co-incidentally* founded on the phantasmatic allure of the outlaw – the Wild West, the frontier, and so on: the errant loner who forges his own rights, in some improvisational fashion, as he goes along (Gourgouris, 1997: 135, original emphasis).

Some may object to associating *Gunfight at the O.K. Corral* with *Henry: Portrait of a Serial Killer*, but any reader of Cormac MacCarthy's classic novel *Blood Meridian* will know that the realization of 'manifest destiny' was, if anything, more violent and bloody than serial murder could ever be. Rather than drawing artificial and untenable distinctions between 'legitimate' and 'illegitimate' types of violence, I propose that we acknowledge that the serial killer is as quintessentially American a figure as the cowboy, and we should acknowledge this fact not least because the intrinsic Americanness of the serial killer has been a feature of writing about serial murder since at least the time of Jack the Ripper, some sixty years before the category of 'serial murder' even came into being. In the words of a 1994 *National Examiner* headline: 'Serial Killers Are As American As Apple Pie.'

Christopher Sharrett has suggested that 'perhaps the fetish status of the criminal psychopath ... is about recognizing the serial killer/mass murderer not as social rebel or folk hero ... but as the most genuine representative of American life' (Sharrett, 1999: 13). Celebrity serial killers provide us with a way of acknowledging the truth of Sharrett's observation in a way that is not too destructive either of our self-image or of our image of America. Our complicated relationship with celebrities, affective as well as intellectual, composed of admiration and resentment, envy and contempt, provides us with a lexicon through which we can manage our appalled and appalling fascination with the serial killer, contemporary American culture's ultimate deviant.

Bibliography

ABC News (2001) 'Killer Collectibles: Inside the World of "Murderabilia"', available at medialab.scu.edu/ratliff/bts/winter01/bts03/abcnews_com%20%20inside%20the%20bizarre% 20world%20of%20'murderabilia'.htm, accessed 14 February 2006.

Abject Films (2003) 'Collectors: A Film by Julian P. Hobbs', available at www.abjectfilms.com/ collectorstext.html, accessed 9 May 2003.

Benjamin, Walter (1986) 'Critique of Violence', in *Reflections: Essays, Aphorisms, Autobiographical Writings*, New York: Schocken Books, pp. 277–300.

Black, Joel (1991) *The Aesthetics of Murder: A Study in Romantic Literature and Contemporary Culture*, Baltimore: Johns Hopkins University Press.

Boorstin, Daniel J. (1962) *The Image: or; What Happened to the American Dream?*, New York: Atheneum.

Braudy, Leo (1986) *The Frenzy of Renown: Fame and Its History*, New York: Oxford University Press.

Bronfen, Elisabeth (1992) *Over Her Dead Body: Death, Femininity, and the Aesthetic*. New York: Routledge.

Business Week Online (2000) 'An Underground Market Moves to Mainstream America', available at www.businessweek.com/2000/00_47/b3708056.htm, accessed 20 November 2000.

Caputi, Jane (1987) *The Age of Sex Crime*, Bowling Green, OH: Bowling Green State University Popular Press.

Cowen, Tyler (2000) *What Price Fame?*, Cambridge, MA: Harvard University Press.

Davids, Diana (1992) 'The Serial Murderer as Superstar', *McCall's*: 84 ff.

Derrida, Jacques (1992) 'The Force of Law: The "Mystical Foundation of Authority"', in Drucilla Cornell, Michael Rosenfeld, and David Gray Carlson (eds), *Deconstruction and the Possibility of Justice*, New York: Routledge, pp. 3–67.

Fisher, Philip (1986) 'Appearing and Disappearing in Public: Social Space in Late-Nineteenth-Century Literature and Culture', in Sacvan Bercovich (ed.), *Reconstructing American Literary History*, Cambridge, MA: Harvard University Press, pp. 155–88.

Fowles, Jib (1992) *Starstruck: Celebrity Performers and the American Public*, Washington, DC: Smithsonian Institution Press.

Giles, David (2000) *Illusions of Immortality: A Psychology of Fame and Celebrity*, New York: St. Martin's Press.

Goldberg, Vicki (1998) 'Death Takes a Holiday, Sort Of', in Jeffrey Goldstein (ed.), *Why We Watch: The Attractions of Violent Entertainment*, New York: Oxford University Press, pp. 27–52.

Gourgouris, Stathis (1997) 'Enlightenment and *Paranomia*', in Hent De Vries and Samuel Weber (eds), *Violence, Identity, and Self-Determination*, Stanford, CA: Stanford University Press, pp. 119–49, 361–5.

Jenkins, Philip (1993) 'Myth and Murder: The Serial Killer Panic of 1983–1985', in Victor E. Kappeler, Mark Blumberg, and Gary W. Potter (eds), *The Mythology of Crime and Criminal Justice*, Prospect Heights, IL: Waveland Press, pp. 53–73.

Justice For All (1999) 'Murderabilia and Serial Killer Art', available at www.jfa.net/petition.htm, accessed 14 February 2006.

Kooistra, Paul (1989) *Criminals as Heroes: Structure, Power, and Identity*, Bowling Green, OH: Bowling Green State University Popular Press.

Krajicek, David J. (1998) *Scooped!: Media Miss Real Story on Crime While Chasing Sex, Sleaze, and Celebrities*, New York: Columbia University Press.

Leyton, Elliott (1989) *Hunting Humans: The Rise of the Modern Multiple Murderer*. London: Penguin Books.

Lowenthal, Leo (1961) 'The Triumph of Mass Idols', in *Literature, Popular Culture, and Society*, Englewood Cliffs, NJ: Prentice-Hall, pp. 109–40.

Schlesinger, Philip, and Tumber, Howard (1994) *Reporting Crime: The Media Politics of Criminal Justice*, Oxford: Clarendon Press.

Serial Killer Central (2003) 'The John Walsh Show', available at joe.skcentral.com/johnwalsh2.html, accessed 14 February 2006.

Sharrett, Christopher (1999) 'Introduction', in Christopher Sharrett (ed.), *Mythologies of Violence in Postmodern Media*, Detroit, MI: Wayne State University Press, pp. 9–20.

Surette, Ray (1994) 'Predator Criminals as Media Icons', in Gregg Barak (ed.), *Media, Process, and the Social Construction of Crime: Studies in Newsmaking Criminology*, New York: Garland, pp. 131–58.

Chapter 18
Madly famous
Narratives of mental illness in celebrity culture

Stephen Harper

In a recent article on contemporary celebrity culture, Jeremy Gilbert describes the psychological appeal of celebrities in terms of Lacanian misrecognition:

> Just as the infant sees in her reflection an image of autonomous and self-contained integrity, so different from the state of confusion which she experiences as herself, so the fan sees in the star an image of perfect autonomy, public agency, smooth-edged self-completion. Lacan famously describes this phantasmatic relationship of subject to reflection as a *misrecognition*. Celebrities in the public domain, according to such a view, function as fantasy objects, images of impossible perfection which hold out the lure of a fully-achieved selfhood to subjects constituted by their perpetual search for just such impossible/absent 'fullness' (Gilbert, 2004: 91).

Unsurprisingly, such seductive images of unrealizable perfection have troubled psychiatric professionals: psychoanalyst Adam Phillips, for example, in a recent *Observer Magazine* article, worries that contemporary celebrities offer 'narrow' and 'superficial' models for behaviour (O'Hagan, 2005: 15). Yet such accounts of celebrity worship rather ignore the complexities of audience understandings of celebrity. Indeed, in his article, Gilbert goes on to question some of the essentialist assumptions of psychoanalytic accounts of celebrity identification, in particular Slavoj Žižek's proposal that the public's interest in celebrity testifies to its innate need for a Master.

Another difficulty with the psychoanalytic account of celebrity worship outlined above is that while celebrities may be regarded as 'smooth-edged' or perfect by some of their fans, they do not appear so unblemished within the less reverential sections of popular media. While public-relations-driven media may focus on the perfection of celebrities, other sections of the media delight in reporting their fallibilities, misfortunes and illnesses. From drug abuse to eating disorders, contemporary media often present the grimy 'reality' as well as the glossy image of celebrity. In a world in which the failures of celebrities are as profitable as their successes, it is vital for media critics to consider how cultural industries and media audiences negotiate and exploit images of celebrity distress.

There have been previous academic studies of troubled celebrity, notably Archer and Simmonds' *A Star Is Torn* (1986). My chapter, however, focuses on a specific, if rather neglected, theme within media discourse about celebrity – mental illness – and aims briefly to consider its significance across several media forms. The brevity of this chapter and the breadth of its textual scope preclude a deep analysis of any of the various media forms (or any of the celebrities) discussed. I shall therefore attempt only an introductory and highly selective survey of popular media representations of celebrity mental distress as a prolegomenon to future studies in this area. I shall argue that mental illness narratives are common in celebrity culture, where they have complex and sometimes contradictory effects. In particular, I shall suggest that these narratives facilitate both the elaboration of meritocratic discourse and the communication of psychiatric risk. Such a reading is consistent with the theory of the 'risk society' proposed by Beck (1992) and supported by the work of Giddens (1991); nonetheless, drawing on examples from celebrity media, I shall argue that any 'risk society' perspective on images of celebrity distress must take account of the ways in which discourses of identity formation are regulated by categories of social difference. Through the examples analysed here, I shall try to indicate how considerations of gender, social class and race mediate representations of mentally ill celebrities.

The concept of the 'celebrity' who is 'well-known for being well-known', to paraphrase Daniel Boorstin (1971), is a relatively recent and, according to Rojek (2001), post-religious (and postmodern) phenomenon. In the contemporary Western media, celebrity, according to Turner (2004) and others, is often 'ordinary', detached from considerations of talent or skill. Nonetheless, the more meretricious notion of 'fame' – and the associated concepts of 'genius' and 'greatness' – has ancient origins, as well as a long-standing association with madness. In the first part of this chapter, I shall suggest that this association can help us to understand contemporary representations of 'mad' celebrity.

As is well known, the Graeco-Roman association of madness with genius was revived in the European Renaissance. In about 1480, the Flemish monk and painter Hugo van der Goes became psychotic during a journey. While theories multiplied about the causes of Hugo's illness, many believed, in the words of Hugo's biographer, that:

> God's all-loving providence [...] had ordained this malady. This brother had been flattered enough in our Order because of his great art – in fact, his name became more famous this way than if he had

remained in the world. But since he was, after all, just as human as the rest of us, he had developed a rather high opinion of himself due to the many honours, visits and compliments which were paid to him. But God, not wanting his ruin, in his great mercy sent him this chastising affliction which, indeed, humbled him mightily. For brother Hugo repented and, as soon as he had recovered he exercised the greatest humility (Wittkower and Wittkower, 1963: 109–10).

This account combines the moralistic medieval view of mental illness as a punishment for pride in worldly honours and the Renaissance obsession with fame and its potential psychological cost. Mental illness is a dire rebuke to the arrogance of fame, and a reminder that all are members of a common, frail humanity. From the Renaissance onwards, and especially during the Romantic era, mental illness – evacuated by psychological medicine of its supernatural import – became increasingly bound up with greatness. Only a tortured artist, according to the Romantic theory of authorship, could produce 'great' art. Susan Sontag notes of the nineteenth-century Romanian writer E. M. Cioran that:

> syphilis-envy figured in his adolescent expectations of literary glory: he would discover that he had contracted syphilis, be rewarded with several hyperproductive years of genius, then collapse into madness. This romanticizing of the dementia characteristic of neurosyphilis was the forerunner of the much more persistent fantasy in this century about mental illness as a source of artistic creativity or spiritual originality (Sontag, 1991: 109).

This supposed alliance between madness and genius contributed to the aura of artists from Vincent van Gogh to Jackson Pollock and strongly influenced the modernist sensibility (especially in the work of writers such as Thomas Mann).

Indeed, mental illness and 'greatness' remain intensely interrelated in contemporary Western culture. The last decade has seen an explosion of self-help books attesting to the giftedness of the mentally ill, ranging from autobiographies such as actress Patty Duke's *A Brilliant Madness* (1999) to psychological investigations such as Kay Redfield Jamison's *Touched with Fire: Manic Depressive Illness and the Artistic Temperament* (1996). In many popular films, meanwhile, mental illness is associated with artistic, literary or academic genius. Scott Hicks's *Shine* (1996) charts the career and mental breakdown of gifted pianist David Helfgott (Geoffrey Rush). *Pollock* (Ed Harris, USA, 2000) depicts the depression of the eponymous Abstract Expressionist painter. *A Beautiful Mind* (Ron Howard, USA, 2001) stars Russell Crowe as the schizophrenic mathematician John Nash. *The Hours* (Stephen Daldry, USA, 2002), *Sylvia* (Christine Jeffs, USA, 2003) and *The*

Aviator (Martin Scorsese, USA, 2004), meanwhile, present the tortured lives and suicidal tendencies of Virginia Woolf, Sylvia Plath and Howard Hughes respectively. Although the psychiatric verisimilitude of these representations may sometimes be questionable (the recovery from, or rehabilitation of, mental illness is rarely so simply or so triumphantly accomplished as many of these films imply), the popularity of these films among Western audiences is undeniable. The onset and development of, and recovery from, mental illness are of course staple fictional themes, since these stages can be neatly mapped onto a classical tripartite narrative structure of equilibrium, disturbance and restitution. But the popularity of narratives of mental illness also indicates the continuing appeal of the 'tortured genius' stereotype in the modern world. Today, as in the Renaissance and Romantic periods, mental illness is a token of both public greatness and private vulnerability; the celebrity, that most visible of attractions, is always imperilled by mental illness, 'the most solitary of afflictions' (Scull, 1993).

Stories about mentally ill geniuses also perform an important ideological role: as narratives about individuals who 'make it through' adversity, such texts support and extend neoliberal ideologies of meritocracy and competitive individualism (compare Horkheimer and Adorno's (1972) useful, albeit somewhat monolithic, view of stars as instantiations of a system of capitalist ideological manipulation). As this reading might suggest, these narratives of 'mad genius' are highly classed (indeed, the term 'genius' itself is generally reserved for writers, artists and intellectuals, and is seldom applied to bus drivers or refuse collectors). It is equally important to recognize that these narratives are differentiated by gender: whereas films with male protagonists – such as *Shine*, *A Beautiful Mind* and *Pollock* – present heroic 'battles' culminating in enlightenment, *Sylvia*, *Iris* and *The Hours* offer somewhat darker, even tragic, visions of partial or even failed personal struggle. This gender distinction is consistent with Christine Battersby's (1989) contention that genius represents a combination of masculine and feminine qualities which has traditionally been defined as attainable only by men. In the films about famous *women*, the heroic and meritocratic connotations of psychological struggle tend to be compromised, if not vitiated, by tragedy, melodrama and hysteria (a point to which I shall return later). Nonetheless, the 'disturbed genius' films mentioned above spectacularly dramatize the inherent psychological risks of artistic self-construction, while reassuring audiences that, far from being a barrier, mental distress may in some sense constitute a rite of passage leading, ultimately, to social and/or professional success. These narratives may have a particular appeal to audiences in what Giddens (1991) calls 'post-traditional' societies, in which subjects increasingly abandon long-established lifestyle scripts structured by class or kinship affiliations in favour of individualized modes of self-fashioning.

So far I have not discussed the subject of celebrity per se (the artists and thinkers featured in the films mentioned above are more properly described as 'famous' or as 'geniuses' rather than celebrities). Moreover, these films often refer to the modernist period or earlier, rather than the present day (there often seems to be a retrospective dimension to filmic representations of 'genius'). I hope, however, to have briefly established a historical context for my discussion of contemporary celebrity and mental distress. In the following discussion, I shall argue that many of the discursive themes and categories mentioned above in relation to some of the 'great' figures of Western culture – authenticity, romanticism, meritocracy, and gender – are also crucial to understanding the representation of mentally distressed celebrities today.

Indeed, the stereotype of the agonized genius is widespread in contemporary non-fictional media representations of mental illness: although the precise state of Michael Jackson's mental health is a matter for some debate, he is frequently endorsed by the media as a genius (see, for example, *The Ultimate Pop Star,* Channel 4, 20 February 2005). Moreover, when psychiatric diagnoses are clearer, attributions of genius are even more likely. A recent British television documentary, *The Madness of Prince Charming* (Channel 4, 17 July 2003), sketched the life of Stuart Goddard, also known as Adam Ant, who developed bipolar affective disorder after becoming famous in the 1980s with the pop group Adam and the Ants. Running throughout the documentary's narration was the assumption that Goddard's mental illness was intimately connected to his creative genius. This connection is frequently implied in journalistic discussions of male rock stars, including Brian Wilson, Keith Moon, Phil Spector, Syd Barrett, Paul Simon, Ian Curtis and Sting. In an analysis of the representation of women in rock journalism, Helen Davies argues that credibility and mental instability go hand in hand for male rock artists, while female artists who discuss psychiatric issues are often ridiculed or ignored:

> Men such as [Richey] Edwards, Kurt Cobain of Nirvana and Brett Anderson of Suede are praised for their exploration of the feminine and, particularly in the cases of Edwards and Cobain, are described as emotional and tortured figures. Edwards was praised for his open discussion of his anorexia and self-mutilation, while the same topics were unpalatable when spoken of by female Riot Grrrls. If men can provide 'the feminine' then women are redundant (Davies, 2004: 172–3).

Like the gendered distribution of heroic attributes in *films* about mental distress, this journalistic approbation for troubled male rock stars who appropriate 'feminine' therapeutic discourses reinforces the patriarchal definition of genius as a combination of male and female qualities reserved exclusively for men (Battersby, 1989).

As well as emphasizing the star's genius, the Stuart Goddard documentary also highlighted the importance of mental illness in the fashioning of self-identity: Goddard is reported to have 'reinvented himself' after his treatment, using his 'music as medicine'. Such references to artistic self-fashioning should not blind us to the reality that, after any celebrity breakdown, media and public relations personnel are often responsible for promoting the 'mad genius' stereotype. This is apparent in reviews of Ian Holm's recent autobiography (2004), in which the actor describes how, after a panic attack before a production of Eugene O'Neill's epic *The Iceman Cometh*, Holm left the production, and abandoned the theatre altogether for many years. Mental illness structures the narrative of Holm's autobiography, as well as critical commentaries about it. For example, a *Sunday Times* review of the autobiography selects for its centrepiece a large-type quotation about the actor's mental illness (Wolf, 2004: 51). This choice, together with the title of the review ('A life less ordinary') presents Holm's acting career as a heroic triumph over mental illness.

This triumphalist and hagiographic tone is typical of popular media representations of all kinds of disabilities; Goggin and Newell (2004), for example, point to the 'saintly numinosity' of the paraplegic actor Christopher Reeve in media reporting both before and after his death. While there may be many reasons for such lionization (not all of them necessarily sinister or exploitative), it is clear that mental illness can be turned to commercial advantage in a media culture in which celebrities must be rendered remarkable. As Anita Biressi and Heather Nunn note, 'although the celebrity is a figure of consumption writ large they must also retain the individualism that marks them apart and renders them remarkable and commercially marketable' (Biressi and Nunn, 2004: 46). To articulate this observation with a discussion of mental illness may seem crude or insensitive, as though mental illness were a cynical, career-enhancing ploy on the part of celebrities. Yet there is no doubt that the sadness that made Romantics 'interesting' (Sontag, 1991: 32–3) also renders contemporary celebrities marketable. My point here is not that the mental health problems of celebrities are exploited by artists as calculated bids for cultural cachet, but that mental illness bears a promotionally and journalistically useful relation to definitions of artistic 'credibility'. In this sense, mental illness fulfils a double function in contemporary culture: not only does it guarantee a celebrity's 'reality' as a suffering subject 'just like us'; it also contributes to the perception of his (for it is usually *his*) artistic authenticity. In the case of male celebrities, at least, mental illness is both a confirmation of ordinariness, and an intimation of auratic uniqueness. Moreover, the examples of Goddard and Holm indicate that mental illness does not necessarily attract media censure, nor need it hinder a celebrity's career; on the contrary, it can generate sympathy and even increase a celebrity's cultural power.

The sympathy evinced in certain media presentations of mental illness is rather underestimated in most of the research on representations of mental illness in the media. Yet stories such as that of Frank Bruno, the working-class black British boxer who rose to prominence as a fighter in the 1980s, indicate that audiences often express compassion for public figures with mental illnesses. When Bruno won the World Boxing Heavyweight Championship title in 1995, the *Sun* heralded Bruno's achievement with the headline 'Arise, Sir Bruno!'. As the *Sun* was well aware, Bruno's success implicitly endorsed the meritocratic dream extolled first by Thatcher and more recently by the New Labour government. Bruno is a well-loved figure in the United Kingdom, not least because of his kindly disposition and polite manner – but also because he has consistently presented himself as a patriotic establishment figure. When, in September 2003, he was admitted to a psychiatric hospital after a manic episode, the *Sun* printed the headline 'Bonkers Bruno Locked Up' (*Sun*, 23 September 2003: 1). Yet the public response to the *Sun*'s affront was extraordinary. Angry radio listeners called in to Radio 5 warning that this might be 'another Hillsborough' for the newspaper (the *Sun* is still widely boycotted in Liverpool following its false allegations about the involvement of Liverpool football fans at the Hillsborough football stadium tragedy in 1988). Elsewhere, copies of the *Sun* were reportedly destroyed in their newspaper stands. The public outcry soon forced the *Sun* to withdraw its headline and later editions replaced it with 'Sad Bruno in Home'. Admittedly, the public response to Bruno's case is not fully representative of attitudes towards black celebrities with mental disorders: after all, the mental illness of the less patriotic black football star Stan Collymore has attracted rather less public (or media) understanding. Nonetheless, *l'affair* Bruno indicates that mental illness is a subject of much public interest that is in no way hostile or stigmatizing. This in turn suggests that media critics need increasingly not only to focus on the old, and continuing, problem of media misrepresentations of mental illness, but also to become more critical of certain assumptions within anti-stigma discourse.

Despite the periodic disgraces of tabloid newspapers, many print publications are quite aware of the public's compassionate identification with stories of celebrity mental distress. Women's magazines, which since the 1990s have been increasingly concerned with celebrity (Gough-Yates, 2003: 136–7), have shown particular interest in celebrity 'breakdowns'. There is, to be sure, evidence that magazine gossip columns do sometimes treat this subject of mental illness flippantly. A recent celebrity quiz in the *Sunday Times Style* magazine asks: 'Which fashion star is too busy to go to the doctor?', continuing 'She gets her assistant to pose as her when she needs a new prescription of anti-depressants and sleeping pills' (*Sunday Times Style*, 19 December 2004: 8). Yet while such ill-considered mockery demonstrates a thinly disguised delight in the notion that a celebrity might require psychiatric medication, many other women's magazines contain detailed and broadly sympathetic perspectives on mental illness. *Marie Claire* journalist Emma Elms, who won an award for her reporting of mental health issues, begins a feature article about the experiences of two schizophrenic women as follows:

> Think of Jane Horrocks, Ruby Wax and Karen Mulder, and phrases like 'creative genius', 'brilliantly funny' and 'glamorous supermodel' probably come to mind. But these women have all been mentally ill. Surprising news, perhaps, in a climate where people with mental health problems are often regarded with fear as 'axe-wielding psychos'. Yet Horrocks, who has obsessive compulsive disorder (OCD), Wax, who is a manic depressive, and Mulder, a chronic depressive, are not exceptions. In Britain, thousands of women with mental-health problems are battling daily to form successful careers and happy relationships (Elms, 2003: 96).

It is interesting to reflect on why such features might appeal to audiences. In her study of the role of celebrity stories in identity formation, Joke Hermes reports that many female magazine readers admit that 'the misery of others made them feel better about their own lives' or helped them to deal with their own frustrations or sorrow (1999: 80). While such feelings of consolation may contain a certain degree of schadenfreude, they may nonetheless make life more bearable for readers. On the other hand, the presentation of psychiatric problems, even here, is problematic for a number of reasons. While magazines such as *Marie Claire* are relatively progressive in their use of celebrity to draw attention to health issues, their understandings of mental illness, and of femininity, remain securely within the confines of a liberal, middle-class framework. The individualistic notion that contemporary life is a personal 'battle' (to use Elms's term), with psychological winners and losers, implies that the problems of life – and the causes of mental distress – are attributable to thwarted romantic and career objectives. Here again we may note the elaboration of meritocratic discourse, albeit here inflected by a somewhat tragic tone. Aside from lending mental illness a rather enigmatic aspect that may not be entirely helpful to sufferers of mental illness (compare Susan Sontag's 1991 critique of the metaphorical language of warfare in the discourse surrounding cancer), the 'battle' metaphor also contributes to the sense of melodrama that often attends the discussion of mental health issues in women's media.

Since mental illness is an increasingly important aspect of mass media narratives of celebrity, it is unsurprising that health awareness media increasingly use celebrity to highlight mental health issues. In July 2004 *there there* magazine was launched to deal with issues such as anger management, stress and addiction problems. Written by health care and media professionals, *there there* is distributed in 6,000 doctors' surgeries in the United Kingdom and is supported by prominent figures in psychiatry. A distinguishing feature of the magazine is that each story relates the issue under discussion to its representation in popular culture or to celebrity. Addressing an implicitly female readership, headlines have included 'Tears in Tinseltown: even Marilyn got the blues' and 'Britney Returns: but is she really ok?' (*there there* 1, 2004: 6–7). The magazine affirms a liberal psychiatric message that mental illness is widespread and that various forms of mental distress can strike anybody at any time. As an editorial puts it:

> In an age when our quality of life is continually under threat, *there there* will be on your side. We'll deal head-on with issues like anxiety, stress, depression and anger. And because we address life in all its colours, you'll also find celebrity interviews and profiles, provocative quizzes, as well as more esoteric features on, say, the effect of colour on mood. (It'll give us an excuse to discuss Carrie's wardrobe on *Sex & the City*). *there there* is passionate about life and how it can be lived better. We'll do it all: genes to jeans, outcasts to Outkast and more. Everything to make *there there* the essential manual for 21st century living (*there there* 1, 2004: 2).

While I shall criticize aspects of *there there* below, the magazine certainly aims to help counteract the lurid tabloid stigmatization of mental illness. The mode of address here is identical to that of many other women's magazines, namely 'one of allegiance to the reader, of being on your side with superior know-how and resources, like a woman-run social service' (Wolf, 1991: 74). *there there* claims to address life in 'all its colours', articulating its coverage of health and lifestyle issues with the staple glossy magazine emphasis on glamour, fashion, and celebrity.

Like the *Marie Claire* article mentioned above, *there there* aims to delve behind the glamorous image of celebrities, using a variety of presentational devices to achieve a reality effect. Jo Littler (2004) has recently argued that audiences are increasingly responsive to presentations of celebrity that use the tropes of intimacy, reflexivity and 'keeping it real'. All of these tropes are carefully contrived in *there there*. The article on Britney Spears, for example, is accompanied by a series of five close-up photographs of the singer crying with her hands over her face. These images are self-consciously presented as instant Polaroid photographs, which posits Spears's depression as a spontaneous psychological breakdown to which we have privileged access. The self-referential character of the photography throughout *there there* – its emphasis on its own status *as photography* – invites audiences familiar with the paparazzi snapshots of celebrity gossip magazines to interpret the photographs as authentic and spontaneous. Thus the magazine makes explicit use of Barthes' notion of the photographic analogue – the 'message without a code' that creates an impression of immediate/unmediated recording of reality (Barthes, 1977: 17). Through this use of photography, the audience is encouraged to believe that it is privy to the truth about Spears. On the one hand, such representations satisfy a public demand for images of what celebrities are 'really' like (for more on this point see Dyer, 1986: 2); but they also, through their seemingly verisimilitudinous mode of address, fulfil the demands of anti-stigma campaigners for more 'realistic' representations of mental health.

Nonetheless, the gender politics of such representations is problematic. These magazine images of Spears and Monroe crying, like the representations of mentally ill heroines of many recent films, mediate mad celebrity through the gendered, or, in Copjec's (1998) Lacanian terms, 'hysterical', form of melodrama. Just as women supposedly identify with the disempowered characters in narrative fictions such as soap operas, so too mental illness narratives seem to offer audiences something like Ien Ang's 'tragic structure of feeling': a melodramatic affect correlating to a particularly female experience of frustration and disempowerment (Ang, 1985). Images of tearful celebrities contribute to what Joke Hermes calls a 'repertoire of melodrama', which:

> can be recognised in references to misery, drama and by its sentimentalism and sensationalism, but also by its moral undertone. Life in the repertoire of melodrama becomes grotesquely magnified. In the vale of tears that it is, celebrities play crucial and highly stereotyped roles, reminiscent of folk and oral culture (Hermes, 1999: 80).

The gendered nature of the repertoire becomes clearer when the attitudes towards mental distress in women's and men's media are compared. While they may reinforce hegemonic definitions of femininity, women's magazines at least keep mental health issues on their agenda, as they encourage their readers to sympathize with Calista's eating disorder or Britney's depression. Men's magazines, on the other hand, show rather less interest in mental health issues, whether they relate to celebrities or otherwise. This relative lack of coverage is unfortunate, since men report symptoms of mental illness in primary care settings far less often than women (despite suffering from mental illnesses with roughly equal frequency). When mental health issues *are* raised in men's magazines, the authorial tone tends to be flippant or ironic and mental distress is discussed instrumentally in terms of 'losing it' or 'losing one's marbles' (on the instrumentalism of men's magazines see Jackson *et al.*, 2001). Thus the April 1999 edition of *FHM* magazine contained the headline 'Are You Going Mental?', while even the usually sensitive *Men's Health*, in December 2001, ran a mental health quiz with the title 'Will You

Lose Your Marbles?'. More pertinently, *celebrity* mental health issues in men's magazines are generally framed in ways that emphasize and validate physical violence. A recent edition of the men's weekly magazine *Zoo* (11 February 2005), for example, carries a feature on the 'Premiership's Top 20 Nutters', which includes a 'madness index' of some of Britain's most famous footballers. In women's magazines the tone is quite different – celebrity mental distress is discussed in highly serious, even lachrymose terms. For all the seriousness with which the topic is discussed, however, female celebrities suffering from mental distress are in general presented tragically, rather than heroically.

The association of celebrity and mental illness, particularly in the magazine publications I have mentioned, can be understood in the context of the postmodern inclination to 'have it both ways' – to offer glamorized images or values *together* with their reversal, critique or flipside. In today's postmodern media, the 'appearance' and 'reality' of celebrity (both equally constructed, of course) are presented *simultaneously*: thus Britney Spears, as we have seen, is presented in *there there* magazine as both glamorous and suffering. Similarly, celebrities appear on talk shows such as *The Oprah Winfrey Show* 'openly' talking about their mental health problems – indeed, television talk shows have been highly amenable to both celebrity and therapeutic culture (Marshall, 1997: 143). The mental illness of celebrities in contemporary media culture reveals the 'truth' about the celebrity concerned, reminding 'ordinary people' (a phrase that has become a media cliché in the United Kingdom and the United States) of what celebrities are 'really like' in a way that does not contradict or undermine their star status. More generally, this seemingly double structuring of the mentally ill media celebrity as both a private and a public being, is typical of a postmodern media culture which offers audiences spectacles of celebrity, while at the same time unmasking them in ancillary texts and spin-off programmes that offer to admit audiences 'behind the scenes' and give them the celebrity 'lowdown' (Wayne, 2003: 147). It may be tempting to eulogize these increasingly common presentations of suffering celebrity as tokens of media democratization. Yet my conclusion is a little less clear-cut than this. While images of suffering celebrities may enable consolatory identifications and even help to destigmatize mental illness, they may also have problematic implications.

In order to identify these implications more clearly, I would like to conclude this chapter by setting the foregoing discussion in a critical and theoretical context. Many media critics have justifiably worried about the misrepresentation of mental illness in the mass media, especially its association with violence. As many critics, including Wahl (1995) and Philo (1996), have shown through analyses of films, television, and popular literature, the mentally ill are often caricatured as violent, socially inept or even evil. Elsewhere, however, I have argued that some of this research is methodologically and theoretically problematic (Harper, 2005). In particular, I have suggested that many researchers tend to overlook sociological and psychiatric evidence about the correlation between mental illness and violence (and that the existing research is too reliant on individualistic definitions of 'violence' and 'mental illness'). Moreover, the claims of many media critics about audience responses to stories of mental illness are somewhat one-sided. The argument that media presentations of mental illness are overwhelmingly negative and foster public hostility towards mental illness has a great deal of validity; yet it does not account for the sympathetic treatment of celebrity mental health stories, particularly in women's magazines, or for the public support for Frank Bruno after the *Sun* slur. As Gilbert Rodman's study of Elvis fandom reminds us (1996: 12–13), celebrity seems to be partly generated 'from below' by the affective investments of 'real people' in celebrities (rather than simply imposed from above by conglomerates), making it all the more difficult for the media to stigmatize celebrity mental illness. At the same time, powerful psychiatric and pharmaceutical interests create pressure 'from above' for increased 'positive' public awareness of mental health issues.

Another shortcoming of existing accounts of mental illness in the mass media is that while they have tended to focus on questions of representation and verisimilitude, they have devoted little attention to how audiences use stories about celebrity mental distress in order to undertake 'identity work'. In the absence of audience research on the texts I have been discussing here, my tentative hypothesis would be that audiences respond to narratives of mental illness, particularly when they involve celebrities, with an uncomfortable mixture of prurience, concern and admiration. As we have seen in the case of Frank Bruno, the public can show enormous sympathy with celebrities suffering from a mental illness. These celebrities become well loved because audiences identify with their 'ordinary' status. This use of mental illness to vouchsafe the 'ordinariness' of celebrity is consistent with what Turner (2004) calls the 'demotic turn' in celebrity culture: as celebrities become less 'God-like', their plights are increasingly presented by the media through intimate and verisimilitudinous modes of address. Mental illness, then, is presented in two ways in popular culture. On the one hand, it is often romanticized as a noble condition linked to refined sentiments and heightened artistic or intellectual sensibility. Yet, as is obvious in media forms with lower cultural value, such as women's magazines, mental illness also symbolizes the trials and frustrations of everyday life.

The increasing presence of this 'demotic' strand of mental illness narratives in the media can be understood in relation to several social and cultural shifts in recent years. The proliferation of mentally distressed celebrities in the mass media may well reflect the growing cultural prominence of mental illness, as the extension of community care, the proliferation of mental health awareness campaigns, and the rise of anti-stigma films thrust psychiatric issues into public view. (Here it is interesting to note a similarity between the mentally ill and celebrities: both seem to be 'other', but both are increasingly presented by the media as being like 'us'. It has been suggested that celebrity is becoming more widespread, and even a normal expectation for some young people (Hopkins, 2002: 189; Turner, 2004: 67). Analogously, mental illness, it is often claimed, will affect one in four adults at some point in their lives.)

From a psychological perspective, meanwhile, media stories about suffering celebrities offer symbolic negotiations of the threats to mental well-being posed by post-traditional lifestyles. The changing nature of the celebrity's social function is a key factor here. Whereas the celebrity was once a distant star, far from the mundane activities of communities, she is now increasingly a part of people's daily lives, at the very time when the psychological support networks offered by state-run psychiatric services are receding in the face of deregulation and individualism. Chris Rojek suggests that the psychological uses and gratifications of celebrity culture can help to explain the appeal of celebrities to audiences in such atomized societies: 'In societies in which as many as 50 per cent of the population confess to sub-clinical feelings of isolation and loneliness, para-social interaction is a significant aspect of the search for recognition and belonging' (2001: 52). Thus, according to Rojek, celebrity provides vital senses of 'belonging, recognition, and meaning' (ibid.) in highly mediated societies, where face-to-face communication is increasingly rare. Psychological consolation, it seems, is a central appeal of celebrity today.

Nonetheless, the celebritization of mental distress cannot be seen simply as a liberating development that contributes to the destigmatization of mental illness. As I have suggested, narratives of mental illness in contemporary culture are allegories of heroism, especially in male-oriented media, which reflect and amplify a meritocratic ideology of competitive individualism. Interestingly, this trend within male-focused celebrity mental illness narratives problematizes (or at least, genders) the argument that celebrity is increasingly conceived in terms of 'ordinariness' (Gamson, 2001). In relation to women, meanwhile, such narratives often offer consolation with a distinctly melodramatic tinge. Yet there are still other, more tangible, problems with the increasing convergence of celebrity and mental distress in the media.

One practical concern is that images of celebrity mental distress may create as many problems as they solve, such as trivialising the experiences of non-celebrities who suffer from a mental disorder and misrepresenting the level of psychiatric care available to them (most people do not have access to private clinics). Moreover, recent research in the field of psychology suggests that an intense interest in celebrities may in itself have deleterious consequences for

the mental health of certain sections (although certainly not all) of the population. As Maltby *et al.* observe:

> Like many attitudes and behaviours, celebrity worship should not be
> a concern when carried out in moderation. However, for those indi-
> viduals who worship celebrities for intense–personal reasons, there
> may be consequences for individual mental health. Within the
> present study, 5% of respondents could be considered as showing
> high levels of intense–personal dimensions to their celebrity worship,
> and as such suggest that some of the population may be at risk from
> the way they consider and focus on their celebrities (Maltby *et al.*,
> 2004: 424–5).

This conclusion clearly problematizes attempts to use celebrities to raise public
awareness of mental health issues in publications like *there there*.

Another troubling aspect of the celebritization of mental distress relates to the
broader cultural implications of emotional investment in rhetorics of personal
trauma. The combination of celebrity and mental health awareness in *there there*
will doubtless be greeted with dismay by those Marxian critics who regard 'therapeutic culture' as a voluntaristic distraction from wider issues of power and
control in society. Wendy Brown (1995) uses the concept of the 'wounded
attachment' to explore how oppressed groups, particularly women, authorize
their right to speak through appeals to experiences of pain and injury; this, she
argues, is a necessary but ultimately individualistic and self-absorbing strategy.
Dana Cloud (1998) also sees 'therapy culture' as a retreat from the radical political activism of the 1960s that is at best palliative or consolatory. In the same
vein, Frank Furedi (2004) bemoans the extension of therapeutic rhetoric (which
he regards as infantilizing) into every domain of human life, reducing first the
desire and eventually the possibility of individuals to shape their own destinies.
These are not entirely new criticisms, of course (see, for example, Habermas,
1977: 355–64; Lasch, 1979: 1991). Nonetheless, these concerns about the
disempowering effects of therapeutic discourse are clearly relevant to any
attempt to make sense of the celebritization of mental distress, warning of the
political and social dangers of combining celebrity and therapy. The infantilizing
tendencies that Furedi finds in therapy culture are certainly clear in the case of a
title such as *there there*. Moreover, the treatment of celebrity psychiatric issues in
women's magazines, as we have seen, is often characterized by the fatalism so
deplored by Furedi.

The politics of the interrelationship between mental illness and celebrity in
popular culture, then, are both complex and disturbing. I have suggested in this
chapter that critics must consider not just the representational 'inaccuracies' of

media images of mental ill celebrities (negative stereotypes, misleading representations of psychiatric conditions, etc.), but also the significance of apparently 'positive' representations. In the context of an increasingly individualized and 'psychologized' (Giddens, 1992) society in which subjects are increasingly concerned with the management of personal risk, it can be argued that stories about the 'battles' and 'triumphs' of mentally ill celebrities are helpful resources in the battle against stigmatization – after all, they do often inspire public sympathy. Yet these resources are neither neutral, nor equally accessible. Just as the 'risk society' thesis of Beck and Giddens can be criticized for its universalism – Skeggs (2004: 52–4), for example, dismisses Giddens's 'reflexive individual' as a disembodied middle-class generalization – so the ostensibly 'positive' and destigmatizing intentions of much celebrity therapeutic discourse are severely compromised by their problematic class, race and gender politics. While more detailed research into such issues is needed, I have suggested here that even socially progressive celebrity mental illness narratives can reinforce neoliberal ideologies of meritocracy and individualism, uphold reactionary class, race and gender distinctions, and cultivate among some (especially female) non-celebrities a melodramatic and fatalistic attitude towards mental distress.

Bibliography

Ang, Ien (1985) *Watching Dallas: Soap Opera and the Melodramatic Imagination*, London and New York: Methuen.

Archer, Robyn and Simmonds, Diana (1986) *A Star Is Torn*, London: Virago.

Barthes, Roland (1977) *Image, Music, Text*, London: Fontana.

Battersby, Christine (1989) *Gender and Genius: Towards a Feminist Aesthetics*, London: Women's Press.

Beck, Ulrich (1992) *Risk Society: Towards a New Modernity*, London: Sage.

Biressi, Anita, and Nunn, Heather (2004) 'The Especially Remarkable: Celebrity and Social Mobility in Reality TV', *Mediactive* 2, 44–58.

Boorstin, Daniel (1971) *The Image: A Guide to Pseudo-Events in America*, New York: Atheneum. Originally published as *The Image or What Happened to the American Dream?* (1961).

Brown, Wendy (1995) *States of Injury: Power and Freedom in Late Modernity*, Princeton, NJ: Princeton University Press.

Cloud, Dana (1998) *Control and Consolation in American Culture and Politics: Rhetorics of Therapy*, Thousand Oaks, CA: Sage.

Copjec, Joan (1998) 'More! From Melodrama to Magnitude', in Janet Bergstrom (ed.), *Endless Night: Cinema and Psychoanalysis: Parallel Histories*, Berkeley: University of California Press, pp. 249–72.

Davies, Helen (2004) 'The Great Rock and Roll Swindle: The representation of women in the British rock music press', in Cynthia Carter and Linda Steiner (eds), *Critical Readings in Media and Gender*, Maidenhead: Open University Press, pp. 162–78.

Duke, Patty, with Hochman, Gloria (1999) *A Brilliant Madness: Living with Manic Depressive Illness*, New York: Bantam.

Dyer, Richard (1986) *Heavenly Bodies: Film Stars and Society*, London: Macmillan.

Elms, Emma (2003) '"I Won't Let Schizophrenia Ruin My Life"', *Marie Claire*, March: 96–100.

Furedi, Frank (2004) *Therapy Culture: Cultivating Vulnerability in an Uncertain Age*, London: Routledge.

Gamson, Joshua (2001) 'The Assembly Line of Greatness: Celebrity in Twentieth-Century America', in C. Lee Harrington and Denise D. Bielby (eds), *Popular Culture: Production and Consumption*, Oxford: Blackwell, pp. 259–82.

Giddens, Anthony (1991) *Modernity and Self-Identity: Self and Society in the Late Modern Age*, Cambridge: Polity Press.

—— (1992) *The Transformation of Intimacy: Sexuality, Love and Eroticism in Modern Societies*, Cambridge: Polity Press.

Gilbert, Jeremy (2004) 'Small Faces: The Tyranny of Celebrity in Post-Oedipal Culture', *MediActive* 2: 86–109.

Goggin, Gerard, and Newell, Christopher (2004) 'Fame and Disability: Christopher Reeve, Super Crips, and Infamous Celebrity', *M/C* 7.5.

Gough-Yates, Anna (2003) *Understanding Women's Magazines: Publishing, Markets and Readerships*, London: Routledge.

Habermas, Jürgen (1987) *The Theory of Communicative Action, Vol. 2. Lifeworld and System: A Critique of Functionalist Reason*, Cambridge: Polity Press.

Harper, Stephen (2005) 'Media, Madness and Misrepresentation: Critical Reflections on Anti-stigma Discourse', *European Journal of Communication* 20/4: 460–83.

Hermes, Joke (1999) 'Media Figures in Identity Construction', in Pertii Alasuutari (ed.), *Rethinking the Media Audience: The New Agenda*, London: Sage, pp. 69–85.

Holm, Ian, with Steven Jacobi (2004) *Acting My Life: The Autobiography*, London: Bantam.

Hopkins, Susan (2002) *Girl Heroes: The New Force in Popular Culture*, Sydney:Pluto Press.

Horkheimer, Max, and Adorno, Theodor (1972) 'The Culture Industry: Enlightenment as Mass Deception', in *The Dialectic of Enlightenment*, New York: Continuum, pp. 123–71.

Jackson, Peter, Stevenson, Nick, and Brooks, Kate (eds) (2001) *Making Sense of Men's Magazines*, Cambridge: Polity Press.

Jamison, Kay Redfield (1996) *Touched with Fire: Manic-depressive Illness and the Artistic Temperament*, New York: Simon and Schuster.

Lasch, Christopher (1991) *Culture of Narcissism*, New York and London: Norton.

Littler, Jo (2004) 'Making Fame Ordinary: Intimacy, Reflexivity, and "Keeping it Real"', *Mediactive* 2, 8–25.

Maltby, John, *et al.* (2004) 'Personality and Coping: A Context for Examining Celebrity Worship and Mental Health', *British Journal of Psychology* 95: 411–28.

Marshall, P. David (1997) *Celebrity and Power: Fame in Contemporary Culture*, Minneapolis, London: University of Minnesota Press.

O'Hagan, Sean (2005) 'That Way Sanity Lies', *Observer Magazine*, 13 February: 12–16.

Philo, Greg (ed.) (1996) *Media and Mental Distress*, London: Longman.

Rodman, Gilbert B. (1996) *Elvis After Elvis: The Posthumous Career of a Living Legend*, London and New York: Routledge.

Rojek, Chris (2001) *Celebrity*, London: Reaktion Books.

Scull, Andrew (1993) *The Most Solitary of Afflictions*, New Haven, CN, London: Yale University Press.

Skeggs, Beverley (2004) *Class, Self, Culture*, London: Routledge.

Sontag, Susan (1991) *Illness as Metaphor and AIDS and Its Metaphors*, London: Penguin.

there there (2004) Online editorial, available at www.theretheremagazine.com/index.php?pageid=editorial_synopsis, accessed 14 February 2006.

Turner, Graeme (2004) *Understanding Celebrity*, London: Sage.

Wahl, Otto (1995) *Media Madness*, New Brunswick, NJ: Rutgers University Press.

Wayne, Mike (2003) *Marxism and Media Studies*, London: Pluto Press.

Wittkower, Rudolf and Wittkower, Margot (1963) *Born Under Saturn,* London: Weidenfeld and Nicholson.

Wolf, Matt, 'A Life Less Ordinary', *Sunday Times Culture*, 29 August 2004: 51.

Wolf, Naomi (1991) *The Beauty Myth*, London: Vintage.

Chapter 19
Celebrity
The killing fields of popular music
Sheila Whiteley

It would seem something of a cliché to observe that celebrities live on for as long as they embody what their fans think they represent, and that death is no barrier to their perceived status as 'gods'. Popular music has always venerated personality, and it is apparent that nostalgia continues to exert a strong presence, as evidenced in the increasing number of Golden Oldies in the album charts, television programmes celebrating 'the best' and musicals that capitalize on past glories. Death, however, takes many forms, and the killing fields of popular music are scattered with the ghosts of young hopefuls who had been promised the stars but found instead that they were simply the fodder for an unscrupulous and voracious monster that thrives on one-hit wonders. In a world increasingly dominated by instant celebrity, success and rejection pivot on the whim of a capricious public whose appetites have been whetted by the ideology of individualism and consumption. Image, style and fashion invite both desire and identification (Gledhill, 1991; Goodwin, 1993) but, above all, it is the intimacies of an individual's personal life that exert such a fatal fascination. The national psyche, it seems, has been nurtured on sadism and sensationalism. The earlier fascination with watching public executions as entertainment is metaphorically realized through reality-pop television and shows such as *The X-Factor* (2004, UK). What is all too often forgotten, as contestants are subjected to the scrutiny of a media-savvy audience, is that fame comes at a price. It can, as John Lennon so tellingly wrote, leave you 'crippled inside'.

The relationship between the iconic and the killing fields of popular music can be attributed to the pressures exerted by the music business, the expectations of fans, and the media, where the reporting of celebrity status in rock and pop is inextricably bound up with issues surrounding sexuality, sensationalism and sexploitation. These, in turn, generate tensions between conformity to expectations and the maintenance of a personal life which can become intolerable. Karen Carpenter suffered from anorexia nervosa, a condition from which she never recovered, the Carpenters' low profile during the 1980s coinciding with her increasingly poor health and weak state. Lena Zavaroni died at the age of 35 having developed an eating disorder at 13 when her agent told her she was too fat (she died weighing three-and-a-half stone). Their fate is not dissimilar to that of Judy Garland whose neurotic addiction to alcohol and pills were the legacy of her years as a child star in Hollywood. According to Gledhill, stardom, 'with its intense focus on the drama of personal identity' (Gledhill, 1991: xviii), invites identification and controversy, gossip and rumour, and my chapter here explores the concept of 'fame damage' and its relation to celebrity status through two related case studies. These focus on hypersexuality and rock, and sexuality and the lesbian muse – raising questions surrounding gender, subjectivity and representation and how these relate to the generic norms of popular music; how celebrity status, as a social sign, carries cultural meanings and ideological values.

Sex and drugs and rock 'n' roll

The association of death with the heroic remains a powerful signifier within rock culture. It confirms the creed that 'sex and drugs and rock 'n' roll is all my brain and body need' (Ian Dury)[1] and situates death as the ultimate form of excess: 'live fast, die young'. While the genesis of the relationship between sex and rock is largely attributed to the gyrating hips, surly gaze and pouting lips that characterized Elvis Presley's performances,[2] the association with 'dope' was initially more covert. Although it was a well-established fact that jazz artists such as Billie Holiday had a heroin addiction, it was not until the mid 1960s, when marijuana and LSD underpinned both the lifestyles and music of many of its most prominent artists, that drug culture and musical content came together[3] – often with disastrous consequences. The extent to which this was a result of 'driving in the fast lane', the need to relax after a late-night gig, or the desire to access the metaphysical, earlier associated with the Romantic poets and such writers as Aldous Huxley, is conjectural. Yet, by the early 1970s, rock lifestyles had proved to have terrifying analogies with the mythical Faustian bargain as iconic figures died from the excesses of superstardom after a magical five-year life span. As such, the release of *Ziggy Stardust and the Spiders from Mars* (1972) provided an apocryphal setting for David Bowie's pop alter ego while evidencing his acute awareness of the more adverse effects of fame.

By 1972, the deaths of Brian Jones, Janis Joplin, Jim Morrison and Jimi Hendrix had provided a chilling testimony both to the morbidity of rock culture and the consuming passion of the media which, zombie-like, fed on their deaths, turning rock icons into celebrity figures whose excesses fuelled both sensationalist journalism and an increasingly repressive legislature. If 1967 is taken as the year when stars such as Hendrix and Morrison first achieved international success, then their deaths suggest that the conceptualization of Ziggy, the Naz of

Bowie's parable, is both an ironic and knowing commentary on the entire rock process. Set in the supposedly drug-crazed world of a future on the brink of catastrophe, Ziggy, like his real-life counterparts, dies from the excesses of stardom when he is killed off in the last track of the album, a rock 'n' roll suicide, five years on.

Bowie is spellbinding as a storyteller and his voice is kaleidoscopic, ranging from the overt, viper-like tones that accompany the verbal caresses of the Stardust Queen, the soulful, preacherman recitative that precedes the big soulful chorus of 'It Ain't Easy', to the intimacy of defeat in 'Rock 'n' Roll Suicide'. The would-be rock 'n' roll star, masquerading as a fictitious pop star, who subsequently becomes a star himself, is both a brilliant piece of wish-fulfilment and a chilling metaphor for the rise and fall of rock icons. While Ziggy's death is wrapped up in a theatricality that evokes memories of Judy Garland, the pressures of stardom continue to drive the insecure to find escape mechanisms – and drugs are clearly one of the most obvious outlets here in that they provide both the necessary stimulants for an exhausting performance programme, and the means to turn off and relax. It is also apparent that the mythologizing of death has situated drugs as the sacraments within the catechism of rock and self-destruction – whether drug-related, suicide or the result of severe risk-taking – and this is curiously related both to the excesses of a rock 'n' roll lifestyle and to much of the litany of its songs. From the cute insinuations about shooting smack often imputed to the Mamas and Papas' lyric 'I'm a real straight shooter, if ya know what I mean', through the Stones' 'Sister Morphine' and on to Generation X's 'shooting up for kicks' (Pattison, 1987: 125), rock's infatuation with narcotics is matched only by its fascination with death itself. Its heroes are those whose emotions have broken out of prescribed limits, endowing them with a godlike eminence which is curiously enhanced by their often ignoble deaths – the inhalation of vomit being but one example. For their fans, however, there is an implicit comparability with the Romantic poets, which manifests itself in the maxim that the good die young, triggered largely by Mick Jagger's narration from Shelley's elegy for Keats as part of a free concert in London's Hyde Park two days after Brian Jones's 'death by misadventure' (3 July 1969):

> Life, like a dome of many-coloured glass,
> Stains the white radiance of Eternity,
> Until Death tramples it to fragments, – Die
> If thou would'st be that which though dost seek.

This sense of romanticism was heightened by the deaths of Jimi Hendrix (18 September 1970, aged 27) and Jim Morrison (3 July 1971, aged 27), whose self-inflicted martyrdom (caused by an excessive addiction to drugs, alcohol and a wild lifestyle) foreshadowed the deaths of such rock icons as Michael Hutchence, of INXS (22 November 1997, aged 37), and Kurt Cobain, of Nirvana (5 April 1994, aged 27). The fact that Morrison was buried without an autopsy or proper identification has fed the legend the he is still alive and that he will, like King Arthur before him, return. As one fan scratched on his headstone at Père Lachaise Cemetery, Paris, 'When are you coming back, you bastard?'

A survey I conducted for *Too Much Too Young: Popular Music, Age and Gender* (Whiteley, 2005) revealed some twenty-five mortalities among leading rock performers,[4] attributable mainly to drug addiction/overdoses, alcohol or suicide, with an average age of death of 30. While it could be argued (given rock's fifty-year history) that this number is not excessive, it is significant to note that my investigation explored only the headline groups and as such, only skims the surface of the casualties inflicted by a rock 'n' roll lifestyle. Again, it might be suggested that their public acts (and rock stars are notorious for trashing hotel rooms, for example) were initially responsible for attracting press attention, and that their subsequent hounding was inevitable. What is evident, however, is that being constantly in the limelight was not always welcome. While fast living argu-ably contributed to their deaths, there is also little doubt that many felt tormented both by the expectations of fans and by an omnipresent media atten-tion. As Bob Hicks wrote:

> The fact that many chose to make [Hendrix] a god was not because he asked to be one. It was because those people needed a god, one they could see and hear and touch, to make their decisions for them; and because modern mass communications provided the means of god-making ... [But] like every man who has ever been worshipped by other men, he knew he was not fit to be worshipped and felt a revulsion and horror towards that mass which so willingly denigrated itself before his ulti-mately frail strength and power (Hicks, cited in Potash, 1996: 208–9).

It is a requiem that could stand equally for Kurt Cobain, who committed suicide in his home in Seattle, also aged 27. His aversion to publicity and the demands of superstardom are well documented, and while responses to his death were diverse (he had pumped his veins full of heroin, written a rambling suicide note and shot himself) many agreed with his mother, Wendy, that 'he'd become a member of "that stupid club" of early rock 'n' roll deaths' (Clarke and Woods, 1999: back cover).

What is apparent from my research is that the icons of rock did not seek or want celebrity status but rather the respect of their fans; and the constant surveil-lance by the media has precipitated moving suicide notes from, among others, Ian Curtis (vocalist, Joy Division) who hanged himself, aged 24, while at the peak of creativity – 'At this moment I wish I were dead. I just can't cope anymore' – and the disappearance of Richey Edwards (guitarist, Manic Street Preachers) who had cut the words '4 Real' into his forearm when his band's authenticity was called into question by *New Musical Express* critic Steve Lamacq. The haunting '4st 7lb', written by the anorexic Edwards, had earlier preceded his temporary admittance to a mental institution.

Clearly there are survivors, but even these bear the scars of their earlier life-styles, Keith Richard, Roy Wood and Eric Clapton to name but a few. It is also suggested that wild boys can become 'de-fanged' by the more extreme connotations of celebrity status. Ozzy Osbourne, the *enfant terrible* of metal, whose band Black Sabbath was notorious for such doom-laden metal as *Paranoid* (1970) and *Sabbath Bloody Sabbath* (1974), was well known for courting publicity, most famously in 1982 when he had to undergo treatment for rabies following an onstage incident when he bit the head off a bat. Osbourne's satanic, werewolf image seemed an unlikely choice for the Queen's Buckingham Palace gig (as part of the 2002 Jubilee celebrations), even though his popular television series *The Osbournes* had become compulsive viewing in Britain (following its huge success in the US). As a hard rocker who had tried every excess and survived, his arrival on stage, replete with black coat and make-up, was met with a certain nervous anticipation. While his performance was inspiring, a question mark remained. Had he become simply a pantomime villain, willing to act out excess for the sake of royal patronage? Had the cult of celebrity (and its attendant publicity) more pulling power than his status as the founding father of heavy metal? Mick Jagger's knighthood (Jubilee Honours list, 2002) can also be interpreted as an acknowledgement of his established celebrity status, although his notoriety and appetite for sex and drugs had earlier led to his characterization as aggressively sexual, insolent and undesirable. At the time, it seemed unlikely that he would join the elevated ranks of Sir Paul McCartney and Sir Cliff Richard, and for many it suggested that he, too, had become 'tamed' and that his 'services to Queen and Country' were more an attribute to his longevity (hence the dubbing by the press of the Rolling Stones as the 'Strolling Bones') than his role in establishing the Rolling Stones as the country's most notorious rock band.

Celebrity status, then, has a sting in its tail. As deCordova has famously elaborated with regard to the establishment of fame in Hollywood cinema, with the emergence of 'the star', 'private lives ... emerge[d] as a new site of knowledge and truth' (deCordova, 1990: 26), something which rapidly came to colonize other media forms. While Jagger has retained his reputation as a womanizer, so situating him within the established heteronormative codes of rock, sexuality and sexual honesty remain a thorny problem. The consequences of being 'outed', for example, are exemplified in the *Daily Mirror*'s jubilant front-page headline 'Zip Me Up Before You Go Go' (8 April 1998). George Michael (founder member of

Wham!, the most successful teen-oriented group of the 1980s, and subsequently a solo superstar) had been arrested for 'lewd' behaviour in a toilet cubicle at the Will Rogers Memorial Park in Beverley Hills, LA, after years of denial that he was a closet gay. The consequences of being 'outed' subsequently prompted Noel Gallagher's caustic comments (on the release of George Michael's single, 'Shoot The Dog') that 'George is trying to make social comment. This is the guy who actually hid who he actually was from the public for 20 years.'[5] While Gallagher's comments can be construed as a somewhat vitriolic reflection on George Michael's sexuality, it is evident that it also effects a less than subtle endorsement of his own honesty as a heterosexual performer in an arena that continues to extol the extremes of machismo. At the same time it is a reminder that popular success continues to reflect the expectations generated by popular music's cultural context, i.e. the continuing bias of normative heterosexuality (Bayton, 1997, 1999; Whiteley, 2000; Reynolds and Press, 1995).

It is also apparent, and important, that women do not enjoy the same mythologizing as their male counterparts, the gods, the kings, the shamans of rock. Wendy O. Williams, of Plasmatics, who paved the way for women in punk, was known for her wild stage performances and for making the Mohawk fashionable. Fearless, rebellious and overtly sexual, she committed suicide on 7 April 1998, aged 48. Mia Zapata of Gits was raped and murdered while on her way home from a Seattle pub on 7 July 1993. Her death prompted friends to start Home Alive, educating women on self-defence and protection. Stefanie Pffaf of Hole overdosed on heroin in 1994, two months after Kurt Cobain's death and Hole's heralded album, *Live Through This*. Bianca Halstead of Betty Blowtorch was killed in a car accident in 2001. Her album *Are You Man Enough?* was released in the same year.[6] With the exception of Hole, there are no biographies on these women in encyclopaedias of popular music, and it would seem that the only woman in rock who has been given mythical status is Janis Joplin. Even so, her death (4 October 1970, aged 27) provided an opportunity for the media to castigate the 1960s for its indulgence and its hedonistic experimentation with drugs. Joplin's fronting of what can be considered an essentially male rock persona – rebellious and 'hard living' – demonstrated that masculinity and femininity are valued quite differently in their sexed context here. Joplin's aggressiveness marked her as uncontrollable, 'unnaturally' active and outspoken on her numerous affairs and drinking habits, and, as such, lying outside the dominant symbolic order. As bisexual, she was confronted with problems of image and representation, and her short career – and a death that ironically established her as a rock icon – situates her as a performer who raised key issues surrounding sexuality and its relationship to celebrity. This was a problem that also confronted, and arguably later destroyed, Dusty Springfield. As Smith argues: 'Despite her courageous, if quixotic, 1970 "coming out" statement, there was no place for Springfield in the highly politicized ethos of lesbian feminism then fulminating, and the rock music world had no place for a "dyke"' (Smith, 1999: xviii).

Celebrity and the lesbian muse

It is something of a paradox that the 1960s counter-culture, despite its challenging stance against inequality and its recognition of music as part of its revolutionary strategy, was largely reactionary in its attitude towards women. In particular, discussions about 'sexual liberation' were framed in terms saturated with male assumptions, including the very male fantasy of 'dope, rock and roll and fucking in the streets'.[7] Attributable in part to the political emphasis on progressiveness, modernization and youth which, in mid 1960s popular music, was reflected in the male domain of progressive rock and the emphasis on fraternal individualism, there was an emphasis on biological determinism and the role of women as mother/nurturer. This was enshrined in the songs of the period which, in turn, provided a commonsense framing of femininity which was both oppressive and reactionary. In essence, women were either cast as stereotypical 'earth mothers' (e.g. the Beatles, 'Mother Nature's Son', 'Hey Jude'; Led Zeppelin, 'Stairway to Heaven') or as 'sexual objects' (e.g. the Rolling Stones, 'Backstreet Girl', 'Under My Thumb', 'Brown Sugar'). Lesbianism remained invisible and relied largely on 'queer' readings of otherwise 'straight' songs (e.g. Tammy Wynette, 'Stand By Your Man'), and despite Joplin's covert bisexuality, she was more commonly associated as 'one of the guys' – an emphasis that reverberated uneasily with her underlying vulnerability.

It is also apparent that the police raid on the Stonewall Inn, a gay bar in Christopher Street, Greenwich Village, did little to assuage the public perception of lesbians as deviant and 'other', or to change the traditional conservatism of the music industry and the media, which continued to have particular expectations as to how its stars should behave. Thus, while rock stars in general could openly engage in often unorthodox heterosexual relationships, 'virtually no highly visible popular performer had – or would – make a public admission of his or her still-taboo homosexuality' (Smith, 1999: 113). In a musical environment that preferred their women performers to subscribe to the ethos of light, romantic, dollybird pop,[8] Dusty Springfield's championing of Motown and R&B and the husky timbre of her voice, situated her as markedly different. This sense of difference was also evident in her high beehive hairstyle, heavy mascara and false eyelashes, which owed much to the Motown groups, the Ronettes, the Crystals and the Marvelettes and which suggested a 'vampy overkill' of femininity and a 'highly ironic lesbian resignification of the gay man in drag – in effect that of the *female* female impersonator' (Smith, 1999: 107). Thus, while her early career had earned her the title 'Queen of the Mods', Springfield's drag-queen image (which has strong parallels with k.d. lang's butch/femme persona) increasingly led to the star-based gossip that characterizes celebrity status (see also Judith Franco's essay in this collection). With the press becoming increasingly curious about her private life, alluding to affairs with both women and men, she escaped to Los Angeles in 1972 where she maintained the loyalty of a large gay following. Her 1985 recording with the Pet Shop Boys (a queer British techno pop duo) can be read as a salutary address to the public, a haunting retrospective on the failure of her albums (*Living Without You,* 1978, and *White Heat,* 1982), and the obscurity of her years in LA:

> You always wanted me to be something I wasn't
> You always wanted too much
> Now that I can do what I want to, forever,
> How am I gonna get through
> > (Pet Shop Boys and Dusty Springfield,
> >   'What have I done to deserve this')

While it may seem that Springfield's 1970 announcement of her bisexuality in the *Evening Standard* was both reckless and courageous, it is salutary to note that k.d. lang did not come out until 1993, when the election of Bill Clinton prom- ised a more tolerant attitude towards gays and lesbians. As Giles Smith wrote in the *Independent*:

> Pop stars stay on the track either by processes of radical self-reinvention or by skating blithely to avoid the ruts. k.d. lang appears to be a skater. It took her a long time to say publicly that she was a lesbian. She finally did so in June 1993, in an interview with the American gay magazine *The Advocate*. She said she was fed up with people asking.[9]

It is certainly worth noting that Lang was, at the time, 32 years old and had been a professional singer since 1982. As such, the 'fed up with people asking' conceals more than it reveals. lang had persistently tantalized her fans with such statements as 'I'm a llll… Liberace fan' but she was clearly aware that 'There's a big difference between not denying it and finally just saying "I'm a lesbian"' (Starr, 1994: 245).

As discussed earlier, it is a salutary fact that the identity of the music industry devolves around the structural subordination of women.[10] The majority of deci- sion-making positions are held by men, and, although women performers are the most visible examples of progress in the history of rock and pop, success often implies a shrewd awareness of the particular demands of the industry – not least its firm attachment to heterosexual desire. Thus despite the fact that many women performers are lesbians, coming out in an industry that invites fantasy, cross-dressing and camp but which predicates female heterosexuality is commercially precarious. Androgyneity is undoubtedly a safer option. To be a declared lesbian in country music, where representations of gender and sexuality are unequivocally heterosexual, and where performer/fan relationships depend on a shared valorization of family values is even more problematic. For lang, it could have been commercial suicide.

The relationship between gender and musical style is important, not least in establishing a point of communication between the performer and her/his fans. In particular, listeners find a sense of their own identity confirmed, modified or constructed in the process. Since both performer and listener are gendered and sexual creatures, the framework is over-determined by these attributes. While it is recognized that this is not a simple process, lang's stylizing of country, which focused attention on both its formal and formulaic features, and her subversion of both the staged and vocal idiom through self-dramatization, is significant – not least in raising questions about the erotics of her performance. For example, while lang constantly changed her stage persona during her 'country' years, thus implying an act, she consistently presented a problematic sexuality which suggested an identity that was gendered and only ambiguously sexed. Like Dusty Springfield before her, there was thus a tension in lang's performance that expressed itself as a dissonance between her anatomical sex, her sexuality and her gendered performance, which communicated itself to her audience (in part instinctively) as different. While this may have been a source of delight to her lesbian fans, her overly dramatic presentation of country, and the playful androgyny of her butch-femme persona, posed a direct challenge to Nashville's traditional codes of heterosexual femininity while constantly attracting the attention of the press in their pursuit of celebrity gossip.

No easy answers

The fact that musical celebrities carry cultural meanings and ideological values which are gendered means that they are often in conflict with the established norms of popular music, and celebrity status all too often involves a betrayal of 'who you are' and a resultant crisis in confidence. Whitney Houston, whose self-titled album (*Whitney Houston,* 1984), situated her as the first female artist to debut at No. 1 on the American charts – a feat also achieved in the UK – and whose awards included Pop Female Vocal and Soul R&B Female Vocal in the American Music Awards (1988), was yet another drug casualty and was rumoured to go through $500 of coke and $100 of marijuana a week, finally becoming little more than a barely functioning junkie. To the outside world, at the time, she was still a pop princess, but as Robin Crawford commented in a recent television programme, 'it's the image that sells, not the real you', and rumours concerning her sexuality ('You can't have a lesbian prom-queen'), her drug addiction, and ill-fated relationship with soul singer Bobby Brown led to an inevitable fall from grace. Kylie Minogue also suffered from an adverse press when she became involved with Michael Hutchence (INXS) and moved to a more grunge-driven sound. His death, in mysterious, possibly sexual circumstances, seemed to confirm that Minogue had been seriously led astray and, together with the new raunchiness of her music ('I want to sing about sex now'), situated her simply as a naïve Madonna clone. Sneered at by Liam Gallagher for her recitation of the lyrics to 'I Should Be So Lucky' at the Poetry Olympics (held at the Royal Albert Hall in 1996), her career foundered, with the media enthusiastically showing photos in which she looked drained, older, and 'past it'. Not everyone has Kylie's ability to bounce back, and in 2002 she won five Brit awards, this time to accolades by the media who, as ever, swam with the tide of public opinion. It appears that she knew all too well that her status within pop music necessitated a return to her earlier fun-image – sexy but clean.

Sinéad O'Connor also attracted adverse media attention and, from the beginning, confused audiences and the media with her mixture of outspokenness and vulnerability. Not least, her visual image, her shaved head, made her a significant target for media interest:

> In 2000 O'Connor intensified this representational tendency by briefly coming out as a lesbian, adding the layer of a lived personal sexual identity to a queerness that had already been established through a career of challenging the normalcy of mainstream society. Controversy erupted when, no sooner had the media declared her lesbian credentials, O'Connor backed away from her previous quoted statements (Mayhew, 2005: 3).

While playing with sexual mores has a long established relationship to popular music (from Little Richard, through to Annie Lennox and Madonna), it is suggested that being interpreted as queer, rather than being a declared lesbian, was a safer option for her mainstream career. Even so, O'Connor has not been slow to challenge the media's obsession with celebrity figures:

> I believe that more so called 'celebrities' should stand up for themselves when subjected to this type of dismissive abuse which I have been the butt of in this country for twenty years now, without really ever standing up for myself. In an intelligent manner. To me, this issue is not about me, but about the freedom God gave all of us, in fact the DUTY

we have, to be ourselves. And we all have the right to be who we are, without being ridiculed and abused every time we set foot out the door to go to work (O'Connor, cited in O'Brien, 2004).

O'Connor's bold declamation of individualism was played out in her physical appearance which transgressed conventional conceptions of female beauty. For Sinéad O'Connor it was the adverse connotations of her shaved head that initially attracted media attention; for others it has been their size. In the 1960s, Elliott Johnson (The Mamas and the Papas) had been accommodated by the pop world by giving her a 'Mama Cass' image – large and lovely. It was something she constantly fought against, not least because co-singer Michelle Gilliam was not afforded the same prefix, being described by the press as the sexy, sylph-like member of the group. In 2003, the second series of the UK reality show, *Pop Idol,* was won by Michelle McManus, a bubbly and decidedly overweight Scottish contestant. This time, it seemed, the press were behind her. To be against Michelle was, it seemed, contrary to a supposed equality of opportunity, despite the omnipresent massive media campaigns and programmes attacking the UK's growing obesity. Holmes argues that such programmes deliberately foster the impression that 'ideological concessions' are being made to challenging discourses with respect to conventionally shared ideals of masculinity and femininity in pop (Holmes, 2004). Indeed, this is integral to their construction of audience agency – the image of the audience as 'authoring' the outcome of the programme (and thus the destiny of the star). Yet this apparent investment (at the level of both economics and audience) is not a guarantee for success. Michelle has yet to produce a massive No. 1 album and it seems that, like Hear'Say before her (the band to emerge from the first UK series of *Popstars,* in 2001), she has simply faded from the music scene.

An important theme which arises throughout my discussion, and which is present throughout the media's production of celebrity, concerns the separation of, and tension between, the 'real' self and its media representation. Thus, while the relationship between the media and popular music is intimately intertwined, the constant pressure to expose and exploit personal traumas demonstrates the way in which celebrity journalism has increasingly impacted on the production of contemporary news. As Dyer explained, the media construction of stardom has always encouraged us to 'hang on to the reality of the star's private self' (Dyer, 1986: 10). Success, it seems, invites non-stop media scrutiny, 'encouraging us to think in terms of "really" – what is [the star] *really* like?' (Dyer, 1986: 2; italics in the original).

Björk's acclaim as an international artist, for example, had been accompanied by the media's running commentary on her private life, including her traumatic break-up with drum'n'bass artist, Goldie, and the letter-bomb sent by fan,

Ricardo Lopez, who had blown his brains out with a shotgun while listening to her song, 'I remember you'. As such, the reporting of Björk's violent reaction to TN News evidences both the pressure associated with celebrity status, the reality/constructed reality of her life, and the way in which the media capitalize on adverse publicity. When reporter Julia Kaufman and camera crew

> '... went for my son, live on air, on TV, and she said "Isn't it difficult to be the son of a pop star who is so self-important that she won't give us an interview?" ... I just snapped.' It was the third time in her life that Björk had hit someone and she acknowledges the fact that 'a lot of shit comes with my job ... but I'd be lying if I said it didn't piss me off when it spills over to my friends and family' (Baker, 1997: 14–15).

Arguably, it is the challenge to the division between the private and public – especially in Björk's transgression of acceptable media celebrity behaviour – that is at issue here. The fascination with the intimacies of musicians' lives and the power of journalism to 'scapegoat' celebrity figures remains problematic. As Yoko Ono comments, 'I was an easy target ... It's very interesting to make a woman into a kind of evil person who has strong evil powers or something. It's a dichotomy in a way in their minds – a strength even. It's a very interesting twist and that's what people loved about it' (Ono, cited in Bracewell, 2003: 135). It is also evident that a scandalous press is often more attractive when it comes to record sales, as shown by the constant media attention to Britney Spears' early career. Her record company, fully aware of the sales benefits of star-based gossip:

> orchestrated a sophisticated guessing game about her level of sexual awareness, alternating apple-pie wholesomeness with brazen acts of sexual provocation, which led to a global obsession with the question of Britney's virginity. One minute she's the bashful girl next door who swears allegiance to her mum, God and the flag, the next she is writhing on stage in a bikini with a python between her legs (McCormack, 2002).

More recently, it was her first (short-lived) marriage that attracted attention but, even so, one is reminded that 'creating the fuckable fantasy woman has long been a preoccupation of pop music, especially now the medium has become so visible' (O'Brien, 1995: 231), and the press is quick to latch on to any scandalous gossip. After all, that's what sells.

'Being' a celebrity is clearly fraught with problems. For the naïve, attracted by the lure of fame and inexperienced in the machinations of the music business, it is doubly so. After all, what is there to accomplish in life if you are famous at 16 and then dropped? What do you do once your musical career and your private life become inextricably mixed up in front-page spreads? For many it has meant a retreat – either into drugs, into a self-imposed exile, or into a refusal to speak – as exemplified in Freddie Mercury's concealment of AIDS, and Rob Halford's (Judas Priest) delay in 'coming out' until 1992. Small wonder, then, that musicians continue to fear the press for their relentless pursuit of celebrity-based gossip. The question remains, however, as to why the public has a right to know everything about a star. Surely it is their music that is important, not the ins and outs of their private lives.

Notes

1 Ian Dury and the Blockheads, 'Sex and Drugs and Rock 'n' Roll', *New Boots and Panties* (Stiff Records, 1977).

2 Presley's simple espousal of black music with hillbilly and his dangerous sexuality marked the arrival of the 'generation gap' of adolescent rebellion. Whereas the stars of the early 1950s did not appeal specifically to the teenage market, the injection of black influences into country music, together with the new emphasis on image and, hence, teen appeal, gave popular music its missing ingredient.

3 For a detailed discussion of how the musical content becomes a metaphor for hallucinogenic experience see Whiteley (1992).

4 My survey focused on rock, metal and punk.

5 *Sunday Times*, 28 July 2002.

6 Thanks to Jeanne Fury (Rocklist) for her list of fatalities.

7 Widgery, D. (1973) 'What Went Wrong?', *OZ* 48: 7–17.

8 Such artists as Petula Clark, Sandie Shaw, Lulu, Cilla Black and Marianne Faithfull exemplify this 'second division' pop status. As Faithfull observes, 'When I finally did run off with Mick [Jagger], I felt I should stop working, because he was such a great star ... I put my ambition on hold and did what was required, which was to be there and to give him everything I had' (O'Brien, 1995: 97).

9 *Independent*, 3 December 1993.

10 This was evidenced by a recent ESF-funded project to explore gender inequalities in the cultural industries. A full report can be found on www.CreativeWomen.org.uk.

Bibliography

Baker, Sarah L. (2003) *Rock On Baby! An Exploration of Pre-teen Girls' Negotiations of Popular Music and Identity in Adelaide, Australia,* unpublished PhD thesis.

Bayton, Mavis (1997) 'Women and the Electric Guitar', in Whiteley, Sheila (ed.), *Sexing the Groove: Popular Music and Gender,* London, New York: Routledge, pp. 37–49.

—— (1999) *Frock Rock,* Oxford: Oxford University Press.

Bracewell, Michael (2003) *The Nineties: When Surface Was Depth,* London: HarperCollins.

Clarke, Martin and Woods, Paul (eds) (1999) *Kurt Cobain: The Kurt Cobain Dossier,* London: Plexus.

deCordova, Richard (1990) *Picture Personalities: The Emergence of the Star System in America,* Urbana and Chicago: University of Illinois Press.

Dyer, Richard (1986) *Heavenly Bodies: Film Stars and Society,* London: BFI.

Gledhill, Christine (ed.) (1991) *Stardom: Industry of Desire*. London/New York: Routledge.

Goodwin, Andrew (1993) *Dancing in the Distraction Factory: Music Television and Popular Culture*, London: Routledge.

Holmes, Su (2004) '"Reality Goes Pop!": Reality TV, Popular Music, and Narratives of Stardom in *Pop Idol*', *Television and New Media* 5/2, May: 147–72.

—— (forthcoming) 'Thank You, Voters': Approaching the Audience for Music and Television in the Reality-Pop Phenomenon', in Graeme Harper (ed.), *The Continuum Reader in Sound and Vision*.

McCormack, N. (2002) 'Britney, goddess of virginity', *The Age*, 25 February, available at www.theage.com.au/articles/2002/02/24/2225britney-mj-sb.htm.

Mayhew, Emma (2006) '"I am Not in a Box of Any Description": Sinéad O'Connor's Queer Outing', in Sheila Whiteley and Jennifer Rycenga (eds), *Queering the Popular Music Pitch*, New York, London: Routledge, pp. 169–84.

O'Brien, Lucy (1995) *She Bop: The Definitive History of Women in Rock, Pop and Soul*, London: Penguin Books.

Pattison, Robert (1987) *The Triumph of Vulgarity: Rock Music in the Mirror of Romanticism*, Oxford: Oxford University Press.

Potash, Chris (ed.) (1996) *The Jimi Hendrix Companion: Four Decades of Commentary*, New York: Schirmer.

Reynolds, Simon, and Press, Joy (1995) *The Sex Revolts: Gender, Rebellion and Rock 'n' Roll*, London: Serpents Tail.

Smith, Patricia Juliana (ed.) *The Queer Sixties*, New York, London: Routledge.

Starr, Victoria (1994) *k.d. lang: All You Get Is Me*, London: Harper-Collins.

Whiteley, Sheila (1992) *The Space Between the Notes: Rock and the Counter-Culture*, London: Routledge.

—— (2005) *Too Much Too Young: Popular Music, Age and Identity*, London, New York: Routledge.

Chapter 20

'Sometimes you wanna hate celebrities'

Tabloid readers and celebrity coverage

Sofia Johansson

On 9 January 2003, an 'exclusive' appears on the front page of the *Sun*, Britain's biggest-selling newspaper. Hollywood film star Cameron Diaz has spots! The brazen headline, 'Why Cameron stayed out of the SPOTlight', is coupled with a large, unforgiving close-up of the actress, her blotchy face exposed for all to see. At the time, the exposé of Diaz's acne attracted a great deal of interest in the tabloids and celebrity magazines, and the actress's skin troubles have since kept resurfacing as a news item in these media. For some, this would epitomize key trends with regard to the role of celebrity in contemporary journalism, where the tabloid focus on this sphere is seen as part of a 'dumbing down' of the media climate. Yet research into the consumption of tabloid celebrity coverage is virtually non-existent. Why is it popular? This essay explores how tabloid stories about celebrities function in the everyday lives of their readers. Based on qualitative research with young readers of the *Sun* and the *Daily Mirror*, the circulation leaders among the popular tabloids, it provides an empirical study of some of the social and cultural functions of this genre where celebrity is concerned.[1]

I begin with an overview of the debate about 'tabloidization', which has raised questions about the role of celebrity journalism in relation to democratic communication. However, it is the perspective of tabloid journalism as a 'cultural discourse' that provides the main basis for this essay as, rather than focusing on inherent reactionary or progressive qualities in the material, it allows for an analysis of the range of functions performed for readers by tabloid celebrity coverage. These are outlined in three sections, starting with perceptions and social uses, followed by an examination of the way tabloid celebrity stories link in with understandings of social mobility. Finally, particular consideration is given to the enjoyment taken from the 'celebrity-bashing' characteristic of tabloids, which calls attention to a more political aspect of their consumption.[2]

Tabloids, celebrity and tabloidization

In the UK, the centrality of the tabloids to the circulation of celebrity is due to two main factors. First, tabloid newspapers dominate the newspaper market, with the popular tabloids (the so-called 'red-tops') holding a majority share of the total newspaper circulation.[3] Second, the news values of these papers are bound up with notions of fame so that, as Graeme Turner explains, tabloid news is 'utterly personalised and dominated by the actions of well-known people – politicians, public officials, sportsmen and women, celebrities, soon-to-be celebrities and wannabe celebrities' (2004: 75). In combination with their wide reach among newspaper readers, this focus on personality corroborates the tabloids' status as a main arena for contemporary celebrity discourse. The popular tabloids have further developed a brand of celebrity journalism that, as compared to its more reverent equivalent in the 'quality' press or television news, focuses on 'exposés' of details the celebrity would like to remain unknown – something that is often the result of invasive journalistic methods such as cheque-book journalism and paparazzi coverage. The *Sun*, the best-seller in the UK since 1978, is generally considered to be the most aggressive in this respect, but it has developed in cut-throat competition with other tabloids, particularly for the same readers as the *Mirror* (Rooney, 2000). With its stress on catching celebrities 'off-guard', the celebrity journalism favoured by these papers is increasingly the province of magazines such as *heat* (see the essay by Rebecca Feasey in this collection, and also Holmes, 2005), which should be seen as a main area of stimulus and competition for the popular tabloids.

These newspapers, then, are clearly part of an extortion of celebrity across contemporary culture, and are often seen as having contributed to a shift towards personalization of the media as a whole. Indeed, a main framework for the analysis of tabloids is the much-discussed concept of 'tabloidization': the (news) media turning to sensationalism, entertainment and the realm of private affairs. Tabloidization is an umbrella-term for a variety of claims about changes within contemporary media (see Sparks, 2000, for a full discussion) which, as noted by Steven Barnett, are often placed in the context of 'a pervasive sense of declining cultural, educational and political standards' (1998: 75). As exemplified in the following quote by Bob Franklin, this is conceived as the diversion of media audiences from 'hard' news and issues of public interest to 'soft' tabloid focuses such as human interest, sport, scandal and celebrity:

> Entertainment has superseded the provision of information; human interest has supplanted the public interest; measured judgement has succumbed to sensationalism; the trivial has triumphed over the weighty; the intimate relations of celebrities from soap operas, the world of sport

or the royal family are judged more 'newsworthy' than the reporting of significant issues and events of international consequence (1997: 4).

Thus, according to this perspective, much of contemporary tabloid journalism would debase democratic communication, in great part due to the prominence assigned to celebrity.

While there are some very legitimate concerns with respect to the impact of commercialization and the concentration of media ownership, there is a tendency here to overlook the ideological tensions and contradictions in tabloid media, as well as to group together heterogeneous media products and developments (Turner, 1999: 68–9). To some extent, the debate about tabloidization can also be seen as a grapple between competing value-systems. For example, it suggests a struggle over the culturally gendered preserves of 'hard', masculine, news and a 'feminized' realm of emotion and intimate life (e.g. Lumby, 1999), with tradi-tional value-systems, such as abstraction over personalization, increasingly subject to challenge. Myra MacDonald, examining the use of personalization in current affairs programmes, argues that, while rationality is important to main-tain critical interrogation, 'personal case studies and personal testimony can enable political insight and understanding through, rather than in spite of, their affecting qualities' (2000: 264).[4] Tabloidization, then, is a problematic concept, whether as an umbrella-term for shifts in media formats, or in terms of approaching media audiences. And while it provides a basis for critical assess-ments of contemporary media, the focus within the tabloidization debate on the informational value of tabloid journalism, frequently discounting tabloid celebrity as little more than trivial 'diversion' from public affairs, has so far done little to explain its popularity and social use. In order to grasp some of the possible mean-ings this coverage has for readers, the next section of this essay will turn to theories of the cultural functions of celebrity.

Celebrity journalism as cultural discourse

In trying to understand the popularity of celebrity journalism, it is important to acknowledge its social uses and interpretative cultural frameworks. Such an approach is outlined by John Langer in relation to 'tabloid' TV news. Langer emphasises that 'viewer linkages to the news [...] may be more ritualistic, symbolic and possibly mythic than informational, and [...] news might better be conceptualised as a "form of cultural discourse"' (1998: 5).[5] This line of enquiry recognizes that news serves at least some purpose beyond conveying information about public affairs – which could be especially true of celebrity-orientated news forms, where some of the main attractions may be found in the way the news fits in with routines and social contexts of everyday life.

Thinking about the appeal of celebrity journalism in these contexts, an apparent social use is as gossip-fodder, stimulating informal talk between members of social groups. Studies have revealed the utility of gossip as supporting group cohesion, and as a means to negotiate and maintain social norms and values (e.g. Jones, 1980; Eggins and Slade, 1997). In studies of the reading of US supermarket tabloids and women's magazines respectively, Elisabeth Bird (1992) and Jokes Hermes (1995) have also shown that media personalities can be added to the 'real' characters populating our everyday life as an extension of social groups, and in this respect the connection between celebrity gossip and the construction of community may be more direct than commonly thought (Turner et al., 2000: 15). Furthermore, celebrity coverage has been viewed in relation to ritual and myth. Langer sees news about famous people as functioning to stabilize news structures which can be called mythic, in allowing for impermanence and change within 'a framework of broader cycles of causality where "real" permanence resides' (1998: 144). Parallels can be drawn between his analysis and the way that celebrity cults may be regarded as a kind of modern mythology, with a spiritual dimension part of their consumption. John Frow, for instance, connects fan cults around dead celebrities such as James Dean and Elvis to religious procedures, arguing that 'religious sentiment [...] has migrated into many strange and unexpected places, from New Age trinketry to manga movies and the cult of the famous dead' (1998: 207; see also Rojek, 2001: 51–99).

Intersecting with the social and spiritual dimensions of celebrity consumption is its potential role in the construction of cultural identities. As shown by Richard Dyer (1979), the public values attached to media personalities mean that they are at the centre of the 'cultural politics' through which we find some of the tools to interpret ourselves and the world around us. An oft-quoted example in this context is the public attention lavished on the Princess of Wales, whereby Diana became a focal point for articulations of British national identity, gendered and family identities as well as notions of political belonging (Turner, 2004: 94–102). An explanation for the attention here seems to have been Diana's ability to tap into these points of controversy in British society, illustrating that the role of celebrity in the construction of identity is 'not a simple matter of finding oneself a role model to emulate' (ibid.: 102) but a negotiation of values within a contested cultural terrain. As the following study of tabloid reading will show, such complexity is evident in many aspects of celebrity consumption, where representations of celebrity within a given genre can take on multiple and contradictory meanings for audiences.

Research methods

For this study, I interviewed 55 London-based, regular readers of the *Sun* or the *Daily Mirror*, either individually or in small focus groups, between May 2004 and January 2005. The focus is not on the affluent, well-educated sections of readers, but on readers drawn from the social segments constituting the majority of the readerships. Participants were aged 18–35,[6] a large and crucial age group in the competition between the two papers (Rooney, 2000: 94), and from the C1C2DE social category (for example clerical workers and skilled and unskilled manual labourers) which represents over three-quarters of both papers' readerships.[7] To get access to 'naturally' occurring groups, such as groups of friends or colleagues, these were recruited through the use of contacts and 'snowball' sampling (see May, 2001: 132). In all, 35 male and 20 female readers participated. Most of these were white and British, with six participants of colour – two non-Western immigrant readers (from Jamaica and Nigeria) and four immigrant readers from countries in the West (Portugal, Greece, Poland, Australia). In total, 11 groups of 3–6 readers were interviewed, with at least two groups of male/female for each paper and one group each of mixed gender. These were semi-structured and taped, taking place where participants were thought to feel comfortable, such as in quiet pubs and cafés and in several cases, the workplace. The individual interviews were arranged in a similar way to the focus groups, but as a research tool, they provided more personal data.[8]

Perceptions and social uses of tabloid celebrity

Talking to readers, it became clear the *Sun* and the *Mirror* were part of a leisurely habit. The most common description of either paper was as 'an easy read', highlighting perceptions of these as accessible and easily fitted into a daily routine. Enjoyment was derived from a range of content, such as horoscopes, agony aunts, to some extent current affairs news, and for male readers, the sports coverage and pictures of scantily-clad girls. Celebrity stories were clearly part of this especially popular reading material. Many female readers even said the main reason they read the *Sun* or the *Mirror* was for 'the gossip', especially the *Sun*'s 'Bizarre' and the *Mirror*'s '3AM' celebrity columns. And while male readers would generally state sport as their favourite element, celebrity stories were the cause of much amusement and animated talk in discussions with both male and female readers.

Yet taking an interest in celebrity was connected to feelings of embarrassment. Men in particular often exhibited a reluctance to admit to a liking for celebrity coverage, with initial reactions either distancing, such as 'Who cares?', or derogatory, such as 'I think it's rubbish'. But as shown in this extract from a group of male *Mirror*-readers in their late twenties, negative perceptions of 'gossipy' coverage did not rule out enjoyment:

Andrew: And it's like, 'who's been seen messing about in Hampstead Heath
               with his boyfriend?' You know? What's the point?
Mike: Yeah, why have it?
Douglas: Having said that I do ... when I buy the *Mirror*, I do read all this ...
Andrew: Oh, absolutely! [...] So, everyone says that, like, they hate gossip,
               but when it comes down to it, everyone reads it.

As noted in relation to the tabloidization debate, taking an interest in 'gossip'
may be seen as contradictory to traditional masculine areas of interest, and such
contradictions can signify a struggle between competing notions of masculinity.
However, experiences of celebrity stories as a 'guilty pleasure' were common
among female readers too. Here this appeared to be determined by social
segmentation, as the white-collar workers in particular were cautious to distance
themselves from such material. Overall, these devaluations may be seen as
shaped by a dominant perspective on celebrity stories as having low cultural
value, and can be linked to Ien Ang's argument that feelings of shame for
enjoying popular culture are representative of a lack of positive ideological basis
for legitimizing this (1985: 110).

Contrary to perceptions of tabloid celebrity coverage as 'pointless', however,
it clearly had social significance in the everyday lives of readers. Tabloid reading
in general was described as a social activity, exemplified in how some of the
participants would read the paper together, for instance 'for a banter at work'
(see also Pursehouse, 1991), and celebrity stories were described as especially
good 'talking points'. As exemplified in the following quote from Nicole, a 21-
year-old unemployed *Sun* reader, one important use of this coverage was to
strengthen social bonds:

> Like, my boyfriend works and I'll ... If I've read the newspaper today
> ... If he phones me, I go, 'have you read the newspaper today?' We
> generally read the same thing or we watch the same news, if we haven't
> seen each other. And, he'll say 'yeah, I heard about so-and-so.' And we
> might discuss it for a couple of minutes. But it's something ... I don't
> know. It's like it's something to talk about. It generates conversation
> between people.

As with Nicole and her boyfriend, where day-to-day experiences provide limited
opportunities for shared insights, news stories about personalities can serve as a
bridge to shared cultural ground.

Celebrity stories can further play a role in the negotiation of social norms. A
major part of the conversations about these focused on morality: how to behave
in society. Topics ranged from what is acceptable in infidelity cases, regarding the

alleged affair of David Beckham, to whether violence is an adequate response to provocation, following Prince Harry's attack on a photographer. Interestingly, readers appeared to view these topics as facilitating conversations across social and cultural divisions – something which was especially emphasized in the interviews with immigrant readers. For example, a Nigerian, Muslim, *Sun* reader described how celebrity stories were a frequent talking point at the building site where he worked, and how joining in these conversations had become a way to bond with the rest of 'the lads'. The discussions about celebrity and morality, then, can serve a normative function, in that a sense of togetherness is established through common evaluation of easily identifiable subjects.

It is my view that a main reason for the social currency of tabloid celebrity stories is just this: they stimulate debates about fundamental moral and social issues, contributing to create an experience of community. It is important to recognize in this context their very public use, at work, pubs, cafés and other public places. Ironically, as a traditional public affairs topic such as politics was sometimes seen as too contentious to bring up in public, the lives of celebrities, as detailed in the *Sun* and the *Mirror*, were very much part of the public realm (for a discussion of tabloid reading and the public sphere see Johansson, forthcoming). However, as we shall see, this did not mean that the essentially political issues of conflict and power were removed from the agenda.

Identification and distancing: tabloid celebrity and social mobility

Langer notes that the discourse around celebrity 'shifts between humanizing the subject and at the same time exalting it' (1998: 49, see also Dyer, 1979: 49–50), a contradictory process particularly evident in talk about tabloid celebrity coverage. On the one hand, readers perceived celebrities as inhabiting a separate, glamorous existence, while, on the other, fundamental human similarities were stressed. Both approaches were integral to the pleasure of reading, as the apparent 'ordinariness' of celebrities appeared to invite a play with identity, allowing readers to imagine themselves in a different role. As shown in the following extracts from interviews with a 32-year-old catering assistant and a group of shop-fitters in their late twenties, this imaginary adventure could serve as a welcome change from the mundane nature of everyday life:

Interviewer: OK, about the celebrity coverage …
Michael: Yeah, yeah. I just suppose that everybody likes to read it at the end of the day. It's glamorizing. It's a very glamorous life, isn't it?
Interviewer: Why do you think it's fun to read about?
Michael: Don't know … I suppose … Why is it fun to read about? It's just …

that you're doing the same job every day, yeah. And you're kind of, like ... it's a bit of fantasy reading, isn't it? And you can kind of like imagine this image of this person that ... you know, there's a photograph of ... You know. I don't know, it's just a fantasy isn't it?

Interviewer: Reading about, you know, David Beckham or other high-profile people, can you somehow relate those to your own lives, or ...?
Ronald: Well, we can relate to their lifestyle. Like, we can wish that we was them, you know?
Adam: Yeah.
Ronald: Yeah, I know what you're saying.
Interviewer: In what ways would that be, then?
Chris: Three girlfriends at once!
[laughter]
Adam: Yeah, you wish!
Ronald: Always.
Ronald: Erm ...
[silence]
Interviewer: But is there anything about those sorts of stories that you can connect to, somehow?
Chris: No ... My life's too boring.
Ronald: Yeah. Same here actually.

Part of the reading pleasure, then, derived from the dissimilarity of the celebrity's life, making the imaginary leap into a different world all the more fulfilling.

While these conversations show the at times ironic distancing from the 'fantasy' of the celebrity, with readers emphasizing the discrepancy between a routine existence and the glamour of celebrity life, others highlight the balancing act between a distancing from celebrities and recognizing aspects of their lives. As in this example from a group of retail trainees (aged 18–21), notions of individual experience, particularly as conceived as personal vulnerabilities, appeared the main area of affinity:

Interviewer: Do you think that celebrity stories somehow relate to your lives, or ...
Helena: No.
Marissa: No.
Helena: I like, I like hearing about how they started, like, before they became famous, yeah. I like to know them things. But when they ... they don't interest me. I don't think their lives are like ours at all.
Joanne: Some of them are though, like Britney Spears. Yeah, she's got her millions and they don't have nothing to do with me, but she's got boyfriends and arguments and ...

Helena: But they have arguments with their boyfriends and they go on TV
            and they can get their boyfriends back by … making a song or some-
            thing, do you know what I mean? And they flippin' got money. They
            split up with their boyfriends, they can go out and spend, cause
            they've got loads of money. When we split up with our boyfriends, I
            ain't got loads of money to go out and spend nothing.

As personal experience provided an identificatory opening into another world,
it is also clear here that reading about celebrities could serve as a grim reminder
of their very different circumstances. Another example of this contradiction can
be seen in an interview with Maria, a 20-year-old laundry assistant:

Interviewer: Do you think, like, some stories about celebrities, do you think they
            somehow connect to your life, or …?
Maria: Some of them do … I mean, I've got a nine-months-old baby …
Interviewer: Oh, really?
Maria: Yeah. So … And I split up with my partner. […] I mean, as mothers,
            like, Jordan again, she split up with her partner, and she's got a son,
            and she looks after him by herself.
Interviewer: Yeah.
Maria: But then, I suppose, in other ways, I don't … I can't really relate to
            the celebrities because they've got the money to support themselves
            and their child and get the … support they need. Whereas I can't, I
            have to work for my money and look after my little girl at the same
            time. Which … can be quite hard, so …

While tabloid celebrity stories offered a way to cope with difficult circumstances,
then, they simultaneously highlighted the poverty of the everyday, coupling the
pleasure of identity play with the pain of its boundaries.

To understand this 'hurtful' aspect of tabloid celebrity coverage more clearly,
a discussion of social mobility is necessary. Anita Biressi and Heather Nunn
(2004) have pointed to a trend in contemporary celebrity discourse toward the
validation of those without cultural capital or elite roles rising to fame – and thus
the dramatization of social mobility. For example, given their disconnection from
traditional structures or hierarchies of influence, this is integral to the popular
impact of many reality TV stars.[9] Tabloid newspapers, similarly, can be seen as
working within the same parameters of 'democratic' fame, in embracing 'downmarket' celebrities, such as soap actors, pin-up girls and reality TV participants,
whose backgrounds may not be dissimilar to that of their largely working-class
readerships. When readers kept emphasizing how celebrities were 'just human'
after all, and especially liked to read about a celebrity's route to fame or about a

sudden transformation from ordinary person to celebrity (for instance through winning the lottery), this can be seen as connected to a hope of social mobility and self-transformation.

Fitting here is Nick Couldry's (2003) argument that the media represent what he calls 'the myth of the [social] centre', with the symbolic power to define our reality. Wanting to be in the media means aspiring to inclusion in main cultural procedures; into 'a "central" space where it makes sense to disclose publicly aspects of one's life' (ibid.: 116). Inclusion through the media, as Couldry has argued elsewhere (2000), seems an engaging idea for those excluded from wider means of social and economic power, especially if other class-based identities appear remote or impossible to emulate. To view tabloid celebrity as related to discourses on social mobility, therefore, may help explain how, rather than aspiring to a different class-based identity, the appeal can lie in the celebrity's perceived proximity to one's own position in the social system. If not gaining access to a central social space through actual transformation into celebrity status, there is at least the suggestion that one's position in the social structure is escapable. However, as shown, such a notion often appeared to be contradicted by the experiences of the readers that participated in this study, drawing attention to the precarious balance between celebrity as both possibility/opportunity and disappointment. In this context, I stress the relevance of a recent analysis of celebrity culture by Jo Littler (2004), who argues that the consumption of celebrity in general can be understood in terms of 'symbolic disempowerment': reading about celebrities may signal our exclusion from the symbolic social centre of the media, but it should also be read 'in the context of economic and social disempowerment: in terms of unequal access to material resource and social mobility' (ibid.:10). Acknowledging such an underlying tenet to readers' relationship to tabloid celebrity contributes to explain the vacillation between identification, disassociation and even aggression. Further, it helps create an understanding for the irreverent treatment of celebrities, which is all about an apparent reversing of power-balances.

'Celebrity-bashing'

As tabloid celebrity stories carry the promise of social mobility, yet invoke restrictions of the social structure, it is not surprising the talk about celebrity in this study was marked by frustration, resentment and anger. Such sentiments have been found in other studies of celebrity consumption (e.g. Hermes, 1999: 80), but are especially prominent in talk about tabloid celebrity coverage. The enmity with which celebrities were often discussed must, however, also be seen in relation to the distinctive tabloid 'celebrity-bashing' exemplified in the introduction to this article: a fault-finding and ridiculing of the celebrities and personalities populating these newspapers. As I will show, this aspect of tabloid celebrity coverage is key to its appeal and further draws attention to the way in which these stories link in with issues of power-struggles and social tension.

Readers were aware that, for the tabloids, celebrities were 'fair game', showing a clear understanding of the particular traits of the genre. The newspapers, for example, were described as 'picking on' celebrities or, as mentioned in the following extract from a group of female clerical workers (aged 28–32), showing them 'making a fool of themselves':

Alexandra: I don't think they [the celebrities] are portrayed as real people in this [the *Mirror*]. They're just portrayed as people on the pavement, walking into or out of a club, or you know, with their shopping bags …

Helen: With a short skirt, falling out of a car …
            [laughter]

Alexandra: 'Oh, look at her knickers!' 'Isn't she looking a bit rough?' You know …

Helen: Or no knickers!

Interviewer: But do you feel that they're kind of being mean then, when they show those kinds of pictures?

Helen: No. No, I don't think so.

Alexandra: I think they're … I think they want to see people fall over, if you know what I mean?

Interviewer: OK. What do you mean … ?

Helen: Yeah, to … to make a fool of themselves, really.

Alexandra: Yeah, like, you've got all the money in the world but you still look rough, or whatever, when you get up in the morning.
            [laughter]

Underscored by the laughter in this conversation, the awareness of celebrity-bashing was often accompanied by a distancing from the celebrities as 'real people'. Some readers, both male and female, expressed concern for how individual characters were treated in the tabloids, feeling 'sorry' for someone like David Beckham or Prince Harry for what they regarded as an intrusion into their privacy. But a more common (and sometimes simultaneous) response was to enjoy this treatment. An example of such pleasure from the misdeeds of celebrities can be seen in an interview with a 34-year-old decorator, whose main enjoyment from celebrity stories consisted of seeing unflattering pictures of 'top celebs':

Daniel: They, cover, yeah, they seem to pick on the top celebs. Catherine Zeta Jones can't move without the *Sun* doing it. Jordan can't change her underwear without the *Sun* knowing about it [laughs]. […] They

> must hang around night clubs 24/7 waiting for a celebrity to fall out
> the door.

Interviewer: Yeah … Is it something you like to read about, or …?

Daniel: Oh, I'd gloss over it. Unless, there's … it's an amusing picture of
              Naomi Campbell or someone, falling over with her legs in a twist
              [laughs].

Again, the laughter here is indicative of a distanced approach, whereby witnessing the celebrity's misfortunes, minor or major, can constitute part of, or even the main, reading pleasure.

This particular appeal must be seen in the light of circumstances of the day-to-day life of readers where, as shown, the perceived glamour of the celebrity's life brings attention to social inequality. Indeed, readers would sometimes ascribe their resentment of celebrities to jealousy, related to dissatisfaction with their own circumstances. Such a connection is evident in this comment from Ronnie, a 34-year-old bus-driver:

> I couldn't care less about them lot [the celebrities]. It just makes me
> jealous. Especially when I'm out there driving a bus picking up all them
> people all day.

From this position, the newspapers' belligerence provides the opportunity for a temporary experience of vindication of injustices, as it allows readers to indulge in what Catherine, a 21-year-old shop assistant, described as a 'hate' for celebrities:

> Sometimes you just wanna hate celebrities, you know? They've got
> money, and the life …

Hating celebrities through these stories may thus be a way to cope with their own situation, as the newspaper exposés of their misdeeds appear to reverse experiences of disempowerment.

Explaining how the resentment of tabloid stars and personalities would be able to perform such a task is further evidence that, for readers, celebrities represent social privilege and power. This is a point made by Ian Connell (1992), who has argued that a significance of tabloid celebrity stories is that privilege is *attackable*, as they 'encourage and nourish scepticism about the legitimacy of the class of personalities to act as they do' (ibid.: 82). There is, as demonstrated, some empirical support for such a hypothesis. The interviews with readers showed that celebrities were understood to represent privilege and these stories did appear to nourish an irreverent attitude to this. As exemplified in this final quote from the interview with Maria, the question of whether celebrities yield social or political power on an individual level is insignificant, as it is the representations of privilege that are torn down and the sentiment that rebellion against social privilege is possible that is nurtured:

Maria: Yeah, they [the *Sun*] are always chasing up celebrities. [...] The things that you don't know about, they tell you. So, I think it's quite good.
Interviewer: So you think it's good to read?
Maria: Yeah, I think it's good to read. I think it is fun to read. I mean, you know ... I mean, the celebrities they think ... You know, they think they're great and ... they've got lots of money and they think they're powerful. But then you find out that they've been taking cocaine for instance, then you think to yourself, 'well, you're not so great are you?' So ...
Interviewer: No ...
Maria: I mean, I think it's good that they do that.

Maria's approval of the *Sun*'s exposure of those who 'think they're powerful' can be seen as symptomatic of a wider questioning of privilege which, in concurrence with Connell's hypothesis, appears central to the enjoyment of reading tabloid celebrity stories.

Through the pleasure taken from 'damaging' celebrities, read as representations of privilege, then, it can be argued that the 'celebrity-bashing' of tabloid newspapers provides a momentary experience of power and control to readers, as they, as spectators and newspaper buyers, are part of dragging the deviant personality down. They are the audience for which the celebrity is sacrificed. They are also part of the 'imagined communities' (Anderson, 1996) of these papers, which appear to have the power to debase the rich, famous and powerful. However, whether a symbolic attack on privilege could in any way be used to challenge real social inequalities is of course questionable as that, as Connell admits, would be dependent on the existence of persuasive alternative socio-cultural arrangements (ibid.: 83). Nevertheless, an explanation of the popularity of the tabloid celebrity story is that, at the very least, it works as a vent for dissatisfaction with situations resulting from social inequality, providing a momentary experience of power to readerships which for the large part can be seen as those which are the least privileged in society.

Conclusion

As tabloid newspapers provide such a major arena for celebrity journalism, it is surprising we know so little about the roles of celebrity coverage in the lives of their readers. In this essay, I have attempted to provide some insights into the kinds of meanings and social uses made out of those stories about stars and personalities that to a large extent populate the pages of the *Sun* and the *Mirror*. A range of work on celebrity and popular culture has been helpful, for instance in pointing to the social currency of celebrity gossip, and the way that individual celebrities are focal points for the 'cultural politics' that can become resources for our cultural and individual identities. However, generic specificity is equally important, and although some of the findings presented may have bearings on the consumption of other media forms, for example celebrity magazines, they are not necessarily relevant to other contexts. Perhaps most related to other kinds of celebrity discourse are the functions tabloid celebrity stories fulfil in the construction of a community and in the negotiation of social norms, as cherished talking-points in a variety of relationships. Likewise, readers have in common with other consumers of popular culture experiences of guilt for enjoying this genre, which, however, did not hinder its highly public use.

Such a contradiction is symptomatic of the complex relationship between readers and tabloid celebrities, marked by a fine line between identification and distancing. As some of the attractions in this relationship lie in its promise of the possibility of social mobility and inclusion into a symbolic power centre, its simultaneous foregrounding of the opposite means that identity construction around tabloid stars and personalities is an ambiguous – sometimes painful – process, framed by discourses of social inequality. The interest in tabloid celebrity stories can therefore be seen as a commentary on some very real social tensions and power struggles in the society in which they operate. I would argue in accordance with Connell that it is incorrect to see these stories as a 'diversion' from such essentially 'political' issues, since on one level they do the opposite by bringing attention to the problematic of social power structures.

The pleasure taken in venomous or revelatory treatment of celebrities, then, must be seen in the light of what they symbolize in relation to the lives of readers – not only, in several cases, dashed hopes of social mobility but also the privilege and power that by and large seemed out of reach for those who participated in this study. Enjoying the papers' irreverent stance on the rich, famous and powerful, if seen as an attack on privilege, helps explain one of the tabloid celebrity story's core ways of providing a connection to the reader. Above all, this is to do with a momentary experience of power and control. Far from revealing a simple desire for titillation, responses to tabloid celebrity stories link in with wider issues of class and identity in relation to celebrity culture.

Notes

1 This research was undertaken between May 2004 and January 2005.

2 I am using the term celebrity in a broad sense, to cover minor celebrities and TV personalities

as well as internationally known 'stars'. Such a broad definition is justified by the approach of the popular tabloids where, while there is a hierarchy in operation of the newsworthiness of different celebrities, this is generally not contingent on achievement or social status. This broad characterization was also applied by readers, where celebrity was taken to include footballers and pin-up girls as well as Hollywood actors and members of the royal family.

3 The average net circulation of the popular tabloids, *Daily Mirror*, *Daily Record*, *Daily Star* and the *Sun* reached 6,464,369 in the period of 3 January 2005 to 30 January 2005. This can be compared with a total of 3,358,359 for the mid-market tabloids and 2,813,551 for the quality newspapers. Figures from Audit Bureau of Circulations, available at www.abc.org.uk.

4 A similar point has been made by Bird and Dardenne (1997), who stress that a 'story-telling' news form, populated by recognizable characters, is most easily absorbed by audiences.

5 '[...]' has been used in this chapter to indicate when words from a quotation are omitted. This is to distinguish such occasions from the use of '...' in excerpts from the interviews, which is intended to denote a pause in speech.

6 Following industry data, the initial age category selected was 18–34, but two group members were aged 35.

7 Figures from National Readership Survey 2004, available at www.nrs.co.uk.

8 All names are pseudonymous to protect the privacy of the respondents.

9 A comparison can be made to Dyer's concept of the 'success myth' in relation to film stars (1979: 48–9), whereby they become symbols for success contingent on discourses of 'ordinariness' and 'luck'. However, the star system Dyer describes is also perceived to reward 'talent', which marks a difference from the kind of celebrity discourse referred to by Biressi and Nunn.

Bibliography

Anderson, Benedict (1996) *Imagined Communities: Reflections on the Origin and Spread of Nationalism*, London: Verso.

Ang, Ien (1985) *Watching Dallas: Soap Opera and the Melodramatic Imagination*, trans. Della Couling, London: Routledge.

Barnett, Steven (1998) 'Dumbing Down or Reaching Out', in Jean Seaton (ed.), *Politics and the Media*, London: Blackwell, pp. 75–90.

Bird, S. Elisabeth (1992) *For Enquiring Minds: A Cultural Study of Supermarket Tabloids*, Knoxville: University of Tennessee Press.

Bird, S. Elisabeth and Dardenne, Robert (1997) 'Myth, Chronicle and Story: Exploring the Narrative Qualities of News', in Dan Bekowitz (ed.), *Social Meanings of News: A Text-Reader*, London: Sage, pp. 333–50.

Biressi, Anita and Nunn, Heather (2004) 'The Especially Remarkable: Celebrity and Social Mobility in Reality TV', *Mediactive* 2: 44–58.

Connell, Ian (1992) 'Personalities in the Popular Media', in Peter Dahlgren and Colin Sparks (eds), *Journalism and Popular Culture*, London: Sage, pp. 64–83.

Couldry, Nick (2000) *Inside Culture: Re-Imagining the Method of Cultural Studies*, London: Sage.

—— (2003) *Media Rituals: A Critical Approach*, London and New York: Routledge.

Dyer, Richard (1979) *Stars*, London: BFI.

Eggins, Suzanne and Slade, Diane (1997) *Analysing Casual Conversation*, London: Cassell.

Franklin, Bob (1997) *Newzak and News Media*, London: Arnold.

Frow, John (1998) 'Is Elvis a God? Cult, Culture, Questions of Method', *International Journal of Cultural Studies* 1/2: 197–210.

Hermes, Jokes (1995) *Reading Women's Magazines*, Cambridge: Polity Press.

Hermes, Jokes (1999) 'Media Figures in Identity Construction', in Pertti Alasuutari (ed.), *Rethinking the Media Audience*, London: Sage, pp. 69–85.

Holmes, Su (2005) '"Off-guard, Unkempt, Unready?": Deconstructing Contemporary Celebrity in *heat* Magazine', *Continuum: Journal of Media and Cultural Studies* 19/1: 21–38.

Johansson, Sofia (forthcoming) '"They Just Make Sense": Tabloid Newspapers as an Alternative Public Sphere', in Richard Butch (ed.), *Media and Public Spheres*, Houndmills: Palgrave Macmillan.

Jones, Deborah (1980) 'Gossip: Notes on Women's Oral Culture', *Women's Studies International Quarterly* 3: 193–8.

Langer, John (1998) *Tabloid Television: Popular Journalism and the 'Other News'*, London: Routledge.

Littler, Jo (2004) 'Making Fame Ordinary: Intimacy, Reflexivity, and "Keeping it Real"', *Mediactive* 2: 8–25.

Lumby, Catherine (1999) *Gotcha: Life in a Tabloid World*, Sydney: Allen & Unwin.

MacDonald, Myra (2000) 'Rethinking Personalization in Current Affairs Journalism', in Colin Sparks and John Tulloch (eds), *Tabloid Tales: Global Debates Over Media Standards*, Oxford: Rowman & Littlefield, pp. 251–66.

May, Tim (2001) *Social Research: Issues, Methods and Process*, 3rd edn, Buckingham: Open University Press.

Pursehouse, Mark (1992) 'Looking at the Sun: Into the 90s with a Tabloid and Its Readers', in *Cultural Studies from Birmingham Number One 1991*, Nottingham: Russell Press, pp. 88–133.

Rojek, Chris (2001) *Celebrity*, London: Reaktion Books.

Rooney, Dick (2000) 'Thirty Years of Competition in the British Tabloid Press: The *Mirror* and the *Sun* 1968–1998', in Colin Sparks and John Tulloch (eds), *Tabloid Tales: Global Debates Over Media Standards*, Oxford: Rowman & Littlefield, pp. 91–109.

Sparks, Colin (2000) 'Introduction: The Panic over Tabloid News', in Colin Sparks and John Tulloch (eds), *Tabloid Tales: Global Debates Over Media Standards*, Oxford: Rowman & Littlefield, pp. 1–40.

Turner, Graeme (1999) 'Tabloidization, Journalism and the Possibility of a Critique', *International Journal of Cultural Studies* 2/1: 59–76.

—— (2004) *Understanding Celebrity*, London, Thousand Oaks and New Delhi: Sage.

Turner, Graeme, Bonner, Frances and Marshall, P. David (2000) *Fame Games: The Production of Celebrity in Australia*, Cambridge: Cambridge University Press.

Bibliography

Abercrombie, Nick, Hill, Stephen, and Turner, Brian S. (1986) *Sovereign Individuals of Capitalism*, London: Allen and Unwin.

Alberoni, Francesco (1972) 'The "Powerless Elite": Theory and Sociological Research on the Phenomenon of the Stars', in Denis McQuail (ed.), *Sociology of Mass Communications*, Penguin: Harmondsworth, pp. 75–98.

Andrews, David L and Jackson, Steven J. (eds) (2001) *Sport Stars: The Cultural Politics of Sporting Celebrity*, London: Routledge.

Babington, Bruce (ed.) (2001) *British Stars and Stardom: From Alma Taylor to Sean Connery*, Manchester: MUP.

Barker, Martin (2003) 'Introduction', in Thomas Austin and Martin Barker (eds), *Contemporary Hollywood Stardom*, London: Arnold, pp. 1–24.

Barthes, Roland (1985) 'The Face of Garbo', in Gerald Mast and Marshall Cohen (eds), *Film Theory and Criticism*, Oxford: Oxford University Press, pp. 650–1.

Biressi, Anita and Nunn, Heather (2005) *Reality TV: Realism and Revelation*, London: Wallflower.

Bonner, Frances (2005) 'The Celebrity in the Text', in Jessica Evans and David Hesmondhalgh (eds), *Inside Media: Understanding Celebrity*, Berkshire: Open University Press, pp. 58–96.

Boorstin, Daniel (1971) *The Image: A Guide to Pseudo-Events in America*, New York: Atheneum. Originally published as *The Image or What Happened to the American Dream?* (1961).

Braudy, Leo (1986) *The Frenzy of Renown; Fame and its History*, Oxford: Oxford University Press.

Carr, Diane (2002) 'Playing with Lara', in Geoff King and Tanya Krzywinska (eds), *ScreenPlay: Cinema/Videogames/Interfaces*, London: Wallflower Press, pp. 171–80.

Carter, Gary (2004) 'Epilogue – In Front of Our Eyes: Notes on *Big Brother*', in Ernest Mathijs and Janet Jones (eds), *Big Brother International: Formats, Critics and Publics*, London: Wallflower, pp. 250–7.

Corner, John and Pels, Dick (2003) *Media and the Re-styling of Politics*, London: Sage.

Couldry, Nick (2000) *The Place of Media Power: Pilgrims and Witnesses of the Media Age*, London, Routledge.

—— (2003) *Media Rituals: A Critical Approach*, London: Routledge.

—— (2004) 'Teaching Us To Fake It: The Ritualized Norms of Television's "Reality" Games', in Susan Murray and Laurie Ouellette (eds), *Reality TV: Remaking Television Culture*, New York: NYU Press, pp. 57–74.

Creed, Barbara (2002) 'The Cyberstar: Digital Pleasures and the End of the Unconscious', in Graeme Turner (ed.), *The Film Cultures Reader*, London: Routledge, pp. 129–34.

deCordova, Richard (1990) *Picture Personalities: The Emergence of the Star System in America*, Urbana and Chicago: University of Illinois Press.

Douglas, Mary, (2002) *Purity and Danger: An Analysis of Pollution and Taboo*, London: Routledge.

Dyer, Richard (1998) *Stars*, 2nd edn, London: BFI.

—— (2004) *Heavenly Bodies: Film Stars and Society*, 2nd edn, London: BFI.

Elliott, Anthony (1999) *The Mourning of John Lennon*, Berkeley: University of California Press.

Ellis, John (1992) *Visible Fictions: Cinema, Television, Video*, 2nd edn, London: Routledge.

Evans, Andrew and Wilson, Glenn (1999) *Fame: The Psychology of Stardom*, London: Vision Paperbacks.

Evans, Jessica (2005) 'Celebrity, Media and History', in Jessica Evans and David Hesmondhalgh (eds), *Inside Media: Understanding Celebrity*, Berkshire: Open University Press, pp. 11–56.

Flanagan, Mary (1999) 'Mobile Identities, Digital Stars and Post-cinematic Selves', *Wide Angle* 21/1, January: 77–93.

Gaines, Jane M. and Herzog, Charlotte (1991) *Fabrications: Costume and the Female Body*, London: Routledge.

Gamson, Joshua (1994) *Claims to Fame: Celebrity in Contemporary America*, Berkeley: University of California Press.

Geraghty, Christine (2000) 'Re-examining Stardom: Questions of Texts, Bodies and Performance', in Christine Gledhill and Linda Williams (eds), *Reinventing Film Studies*, London: Arnold, pp. 183–201.

Giddens, Anthony (1991) *Modernity and Self-Identity*, Stanford, CA: Stanford University Press.

Giles, David (2000) *Illusions of Immortality: A Psychology of Fame and Celebrity*, London: Macmillan.

Gledhill, Christine (ed.) (1991) *Stardom: Industry of Desire*, London: Routledge.

Goffman, Erving (1974) *Frame Analysis: An Essay on the Organisation of Experience*, Boston: North-eastern University Press.

Grieveson, Lee (2002) 'Stars and Audiences in Early American Cinema', *Screening the Past*, available at www.latrobe.edu.au/screeningthepast/classics/cl0902/lgcl14c-2.htm, accessed 23 July 2005.

Hills, Matt (2003) 'Putting Away Childish Things: Jar Jar Binks and the "Virtual Stars" as an Object of Fan Loathing', in Thomas Austin and Martin Barker (eds), *Contemporary Hollywood Stardom*, London: Arnold, pp. 74–89.

Hilton, Boyd (2004) 'How I Learned To Stop Worrying and Love Celebrity Culture!', *Four Magazine*, December: 21.

Holmes, Su (2004) '"All you've got to worry about is the task, having a cup of tea, and what you're going to eat for dinner": Approaching Celebrity in *Big Brother*', in Su Holmes and Deborah Jermyn (eds), *Understanding Reality Television*, London: Routledge, pp. 111–35.

—— 2005) '"Off guard, Unkempt, Unready?": Deconstructing Contemporary Celebrity in *heat* Magazine', *Continuum: Journal of Media and Cultural Studies* 19/1: 21–38.

Jeffords, Susan (1994) *Hard Bodies: Hollywood Masculinity in the Reagan Era*, New York: Rutgers University Press.

Langer, John (1981) 'TV's Personality System', *Media, Culture and Society* 4: 351–65.

Liddiment, David (2005) 'Opinion', *Guardian*, 6 June, available at media.guardian.co.uk/mediaguardian/story/0,,1499793,00.html, accessed 16 February 2006.

Littler, Jo (2004) 'Making Fame Ordinary: Intimacy, Reflexivity, and "Keeping it Real", *Mediactive* 2: 8–25.

Llewellyn-Smith, Caspar (2002) *Poplife: A Journey by Sofa*, London: Sceptre.

Lowenthal, Leo (1961) 'The Triumph of Mass Idols', in *Literature, Popular Culture and Society*, Palo Alto, CA: Pacific Books, pp. 109–40.

Lury, Celia (1996) *Consumer Culture*, Cambridge: Polity.

McDonald, Paul (1995) 'I'm Winning on a Star: The Extraordinary Ordinary World of *Stars in their Eyes*', *Critical Survey* 7/1: 59–66.

—— (1998) 'Supplementary Chapter: Reconceptualising Stardom', in Richard Dyer, *Stars*, 2nd edn, London: BFI, pp. 177–200.

Marshall, P. David (1997) *Celebrity and Power: Fame in Contemporary Culture*, Minnesota: University of Minnesota Press.

—— (2004) 'Fame's Perpetual Moment', *M/C Journal* 7/5, available at journal.media-culture.org.au/0411/01-editorial.php, accessed 16 February 2006.

Mercer, Kobener (ed.) (1994) *Welcome To The Jungle*, London: Routledge.

Mole, Tom (2004) 'Hypertrophic Celebrity', *M/C Journal* 7/5, available at journal.media-culture.org.au/0411/08-mole.php, accessed 16 February 2006.

Mulvey, Laura (1975) 'Visual Pleasure and Narrative Cinema', *Screen* 16/3: 6–18.

Negra, Diane (2001) *Off-White Hollywood: American Culture and Ethnic Female Stardom*, London: Routledge.

Pateman, Carole (1988) *The Sexual Contract*, Cambridge: Polity Press.

Rojek, Chris (2001) *Celebrity*, London: Reaktion Books.

Schickel, Richard (1985) *Intimate Strangers: The Culture of Celebrity in America*, Chicago: Ivan R. Dee Inc.

Sconce, Jeffrey (2004) 'See You in Hell, Johnny Bravo!', in Susan Murray and Laurie Ouellette (eds), *Reality TV: Re-making Television Culture*, New York: New York University Press: pp. 251–67.

Spurgin, Tim (2001) 'The *Times Magazine* and Academic Megastars', *the Minnesota review* 52–4, found at www.theminnesotareview.org/ns52/spurgin.htm, accessed 30 June, 2005.

Stacey, Jackie (1994) *Star Gazing: Hollywood Cinema and Female Spectatorship*, London: Routledge.

Stevenson, Nick (2005) 'Audiences and Celebrity', in Jessica Evans and David Hesmondhalgh (eds), *Understanding Media: Inside Celebrity*, Berkshire: Open University Press, pp. 135–72.

Storey, John (2001) *An Introductory Guide to Cultural Theory and Popular Culture*, Hemel Hempstead: Harvester Wheatsheaf.

Tulloch, John and Jenkins, Henry (1995) *Science Fiction Audiences: Watching Doctor Who and Star Trek*, London and New York: Routledge.

Turner, Graeme (1996) *British Cultural Studies: An Introduction*, London: Routledge.

—— (2004) *Understanding Celebrity*, London: Sage.

Turner, Graeme, Bonner, Frances and Marshall, P. David (2000) *Fame Games: The Production of Celebrity in Australia*, Cambridge, Cambridge University Press.

Williams, Linda (1990) *Hard Core: Power, Pleasure and the Frenzy of the Visible*, Berkeley: University of California Press.

Index

Page numbers in *italics* indicate illustrations